GW00771402

UNEVEN MOMENTS

ASIA PERSPECTIVES
WEATHERHEAD EAST ASIAN INSTITUTE, COLUMBIA UNIVERSITY

ASIA PERSPECTIVES: HISTORY, SOCIETY, AND CULTURE
A SERIES OF THE WEATHERHEAD EAST ASIAN INSTITUTE,
COLUMBIA UNIVERSITY
Carol Gluck, Editor

UNEVEN MOMENTS

Reflections on Japan's Modern History

HARRY HAROOTUNIAN

Columbia University Press
New York

Columbia University Press
Publishers Since 1893
New York   Chichester, West Sussex
cup.columbia.edu

Library of Congress Cataloging-in-Publication Data
Names: Harootunian, Harry D., author.
Title: Uneven moments : reflections on Japan's modern history /
    Harry Harootunian.
Description: New York : Columbia University Press, [2019] | Series: Asia
    perspectives : history, society, and culture | Includes bibliographical
    references and index.
Identifiers: LCCN 2018025228 (print) | LCCN 2018040820 (ebook) |
    ISBN 9780231548779 (electronic) | ISBN 9780231190206 | ISBN 9780231190206
    (cloth : alk. paper) | ISBN 9780231190213 (paperback) | ISBN 9780231548779
    (electronic)
Subjects: LCSH: Japan—Civilization—1868– | Japan—Intellectual life—1868–
Classification: LCC DS822.25 (ebook) | LCC DS822.25 .H357 2019 (print) |
    DDC 952—dc23
LC record available at https://lccn.loc.gov/2018025228

Cover image: The Central Station at Tokyo, circa 1930s. © Private Collection
Peter Newark Pictures/Bridgeman Images

In memory of some old friends: Arif Dirlik, Masao Miyoshi, Bernie Silberman, and Hayden White ∽

CONTENTS

ACKNOWLEDGMENTS

I would like to express my immense debt of gratitude to Carol Gluck for first suggesting the collecting of some of my essays for publication, initiating the project, and seeing it through to its completion. I want also to thank Carol for reading an early draft of my introduction and for her perceptive remarks, which I have incorporated. I want also to thank Ramona Bajema for expending personal time and effort in locating, collecting, and reproducing the various essays, many of which I no longer have in my possession. None of this would have happened without her speedy labor.

I have benefited from the help provided by Columbia University Press, particularly its editors Caelyn Cobb, Leslie Kriesel, and the staff of the Weatherhead East Asian Institute, especially Ross Yelsey, who made many contributions that eased the path to production. Thanks to Bill Mihalopoulos for indexing the book. I also want to remember and thank for their generosity Kim Brandt and Marilyn Ivy for reading the penultimate draft of the introduction and their valuable suggestions, which I have followed in the final version. Finally, I owe a great thanks to two anonymous readers who had a clearer idea than I of how these essays might be explained, which, again, is inscribed in the introduction.

UNEVEN MOMENTS

INTRODUCTION

Uneven Moments from Japan's Modern History

There is no world for which I was fitted, least of all the one I was to enter.

—C. L. R. James

Aspirations

The essays gathered in this volume span a duration of time that stretches over more than four decades. They have grown out of my belief that the history we study is not simply what happened in the past as it yields to a new present but a constant intermingling and interaction of pasts in the present. Nothing is ever sharply delineated in the historical divisions of tenses like past and present, even though most historians cling to such divisions as if they were in danger of drowning. Moreover, nothing is ever completed, as we are reminded by the repetitively periodic demands reverberating throughout Japan's modern history for completing the restoration inaugurated in 1868. More often than not it is difficult to know when the present has begun and the past has come to a close. History, because its putative recovery or reconstruction occurs in practices that take place in the present, is ceaselessly mediated both by the nature of the present's changing political landscape and by the forms of cultural expression that accompany it. While these essays were produced in different academic environments reflecting differing political and cultural moments, in the context of changing historical presents in the United States and Japan, their diverse spatial locations still convey an overriding thematic preoccupation with time, especially the spectacle of uneven and mixed temporalities that constitute the different presents of Japan's pasts and the way the everyday has occupied the position of providing it focus in the figure of a minimal temporal unity. This is not to say that the writing of these essays has remained immune from precisely the mixed and uneven temporalities that have dominated the presents in which they were conceived and composed. These moments not only indexed their respective historicities but, at the same time, required an interrogation of the terms of the historical present, referring to the relationship of a present to those traces of pasts that coexist in it, in which they were produced or made possible. In brief, we are always obliged to account self-critically for their immanent appearance and acknowledge its difference from the "practical present,"[1] the ordinary routines of everyday life that regulate the rhythms of day-to-day existence. It has been my conviction that the regime of capital, wherever it prevails, not only points to the unevenness it creates and the various combined presents it continuously generates but also embodies the force that shapes lives and causes events manifesting the fissures of discordant temporalities.

The chronological span of the essays ranges from the crucial moments of Japan's transformation into a modern political and economic order beginning in the late Tokugawa period to the interwar years of capitalist modernization, and finally to the uncertainties of war's defeat and ruin after World War II, efforts to reconstruct a broken nation-state and its successful return to worldly economic status. Many of the essays, like "Cultural Politics in Tokugawa Japan," "Overcome by Modernity: Fantasizing Everyday Life and the Discourse on the Social in Interwar Japan," and "Reflections from Fukushima: History, Memory, and the Crisis of Contemporaneity," emphasize the discrepancy between politics and culture and how the instance of often new proliferating cultural practices appears to demand a different and new politics capable of metabolizing new social relationships and subjectivities. But they also show the initial unevenness between politics and culture, whereby the former is always limited to actualizing fewer possibilities while the latter seems to possess a capacious propensity for producing new and different forms. Above all, what these essays show is a validation of the Gramscian insight that politics and culture are invariably destined to remain at odds with or distant from each other, and from the discrepant perspective of each, the other is either too broad and too excessive.[2] Yet they are also fated to constantly rub up against each other to produce frictions necessitating resolution. It is this form of unevenness, often coded by mixed times in the example of Japan's presents, that calls attention to the possible prospect of historical and national crises in the economic and social domains.

The essays often revisit what appears to me as the historical watermark of such crises in the production of discourses on culture (thought and art). These discourses were usually dedicated to reshaping or bending a cultural relationship to politics in such a way as to resolve or overcome manifest rupture, discontinuities, observable unevenness, and the collision of different temporalities that coexisted with each other. With capitalism, concepts like culture, representation, and modernity, etc. were rapidly recruited to supply mediation in a sociohistorical environment marked by the ceaseless production of new forces of production and social relations that threatened to end in furthering division and conflict, well into the extended postwar years.

While the essays represent a broad range of interests involving Japan's cultural and intellectual history and related problems of metatheory and strategies of interpretation over a long duration of time, they also reveal an abiding lifetime's preoccupation with a single question, the everyday and its claim on historical knowledge. This has been the necessity of recognizing the importance of working through the encounter and frequent collision of history and memory, event and experience, world historicality (as condensed in the nation form) and the everyday. Memory had been banished from history long ago and is still distrusted by historians. But the witnesses of holocaust and other catastrophic events have demonstrated that perhaps it is not so easy to separate the historical from memoration. Behind this working through, what clearly fueled this recognition was the perceived distance between historical narrative, dominated by world-historical eventfulness enacted by and among nation-states on a global stage, and an everydayness, anchored in repetitive routines and a scarcity of events, whose rhythms remain unassimilated to the nation form. If the former lays claim to the acquisition of a verifiable historical knowledge, the latter stands as the repository of transient experience and memory. The distance between these two different modes of retention and cognition, driven to be separated from each other, was recaptured at a more basic level between what Kristin Ross has renamed the "conceived" and the "lived."[3] Ross has envisioned a historical scene as a "landscape," in this instance the Paris Commune of 1871, constituted of the lived and the conceived. The former refers to the materials utilized for her composition, comprising the attitudes and actions realized by the communard insurgents, while the latter points to the conceptual imaginary reflecting the logics authorized by things said, speeches made, and actions taken that guided the paths of the combatants. With Benjamin, she is persuaded that if the past never yields lessons, it nevertheless produces moments where a particular event or struggle forcibly enters the "figurability of the present."[4] It is at this moment that capitalist time is interrupted by the unscheduled arrival of an untimely temporality. I would add, in this regard, that this forcible entry of past into present or presence echoes Marx's earlier observation of how the "train" of "inherited evils arising from the passive survival of archaic modes of production," equally accompanied by "anachronistic social modes and political relations," unwanted residues of the past constantly buffeting the present, leaves its indelible imprint of unevenness and combined development on the structures of social formations.

Yet the conception of everyday that has caught my attention is not simply the place where nothing happens because it lacks significant eventfulness inscribed in world history. Why it can claim equal importance with history is found in the capacity of its mode of cognition to authorize reversible times that run counter to history's insistence on the irreversibility of temporal linearity. The collision between them occurs in the nation's dedication to linear progression—Walter Benjamin's "one-way street," whereby the past remains passed, while the everyday remains imminent, filled with coexisting traces of pasts constantly mingling and interacting with the present moment. In this collision the everyday discloses the specific singularity of an unnoticed unevenness and inequality lived daily by large numbers of the anonymous under the claims of national history that seek to produce and project the image of evenness, which always moves to efface the spectacle of mixed temporalities and displace the scandal of lived inequality or difference.

While this collision has appeared everywhere capital has established its production process it is particularly evident in societies outside Euro-America and especially in former colonies and latecomers to national independence and capitalism. But, it is important to repeat that this occurrence of unevenness was no less true of societies that had already attained a level of mature capitalist development. It is this experience that is bypassed in most historical narratives, averaged in such a way that the unnoticed remain anonymous if counted. Instead, the national history eclipses the everyday, making it history's lengthened shadow, and as its enabling condition of concentrating on eventfulness on the stage of world history to the exclusion of all other considerations. The presumption is that the impact of eventfulness supposedly will trickle down to the everyday, a little like bad economics that believes that increasing wealth of the rich will drip downward and benefit the rest of us. The everyday, in this way, gets left out of history, and its rich reservoir of memory and experience embodying mixed times of different pasts is confined to a present where they, like Poe's purloined letter, are constantly before us but rarely seen. The reason for this failure to see unevenness and inequality as a permanent condition of daily reality among the majority of unnoticed lives all over the globe derives from the conviction that it was wrongly grasped as merely a temporary phase in a theory of economic development that would, in time, evolve into a final stage of even development. At the same time, this misrecognition became a measure of scheduled comparative growth and locked late developing societies in a trajectory of endless catch-up, which would happen only in the last instance.

Since World War II we have seen the production of an excess of memory and experience, demanding, as never before, recognition. The confrontation of history and memory was first inscribed in an emergent configuration made up of a new social space signifying the lived everyday (as against the nation) in the expanding sites of both center and colonial periphery. Before the war considerations of experience and memory were confined to a few theorists like Freud, Halbwachs, and Benjamin but clearly were proscribed by history. This explosion of memory and experience had been already perceived by Benjamin as a characteristic response to the shock of modern capitalist life and its rhythms of creation and destruction. The post–World War II era became flooded with expressions of memoration devoted to retrieving the instance of mass murders from the immediate past to challenge historical practice. Memory's challenge seemed to exact more persuasive explanations of events whose scale, it was believed, was better understood at the level of the every-dayness in the register of experience, both of which had remained recessive and external to conventional historical narratives.[5] The inexhaustible inventory of the crimes of the past has managed to wedge its claims into the forefront of our historical awareness and exceed the conventional boundaries of historical research, spilling over and even occupying the public realm to interpellate our present.[6] Not only the crimes of the past but also the vast transformations of the world outside Euro-America demanded by the expansion and penetration of capitalism have added to this continuing collision of pasts that no longer wish to pass and the formation of a new historical consciousness in which collective memory now commands a central place requiring serious attention. These stubbornly persisting pasts have generated a crowd of memories belonging to diverse groups in different places, which have survived struggles for national liberation and the massive dislocations of decolonization. The subsequent formation of nations produced a surplus of new historical claims that have strained the capacity of received historical practice to continue telling one kind of familiar story.

The essays in this collection I hope show how I've tried to address this problem of repairing the emergent dichotomy of history and memory, event and experience that sought resolution through bringing together their different forms into an uneven and not entirely suitable fit producing a hybridity of form. What has guided me in this effort has been the not always successful attempt to overcome or put into question a binary logic of couplings like subject and object, individual and group, text and action in order to evade slipping irretrievably into unbridgeable antinomies and incurring the risk of permanent contradiction. If the goal of historical and cultural analysis has been to find a way to rejoin a public history of events to memory, then its pathway consists in recognizing the existence of a matrix founded on a kind of ontological ground that authorizes a shared differentiation, rather than a division, of interpretative labor linking the conceived and lived. According to the philosopher Paul Ricoeur, history is committed to the search for truth, objectified in a veritable chronology capable of moving only one way, whereas the appeal to memory must be preoccupied with faithfulness and unconstrained by time's direction. If perspective is dominated by history and the historical, the everyday fades into an indistinct shadowed silhouette whose contours are barely visible; if the standpoint privileges the everyday, experience, and memory, the historical is blurred. We face two different cognitive modes and temporalities that must be put into constant articulation with each other: history with its mission to retrieve and its findings placed in ordered linear succession on the one hand and memory's reversibility of time on the other.[7] The articulation must include both in the opposing forms of narrative and montage.

In circumstances in which the claims of historical knowledge have confronted expressions of experience and recollections of memory, the former invariably led to verifying facticity over subjective intimations derived from sensory impressions. Experience thus proved to be immediate, transitory, and memory temporally imprecise, while history's knowledge could declare superior status owing to its correspondence to measureable time, which constituted one of its principal supports of empirical authority. The competition between these conflicting forms of time was conveyed through categories of the nation-state (history) and the new everyday of industrial capital (memory, experience); the latter standing as both the locus of an experience rarely, if ever, completed and the place where collective memory gathered to determinedly remain unassimilated to the rhythms of the nation-state. Yet both, paradoxically, shared the same space of the present, history looking back to what had passed and memory and experience insisting on their continuing presence.

✳ ✳ ✳

In our time it is this remaindered force of memory, not yet erased, that manages to momentarily elude the negativity of the new produced by capitalist modernity and its relentless aptitude for creative destruction. In fact, the uneven layering of times within social formations provides entry into grasping the role played by the unequal relations and development deposited within the synchronic framework of the present. The historical present, as it might be named, offers the prospect to unspool or unwind a present filled with the mixed and entangled times of history and memory, showing itself, above all else, as a sort of noncontemporaneity or temporal discordance. This recalls Eelco Runia's perceptive observation that the retention of prior practices and experiences in the present is the "unrepresented way the past is present in the here and now."[8] The best material example of this kind of layering and unevenness deposited by historical time are the great historic urban spaces like Rome, Istanbul, Kyoto or islands like Sicily, where the most remote but preserved archaic presences coexist side by side with the fittings of modern city life. In short, these essays have been steered by a conviction that knows no one-way street, as such, whether a linear progression, "following the sequence of centuries," or transversally, "when one society lives the life of another in thought, while the latter acts out the thought of the former, without philosophy and history, economics and politics. . . . Construed as 'backwardness' in relation to an imaginary temporal norm, anachronism ends up imposing itself not as a residual anomaly, but as an essential attribute of the present. Non-contemporaneity is not reducible to the immaterial unevenness of its moments. It is also their combined development in a novel historical space-time."[9] Hence, the spectacle of backwardness is no reflection of degraded archaic remainders, leftovers, or even failed past resolutions but rather signifies an "integral part of the way modern society" is constituted and "reproduces itself, or . . . as evidence of perverse forms of progress." For historians of Brazil, in agreement with the literary critic Roberto Schwarz, and putative latecomers like China, India, and Japan, this perspective empowers a mode of "deprovincializ[ing]" that "inscribe[s] these once peripheral regimes on the present." Though once denied entry and assigned to the impossible category of catch-up, they are now placed within the current global configuration, which had previously "seemed to distance [them] from it and confined [them] to irrelevance."[10] The function of this statement of my perspective on history is what many of the essays in this volume aspire to exemplify. Although they might not always clearly or successfully realize this aspiration they nevertheless strive to be counted within the spectrum of its perspective. But it does not account for the specific phases characterizing my interests and the accompanying mediations shaping my outlook, which I will try to supply in the following section.

Actualization

In any effort engaged in trying to envisage and account for a personal trajectory informing these essays and the moments when significant terms of political and cultural direction occurred, it seems always the case that the imperative appears to automatically look backward to origins by uncoiling an individual's narrative chronology. Instead of starting from the present and actually working back through more immediate mediations, the received convention makes it appear that biography should start from the origins of the subject or her/his beginnings on the assumption that the later achievements will be prefigured and prescience mirroring its future revealed. Yet the achievement of a mature life belongs to a later present, its lived present, which should be the true starting point for biographical explanation, rather than a distant childhood or adolescence, which can hardly demonstrate what came later in the individual's life. This conventional strategy comes closest to what Pierre Bourdieu once named as the "biographical illusion." While Bourdieu undoubtedly had his own hobby horse to ride in privileging the concept of habitus that excluded the agency of individual subjectivity and diversity, he was nevertheless right to call into question the totalizing claims of biography/ autobiography that presuppose that a life obeys the dictates of a story. He objected to a view that saw in the story of an individual the totality of events, driven by a "subjective intention" unfolding in chronological steadiness, from a prescient origins to a mature present, sandwiched between a beginning and end. What he warned against was the desire to make individuals the "ideologist[s] of one's own life," a "rhetorical illusion," of another's by settling on a singular and unitary purpose founded on "significant events" through "relations" capable of providing them with meaning.[11] In brief, Bourdieu was objecting to transmuting the individual's life into the microcosm of historical narrative. Even if individuals are thus denied the actuality of authoring their events, it is still possible to identify significant turns in outlook or rather the occasions that move them on. Some combination of forms of socialization I was subjected to experiencing at different times and in quite different places have obviously constituted and are reflected in the course of the essays collected in this volume. My undergraduate education was carried out at Wayne State University and, as I look back, where I possibly received the best and most exciting education imaginable. It emphasized the singular importance and dignity of the life of the mind and centrality of human consciousness in history over the protocols of mere professionalism. Graduate school was its opposite and was what managed to barely bring me into the field of Japanese studies (or pompously Japanology). Graduate school was my first encounter with the larger postwar institutional referent called area studies, which was still in an unfinished and embryonic stage being organized in a number of major universities. Area studies programs sought to provide general, multidisciplinary coverage in specific world regions and apparently represented a delayed response to the awareness of an earlier acknowledgment of entering a war and not knowing anything about America's enemies, pointing to an unpreparedness and the paucity of having only a few specialists who could command some mastery of languages outside the European spectrum. But area studies never completed its trajectory and failed to live up to its principal aim to supply integration of its constituent disciplines. Although this failure of regional totalism, in haste to establish programs and begin enlisting funds for their reproduction, may have been diverted from its original course, it also stemmed from the absence of any serious consideration of how disciplines of knowledge might be put together, which would have enabled working out subsequent procedures for carrying through diverse agendas of comparative research, another missed aspiration. It was evident that all these programs were initially dedicated to serving the needs of an emergent national security state by offering trained specialists in a specific and strategically defined region, who knew both the requisite language and could conduct research in it and how its culture was put together. Knowing one's enemy, real or imagined, was superseded by implanting strategies promising growth and development for new nations that had been former colonies and countering the politics of revolutionary insurrection that appeared in the wake of decolonization. Japan studies offered a slight difference—a noncolonized Asian society that launched a war against the United States and lost. But this historical experience provided a different model, as an already more or less successfully developed example of capitalism existed, which, once rebuilt, could serve as a textbook template for emerging nations in the Cold War struggle for the nonaligned. At the core of the formation of Japan studies an army of occupation officials had already implemented an inventory of ambitious reforms to remove what planners believed were the structural sources that had caused war to remake the country into a proper democratic order. This narrative, never fulfilled, was conveyed by a generation of Japan-related scholars and teachers, many of whom had worked in the military occupation, to reconfigure the occupation's program to showcase Japan as a model of political and economic modernization of non-revolutionary change. Some of the essays in this collection—"Tracking the Dinosaur: Area Studies in a Time of 'Globalism' " and "Memories of Underdevelopment after Area Studies"—address this question of the formation of area studies and its working through in Japan-related studies. Briefly, it might be said of Japan-related studies that there occurred a rapid reconfiguration of the Occupation's schedule of reforms aimed at democratizing the country and reconstructing its capitalist endowment into a scholarly program dedicated to the examination of Japan's historic modernization makeover. The economic theory of modernization was based on the premise that backwardness brought advantages: underdeveloped societies could take over and build on the advances already made elsewhere, as Japan showed in the Meiji era. It was also evolutionary, in as much as it envisaged growth as a slow but steady process that would utilize practices and values surviving from the past to serve capital's accumulation of surplus value to assist Japan's modernization. The real difference from this received evolutionary narrative among latecomers like Japan was manifest in how modernization theorists envisioned an appropriate politics for the new capitalist order, which invariably led to forms of authoritarianism masquerading as democracies founded on the preservation of mythic traditional values. Its most extreme form was fascism.

At one level, I was never fully or even partially assimilated to the protocols of area studies or what came to be defined as the principal vocation of Japan-related studies, of Japan's successful modernization as a textbook model for nonaligned new nations in the Cold War to emulate. I was particularly struck by the contradiction of putting learning at the disposal of the security state and its simultaneous claims that it was value-free, beholden to no ideology, and supremely committed to objectivity. Moreover, it should be added that my relationship to Japan differed from that of many of my contemporaries. Some, owing to military language schools and experience living in the country and working in the Occupation, were already experienced in things Japanese, and still others came to Japan even earlier through missionary experience. And there may also have been a mix of motives prompting people to specialize in Japan studies, including emotionality and experience, delayed exotic desire that led to embracing religion or aesthetics or simply the customary way Japanese lived. None of these applied in my case, which undoubtedly immunized me against successful domestication by area studies and worked to exempt me from seeing Japan as a field of knowledge rather than a way to exemplify and instantiate disciplinary knowledge, history. Gathering data for a totalized view of a region would strongly discourage criticism because of the necessity to fill in the whole picture. In this way, area studies tended to resemble what Japanese called *Nihongaku*, "Japanese learning," a modern gloss of nativist knowledge (*kokugaku*), dedicated to showing the country's exceptional uniqueness. I suppose my orientation came from my undergraduate education, which trained me to see historical studies principally as an intellectual encounter, rather than following the vocation promoted by area studies that privileged the region as the subject of knowledge. If pursued, this route could lead historical practice to reinforcing the reified figure of national history and accepting its accompanying risk of promoting national amour propre to become a patriot of somebody else's history.[12]

Here, I believe, the historian Umemori Naoyuki, who translated my book *Overcome by Modernity*, best describes my departure from many of my contemporaries in what I have been trying to do. In his interpretative essay at the end of the translated version he asks the question, History for whom? and explains that "*Kindai ni yoru chōkoku* [Overcome by Modernity] is a text that has a different feel [about it] from Japanese intellectual history as it has existed until now." It is less a matter of whether the book is original or correct with respect to the individual thinkers it seeks to represent. For Umemori, this text derives its meaning from separating itself from the field of learning constituted as the history of Japanese thought. This departure clearly aims at the basic problem of determining the question of at whom Japan's history of thought is directed and what it is written for. In a word, the history of Japanese thought is written by writers and directed toward readers who share a concern for Japan and a common understanding of it. "With Harootunian's *Kindai ni yoru chōkoku*, the self-evident and tacit premise throughout the book seeks to shatter the silence. Speaking frankly, the writer holds no concern for Japan, as such, and it is a text on Japan's intellectual history for readers who bring no concern for Japan, with respect to things outside Japan. . . . At the same time that it is a basically critical text toward the existing history of Japanese thought, it opens up new possibilities."[13] It is worth recalling that Tosaka Jun had already, in the 1930s, recommended this critical perspective as an antidote to metaphysics and hermeneutics and a reliance on unhistorical categories like *minzoku* (folk), the Japanese thing (*Nihonteki na mono*), and reified concepts like Japanese culture that worked against a material history that must originate in the present rather than the past.[14]

It is important to acknowledge that despite all else the project on Japan's modernization and the series of volumes it produced in the context of the Vietnam War and the American vocation to reorder the globe made a lasting impression on my work, turning me toward envisioning a critical account of area studies on the one hand and an analysis of how the modernization paradigm mediated our understanding of Japanese society and history on the other. In both cases, there seemed to be a shared absence of critique, especially an accounting of the historical and political stakes implicit in representations of area studies and Japan's history and society. Writing history without accounting for the layers of mediations constituting historical moments, as well as those making up the contemporary perspective in which the essays were produced, resembled thinking of capitalism as derived from nature and not history. If in the case of Japan's modernization process a wide gap appeared between an alleged neutral description of development and its content—the capitalist system—the Vietnam War opened the way to dramatize the conflict between politics and scholarship. This conflict was ignited by the growing accusations of student groups—namely, the Committee of Concerned Asian Scholars— which not only protested the hypocritical articulation of the American state's war aims and its expansion but eventually raised the question concerning the role played by scholarship. The student cohort was composed primarily of graduate students specializing in various aspects of Asian studies and their target was an older generation of scholars of Asia who were also their teachers. The principal point of student discontent charged an older generation of scholars with having bracketed the politics informing their scholarly work, which they saw as authoritatively empirical, scientifically neutral, and free from ideological distortion. Under the direction of the Committee of Concerned Asian Scholars, the critique swung broadly to include East Asia and Southeast Asia and consisted of leveling claims and complaints of complicity against well-known scholars of Asian studies, the American state, and its emergent programs of mounting wars of imperial intervention. The protest organization slowly disappeared from the academic scene, especially once the Vietnam War ended.[15] It occurred to me that perhaps the reason for its demise derived less from the war's end than its distrust of or indifference to theory. Yet we should keep in mind that the war provided the occasion of discovery of complicity, which had been at the core of area studies from its beginning. The absence of some commitment to the form of a larger sense of critique might have reset for the group a future agenda capable of sustaining them beyond a temporally momentary and single issue. Its residual trace exists only in a journal titled *Critical Asian Studies.*

In those years, what did survive was the momentum devoted to exploring Japan's modernization. It is important to note that the several volumes in this project appeared in the 1960s and 1970s. There are a number of things that stand out about this series: there is rarely the possibility to catch sight of any contributing essay that actually refers to the role played by capitalism, as such, or its negative consequences in Japan's modern history; by the same measure there is no real awareness of subjectivities of gender, sexuality, or even class; the principal events in Japan's modern history like the Meiji Restoration received little attention and the drift to fascism was consensually ignored; the same people involved in staging the various conferences that produced the volumes controlled funding in a number of agencies like the SSRC (Social Science Research Council), Japan Foundation, and others, positioning them to influence the sponsoring of favored programs of research; while the initial conferences of Japan's modernization were financed by the Ford Foundation and other American foundations, in the 1970s these were gradually replaced by official and private Japanese agencies; and lastly, this series, which never mentions the great Marxian debate in Japan on the origins and development of Japanese capitalism of the 1930s, must be seen as its darkened mirror opposite, resembling a negative photographic print, inasmuch as it was dedicated to the successful development of capitalism and its baleful social and economic consequences in Japan without actually saying so. If the Japanese historical debate exercised a sustained critical approach illustrating an uncompleted capitalism and the political consequences wrongly attributed to it, its American counterpart valorized its achievement and successful completion by reinforcing Japan's claims to exceptionalism, which undermined any utility of the experience as a model for other societies to follow. Over the years, I felt that the conferences devoted to Japan's modernization and its principal proponents overstated the importance of Japan, instead of exploring forms of distancing that saw Japan from the angle of vision of a broader world perspective. Such a standpoint leading to the possibility of comparability would have been preferable to clinging to a view that originally derived its significance from Japan's status as an enemy of the United States, which seemed to diminish once the country became a client of the American imperium and passed into the shadows it had begun to cast. It was hard to separate this representation of Japan studies as an "important national resource" from the career ambitions of this earlier generation of specialists. This progressive diminution not only explains Japan's postwar reluctance to enter the world, until very recently, but also allowed the country to slip back into what might be called a twilight isolation reminiscent of the Tokugawa period's policy of *sakoku*, strangely fulfilling the desire implicit in Watsuji Tetsurō's important postwar book (*Sakoku*) on the isolation effect. The result significantly narrowed the compass of research on modern Japan, instead of seeing in it the possibility and terms of a larger world-historical referent and prevented it from delivering the comparative perspective once promised by area studies. In this way, Japan was rendered into a small subject Masao Miyoshi once described as "uninteresting." What Miyoshi was pointing to was how narrowness from withdrawal from the world was inflected in the absence of any genuine critical practice in contemporary Japan, overtaken by a preoccupation with self-referentiality, signaled by the constant concern with themselves as uttered in the repetitive invocation *warera Nihonjin*, "we Japanese."[16]

✳ ✳ ✳

Finally, many of the essays were written during the long period I spent at the University of Chicago. Chicago was an intellectually charged catalytic environment that taught me more than I can say. In many ways it provided the academic space for extending the undergraduate education I had received earlier at Wayne State. I feel fortunate and even privileged for having been in such an environment, at perhaps the high point of American universities, which now seem to have passed into becoming holding pens for the children of the rich and famous, indebted students, and professional administrators who see themselves as managers pitted against the laboring classes of teachers, principally dedicated to disciplining them. Now shorn of the intellectual freedom and encouragement of diverse forms of learning higher education once cherished, I was lucky to fall in with good colleagues and friends in the Japan-related fields and the opportunity to teach some of the most interesting students I've encountered. I've purposely used the term "teach" advisedly since I received as much, or more, than I was able to give. For me, Chicago permitted a release from responsibility of strictly adhering to the Japan field and opened the pathway by encouraging the pursuit of different kinds of teaching and research subjects often directly unrelated to Japan. It was, by its nature, the most obsessively interdisciplinary university I have ever experienced. It was in this environment I was able to formulate and teach a number of courses that widened and deepened my commitment to intellectual history. Specifically this entailed organizing and teaching with colleagues in European studies comparative seminars on history and literature, intellectual history, which became the basic course for students wishing to specialize in the field, workshops that invariably brought different area specialists and historians together, and a decadelong reading course composed and organized with graduate students from various disciplines, which met weekly on Friday afternoons to discuss a reading assigned from a philosophical or theoretical text. Our goal was to read and discuss whole texts rather than snippets and it was open to anyone interested in participating.

There was no hierarchic leadership, no exclusions of anyone, and discussion was generated from within the participant group, without mediating guidance. This, in itself, was a priceless education for me and, I believe, all who stayed the course with it during their time in Chicago. Happily, Chicago had always been different from most American universities and there was a certain truth in its official ideology that it was the last of the great German universities. (Edward Shils never seemed to tire of remarking it was the best second-rate university in the world and he knew of no first-rate universities!) But it should be said that none of us in the Japan field ever self-consciously fixated on the formation of something called the "Chicago school," a label that was tacked onto us by outsiders, many of whom disapproved of some of the things we were doing or stood for. In some instances the label acquired associations of criminality, thugism, and racism when it was altered into the "Chicago mafia."

From the Occupation to the modernization project, it was evident that the dominant American view of Japan was based on the assumption that Japan stood in a client relation to the United States. It was this premise that supplied the basis for the construction of an image presumably based on objective and value-free scholarship, even though there were values all over the place that were hardly neutral. American values were being pressed on the Japanese, as Etō Jun once correctly observed, even though he wrongly exemplified it with the North's forcible imposition of its values on the American South after the Civil War. As former Occupation officials the first postwar generation of Japan-related scholars undoubtedly believed that serving one's nation was a natural duty. This meant they were unable to see the "bent" nature of their scholarly interests as politically saturated, and instead identified politics with the Marxism and Leninism they so opposed. Built into this legacy was a subsequent attitude toward Japan that discouraged and opposed any sign of criticism of what came to be considered the accepted image of Japan as now a democracy. Later, critical views on Japan were reduced to expressions of "Japan bashing."

Much of the work in which I was interested aimed at trying to get behind or beyond this image of Japan to see what was being bracketed and displaced. Many of the essays are spin-offs from books I was writing or editing with others. It was during these years that I focused on three distinct periods in Japan's history, late Tokugawa, the interwar, and postwar. What held this chronology together was the appearance of the collision of new cultural forms, with political implications, and the response of political modes of organizing social relationships, which, in many ways, reflected our historical conjuncture with its own, constant conflict between culture (and identity) and politics down to the present. In the case of Japan, I was particularly concerned with the role played by the development of capitalism from its incipient occurrence in the late Tokugawa, its acceleration in the interwar years, and its domination in the postwar reconstruction. But apart from trying to show that the consensual image needed to be contested for what it had left unsaid or unstated I was committed to showing that Japanese society since the late Tokugawa years leading into the Restoration was violent and chaotic and this tradition of conflict continued to scrape against any image seeking to uphold the consistency of a society run according to smooth and orderly consensus. But this image, reaching its most intensely phantasmagoric moment in the book *Japan as Number One*, easily betrayed itself when people began to look behind it and determined the modes of coercion necessary to maintain it and, in recent years, the violence exercised against those who dared to be different. In my most recent work I have begun to look at the role played by the figure of the emperor, restored by the American Occupation as a symbolic presence of "national unity," actually representing a second restoration, instead of targeting the imperial system (*tennōsei*), which simply was a convenient displacement to bureaucracy necessitated by fascist censorship in the 1930s. It should be recalled that in the prewar years, state censorship constrained any criticism of the emperor, which forced Marxists to develop a coded language and to substitute the retention of feudal remnants for the imperial household. In the postwar period, when constraints on criticism were lifted, Marxists continued to use the older idiom associated with *tennōsei*, rather than inaugurate a national discussion on the status of the imperial figure. Instead they exhumed the old bogey of bureaucratic apparatus that administered its realm, trying to resuscitate worn-out clichés like feudal remnants while the so-called modernists turned to promoting an overdetermined discussion on male bourgeois subjectivity. But what was being restored by the Occupation was more than a symbol, since even as a symbol the figure was no less empowered than it had been before the war. Since the restored emperor, Hirohito, retained all the ceremonial and ritualistic functions identified with the throne, he still embodied the conflated power of politics (governance/ceremony, *matsurigoto*) and the social body (ethnicity linked to the gods who created the islands and its peoples). My own interest, in this respect, was to examine why fascism was so quickly extinguished in the early postwar and literally forgotten, even though its archaic presence remained intact in the restored monarchy and its narrative and its imminent readiness, poised to make a comeback under certain historical circumstances, as we can observe elsewhere. Yet we must consider the consequential importance of a second restoration of an archaic imperial presence that still presides over the religiopolitical calendar of rituals, rites, and ceremonial observances linking the earthly emperor and the Japanese people to their ancestors and national deities, reminding the population of the unity demanded and signified by the national body (*kokutai*). This consideration has brought me back to the Meiji Restoration, where I literally began my uncertain intellectual adventure and which seems to have disappeared from the screen of historical practice in Japan and abroad. What I am particularly interested in of the Meiji

Restoration is the inherent repetition associated with the subsequent calls for another restoration to overcome historical time and complete the unfinished business of returning to the present an imperishable ancient endowment which, like the emperor bonded to this operation, remains outside time and supposedly immune to history's erosions. Any call for an imperial restoration to complete unfinished work of the immediate past embodied both an archaic presence and the temporality of anachrony or claims of timelessness recalling a mythic moment of origin. Yet the figure of the archaic also recalls Marx's support of retaining certain archaic elements like the Russian commune to circumvent the more baneful aspects of capitalism. The principal difference was the absence of history in the Japanese appeal to the archaic origin as against Marx's insistence on the historicality of the Russian commune. It was in fact this privileging of the figure in the Meiji Restoration that transformed the late Tokugawa process of multiple secessions withdrawing from the central authority of the *bakufu* and the possibility of plural restorations implying a federal form into a singular event and centralized state. This possible interpretation of the Meiji Restoration is introduced in the conclusion of the essay "Late Tokugawa Culture and Thought," which seeks to show the force of proliferating new cultural forms introduced in the late Tokugawa period (*bakumatsu*), and demanding attention to finding adequate political arrangements to accommodate them. What in the Tokugawa period gestured toward reconfiguring the body for pleasure and different political possibilities was transmuted into a body singularly dedicated to work and self-sacrifice in the Meiji. The problem that now has to be worked through is the consequential and defining contradiction of the combination of an archaic emperor and capitalism in the unevenness in modern Japan.

This critical impulse was accompanied by an additional concern. So much of my writing dealt with discursive texts, the staple of both intellectual and certain kinds of cultural history, I found, given my interest in Marxian modes of analysis, it was necessary to try working through a way that might join Marxian analytic formulations and the production of intellectual and cultural histories without reducing one to the other. This was true of some my larger or longer works, and I was able to envisage how instances of unevenness and the bringing together of past practices with newer ones in the present required by capitalism's production process (what Marx described as subsumptive appropriations) might provide a productive perspective. I was particularly concerned with the recognition that Marxism of the vulgate version had always eschewed and often discounted thought and culture as merely effects reducible to a material base and had often neglected the relationship between thought, discourse, culture, and materiality. This was especially true of Marxists in Japan, excepting the historian Hani Gorō, who was perhaps the most gifted practitioner of a Marxian intellectual and cultural history before and after the war.

Part of this impulse was supplied by new interpretations of Marx from the 1960s that drew away from vulgate versions originating in the Second International. But a more important circumstance was the collapse of the Berlin Wall in 1989 and the dissolution of Soviet Marxism in its Stalinist inflexion. Under these conditions, it was not surprising that there was a return to the founder's texts and a program of rereading them that opened new possibilities and extended older intellectual horizons to include more of the world rather than Euro-America. It was, again, Marx who forged this global pathway with his striking observation of the formation of the world market in the nineteenth century and his acute advice in *Capital* that what he was describing was not limited to England and Germany but the world. Quoting from Horace, Marx proclaimed, "The tale is told of you" (*De te fabula narrator*).[17] It was this historical environment that saw Japan as part of a larger global configuration (noted by Tōyama Shigeki in his classic book on the Meiji Restoration) marked by unevenness and forms of combined development in which capital actively utilized older practices from the past to enable its own production system, and which became the basis of my book *Marx After Marx*. This thematic thread, exemplified by Japan's history, shows that the experience of uneven development is not limited to capitalist latecomers but implicates all societies committed to its production agenda. For this reason, we are, I believe, obliged to respond to its demand of a global perspective because there is no "pure development" of capitalism as supposed by earlier versions of Marxian discourse or a modular form that prescribes for all a unitary linear developmental trajectory divided into progressive stages. Unevenness thus pointed to plural societies, relationality, a multiplicity of different pathways of the historical development of capitalism that made each manifestation intrinsically worldly.[18] It also brought "with their accompanying train" manifest noncontemporaneous or nonsimultaneous temporalities that coexist with one another indexing historically different formations each has utilized. The point here is to broaden the logic of subsumption to account for it as an ongoing global process that must be seen to involve the incorporation of other dimensions like the cultural, political, religious as necessary conditions for the social reproduction of capitalist society. Grasping the actualization of subsumption as a global process beyond the economic and its relationship to plural determinations opens the pathway to seeing the production of history as the record of uneven and combined development.

It is precisely this dialectical encounter between history and capital logic, the capacity for producing combinatories out of what appear as incommensurables, that brings us to its possibilities for producing history or its concept and, eventually, back to the Japanese experience. It is precisely capital's incessant desire, if not persistent goal, to ultimately convert all difference and uniqueness into quantifiable commensurability that the labor of intellectual history and reinstatement of rememoration preserved in the everyday seeks to restore the true meaning of the incommensurate.[19] Paraphrasing Samir Amin, world history is always driven by different unequal and uneven developmental situations that produce diverging forms of combinations.

Notes

1. Michael Oakeshott, *On History and Other Essays* (Indianapolis: Liberty Fund, 1999), 1–48.
2. Francis Mulhern, *Culture/Metaculture* (London: Routledge, 2000), 171.
3. Kristin Ross, *L'imaginaire de la Commune*, trans. Etienne Dobenesque (Paris: La fabrique, 2015), 1–18.
4. Ross, *L'imaginaire de la Commune*, 2.
5. Enzo Traverso, *Le passé, modes d'emploi: Histoire, mémoire, politique* (Paris: La fabrique, 2005), 22, 87.
6. Traverso, *Le passé*, 40.
7. Paul Ricoeur, *Memory, History, Forgetting*, trans. Kathleen Blamey and David Pellauer (Chicago: University of Chicago Press, 2004), 141–45, 508.
8. Eelco Runia, *Moved by the Past* (New York: Columbia University Press, 2014), 154.
9. Daniel Bensaïd, *Marx for Our Times*, trans. Gregory Elliott (London: Verso, 2002), 24.
10. Roberto Schwarz, *A Master on the Periphery of Capitalism: Machado de Assis*, trans. John Gledson (Durham, N.C.: Duke University Press, 2002), 3.
11. Pierre Bourdieu, "L'illusion biographique," *Actes de la recherche en sciences sociales* 62/63 (June 1986): 69–72.
12. Harry Harootunian, "Other People's History: Some Reflections on the Historian's Vocation," *Japan Forum* 29, no. 2 (2017): 139–53.
13. Umemori Naoyuki, "'Kindai ni yoru chōkoku' no setsudan," in *Kindai ni yoru chōkoku*, by Harry Harootunian, trans. Umemori Naoyuki (Tokyo: Iwanami shoten, 2007), 2:321–22.
14. Tosaka Jun, *Tosaka Jun zenshū*, 5 vols. (Tokyo: Keisō shobō, 1978), 4:203–9.
15. Fabio Lanza, *The End of Concern: Maoist China, Activism, and Asian Studies* (Durham, N.C.: Duke University Press, 2017).
16. Harry Harootunian, "Warera mishi mama ni, Masao Miyoshi to hihanteki tatakai to iu shimei," trans. Hirano Katsuya, *Misuzu* 664 (October 2017), part 2:62.
17. Karl Marx, *Capital: A Critique of Political Economy*, trans. Ben Fowkes (London: Penguin, 1990), 1:90.
18. Etienne Balibar, *The Philosophy of Marx*, trans. Chris Turner (London: Verso, 1995), 110.
19. I am grateful to Marilyn Ivy for this observation and indebted to her for reminding me of it, from a personal correspondence.

PART I

IMMINENT CRITICISM AND ACADEMIC DISCOURSE

Area Studies

CHAPTER 1

TRACKING THE DINOSAUR

Area Studies in a Time of "Globalism"

You've established a wonderful thing here with Hitler. . . . Nobody on the faculty of any college or university in this part of the country can so much as utter the word Hitler without a nod in your direction, literally or metaphorically. This is the center, the unquestioned source. . . . It must be deeply satisfying for you. The college is internationally known as a result of Hitler studies. It has an identity, a sense of achievement. You've evolved an entire system around this figure, a structure with countless substructures and interrelated fields of study, a history within a history. I marvel at the effort. It was masterful, shrewd and stunningly preemptive. It's what I want to do with Elvis.

—Don DeLillo, *White Noise*

I t has been one of the enduring ironies of the study of Asia that Asia itself, as an object, simply doesn't exist. While geographers and mapmakers once confidently named a sector on maps, noting even its coordinates as if in fact it existed, this enmapped place has never been more than a simulacrum of a substanceless something. It refers only to itself in the expectation that something out there will eventually correspond to it or be made to align with it. The cartographers' art has been produced by an age-old fantasy and then reinforced by requirements of World War II. Nonetheless we have in this country professional organizations devoted to the study of this simulacrum, and educational institutions pledged to disseminating knowledge of it, even as the object vanishes before our eyes once we seek to apprehend it. I always felt that a professional organization like the Association for Asian Studies periodically brought specialists together in order to reaffirm the existence of what clearly is a phantom. So confident in its existence, this professional body years ago decided to change its name from the Far Eastern Association to the Association for Asian Studies in order to stake out an even larger territory, however phantasmagoric. But these names are as lifeless as the social science—geography—that once declared their reality and named its presence. What seems so important is the way the association tries to sustain the fictional phantom even as its mode of organizing and operating disperses Asia as a coherent figure of knowledge. Anybody familiar with the workings of this association or who has had a glimpse of its journal or the programs of the annual meetings will immediately realize that if Asia is absent, smaller geographic units such as Southeast Asia, East Asia, and South Asia are everywhere represented. A closer look will show that even these satellite units have shrunk into smaller categories of the nation-state.

Although the association's committees are divided along area lines, its membership and officers serve as metonyms—stand-ins—because they are, at bottom, not specialists of Northeast Asia, South Asia, or Inner Asia but of nation-states. In every year's abstract there is a section near the back of the volume devoted to "inter-area," yoked to the categories of library and teaching, marking its location of "in-betweenness" and suggesting both expedience and afterthought. All this signifies the recognition that an association committed to the study of Asia is not an "inter-area" when in fact its true vocation would be to extract or produce knowledge that could be only inter-area. Nobody ever questions the directional tyranny that names as East the place we go to study. East is, rather, where one ends up when starting from the geographical West, which implies that movement can proceed in only one direction. But this inversion of the earlier Hegelian itinerary of freedom's unfolding as it moves slowly from east to west confirms its intellectual trajectory favoring the place of the West which, because of its full and completed development, can view the East from this privileged site. But where do we really start from, where is the place of enunciation?

When we try to account for how an association devoted to Asia determines the principles on which panels are "selected for its annual meeting," we learn that apart from the exercise of political interest—invariably denied—no other criteria seem to inform the breakdown besides the traditional disciplines and national societies. Panels belong to either a discipline or a national society around which papers have been organized. A few years ago, a proposal for a two-part panel dedicated for the first time to examining area studies was reduced to one part by the selection committee, and its placement suggested that the association was indifferent, if not outright hostile, to self-reflection. In 1996, a president's round table was scheduled to discuss the status of area studies in a profession that has never shown the slightest interest in its enabling epistemology and the structure of organization it has authorized. But multipart panels still continue to be formed to examine arcane subjects like medicine in Tokugawa Japan as if such a subject, and others even more remote and specialized, were so compelling that students were actually waiting in line to get the latest word. I always suspected that this arrogance could be traced to the association's desire to appear "unpolitical" and functioned to repress its political origin, which plainly was generated by political considerations after World War II. While this newly articulated, self-reflexive interest in the status of area studies stems from the widely acknowledged bankruptcy of the model, it was undoubtedly prompted by the Ford Foundation's recent program to fund the effort to rethink area studies in fifty colleges and universities.

Once the organization of area knowledge was fixed, soon after World War II, all that remained were periodic adjustments to the changing political realities throughout the world and discussion of how the structures it sanctioned could be sustained. This anxiety was expressed in the obsessive search for money here and abroad, which has become the principal preoccupation of area studies in the established universities and colleges of the United States and probably the United Kingdom.

The reluctance to cross the administrative/geopolitical and disciplinary grids that partition knowledge means only that the informing principles of a dominant tradition in the social sciences and the humanities continue to authorize the still axiomatic duality between an essentialized, totalized, but complete Western self and an equally essentialized, totalized but incomplete East. Yet we can see that this refusal to tamper with epistemological and organizational categories is at the heart of the Asia profession and its institutionalization into the model of area studies. Fifty years after the war, we are still organizing knowledge as if—in the case of Japan, China, and the former Soviet Union—we are confronted by an implacable enemy and thus driven by the desire to know it in order to destroy it or learn how to sleep with it. While nobody would deny that this tireless industry has produced mountains of empirical data on the peoples of these societies, this accomplishment has kept these areas from being assimilated into new theories of knowledge and categorizations that promise to end their isolation. The paradox has been that even while we go from a place marked as the West to study the East, we—as Westerners—conspire to keep the two sectors of the globe from encountering each other, shadowing the Hegelian conceit that once spirit left its abode in the East to reveal itself fully in the West, nothing more needed to be said about that part of the world and history, which would remain incomplete until it remade itself in the image if its "other," the self. Like the exotics of an earlier generation, we still seek to penetrate the East and unravel its mysteries, despite knowing that there are none, but we never bring the East back to the world we started from, thus making sure that the East remains the East. In doing so, we preserve the "mysteries" and become its custodians. Perhaps like the intrepid Victor Segalen, we discover there is no there, no mysteries to behold or to report back, and so we have no choice but to preserve the aura by resorting to separation and isolation.

This is, in fact, an apt description of area studies practiced in universities and colleges as their proponents have sought to maintain them in a world increasingly more global and culturally borderless than when they were introduced into the academic procession. What started out as a convenient way to get courses and languages of distantly foreign countries into college and university curricula after the war became, in time, an enormous organization, resembling more a huge holding company with a tight grip on its subsidiaries, monopolizing its product—knowledge of a specific area—and thus controlling its distribution and consumption. Like those temporary dwellings hastily assembled during World War II, presumably to be replaced by something more permanent in the near future, area studies have outlived their original purpose and temporary function to become an entrenched structure that has maintained the separation of knowledge of an area or region from being integrated into a general pedagogy and curriculum, as it was once supposed to do. As a result, they have become like fossils entrapped in amber, and today, they still behave more like a dinosaur whose immense body incessantly demands food but whose small head is no longer adequate to control its movements.

Even though the structures representing area studies in colleges and universities are both well staffed and well financed these days, intellectually they are nothing more than worn-out hovels, like the corrugated Quonset huts left on American campuses by the military that served as temporary classrooms and offices well into the 1960s. Even after those structures were eventually dismantled, we still have area studies to remind us of another and a different world, dinosaurs in an intellectual Jurassic Park, where creatures with large bodies and small brains are on display.

The development of area studies programs after World War II grew out of a wartime necessity. Readers of Ruth Benedict's *The Chrysanthemum and the Sword* will recall her acknowledgment that the book was commissioned by the Office of War Information and that its purpose was to better understand the enemy we were fighting.[1] Likewise, the systematic formation of area studies in the major universities was a massive attempt to relocate the enemy in the new configuration of the Cold War. This relocation was made possible by large infusions of money from private corporations, scholarly organizations like the Social Science Research Council (SSRC)—"brokering" (pimping might be a more apt description of its role) for both government and private funders—and businesses. This intervention was not simply limited to American universities. The Rockefeller Foundation poured a lot of money into reorganizing the social sciences in France to give the French a new and more scientific social science capable of combating the claims of Marxism. During the Vietnam War, the Ford Foundation tried to support Southeast Asian studies at Kyoto University and for years has been active in both India and Indonesia. In fact, the Cold War easily replaced the wartime necessity of learning the enemies' languages and customs by establishing a closer link between the task of identifying the foe and gathering knowledge—intelligence—about it.

As a field of inquiry finding its own place at the end of the academic procession in colleges and universities, area studies were a response to the wartime discovery of the paucity of reliable information concerning most of the world outside Europe. In the immediate postwar period, the recognition of this deficiency was made more compelling by the military, political, and economic expansion of the United States in its effort to reconfigure the world. Underscoring this new urgency and giving it force were a number of reports issued by official and semiofficial commissions immediately after the war that called for the rapid installation of multidisciplinary programs, composed of specialists in various disciplines to train area specialists and provide policy making and business strategies with informed, socialized knowledge of specific areas. This mode of reporting has characterized the development of area studies and has—in the case of Japan, where responsibility has passed from the SSRC to the Japan Foundation and the Japanese Ministry of Education—become a form of surveillance and even censorship, about which I shall say more later.

The University of Michigan geographer Robert B. Hall headed the SSRC's Committee on World Area Research, which emphasized the need for an "integrated" approach and the primacy of contemporaneity, suggesting that an interest in historical cultures was no longer useful to government and business.[2] Hall, it should be recalled, had been the president of the Association for Asian Studies and also one of its founders, who subsequently established the Center for Japanese Studies at the University of Michigan and ended his career as the director of the Asia Foundation's office in Tokyo, which sponsored clandestine activities in East Asia. The Commission on Implications of Armed Services Educational Programs, sponsored by the American Council of Learned Societies (ACLS), recommended the establishment of area specialists, recruited from graduates of the service language schools, to supply reliable knowledge on specific areas. Corporate interests were early reflected in the active involvement of private foundations, like Rockefeller's inaugural gifts to Yale to establish Far Eastern and Russian studies and the University of Washington's program in Far East studies and Columbia University's Russian Institute. The Carnegie Corporation gave Harvard $740,000 to establish its Russian Research Center in 1947 and, later, almost as much to the University of Michigan for Japanese studies. Between 1953 and 1966, the principal private funder for area studies was the Ford Foundation, which awarded more than $270 million to thirty-four universities and also financed projects like Princeton University's "Modernization of Societies" and the University of Chicago's "New Nations" project in the 1960s. Even after the government took over this responsibility with the passage of the National Defense Education Act in 1956, private foundations continued to underwrite established area studies programs and, in time, were joined by overseas foundations associated with foreign governments and private organizations.

I should point out that the establishment of area studies programs promised to "transcend" disciplinary boundaries—partitioned knowledge—to provide holistic and integrated accounts of different societies. But because of the relentless kinship that area studies formed with policy making, serving national interests and, according to Ravi Arvind Palat, "contract research," they could never free themselves from the pursuit of a knowledge bonded to an original purpose. In a 1970 report on Japanese studies for the SSRC, John W. Hall, formerly of Yale University, described Japanese area studies programs and the area specialists as a national resource.[3] During the Vietnam War, Professor John K. Fairbank of Harvard University, literally the last emperor of Chinese studies in the United States, reiterated the instrumentalist theme that the war dramatized how little Americans knew about Asia and that it was important to both government and private business to support Asian (Chinese) area studies. But this was an already exhausted echo of the plea for area studies to meet the challenges of the Cold War in the years immediately after 1945. Yet it was precisely this division of intellectual labor marking area studies—their service to the state and business and even to foreign governments—that discouraged the discussion of an integrated knowledge of the area and instead encouraged its continued partitioning and fragmenting. The importance of Hall's study, a model for subsequent surveys, is that it prefigured all future efforts to transfer scholarly and pedagogical considerations to the problem of funding area studies programs.

Area studies during the Cold War managed to reduce the region under study to the category of national society, as if China, Japan, or Korea could serve as a stand-in for East Asia, or Mexico and Brazil for Latin America, or Bengal for South Asia. With few momentary exceptions like the old New Nations program at the University of Chicago, funding agencies like the SSRC and ACLS and university teaching and research programs have been organized along the lines of national societies throughout the Cold War and after. But even the New Nations project employed the model of the nation as an emergent unit. Despite the SSRC's recent warning that the time has come to "become conscious" of how the organization of international scholarship is patterned on past public and foreign policy and funder priorities, its committees still follow the national model. Even though a recent report announced a shift from country toward "a range of themes," the SSRC was delegated the task of envisaging new models for international scholarship to the very national committees that are supposedly being phased out. This hypocrisy is compounded by the fact that the SSRC has periodically called for reforms and revisions only when "funders' priorities" change and money for area studies stops flowing into its coffers.[4] Like Hegel's owl, it is always too late.

In the immediate postwar era, calls for the establishment of new area studies programs revealed the kind of knowledge desired. William Fenton's *Area Studies in American Universities* of 1947 observed that the very methodology of integrated studies was a new challenge. "In taking a functional view of contemporary civilizations," he wrote, "it jeopardizes the strong position which the historical method holds in academic thinking." The new functional approach concentrates on the present situation with its "latent historicity, in place of long developmental curricula running from Aristotle to modern times." And "it calls on the method of the cultural historian to develop the major themes in the civilization, delving deep enough into the past only to make the present understandable."[5] In time, this became an invitation to abandon history altogether, as functionalist social science explicitly demanded in the 1950s and 1960s. Although the older social science, focusing on the interaction of culture and the formation of personality—exemplified at war's end by Benedict and Francis Hsu—cooperated with this recommendation to eliminate the long duration of history, or even historical specificity, it could not adequately account for explaining the processes of change and development considered so vital to Cold War policy strategies designed to win the hearts and minds of the free and unaligned world. Indeed, it had no way to provide for a society's capacity to change and thus risked making modern social groups appear identical with their Stone Age predecessors.

Because of this epistemological weakness, a different kind of social science, capable of explaining development and change, was needed, especially one that could offer an alternative to Marxian conflict models and the conception of revolutionary change. It was provided by structural functionalism, which rearticulated the social Darwinist conception of evolutionary adaptation and development and was reconfigured into an export model of growth called *modernization* and *convergence theory*. What was eventually offered as both a representation of and a prescription for development was an evolutionary model of growth, as opposed to a revolutionary one, which, if followed, would lead to the peaceful development of capitalism and, presumably, democracy in the non-aligned world. Even today, the *New York Times* regularly reports, as it did on Sunday, March 9, 1997, quoting President Clinton's former economic adviser Laura D'Andrea Tyson, that American policy is based on, and is thus served by, the conviction that the growth of capitalism and presumably a middle class in China will lead to a "stable evolution toward a more open, more democratic, more market-oriented system based on the rule of law."

Claiming a normative status but appearing more as an idealization scarcely reflecting any recognizable American society on which it was supposed to be based, this theory was inspired by Talcott Parsons's theoretical patternings and Marion Levy's unusable applications that often recalled a Rube Goldberg drawing rather than an analysis of a specific social system. Its theory of knowledge rested on a number of ideal typical traits: societies as coherently organized systems whose subsystems were interdependent and on historical development (divided into modern and traditional) that determined social subsystems (in this scheme, modernity meant rational, scientific, secular, and Western; historically, modernization was evolutionary). Last, traditional societies, owing to the success of modernization, would undergo adaptive upgrading.[6] Modernization theory shared with Marxism and, later, postcolonial discourse its refusal to recognize modernity as a specific cultural form and a consciousness of lived historical time that differed according to the various social forces and practices that depended as much on the experience of place as they did on time.

In the scholarly world of the 1950s, 1960s, and early 1970s, this strategy generally dominated research agendas related to area studies, as they still do in policy consideration, even though the cold war has officially ended. During this time, marked by the Vietnam War, its most spectacular success was supplied by the example of Japan and the singularity of the national model. Modernization theory seemed to be able to validate the category of national society more easily than could a heterogeneous area like East Asia and show how a country like Japan could successfully reproduce the necessary patterns when others, like India and Turkey, could not. It was for this reason that Japanese political arrangements have consistently been represented as a democratic stand-in for capitalist development when, in fact, they are driven by a single party devoted to managed capitalism rather than the "free play" of the market. Japan has had to enact a narrative free from conflict and contradiction, in which traditional values could adapt to new exigencies and perform as rational agents. It is important to notice that the category of the nation is made to stand in for the area or region and that the efforts to present a coherent East Asia appeal to the binding power of a religion or an ethic as they fuse comfortably with capitalism (usually referred to as "Asian values"), which stretches the imagination as much as it insults the intelligence. The force of national or ethnic metonyms seems also to have migrated to postcolonial studies, in which Bengal is made to represent the subcontinent.

One effect of modernization theory was to transmute a prescriptive into a descriptive, the rational into the real, an ought into a what is, as the former ambassador to Japan Edwin O. Reischauer put it in numerous speeches to

Japanese audiences during his tenure in the early 1960s.[7] One consequence of this tactic for the study of societies like Japan has been to discourage the importation of newer theoretical approaches (sensitive to knowledge/power, cognizant of colonizing experiences, and the like) in order to defend the representation of what has been naturalized as a sign of empirical research. According to modernization theory, Japan has thus become a walled enclave resisting newer theoretical approaches. In fact, Japan's "success" as a modernizer exceeded the expectations of its formulators to the extent that Japan, as Reischauer early and ceaselessly reminded audiences, is really not like other Asian countries but is closer to the advanced Western societies it has emulated. For this reason, the Japan field has never shown much inclination to "validate," theoretically or methodologically, the field,[8] which itself never questions the conceptual status of a "field" called "Japan" but, rather, continues to serve a national interest, first that of the United States and then of Japan. Organizations like the SSRC, especially, and the Japan Foundation, presumably devoted to "cutting-edge" methodology, have made sure that the national committee structure directing their respective activities (distributing funds and controlling research) are positioned to serve as the sole directors of and vigilant guard dogs against particularly the kinds of theoretical and methodological innovations they purport to promote. Instead of encouraging greater integration of differing knowledges and intellectual agendas, they have only partitioned and dispersed them, supported by the national committee structure with its received views of region. The jealously guarded defense of a particular view of an area, say Japan, is matched by the reproduction of institutional and organizational structures (like the composition of committees distributing funds for fellowships and research) that reinforce claims of "normativity." It is here that the negative desire for theory at the heart of area studies is defined and repressed.

If it is hard to take seriously the SSRC's recent declarations that the area studies model is no longer operable, it is even more difficult to believe a plan that places responsibility for implementing the needed changes in the very committees that created the problem. The worst consequence of this repetition is the aggressive dismissal of new theoretical and methodological approaches that might disturb the representation of Japan as signified and its sponsored study by organizations like the SSRC, the Japan Foundation, and that durable instrument of the Japanese Ministry of Education, the International Research Center for Japanese Studies in Kyoto. What I am suggesting is that these and other entrenched agencies are committed to sustaining a particular (and uncritical) conception of Japan and how it should be studied and taught. This conception is linked to institutional structures and sources of funding. More often than not, the same people who represent the interests of large programs have replicated that venerable Japanese practice of "lifetime job security" and sit for long durations on the various national and binational committees distributing money. At one time, this feudal arrangement made no effort to disguise its operations and simply brought the same faces to the same windows.

Apart from the large institutional and financial inducements that encourage the study of the area from the optic of the nation, the nation as a category often determines how people will study it. Many who rushed to a study for personal reasons (missionary connection, service experience, delayed and infantile exoticisms) usually masked such emotional attachments with appeals to empirical and "scientific" authority. The early generation of Americans who raced to study Japan after the war, for example, were committed to showing how the nation's history disclosed the rule of reason (which apparently had been on holiday a few years earlier) and how closely the modernizing experience resembled the example of the United States. (In this project, scholars were assisted by the experience of the U.S. military occupation, which saw Japan as a social laboratory for social democracy and an opportunity for fine tooling and thus improving on the American experience by removing its defects.) This fantasy was projected by the work of modernization studies, sponsored by the Ford Foundation, which effectively sought to transform former foe into friend and trading partner.

Yet this project also disguised or misrecognized the semicolonial status of Japan (it had already forgotten about Japan's fascism and its recent history as a colonizer) after the U.S. occupation ended. The consequences of this transformation were revealed in subsequent teaching and research showing that Japan most nearly replicated the development of the capitalist and democratic West, despite its brief affair with fascism. When relations between the two partners began to fall apart over trade in the 1970s, critics of this rosy representation were denounced as Japan bashers, usually by professional Japanologists who unwittingly betrayed their own carefully hidden stakes in maintaining an "upbeat" version by trying now to preserve what experience had already repudiated.

China studies seemed to be dominated by the paradigms of challenge and response (actually an old Toynbeean idea recycled by Fairbank and his personal army of students) that saw China responding to the West and failing, owing to retrograde institutions and intellectual traditions, often described negatively as the "nondevelopment of science" and the "nondevelopment of capitalism," paralleling the non-Western outside Euro-America. Early interpreters of South Asia (in what used to be called "empire studies") easily and enthusiastically overlooked colonialism and attributed all of India's postcolonial problems as a fledgling democracy to the dead hand of religion and overpopulation, as if the subcontinent had never been colonized. With South Asia, the approach to the region still seemed to be clouded by Hegel's dim assessment of the negativity of Indian life.

If the link between professional Japanologists and the field of study appears more prominent and overdetermined than in other area studies, it is, I believe, because of the overwhelming production of native knowledge and thus self-consciousness that has marked Japan's own modernity. But this enhancement of native knowledge is also a kind of occupational handicap that dogs the study of Asia especially and other parts of the world outside Euro-America. Area interest is powered by a mix of exoticisms, however displaced, and a desire for nearness, closing the distance between there and here and the promise of difference. During my first trip to Japan, I met all kinds of Americans fulfilling their exotic and erotic fantasies for reidentification, ranging from obsessive "kanji sharks," as they were called (the craze to learn as many Chinese ideographs as the mind was capable of retaining, especially those with several strokes), to those who wore baskets on their head, carried rice bowls, and pretended they were itinerant Buddhist pilgrims. We might call this hermeneutic strategy the "Pierre Loti effect," which is easily recognized as a way of making contact with otherness through a reliance on costume and performance. Since then, only the objects promising identification have changed. (The latest example is the tirade of an American who, after a brief stay in Japan, has written a novel from the viewpoint of a geisha, which is about to be made into a movie by Spielberg!) With China, there was the "helping hand," the vanished missionary vocation, and the seeming helplessness of the Chinese people in the face of Japan's aggression. Later, for a moment, it was the romance of revolution. With Japan, there is, of course, the legacy of the American occupation and the romanticization of this partnership to rebuild a free and prosperous Japan. Many postwar Japan specialists had come from either missionary families or service language schools; others experienced the occupation as a colonial opportunity. This gave Japan a special status, a uniqueness that was built into programs that always required trainees to go to Japan to do their fieldwork.

When I was a graduate student studying history, I was puzzled by the way Japan was presented as a field where one went to do fieldwork, even if one's purpose was archival rather than ethnographic. People were always off to the field or just returning from it. Even so, they were not as clothes conscious as today's news correspondents, who always seem to be outfitted by Banana Republic when on assignment in the "field." But by the same measure, I knew that France, Italy, and England were countries where people went for study and research, whereas Japan, Asia, and Africa were simply fields, places that required observation, recording, and, in some instances, intervention. Perhaps this sense of the field revealed the deeper relationship of these regions to a colonial unconscious, which still approached them as spaces occupied by "natives" who needed to be observed and thus represented. This differentiation between field and country suggested both distance, physical and figural, and the existence of different temporalities marking the boundary between modern and premodern. As students, we were encouraged to spend time in the field to observe societies that belonged to a different temporality, even though we all inhabited the time of the present. It was a Western present, however, established according to "modern" timekeeping. Its most important effect was to classify the field as inside and native and us as visitors from the outside and nonnative seeking entry in order to penetrate and thus grasp the secrets of native knowledge, which would always be beyond reach.

The conceit of transforming a place into a "field" was a custom long practiced by anthropologists and ethnographers, who saw the field as a code for the laboratory; now it became a commonplace among historians, political scientists, sociologists, and students of literature. Persuaded to view Japan or China (which at the time was closed to Americans, who had to use surrogates like Taiwan and Hong Kong), India, and Southeast Asia as ethnographic scenes, students were required to take intensive language courses and to experience living among the natives. These two conditions were considered—and still are—as more than adequate substitutes or replacements for theory and methodology; in fact, they were seen as functional analogues of both. Moreover, trainees in Japanese studies since the end of the war have regularly acquired wives who could double as native informants and stand in for field experience during their time away from the "field." If this often constitutes a kind of rite of passage, it also sealed an identity with Japan that further foreclosed the possibility of critique. I should also say that this relationship was usually one way, with men acquiring Japanese wives.

This relationship revealed a deeply embedded hermeneutic that had always promised to promote empathic immediacy and identification as the most appropriate and authentic mode of studying Japan and, I suspect, Asia. It is for this reason that so much emphasis was placed on translation, which apparently produced access to a transparent reality. This epistemological assumption betrays its own racist conceit in the belief that only natives are able to stand in the place of the native. (I remember being reminded by Japanese scholars that I would never truly understand either their language or their culture, which were seen as interchangeable. Although they were probably right for the wrong reasons, the charge presupposed the totally indefensible, if not impossible, acquisition of perfect-transparent knowledge as the only condition for gaining access to the real!) It is important to remember, too, that this conception of a hermeneutic, based on the primacy of and experience in the field ("field time," we should call it) and the "desire" for native or near-native language proficiency and identification, has marked both the way regions are studied and the conditions that inhibit the practice of theory in constructing research and intellectual agendas, which are dismissed out of hand and even denounced in "field" journals like the *Journal of Japanese Studies*, *Harvard Journal of Asiatic Studies*, and *Monumenta Nipponica*.

Terrorist denunciation has become one of the main vocations of such field journals today, which notoriously act solely as custodians of what can only be described as the authenticity of native knowledge and native concepts, as if native experience anywhere, much less Japan, remained immune from the threat of modernity's promise to eliminate all received cultures of reference. Indeed, the very persistence of field journals devoted to the singularity of a national state like Japan or China or the broader region as it was once envisioned by "Orientalist" scholars confirms the long-standing practice of keeping their study removed from the wider world of which they are a part and to maintain the quarantine against new theory and methods that would deghettoize these "fields." The appeal to native knowledge, even by those who do not qualify as natives, promises to retain the sense of immediacy capable of resisting all mediations. Paul Cohen's earlier call for a sinocentric history of China (an idea whose enunciatory location was the West) reaffirms this desire.[9] If the claims of this unstated hermeneutic rejects theory for the authority of native knowledge and experience, it has also forced its adherents to repeat native pieties and serve willingly as foreign amanuenses interpreting the truths of a native knowledge to their countrymen and -women, faithfully conveying the dictations produced on the native ground of cultural authenticity. But this appeal, which still prevails among students of Japan, if not of other areas like China and South Asia, contrasts dramatically with the received traditions of studying regions like Europe and Latin America, which are geographically and culturally closer to our own national experience. Unfortunately, Jonathan Culler has recently called for a reorganization of European studies along the lines of this area studies model and its theory of knowledge and thus the repackaging of pedagogy and research as discrete national studies. This is what Adorno once described as a reification of reification, since both the national unit and the multidisciplinary approach to its study succeeded only to reify further a set of practices that long ago lost any enabling purpose.

As a model, area studies have produced a theory of knowledge and its practice based on the authority and authenticity of native experience in a world where the native is no longer on the outside, as once imagined but, rather, is subjected to the same political-economic processes and structures that all of us encounter in our everyday lives, everywhere and anywhere. The distinction between West and non-West and the privileged geopolitical identification between modernity and a specific place is a Western concept that has been used to establish and maintain Western unity and superiority and can no longer be taken for granted. Any critique must now be positioned not inside or outside the "West," since the West can no longer be thought of as a dominant geographical concept structuring the non-West. Rather, it must be located immanently within the temporality of a modernity embracing new cultural forms that have been and are still developing in what used to be the non-West and that now offer an occasion for dialectical encounter.[10] Owing to its obsessive desire to identify with native knowledge, the practice of area studies risks strangely being linked to more recent efforts to elevate identity and cultural difference as the true vocation of cultural studies seeking to succeed the study of the area. The irony of this move comes with the recognition that area studies have historically sought to separate the study of the home country from its immigrant and diasporic inflections.

The most important consequence of these patterns of identification with the "field" has been to prevent its practitioners from reflecting on themselves as specialists in the field, from seeing the field of practice itself as an object of knowledge production. Instead, it has relied on the natural identification with the native's knowledge and fluency in the cultural idiom as a more than adequate substitute for theoretical self-reflection. But this is simply desire, not a method, which aims to conceal the absence of theory and method that postcolonial studies, the true successor of area studies, have more than satisfied. Such considerations would help explain the intense hostility Japan specialists have shown toward theory and criticism and why they have consistently resisted all efforts dedicated to exploring the necessary relationship between theoretical exposition and the immediacy of empirical facticity with the determination of earlier "know-nothings."

So far, I've been concerned with the question of why area studies, relying on the unit of the nation form, have been notably isolated from other fields of inquiry and categories of research and teaching that validate a self-fulfilling representation. Moreover, in this desire to isolate their knowledge and representations, area studies have overlooked their complicity with a deeply rooted ethnocentrism in the social sciences and humanities.[11] Periodic surveys of the "field" have worked to sustain the identity of the field as such and to give it definition where there has been none, by inventorying personnel, curricula, and institutions. Begun by the SSRC, these surveys have often been indistinguishable from maintaining a system of simple surveillance. In recent years, the Japan Foundation and other Japanese governmental agencies have taken over their funding.

In the most recent survey, supported by the Japan Foundation, one of its organizers reported, without a shred of irony, that Japanese studies, unlike China studies, possess a "remarkable" degree of self-reflection that derives only partially from the "availability of outside financial support" and just as much from the apparent recognition that, quoting the sociologist of Japan R. P. Dore, "area specialists acquire the characteristics of the area they study." "Like our Japanese counterparts," the report continued, "American Japan specialists have acquired the habits of systematic information-gathering and long-range planning."[12] I hope this Japanese genius for planning doesn't include earthquakes, poison gas attacks in subways, and political and financial corruption bordering on incompetence and criminality. This expression of identity belongs to an older model of gathering information in the field that, we're reminded, comes from a time when Japan was "irrelevant" to the United States. If Japan studies were irrelevant in the decades after the war—and I do not believe they were, as I've already explained—it is because they resisted any effort to look beyond the mission attending their inauguration and the representations that best served them. The unintended irony is the belief that Japan studies are now relevant, according to the report, precisely when area studies are being abandoned because they no longer speak to or on, if they ever did, the world we occupy and must try to understand.

While the periodic survey constitutes the sign of surveillance, punctually cementing the identity of the "field," it also calls attention to the larger apparatus of reproduction and the primary role played by funding. In the first reports issued by the SSRC, under the direction of the Joint Committee on Japanese Studies, the funding of and for the "field" became an urgent and early priority. Hall's report, as it was subsequently labeled, pointed to the great strides achieved in the development of Japanese studies in the United States from the end of the war until the 1970s as evidence of momentum that could be sustained only if reliable and stable sources of funding could be identified and tapped.[13] What is striking about Hall's 1970s report, and its successors, is the absence of any attempt to articulate a new or even different intellectual and pedagogical vision that might justify the prioritization of funding.

Following this recommendation, the ensuing search for cash looked to Japan for both public and private sources. A generation of "occupationaires," old Japan hands, and sons of missionaries cashed in their chips, and probably more, to recruit money from both private and public donors in Japan to finance Japanese studies in the United States. This strategy has often gone outside the small world of area studies to encourage business schools, scientific institutions like MIT, and law schools to seek donations for chairs that have nothing to do with Japanese studies as such but everything to do with Japan. Hence, the resistance to theoretical self-reflection has been compensated by the scramble among proponents of area studies to take money from any willing donor, domestic or foreign, without asking too many questions or worrying too much about finding new ways to think through the more difficult task of constructing a knowledge of Asia and teaching it. The seemingly mad pursuit for endless sources of funding often resembles the campaigns of those earlier adventurers/archaeologists who were always trying to find enough capital to put together one more dig that would complete the picture in some simpleminded positivist fashion, knowing of course that they were concerned only with getting back to the site and staying there indefinitely. Far from serving any pedagogical or epistemological purpose, the real intention behind this craze to find funding seems to have no other reason than sustaining the structure of area studies and maintaining what can be described only as a dinosaur whose head can longer support its body.

We are reminded by administrators and cooperative academics that universities often claim they are taking money from a foreign government in order to do research, which is always presented as neutral and unaffected by the politics associated with the donor. But this explanation is about as convincing as recent declarations of the president and the Democratic National Committee that financial gifts do not influence policy. Area studies rarely engage in collaborative research projects necessitating large outlays of capital (the last and only significant exception was the University of Michigan's Village Japan project), and individual research will still be carried out without large capital contributions from foreign governments. Princeton University's recent acceptance of money from the Turkish government shows the risks entailed in taking money from a foreign government with a stake in effacing a history of Armenian genocide (fashionably called today "ethnic purification") and the kind of predictable relationship between the expectation of the foreign donor and the willing complicity of American college administrators. The University of California at Berkeley's momentary declaration of intent to name a library after Chiang Ching-kuo—former head of the secret police in Taiwan, among his many vocations—was simply a repeat performance of the University of Chicago's earlier madness to name an institute after the Pahlavi family after receiving $2 million in the early 1960s, which it speedily returned.

Although the search for funding, ostensibly to sustain the structure of area studies and their knowledge and curricula, still characterizes its principal calling, it has also strengthened the resistance to incorporating new cultural strategies that can resolve the deficiencies of an approach driven obsessively by the search for money. This approach manages only to recuperate the lost historical world of its own origins as a program of study and research. While the newer cultural studies promise to find new ways to a more productive understanding of how to integrate local experiences into the larger world, they might also help restore the relevance of national societies by alerting us to models that will permit researchers to resituate the role of critique and local experiences as instantiated inflections of larger processes sharing the same temporality. The importance of cultural studies is the recognition—completely overlooked by area studies—of knowledge as production that demands an abandoning of what Louis Althusser once referred to as the "mirror myths of immediate vision." If area studies employed a strategy driven by a holistic conception of knowledge—Japan as signified so dear to Japanologists—and emphasizing enduring cultural values ("core values") and political and social normativity, the method it used was based on a multidisciplinarism that too often was misrecognized as interdisciplinarism. Most area studies programs still presume to cover the waterfront, which means making sure only that the region in question is approached comprehensively, with all disciplines represented. This means that understanding the area as a totality is possible only when and if all the disciplines are accounted for. Yet the assumption of this approach to understanding the whole has never been questioned as long as the disciplinary parts have been lined up like ducks ready to speak their partial truths. Instead, this strategy promoted the systematic gathering of information that ultimately would reflect an invariant reality rather than encourage a critical practice made possible by producing knowledge from the act of reading and writing. The one truth that area studies never spoke was the condition of empowerment that produced a particular knowledge of an area or region to serve the national interest, whether it was the national security state or multinational corporations.

By contrast, the newer cultural studies have tried to break with both holism and a concern for core values in favor of an approach that has consistently turned from knowledge to power and domination. While it has aimed at breaking down disciplinary boundaries to better examine the locus of power and its migrating habits, it has not always managed to replace an earlier and discredited multidisciplinarism. Rather, this obsessive Foucauldianism has often found power everywhere, as well as an opportunity for resistance everywhere. Too often this has resulted in lavish declarations of resistance by the powerless and weak and those consumers who are made to appear as if they are exercising agency when buying a commodity or changing a TV channel. Sometimes the mere enunciation of cultural difference and thus the claim of identity is made to appear as an important political act when it usually signals the disappearance of politics. The politics of identity based on the enunciation of cultural difference is not the same as political identity whose formation depends less on declarations of differences than on some recognition of equivalencies.

All this, however, is an immense improvement over an approach that led its practitioners to acquire the characteristics of the field they study, without thinking about what it meant to invade, inhabit, and "snatch" the body of the other. Because of the implementation of either a Foucauldian desire to locate power everywhere but nowhere specific or a Habermasian dependence on the installation of a public sphere that nobody seems to inhabit yet, the newer cultural studies risk the same reluctance noted in the earlier area studies approach to link power and domination in specific configurations to the role played by capitalism and the state. If the older area studies promoted descriptions masking prescriptives for development in order to export capitalism and its value system to the Third World and to defeat the Second (to open up markets and so on), the new cultural studies often risk the same by concentrating on microtechnologies and displacing state and capital with indeterminate loci of power and their local variations. Moreover, they sometimes slip into the role of becoming a cheerleader for runaway "globalization" and its propensity for border crossings. The new cultural studies do this by emphasizing discourses of power and their slippage, splitting subjectivities, and charting their subsequent dissemination as if the movement were a natural function of an already existing, unnamed conception of social order, even though those who carry out this practice disavow totalities. In more recent efforts to imagine a "globalization" process to account for the local, we see what often appears as a rearticulation of modernization theory in a different register. This neomodernization theory celebrates cultural difference enthusiastically, very much in the manner of the united colors of Benetton, yet fails to recognize that the production of plural identities is consistent with the propensity of global capitalism to undermine all fixed positions for a fetishized "narcissism of small differences."

Finally, we have the promises offered by postcolonial theory and its desire to account for the complex relationship between colonizer and colonized, metropole and colony, and chronology and epistemology. It has, first and foremost, given English literary studies a new lease on life once it was recognized that the received canon was too narrow and there were far too few unedited texts to accommodate the swollen army of graduate students recruited in the 1970s and after. In a certain sense, area studies missed the opportunity first made available to them when Edward Said argued in his *Orientalism* that their knowledge of region was already mediated by the power/knowledge considerations of colonialism and colonial discourse. Said—correctly, I believe—wanted to assimilate the practice of area studies to colonial discourse, which would have endowed area studies with a desire to explain the relationship between colonizer and colonized, metropole and colony, inside and outside, a world shaped by the forces of Western imperialism, as well as the often forgotten observation of Frantz Fanon that hegemonic cultures also colonize the mind.

As for the significant but missed opportunity, it is important to say here that the indifference of area studies to Said's strategic observation meant that they remained locked in their own enclaves of knowledge. The mission of rethinking regions outside Europe—that is, what had become known as the Third World—passed to English studies and the humanities, privileging the textual over the social scientific and the role played by the political economic, even though they shared the older discipline's preoccupation with culture. We should applaud this sensitivity to both the dominated and the margin (nowhere to be found in the older, scientifically "neutral" area studies) and to what Fanon sadly recognized as the "sacking of cultural patterns," or at least the conditions implicated in the act of sacking, in which "the social panorama is destructured; values are flaunted, crushed, emptied."[14] In this regard, postcolonial theory's promise to supply a critique of Eurocentric conceptions of knowledge and provide a forum for the hitherto excluded to speak in their own voice from the margins where domination and power had held them silent since the beginning of modernity—now reread as colonialism—stands as the true successor of area studies, which can be seen as a kind of prehistory or even prefiguration of what would become area studies. Yet the search for the excluded voice often leads to the futile pursuit for authenticity and restores the Eurocentric claims of the sovereign subject it wishes to eliminate. In this sense, it reveals its own historical myopia and consequent incapacity to see beyond the horizon of a specific colonial encounter—namely, British India—and the retrospective illusion that comes with occupying a position after the colonial moment.

A consideration of the longer duration of history elsewhere would supply examples of different kinds of colonizing and deterritorializing experiences and how the loss of cultural reference, as experienced, say, by the Japanese—even though they did not lose any territory—signified a relationship between colonization and capitalist modernization. Capitalism was seen by the Japanese between the wars as a totalizing process that affected every part of society; this historical experience is crucial to understanding the colonial episode that postcolonial theory currently wishes to theorize. If, for example, this history had been consulted, which actually was contemporary with British colonial rule in India, not to mention Africa and Southeast Asia, it would have shown the impossibility of imagining what Partha Chatterjee has identified as an "anticolonial nationalism" capable of demonstrating that the colonized were not merely, in his memorable words, "consumers of modernity."[15] Chatterjee was suggesting—shared by others who insisted on seeing the availability of uncontaminated autonomous cultures as a reservoir of anticolonialism—the conviction that the disempowered in India seemed to have involuntarily recuperated the space of nonreification that Lukács once invested in the proletariat because they were involved in manual, not mental, labor. In making this move, adherents of postcolonial theory misrecognize the identity between capitalism and its claim of universalism; rather, they elide homogeneity with universalism. The point is, as Pierre Vilar reminded us, that capitalism was "born of colonization and the world market" and has subsequently "universalized" history, inasmuch as it has established systematic relations of social interdependence on a global scale that have eventually encompassed noncapitalist societies. In this regard, capitalism has managed to fix a standard of measurement—world time—produced by a "single global space of coexistence," within which action and events are subject to a single, quantifiable chronology. But because different social practices remain outside this abstract measure, capitalism has not "unified" history.[16]

The difference between the Japanese, who were not physically colonized, and the Chinese and Indians, who were, is instructive because they responded to their situation in a way comparable to Chatterjee's description of an uncontaminated anticolonial rationalism, constructing cultural imaginaries rooted in the primacy and authenticity of native cultural patterns and reinventing the culture of reference that Fanon observed had been sacked and emptied. For postcolonial theory, what became the sign of an authentic anticolonial cultural nationalism, uncorrupted by the West, was for the Japanese, Chinese, Indians,

French, Germans, and Italians the irreducible mode of a modernist critique of the devastation caused by capitalist modernization and the need to find a location for historical difference. The appeal to native culture was, in fact, the very sign of capitalist modernity and its modernist ideological program rather than resistance to it. The appearance of the uncanny, out-of-time, a ghostly repetition that erupts from the surplus of what had been suppressed to trouble the stable boundaries between past and present, the past in the present, demonstrated that these societies were, in fact, "consumers of modernity" because there appeared to be no other alternative to the deterritorializing wealth of capital and the labor power of the deterritorialized worker. The appeal to such autonomous resources, immune to capitalism even in the colony, is a fiction not worth "delving into," as Fanon recognized long ago: "A national culture is not a folklore, nor an abstract populism that believes it can discover the people's true nature. It is made up of the inert dregs of gratuitous actions, that is to say actions which are less and less attached to the ever-present reality of the people."[17]

When contemporary postcolonial theory celebrates an anticolonial nationalism based on an undefiled spirit made to stand as a sign of genuine nativism—uncontaminated interiority—as a form of resistance unmarked by the "consumption of modernity," it is, I believe, unintentionally reviving the response of Japanese modernists to the culture of capitalism in the interwar period. But this repetition, what Raymond Williams named "modernists against modernity," comes now with a difference and a disavowal. In mapping this projection of authenticity onto an earlier moment—the colonial era—they themselves become seekers of the authentic, the inward, the unspoiled, and inadvertently the learners of a "capitalism without capitalism" and everything that such a gesture implies politically. Moreover, this return to the pursuit of cultural authenticity loops back to form a symmetry with the desire of an earlier area studies program to stand in the place of the native.

Worse, postcolonial theorizing often slips into a kind of necessary ambivalence and indeterminacy that, in the case of Homi Bhabha and Gayatri Spivak, grows out of a methodological desire to exploit the splits and contradictions embedded in the Enlightenment discourse on rationality.[18] Although such a strategy is aimed at unsettling readers and turning them away from the promise of epistemological certainty—because it is a critique that has eschewed consciousness and experience—it is hard to know, unlike the practiced examples of Fanon and Said, who, in fact, is being addressed and the location of its enunciation. By resorting to the division marked by the colonial experience and its aftermath, it has created a binary no more productive and exempt from charges of essentialism than the older polarities it has held up for derision.

We can recognize the working of this binary in those categories constructed by Homi Bhabha to explain the encounter between the colonizer and the colonized and to signify its complexity. While he was correct to show that the relationship between colonizer and colonized was not simply an instance of a hegemonic discourse representing the other and that this relationship was filled with anxiety and possibilities for slippage, the terms of the encounter still expressed the self and the other recast as pedagogy and performance. Although postcolonial theory has offered through the strategy of compelling dominant structures to restore history as a mediation capable of accounting for differences that older strategies had overlooked, it is, because of the circulation of its own binary terms, often as ahistorical (anahistorical?) and blind to the temporal and spatial differences lived and experienced by those voiceless, excluded, marginalized peoples it seeks to redeem.

The chronology of the colonizer is not always the same for the colonized; Bengal under British rule was different temporally and spatially from Korea under the Japanese, even though they were contemporary, and the forms of colonial domination differ widely from Africa and Asia, demanding sensitivity to the specific political and economic histories that postcolonial theory rarely, if ever, manages to mention. Only history shows the range of such differences and helps us avoid the essentialisms and exceptionalisms that postcolonial theory produces in lifeless stereotypes. In its desire to turn away from the global forces of capitalism—another Western narrative—postcolonial theory trades in stereotypes and holism and the fantasy of genuine, anticolonial nationalism uncontaminated by either the contagion of the colonial epoch or capitalist penetration. It moves ceaselessly from cultural essentialism to an indeterminate social system that need not necessarily be colonial, even though it is named as such, and whose subjects are grasped through a psychoanalytic framework that is culturally specific to the hegemonic culture that the colonized are supposedly trying to resist despite recent efforts to authenticate this psychologizing of other by appealing to the authority of Frantz Fanon as endorsement. With this vacillation, according to Aijaz Ahmad, postcolonial theory has "become transhistorical, always present and always in process of dissolution in one part of the world or another, so that everyone gets the privilege, sooner or later . . . of being colonizer, colonized and postcolonial all at once." Postcolonial theory "levels out all histories, so that we are free to take up any of a thousand of available micro-histories, more or less arbitrarily, since they all amount to the same thing, more or less."[19] We can also employ the power of metonymical example (one of Bhabha's two tropes of fetishism) so that Bengal can stand in for all of Asia or, indeed, the entire colonial world. But if it comes down to this, then postcolonial theory has merely smuggled back the narrative of capitalism under a different name, what Žižek termed a "capitalism without capitalism"—that is, capitalism without social divisions, a utopian model of a hybridized globe.

It seems to me that what's left in this endless deconstructive subtraction carried out by postcolonial theory is an innocuous "cultural respect" as its current response to the question of human rights. Now that its initial theoretical splash has turned into a puddle, when researchers have found theory and criticism outside their endless self-referrals, postcolonial might return to its prehistory in area studies as a step toward enriching both. This would mean coming to grips with postcoloniality's epistemological claims and rewinding them through its original chronological identity as the post to colonialism. By returning to its incipient origins in area studies, postcoloniality might recover the moment when the Third World was viewed from its colonial past but not necessarily from the perspective of its later unwanted heritage—the apparent price it has had to pay for decolonization. This reunion might impose on postcoloniality memories of uneven political-economic and cultural development and a reminder of the powerful presence of capitalism and its secular, historical totalization we call modernity as the principal deterritorializing agent and the determinant of a bounded narrative. By the same measure, postcoloniality might infuse into a moribund area studies the memory of a desire for theory that was early repressed in the scramble to recruit funds rather than ideas. What this points to is how postcoloniality might be refigured into an act of memory rather than merely a chronology or critique masquerading exceptionalisms and unnamed social theories that might help us discriminate among current claims identifying history with memory and restoring to each their own order of knowledge and experience.

Beyond this move to memoration, we might look to a new candidate for cultural studies that would cloak history in the form of everydayness in the larger and immanent framework of capitalist modernity and its transformations. Such a study might redirect our attention to the role of capitalism throughout the world, rather than merely cheering it on or repressing it, and alert us to the relationship between the experience of everydayness and the regime of the commodity form, surely one of the principal agencies of the production of contemporary historical formations. Such a consideration might also allow the current practice of cultural studies in the United States and the United Kingdom to venture beyond its vocation of reproducing the kind of Euro-American centrism it was supposed to overcome.[20] Perhaps the time has come, as Žižek proposed, to "resuscitate the Marxian insight that Capital is the ultimate power of 'deterritorialization' which undermines every fixed social identity, and to conceive of 'late capitalism' as the epoch in which the traditional fixity of ideological positions . . . becomes an obstacle to the unbridled commodification of everyday life."[21] Žižek's observation corresponds to Deleuze and Guattari's earlier reminder (in *Anti-Oedipus*) that capitalism constituted the determining motor of colonialism.

What is important in these cases is that our attention is redirected to capitalism's role in colonialism and, in the case of Žižek, to the relationship between the experience of everydayness and the process of commodification. In this connection, even Homi Bhabha has distinguished between what he labeled the "epochal" and the "everyday" (echoing Henri Lefebvre's earlier pairing of "exceptional" and "everyday"), in which the latter breaks off from the former in order to negotiate the meaning of the modern in "the 'enunciative' present of the discourse." It is in this lag that he proposes "a temporal caesura" that separates the "epochal event" of modernity as the symbol of the continuity of progress from the "contemporaneity of the everyday."[22] Yet the epochal event is merely another way of naming the pedagogical, whereas the everyday becomes the performative, the "time lag," and thus the movable furniture in an endless game of musical chairs attesting to the functions and functioning of an absent social system that is present in its operations. In this way, Bhabha slips into ordinary functionalism, failing to masquerade performance as mere function in an unstated social system. Bhabha also argues that the power of the "performative," its "deformative structure," introduces another "hybrid." But here, as elsewhere, the hybrid merely masks a more corrosive and destructive unevenness that distinguishes the everyday. That is, the realization of hybridity, the "in-betweenness," conceals the mix of elements that are being hybridized and thus works to smooth the experience of unevenness of both the colonized and the noncolonized everyday. Despite the elaborate rhetoric, or because of it, he ends up as a satisfied customer of colonialism.

Everyday life refers to the experience of the lived reality that marks the appearance and expansion of industrial capitalism and its propensity to install similar conditions everywhere it is established. Everyday life has the impressive and probably unparalleled credential of standing at the intersection of four intellectual movements that are at the heart of our own, contemporary historical conjuncture: Marxism, surrealism, existentialism (especially its phenomenological perspective), and cultural studies.[23] I am not referring to the conception of the everyday as it was envisioned by Michel de Certeau in *The Practice of Everyday Life*. Although this conception informs many agendas in cultural studies today, it never has escaped the opening perspective of part 3, which looks down on New York from the heights of the World Trade Towers and makes the topography of the everyday appear as a lifeless, deserted space punctuated by the endless circulation of strategies by the powerful and tactics by the disempowered. This conception also conforms to an unnamed functionalist social conception that permits the expression of forms of resistance that act to defuse the excesses of conflict, like a safety valve, and ensure the maintenance of the social order. Nor am I recalling the everyday that has existed in history since time immemorial which Henri Lefebvre discounted because the prose and poetry of life were still identical.

Because everydayness is different from the daily life lived before capitalism and an epochal modernity, it is, first and foremost, a secular historical concept, a temporality, and not a geopolitical space that until recently—that is, until Japan and then other societies embarked on programs of capitalist modernization—identified modernity with North America and western Europe. In this instance, everydayness constitutes a cultural form that shares with modernity the experience of capitalism and is thus coeval with it. Both are also temporal categories that derive their broader importance from their respective historical forms. Modernity is represented here as the new, and everydayness is seen as the durational present, incomplete but "situated at the intersection of two modes of repetition: the cyclical, which dominates in nature, and the linear, which dominates in processes known as 'rational.'" For Henri Lefebvre, the everyday consists of cycles, nights and days, seasons and harvests, rest and activity, and so forth, and it also requires the repetition of work and consumption. In modernity, work and consumption "masked" and destroyed the cycles. Despite the predictable monotony of repetition, everything changes, especially when control falls into the hands of the "bureaucratic society of controlled consumption" that oversees planned obsolescence. Lefebvre once distinguished between the everyday and the lived—later called modernity and the everyday. The former refers to the global structure or "totality," work, leisure, family life, private life making up the whole yet always marked by its historical, circulating, shifting, and transitory nature. The latter refracts this experience in countless, individual, and contingent ways, attesting to how the everyday is encountered. Everyday life and modernity "crown" and "conceal" the other, "revealing and veiling it." "Everyday life," Lefebvre continued, "a compound of insignificances united in this concept, responds and corresponds to modernity, a compound of signs by which our society expresses and justifies itself and which forms part of its ideology."[24]

Indeed, the "quotidian and the modern mark and mask, legitimate and counterbalance each other." It is the space where the "riddle of recurrence intercepts the theory of becoming,"[25] according to Peter Osborne, the incompleteness of the present that Lefebvre believed demanded continuation is, at the same time, an "incomplete de-historicization" that supplies the place of the everyday with the "potential" for historicizing experience.[26] Moreover, this space of everyday life permits us to negotiate relationships between the global and the local, between the rhythms and routines reproduced everywhere that capitalism spreads and the lived or local and contingent experiences mediating them. In this regard the everyday might function like the Bakhtian chronotope, obliging us to measure the differing relationships between time and space as societies undergo the process of capitalist modernization. "The everyday," according to Lefebvre, "is therefore the most universal and the most unique condition, the most social and the most individuated, the most obvious and the best hidden." It is, as Simmel observed, always immediate, filled with the sedimented layers of countless routines and repetitions that give the present a sense of eternity. But because it always remains incomplete, it is open to the

contingent, the unexpected, the eventful, and the possibility for constant refiguration that both time and place necessitate. If the commodification of everyday life leads to dehistoricization, we must understand this as a sign of the
historical process always found in a specific time and place.

The continuing contradictions among the repetitive cycles that everyday life
must constantly negotiate, the ceaseless interactions between modernity and
everydayness everywhere, and the refigurations they produce will disclose the
operation of that unevenness distinguishing the modern (the regime of the
"new") from the cultural forms of everyday life. As different social subjects constantly redefine modernity, these contradictions will also attest to the emergence of new configurations of modernity in what used to be the West and the
non-West. In this respect, an examination of everydayness as the site of unevenness will deprivilege the usual cultural emphasis by cultural studies and its
text-based orientation for one that at the same time must be sensitive to the
materialities of lived political and economic experience. Fredric Jameson alerted
us to how cultural studies in the United States is currently a substitute for Marxism and to everything this displacement may imply politically.[27] An appeal to
the study of everydayness as the site producing unevenness everywhere will not
only remind us of what the practice of cultural studies do not do but also force
their practitioners and us to see the relationship of immanently based, different forms of historical temporalization throughout the world. This means that
if cultural studies have, as I believe they have, ignored the world outside Euro-
America and centered the "articulation" of cultural texts at the expense of political economic considerations, they have done so at the risk of merely recuperating the formalisms they swore to forgo.

At the heart of the everyday life, then, is the figure of uneven development
generated by capitalism as it enters societies at different moments and different rates of intensity. Subsequently produced are the differing temporal terms
and cultural spaces and the coexistence of differing modes and forces of production. In the 1920s, the Japanese native ethnologist Yanagita Kunio named
this combined development "ruined or hybrid civilizations" that could be found
throughout East Asia. But he could just as easily have been describing that process everywhere by which modernity and everyday life respond and correspond to each other. What drives this approach is a critical agenda that seeks
in the everyday the place where alienations, fetishisms, and reifications produce
their effects. While this combined development easily replaces the space occupied by a phantom called Asia—a geographical referent that still fails to conceal
its status as the second term—it also shifts our attention away from the singularity of the nation and its counterclaims to uniqueness that, it now seems, are
trying to bridge the difference between modernity and everyday life. In a certain sense, it always calls attention to the structure of temporal immanence it
shares with other societies even as we concentrate on a local experience. Finally,

it will end the long practice of partitioning, which area studies and their principal mode of inquiry—multidisciplinarism—sustained, and their consequent ghettoization in academia to make way for a return to exploring experiences that cross the boundaries of culture areas. For if categories of historical analysis like capital and modernity are to have a particular effect, they will have to be examined in the cultural forms in which history is lived everywhere as a continuing temporalization of existence.[28] But it would have been everydayness, as both Japanese in the interwar period and Europeans began to realize even before the war, lived as a formation rather than a core value. In this way, it just might be possible to make the transition from area studies to cultural studies that DeLillo's hero Gladney made with such dazzling skill from Hitler to Elvis in one easy jump.

Notes

1. Ruth Benedict, *The Chrysanthemum and the Sword: Patterns of Japanese Culture* (New York: Riverside Press, 1946).
2. Ravi Arvind Palat, "Fragmented Visions," unpublished manuscript, University of Hawaii, n.d., 62–63.
3. Joint Committee on Japanese Studies, directed by John W. Hall, *Japanese Studies in the United States: A Report on the State of the Field—Present Resources and Future Needs* (New York: Social Science Research Council, 1970), 7.
4. Stanley J. Hegenbothan, "Rethinking International Scholarship," *SSRC Items* 48, nos. 2–3 (June–September 1994): 33–40.
5. William N. Fenton, *Area Studies in American Universities: For the Commission on the Implications of Armed Services Educational Programs* (Washington, DC: American Council of Learned Societies, 1947), 81–82.
6. Jeffery Alexander, *Fin de Siècle Social Theory* (London: Verso, 1995), 11.
7. See H. D. Harootunian, "Aimai na shiruetto" (2), *Misuzu* 441, no. 5 (May 1998): 78–79.
8. Palat, "Fragmented Visions," 23.
9. Paul A. Cohen, *Discovering History in China* (New York: Columbia University Press, 1983).
10. See Peter Osborne, *The Politics of Time* (London: Verso, 1995), 18; also see Naoki Sakai, "Modernity and Its Critique: The Problem of Universalism and Particularism," in *Postmodernism and Japan*, ed. Masao Miyoshi and H. D. Harootunian (Durham, NC: Duke University Press, 1989), 106.
11. Palat, "Fragmented Visions," 34.
12. *International House of Japan Bulletin* 13, no. 1 (Winter 1993): 1.
13. Joint Committee, *Japanese Studies*, 32, 36.
14. Frantz Fanon, *Toward the African Revolution* (New York: Grove Press, 1967), 33.
15. Partha Chaterjee, *The Nation and Its Fragments: Colonial and Postcolonial Histories* (Princeton, NJ: Princeton University Press, 1993), 5. It should be pointed out that Chaterjee, living in a chronologically postcolonial time, was seeking to rescue "imagination" and the prior claims of an inner life that were exempted from the corrosive effects of (colonially inspired) nationalism and modern capital. This strategy recalls

the discourse on the social Japanese, especially, constructed between the wars to escape the performative present in which they experienced capitalist modernization for an authentic but indeterminate past before capitalist modernization. Through the alchemy of authenticity, thinkers and writers believed they were able to change the baser metal of their present into the pure gold of an eternal experience unaffected by history.

16. Pierre Vilar, "Marxist History, History in the Making: Towards a Dialogue with Althusser," in *Althusser: A Critical Reader*, ed. G. Elliott (Oxford: Blackwell, 1994), 10–43.

17. Frantz Fanon, *The Wretched of the Earth* (New York: Grove Press, 1968), 233.

18. Robert Young, *White Mythologies* (London: Routledge, 1990), 174. Young and others argue that Bhabha and Spivak seek criticism by "exploiting" the indeterminacies within rationalism itself, whereas Said and Fanon proceed from experience and consciousness. In her recent book, *Critique of Postcolonial Reason,* Gayatri Spivak pursues this program, which, unfortunately, suffers from her propensity for self-interruption and constant self-referral. The average number of pronouns indicating the "I" on any randomly selected page suggests that her critique owes more to experience and consciousness than she has admitted.

19. Aijaz Ahmad, "Postcolonialism: What's in a Name?" in *Late Imperial Culture*, ed. Roman DeLaCampa, E. Ann Kaplan, and Michael Sprinker (London: Verso, 1995), 31.

20. L. Grossberg, C. Nelson, and P. A. Treicher, eds., *Cultural Studies* (New York: Routledge, 1992), 476. Meagen Morris rightly observes that in a volume of more than seven hundred pages mapping out cultural studies, large parts of Asia, Africa, and Latin America are absent. In fact, it is astonishing, if not a Herculean feat, how a volume of such size and scale, dedicated to the catholic promises of cultural studies, could have so consistently ignored the very world that the new "discipline" supposedly occupies.

21. Slavoj Žižek, *Tarrying with the Negative* (Durham, NC: Duke University Press, 1993), 216.

22. Homi Bhabha, *The Location of Culture* (London: Routledge, 1994), 242, 245.

23. The idea is from Osborne, *The Politics of Time*, 190.

24. Henri Lefebvre, *Everyday Life in the Modern World* (New Brunswick, NJ: Transactions Publishers, 1994), 24.

25. Lefebvre, *Everyday Life in the Modern World*, 25, 18.

26. Osborne, *The Politics of Time*, 196.

27. Fredric Jameson, "On Cultural Studies," in *The Identity in Question*, ed. John Rajchman (London: Routledge, 1995), 253, 264.

28. Osborne, *The Politics of Time*, 200.

CHAPTER 2

"MEMORIES OF UNDERDEVELOPMENT" AFTER AREA STUDIES

The Desire Called Area Studies

In this essay, I examine how the "desire" called "area studies"[1] was founded on the privilege attached to fixed spatial containers, such as geographic area, culture region, or directional locality (East Asia, Southeast Asia, Northeast Asia). The model for these spatial regularities has undoubtedly been the nation-state—itself a spatial figure—and its capacity for modernizing makeovers. These have led to the formation of rationalities such as the liberal-democratic state, capital accumulation, and the primacy of the "self-regulating market," which have come to collectively signify an unchanging modern structure.

Even the transmutation of area studies into its most recent avatar—identity studies, which presumes permanent ethnocultural determinations—persists in privileging the spatial over the force and forms of time. This "end of temporality" excludes time's agency (although not chronology) and spatializes certain world regions, transubstantiating multiple temporalities (with their different histories and modes of production) into a singular temporality that marks the distance between developed and undeveloped. This spatial privileging converts a purely quantitative measure of time—chronology—into a qualitative yardstick, whereby a different temporality becomes a symptom of backwardness. What was misrepresented as "modernity" with the concentration on the new is in fact a misrecognition of capitalist accumulation, whose repetitive functions seek to mask, if not eliminate, the regular cycles of existential time in everyday life.[2] Capitalism's immense conceptualization of time accountancy produced the temporal coordinates of the modern nation-state, which then became the placeholder of capitalist accumulation.[3] I offer instead a containment strategy that seeks to identify specific space-time relationships, recalling M. M. Bakhtin's chronotope, which aims to restore time to any consideration of space and opens up the possibility for conjunctural analysis of multiple and distinct forms of temporality, drawn from social formations and modes of production, despite the dominance of capitalism. Louis Althusser associated this idea of conjuncture with the "material philosophy of the encounter," an optic through which to understand the historical reality of those moments when diverse circumstances confront each other and create a "world, torn between powers in collusion and the 'crises' which unite them in a circle." Althusser was convinced that while historical periods have their laws, "they can also change at the drop of a hat revealing the aleatory basis that sustains . . . without reason . . . without intelligible end."[4] This is the history of capitalism: a series of contingent encounters that produce practices, subsequently recoded as categories, into a logic of relationships that becomes the mature form of capitalism. By uncovering heterological temporalities and histories—recognizing uneven flows and the never-ending prospect of untimeliness—"progress" is released from its unilinear mooring and rethought as a relative term that considers missed opportunities and defeated possibilities.

Since the collapse of the Berlin Wall in 1989 and the end of the Cold War, scholars have nervously scrambled to rethink the university's long-standing commitment to the study of societies geographically and psychologically consigned to the outside of Euro-America. This frenzied search for new pedagogical purpose was prompted by the recognition that the circumstances that had authorized area studies programs had virtually disappeared, and the need to justify the rather large investment in an institutional infrastructure that appeared to have no place to go. Dazzled by the prospect of unlimited market access, private corporations momentarily seized the opportunity to make sure that universities, especially business schools, were prepared to train people to meet the challenges of a globalized environment. Area studies faced the problem of reacquainting a new generation of students with the task of changing the received image of a peripheral world filled with known enemies, potential foes, and societies seen as incapable of vocalizing their own interests. If area studies ignored the historical experience of colonialism, it dismissed the destinies of decolonization by affirming the Cold War strategy of sandwiching new nations between the monologic discourse of two superpowers. For a brief moment in the 1950s, countries recently released from colonial bondage sought to find their own way in the world, by appealing to an autonomous form of regionalism captured by the classification "Third World." Yet this effort to avoid being overtaken by either the "free world" or the Soviet bloc became one of the first casualties of area studies programs looking for ways to serve the national security state. Later, it became the vocation of postcolonial discourse, which presented the voiceless as capable of enunciating tactics of resistance and negotiation, elevating them as subjects worthy of study and inclusion.

But while this effort to breathe new purpose into area studies has produced no paradigmatic or conceptual breakthrough, the aggregate activity suggests an overdetermined concern that, perhaps inadvertently, acknowledges the obsolescence of older models and the bankruptcy of their knowledge systems. In fact, area studies were always constrained by an instrumental purpose to supply the national security state with accurate information concerning the United States' enemies.[5] This displaced both the necessity for criticism (since its purpose was not necessarily understanding but policy objectives)[6] and an explanation of the unwillingness of the targeted to be won over by the assumption that they were pale reflections of ourselves—surrogate U.S. citizens fulfilling the desire for modernizing makeovers of their societies. The goal of modernization was to remake former colonies into replications that reflected the logic of the Same, whose content derived from an idealized representation of the United States that required conformity to its demands for democracy and the free market.

The ideological binary that divided the world was inscribed in area studies programs, bolstering U.S. capitalism as the natural expression of democracy, although actually cementing contradictory claims of equality and inequality. While modernization theory served the U.S. security state and implemented development and aid policies to win the hearts and minds of the unaligned, barely concealing its own imperializing impulse, the Soviet Union was forced to offer a competing model that, in its own way, risked cleaving to forms of colonialism. In this respect, modernization theory "endowed" a world-historical narrative (Hegel) with a "civilizing grammar and direction" and the task of overseeing a transnational experience by administering capitalism as it "ideologically captures historical time and deploys it as means."[7] During the Cold War, modernization theory aimed to "manage" life in the Third World through the imperial instrument of developmentalist policy, which was perceived as a form of neocolonialism.[8] This involved tolerance for the worst kinds of political anomalies among U.S. allies, including the brutal authoritarian regimes of Central America and the Middle East and the oxymoronic single-party democracies of Mexico and Japan. Since the fall of the Berlin Wall, the U.S. model of capitalism, unconstrained by a "free market" that defines freedom itself, has proceeded on an unchallenged rampage throughout the world to realize what momentarily and euphemistically was described as a "pure form of economic liberty" and "free market fundamentalism." Ironically, the brutality of this savage, neoliberal capitalism was matched by a U.S. aptitude for torture against its last standing foes. The loss of purpose in area studies after the Cold War has been imprinted in the wreckage of a misshapen mission to provide expert knowledge of "strategic world regions." In this regard, area studies has been a silent accomplice, duplicitous in its capacious desire to serve a state that sought to refashion the world through unbound capitalism, whose destructive effects have been amply dramatized by an explosion of excess that now threatens to take everybody down.

It is, of course, easier to describe a regime of knowledge that prevailed throughout the Cold War than it is to portray what has taken its place since. The paradigm that authorized the system of knowledge for area studies during the Cold War was more systematically conceived than its putative successor and was driven by explicit instrumental goals. Its successor revealed itself at first as a vague silhouette, occupying the vacated space of area studies, just as nature gradually encroaches upon an abandoned settlement. But while nature's return is a reconquest of space from which it had been driven, the new knowledge system can make no such claim. In fact, the paradigm is simply an inversion of the old practice—promising inclusion of the formerly excluded, whereby the object now occupies the position of subject, and equal status replaces the hierarchical classification that separated the West from the Rest. Area studies has drifted from its initial purpose of gathering useful information for the national security state into its capture by identity studies, which had already established its presence in the academic procession of disciplines. In the wake of the Cold War, the United States realized its postwar aspiration of global hegemony, at last unhindered by military rivals. Among social scientists and allies in business, globalization evoked notions of a utopian borderless world of commodity flows, underscored by respect for difference among a vast army of global consumers. This appeal to the multiplicity of subject positions had all the force of a Benetton advertisement, masking the reality of homogenization with symbolic representations of world heterogeneity.

Area studies was infiltrated by a gush of identity studies, which valorized difference and Otherness, challenging the logic that had been dedicated to the Same.[9] This putative transfer of logics announced the return of the native, so to speak, and with it the authority of knowledge claims steeped in cultural authenticity and lived experience. This transformation was accompanied by a profound move from a social scientific theorization of modernizing societies to a revival of the humanities through the expansion of cultural studies, with its emphasis on identity and the reconfiguration of Otherness. Both logics share a concern for inclusion: the older modernizing strategy called for the development of an Other that lacked fullness and completion into a modern self, whereas the newer theory authorized a complete, full Other to press its claims for equivalence. (Here, "equivalence" means "sameness," though there are contexts in which it actually implies "difference.") Ironically, the logic of the Same paraded its dedication to the figure of demos, as promised by the spread of democracy and capitalism for the multiplicity of ethnos. But this has merely led to the quest for analogues, such as the heralded "Asian values," to show how cultural endowments result in economic success (a vulgar Weberianism, which, in the hands of more practiced contemporary proponents, still sounds like the shrill announcements of an older Pan-Asianism), as well as appeals to native theory, cloaked by something called "East Asian theory," which supposedly reverses the inordinate privileging of a Western perspective.[10] This return of the native is less a settling of accounts than an overcompensation and repayment for neglect and exclusion. But it is also a natural response to the interpretative strategies of narrow national and imperial interests, which had previously posed as scientific and universal.

The residues of modernization theory and its post–Cold War political strategy resulted in efforts to substitute China for the vanquished Soviet Union, to maintain continued support for the "free world," which was the United States' client states. But once the need for development exhausted its productivity in the new global environment (with the removal of the Soviet competitor), attempts appeared that sought to envision and reconfigure the globe. Showcase clients such as Japan and, to some extent, South Korea, claimed textbook status as models for less-developed societies but were eventually dropped, despite the former enthusiasm for their miraculous modernizing achievements. This was particularly true of the accomplishments attributed to Japan, which included managerial genius and a harmonious consensus society. Its image frayed into that of a fading global power, exporting a banal popular culture and steadily increasing its inventory of social problems. Japan, which had long exemplified successful modernization, was one of the first casualties of the post–Cold War world. Today, Japan appears regularly as a static economy teetering on the edge of deflation, dragged out as a warning of what the United States must avoid. This is especially the case now that the country has been thrown into a tailspin by a massive earthquake and devastating tsunami. Yet, once the tremors passed and the waters receded, the scene was not simply a ruined landscape of destruction, littered with debris and thousands of displaced people (resembling the plight of poor African-Americans in New Orleans after Katrina), but a region that had been marked by historically uneven development, dating back to the nineteenth century. The construction of nuclear facilities along the perilous Sanriku coast in the early 1960s was a belated attempt by the state to promote development in the regional economy, even though much of the power they generated was sent south to Tokyo.

In the new disposition, the reorganization of global hierarchy positioned societies according to their emergent economic power. But appearances by India, China, and South Korea have been accompanied by the recognition that their new standing also reflects ethnic proficiency, often resembling arguments around Japanese culture in the 1970s and 1980s, which repeatedly congratulated that country's native aptitude for technological success and ascribed political and economic achievement to a transhistorical cultural proficiency that had remained unchanged since the Stone Age. Like the earlier portrayal of Japan as a treasure trove of untold wealth, which lured young U.S. business majors to learn Japanese, today's representation of China's inexhaustible riches recruits students into Chinese language courses and deludes university administrators with repackaged fantasies of Cathay's treasures dating back to the time of Marco Polo. Universities now seek funding to establish campuses in China, India, and South Korea, when before interest was underwritten by the U.S. government and some private foundations. Conversely, the frantic pursuit of foreign financing has often resulted in accepting, if not inviting, to American campuses foreign-sponsored and even foreign-administered programs dedicated to disseminating the specific language and culture among American students. The most prominent, if not notorious, has been the establishment by the People's Republic of China (PRC) of a number of Confucius Institutes on American university and college campuses, as well as foreign ones, which not only fund the teaching of language and culture but also usually place a representative of the PRC on the local administrative committee. If this rush to accept foreign funding shows anything, it is greed at any price or questioning that has infected area studies and the transformation of their prior vocation devoted to scholarship and teaching to the endless chasing of funds anywhere. On its part, the Korean National Research Foundation has been energetically active in encouraging diasporic Koreans to carry on Korea-related research projects, which inevitably favor studies reinforcing the South Korean nation form and national identity. But these countries are also exporting more students to the United States to study not just the sciences, as had been the case for many years, but also the history, culture, and literature of their own societies. It is interesting to compare this recent trend among Chinese, Indian, and South Korean students with the Japanese students who came to study science and technology and then invariably returned home. The consequences of this shift in audience for the teaching of areas like Asia will no doubt be far reaching, with critical effects on research, which is already showing a disturbing revival of reductionist strategies authorized by appeals to cultural authenticity and exceptionalism.

The idea that identity should be the vocation of area studies threaded its way through cultural studies and ethnic studies programs that emphasized the hyphenated experience of immigrant groups and minorities in the United States. American studies programs enabled this diffusion, aping the imperial expansion of English departments that had responded to Saidian calls for colonial discourse, by housing diverse hyphenated programs where administrations were reluctant to establish new departments, claiming them as a necessary intellectual and curricular enhancement of their commitment to study an area. While English departments expanded their reach by including the literatures of certain world regions such as South Asia and Southern

Africa—Anglophone literatures—the compass of American studies broadened to accommodate the distinct experiences of certain groups in the United States. The emphasis on different ethnic experiences within a single society meant expanding disciplinary treatment to cover diverse experiential terrains and a continuing effort to link up with metropolitan communities.

This fusion of area studies and ethnic studies reinforced the nativist claims of both the metropole and newly configured studies of diasporic communities. As China, India, and South Korea became emergent economies, driven by massive outsourcing from the United States, Japan, and even Europe, the headiness of new expressions of nationalism and national amour propre further secured the relationship between home cultures and their diasporas, reducing the geographical distance between them by recalling inclusion and irreducible forms of identification.

If area studies diminished after the Cold War by failing to overcome barriers of its own making to engaging the hyphenated identities of the new world order or addressing postcolonial disappointments, it was also complicit in its own subsequent colonization by identity studies. This capitulation was noticeable in its approach to language training and the gradual empowerment of the figure of the native informant and constituted a hangover from an earlier practice in area studies, whereby scholarship relied on the cheap, exploited labor of the native informant to read difficult texts and serve as interpreter in the field. In fact, the activity of "fieldwork" derived from an imperial anthropology that believed it was encountering primitive, premodern societies. The model predominated in research devoted to China, India, Africa, and Japan after World War II, and it generally guided socialization in higher education. In this regard, the change from prewar patterns of training was considerable, since scholars of that generation were less anthropological than philological.

Unlike students of the United States or Europe, who consult libraries and archival collections, the first students in area studies went out to the field to observe, record, and report back what they saw and heard. This research often required knowledge of the local language and reflected the switch from a text-based study of the Orient to daily contact with native populations. The model for area studies was anthropology, which emphasized immediate experience, proficiency in the spoken language, and recruitment of a native speaker as junior partner in the research team, a reflex that, in time, became an unquestioned criterion in job descriptions for language instructors. In principle, the criterion was necessary, so long as language styles and diverse historic modalities remained part of disciplinary training programs, where learning how to speak a language was separated from cultural ideologies derived from the study of its literature, philosophy, religion, and so forth. By opening the portals of area studies to identity, and making native language proficiency its irreducible authority, the way was clear to reconfigure the vocational paradigm by validating the authenticity of identity and the qualification to speak for its idiom. All this began with the simple advertisement, "Native and near native fluency desired."

As in the older form of area studies, with its prescriptive modernization theory, the newer emphasis on identity has been driven by an unacknowledged theory of ethics and rights. We catch glimpses of this impulse in postcolonial discourse, such as the self-vocalizing subaltern subject, previously drowned out by the din of colonial coercion and violence. This theorization often relies on poststructuralist (Derridean) notions of indeterminacy and the sign, Lacanian subject formation, and a postcolonial distancing from both the colonial past and subsequent disappointments of decolonized nationhood, with its ceaseless melancholia.[11] But the most current practice derives from an ethics that demands respect for difference.[12] In earlier area studies, the native informant mediated the relationship between subject (colonizer/researcher) and object (subordinate), but only as a "vanishing mediator"—like the *kuroko* of Japanese Kabuki theater: stagehands dressed in black who move the scenery around while the drama unfolds and are not supposed to be noticed by the audience. By contrast, in the new paradigm the shadowy figure of the native informant is now in full view on center stage and no longer moving scenery.

If the dialectic of the Same and Other ensures the absence of the Other in thought and suppresses all genuine experience of it, then today the Other has returned, challenging self-Same identity with its claim of difference. This return has been enabled by an appeal to an ethics that conceives the Other as anterior to the construction of self-Same identity, to a prior law of founding alterity.[13] But if the former modernization logic of area studies has been replaced by an enunciation on difference as ethical imperative but retained within the privilege of capitalism, we have a case of fetishistic inversion. This inversion of logic from Same to Other is simply a return to what had once prevailed in a different historical register. For Alain Badiou, what lurks behind this conceptualization of Otherness—and what contemporary proponents of it no longer wish to see—is the religious prescription of an Other so remote that it commands devotion, in the place of a deity—the altogether different—and the piety of belief accorded to it.[14] While this "god" remains hidden at the heart of Otherness, appeals to identity and cultural necessity have filled its place. The distant Other has vanished, leaving a call to Otherness that any identity can satisfy. The appeal to difference thus produces a pervasive culturalism that insists on unmediated absolute difference and knowledge putatively derived from the humus of native history. No real light is thrown on any concrete situation by an insistence on recognizing the Other, and valorization of difference does no more than remind us that "differences are what there is, and precisely what truths depose or render insignificant."[15]

We can only guess what it means to place even more emphasis on difference and the qualifications to speak for it. Apart from the antidemocratic reflex

implanted in such privileged knowledge, bespeaking the recruitment of personnel to vocalize and reconfigure the content of area studies, it further spe-
cializes our research agendas and curricula, more than we should accept in this
moment when specialization and splintering is the problem we must overcome.
Even worse are the appeals to resuscitate native theories, as if they remained
uncontaminated throughout the long duration of modernization, waiting to be
summoned once the culture in question was retrofitted with alternative modernity and capitalist wealth. The new paradigm puts up even higher barriers
than the attempts of older area studies to return to a historical singularity and
specificity indifferent to difference, as a condition for thinking about comparative possibilities. One of the failed promises of area studies was comparative
study, before it disappeared in the frenzied desire to solve the problem of comparability by making everyone look like us, which only revealed the bankruptcy
of situating societies hierarchically according to their proximity to the modern. Reversing this demand can only reproduce the earlier failure and recall
what still needs to be done.

The inversion has unleashed a strident call for greater attention to the relationship between subject formation and identity and native expressions of
address, as the voice of the subaltern asserts its claim to inclusion (in what or
where is rarely clarified). The growing support for "native theory" and core cultural values calls for hitherto nonnatives who monopolized enunciation (and
theory) to show greater sensitivity ("respect for difference")[16] toward representatives of the Other and to practice interdisciplinarity, once identified with older
area studies, though it never went beyond simple coverage.

All this is simply a redressing of older practices to appear different. While
this reverse course reinforces a critique of the privilege enjoyed by the fiction
of a unified West and its putative universalism and promise of achieving a "universal history," its goal has been to shed the charge of incompletion and the
stigma of unrealized self-representation. Whether deconstructionists project
Western "unity" in their endless routine to undermine it, as if it had no outside (likewise for "Western Marxists," whose horizon of the perceptual seems
constrained by the same geographical limits), the promotion of its opposite can
offer no improvement. Any program that invites the nonnative to collude with
a nativist enterprise in the name of core Asian values can only lead to the worst
example of what Herbert Marcuse described as "affirmative culture," fusing liberal philosophical idealism with fascism that traded facticity and materiality
for transcendence and timelessness.

Moreover, the demand for recognizing native theory has frequently presumed that, since the West has monopolized theory as a condition of its claim
to subjective status, the East must now rescue native resources of theory to assert
its own subjectivity. Too often this inversion spills over into an embracing of
regionalism. But this move also presumes geographical contiguity as a promise

of cultural commonality. Here, too, is the desire to overlook the configuration of regions by the global expansion of capital and the mediation of the geography and culture that mark a region's claim to sovereign autonomy by economic and political forces and the dialectic pulsations of global-local relationships. In fact, the category of "regionalism" only works if we take into account the specific encounter of time and place, historicality and contemporaneity, between capitalism's expansion and the conditions it generates or confronts, such as colonialism, semicolonialism, and national independence; only then is it possible to envisage the totality to which these regional inflections seek to summon.

James Scott's recent book, *The Art of Not Being Governed*, is an illustrative and imaginative departure from conventional expressions that have appealed to the irreducibility of regional cultures as an alternative to the nation-state, or those tired declarations of new regional cooperatives that invariably recall the dubious heritage of the Greater East Asia Co-Prosperity Sphere.[17] Ultimately, regional cooperatives rely on the authority of one "national culture," reduced to a locality. Scott's study offers a critical regionalism, manifested in an anarchist politicality that avoided the nation-state form and its model for a new area studies.

The recent chain reaction of revolutionary demonstrations in the Middle East (Tunisia, Egypt, Libya, Yemen, Bahrain, Syria), which shook up long-encrusted despotic dictatorships, may well disclose another possibility for critical regionalism, resembling what has also occurred in Bolivia and Venezuela and signifying a movement away from, or at least a breakdown of, the neoliberal global order. It is equally possible that such movements may lead back to atavistic forms of religious reaction. What once seemed years away—that is, what would come after the global pretension of neoliberalism—has become immediate. Though it might only mean a lot of educated people searching for employment, this move underscores the prospect of greater unevenness in the development that neoliberalism has accelerated, to the extent that it will no longer be possible to conceal its role in making the present, and concealing what its socioeconomic system of classifications had displaced or simply dismissed.

Uneven Presents, Unpredictable Pasts

Recognizing unevenness requires a moratorium on the endless discourses that recuperate categories of East and West, North and South and all their dire combinations that classify underdevelopment, despite their critical intentions and professions of solidarity with Otherness. This moratorium must also include claims to a pristine, unmediated native theory, as if it had interpretative and explanatory force outside East Asia. More often than not, calling upon unmediated native theory from its grounding in a historyless culture is as unimaginable as the binaries of East and West that still manage to generate the desire for Otherness. A swing in this direction might finally bring a welcome end to area studies itself.

Instead, we must look at specific experiences of uneven development that occur everywhere, not as societies waiting their turn to move along a linear trajectory and catch up to the head of the signifying chain but as expressions of untimeliness and thus temporalities that belong to the register of difference, but not to the classification of "before" and "after." The charge of unevenness has always been leveled at sites outside Euro-America, even though it is an active and unwritten law of capitalism from which no region can claim exemption. In this regard, uneven development is more than a memory of the experience of defining the Third World. It is a historical process that has been present everywhere, especially in those societies that exported their own unevenness and thus masked their complicity with a development that supposedly represented the maturation of a singular temporality—the fullness of time itself. We know now that the memory of underdevelopment was really the history of untimeliness, of how societies have lived and negotiated their temporalizing effects, and the noncontemporaneity that capitalism produces in various social formations, where people live not in the same present or past to our present but in their own presents that are different from ours, yet which share an immanence that Marx recorded in the *Grundrisse*. Gilles Deleuze's observations on time are useful here, because the past and the future constitute temporal tenses of the present rather than autonomous times. This would be true of any "present." But it is ironic that once the capitalist present became the normative temporality, it sought to classify societies that were backward as belonging to a separate past.[18] The production of unevenness is still a law of capitalist accumulation, in its continued reproduction across spatial and temporal registers. In this regard, capitalism has yet to resolve its own past.

In acknowledging that the paradigms of area studies have arrived at an endgame, it is still reasonable to propose that its dedicated commitment to interrogating the subject of how modernity has been constituted among late-developing societies represents a legacy of lasting value. By linking this preoccupation with forming the modern to the conditions implicated in the constant production of contemporaneity—capitalism's penchant for creating unevenness, especially now that it has been quickened by neoliberalism—we can see an exit from the endless play of binaries, trading places with each other in a global game of musical chairs that always ends up reaffirming a logic of the Same. Such a move brings back the political imperative into any subsequent attempt to make sense of the spectacle of contemporaneity, in view of a historical present always filled with reminders of mixed temporalities generated by uneven development, poised to disrupt stability and fixed identities and shatter any complacency in the unity promised by homogeneous time. Hegel's invocation of the Greek myth of Zeus and his decision to establish the State to counter the ceaseless destructions inflicted by Chronos—Time in the form of change and thus negativity—identified the modern nation-state as timeless, complete, and thus obliged to oppose any instant of temporal heterogeneity as a challenge to its changeless eternity.[19] Where these heterogeneous and discordant temporalities collide is both the moment of politics and the vocation of history.

In my own work I have tried to locate Japan within larger conjunctures, especially during the interwar period, to explain the formation of an uneven modernity and its temporalizing consequences, marked by a late entry into capitalist modernization. By concentrating on Japan as a local inflection of capital's international extension, my aim has been to see it, as Tosaka Jun advised in the thirties, "as a fragment of the world." But even though Japan reproduced capitalism's unevenness, it did so through the mediation of a historical and cultural endowment that aligned with capital and at the same time generated what economist Yamada Moritarō called in the 1930s Japanese-style capitalism.[20] This was the beginning of capitalism's attempts to resolve its specific past in Japan, as in other regions where it prevailed, without ever completing the task. While capital has increasingly subsumed its Other—labor—to complete the commodity relation, it has never really resolved the question of its own history to the extent that "real subsumption" has overtaken history; its traces remain stubbornly embedded in the present. In postponing such a resolution, capitalism, perhaps accidentally, provided a way to see how history failed to correspond to either the temporal rhythms of everyday life or to the narratives of the nation-state. The inability of capitalism to resolve its past validated Marx's observation that archaic traces in the present coexisted with new economic, political, and cultural practices. Yet during the interwar period, Japan accepted Western judgment of its late development to thus occupy a position of relative backwardness in an imaginary trajectory where completed development was realized only in Euro-America. This verdict entailed living the fiction that capitalism (modernity) would eventually realize self-completion and eliminate all traces of its antecedents, thus authorizing the claims prompted by a later aesthetic and literary modernism. In this way, Japan and societies on the colonial periphery confronted the stigma of a time lag that signaled their "backwardness," "late development," or "underdevelopment," according to a singularizing temporality, and thus the necessity of catching up to the present.

During the Cold War, this categorization was revised to accommodate the unaligned nations that the United States targeted for modernizing makeover—development—as its principal strategy against Soviet Marxist revolution. The result was a representation of the world outside Europe and the United States as having failed to join the temporal rhythms of capitalist production, and thus a judgment that it was unworthy of equivalence. What occurred between pre-war and postwar conjunctures was decolonization and the willingness of larger powers to assist in the makeover of the "new nations." The trajectory became more linear and progressive, its measures quantitative rather than qualitative, whereby historical time could only be successive and could tolerate no other temporality. With time's naturalization into nationalization and dehistoricization came the possibility of bridging the distance between the self-declared advanced (imperializing) societies and the Rest, but only if development imitated a logic of the Same. This strategy required transforming qualitative and different temporalities into a single, measureable, quantitative time as the privileged component in a comparative method that authorized the "treatment of human culture in all times and places."[21] But its axis was simply the temporality of before and after. The commitment to a natural evolutionary time enabled the classification of past cultures and living societies, such that some were consigned to the distant past, struggling to move upstream to the present they empirically shared with more advanced societies. Such societies, despite being in the Now, were considered to be in an earlier time.[22]

During the interwar period, Japan so thoroughly absorbed this standard of evaluation that the country was convinced that contemporary Okinawa exemplified its own seventh-century past—even though in the present, the Ryukyus possessed a cultural form that had been shaped by the state in the late nineteenth century to maintain older social and land relationships so necessary for the production of sugar.[23] While the evaluative scheme provided justification for colonial expropriation, it was formalized into a theory of modernization and convergence (in contrast to the Marxian category of "uneven and combined development") that offered societies not yet in the (capitalist) present the prospect of catching up without incurring the dislocations of a wrenching, revolutionary transformation. Catching up implied the status of temporal latecomer, existing in the parenthesis of the time gap, and facing a distance that had yet to be covered.

This perception of a time lag is a reversed cultural diplopia—the defect that sees two images as one. Reinforced by a dematerialization and singularization of time, this reverse diplopia eliminated both the spectacle of coexisting, multiple temporalities and the possibility of seeing them as agentic forms of time. In interwar Japan, the figure of the untimely was reduced to the uncanny—a ghostly reminder of the past—a dangerous anachronism that challenged the settled boundaries of the present, a spectral, irrational presence at the heart of a rational society. This transmutation of qualitative into quantitative time and the dematerialization it demanded were already an established principle in the Western temporal project before the war, renamed as "modernity," which social theorists employed to replace the repetitive process of capitalist accumulation. In time, the visibility of capitalist accumulation was effaced (or superscripted) by systems of values and styles of life and a discourse of "civilization," and identified with the timeless and spatial countenance of the nation-state form, whose enclosing narrative became capitalism's placeholder.

Postwar attempts to configure alternative and multiple modernities, as in the Japanese example before the war, or to privilege irreducible difference and detemporalize and dematerialize it into the moment of subaltern verbal address, as in the stronger versions of postcolonial discourse, invariably recuperated capitalism's conception of time accountancy and the time lag it produced, even as they occupied two different global conjunctures. In both prewar Japan and the later era of decolonization, the quest for the modern was based on values associated with specific cultural experiences, rather than capitalism and its economic and social structures. The imperative of catching up was displaced to identification with a modernity drawn from different cultural experiences, instead of the materiality that separated one society from another. Yet this conception of the modern, perhaps most powerfully articulated by Max Weber, was in fact founded on a misrecognition derived from the experiences of manufacturing and technology, which established the primacy of uniform, linear time over circular and cyclical rhythms—the relationship of living to dead labor in the modern factory and city. Hence the calendar and clock measured the ceaseless passage from moment to moment, day to day, year to year, fixing before and after, then and now. Despite its claim to neutrality, the measure was marked by a developmental narrative that located societies on an imaginary, flattened, temporal grid in relationship to the present.

We can see how this strategy, in which claims of culture and quality veiled materiality and quantity, sanctioned imperial interventions before World War II. This surely explains the prewar Japanese call to "overcome the modern" and the later postcolonial demand for an alternative modernity, which valorized cultural identity to attain some sort of recognition of equivalence for having been assigned to the precinct of temporal unevenness. In Japan during the 1930s, the call to overcome the modern was linked to the effort to resolve what Ernst Troeltsch named the "crisis of historicism." Japanese thinkers of the Kyoto school reinforced the conviction that they were living through a crisis in historical thought, evidenced in the production of an excess of history and the runaway relativization of values that modernity had unleashed.[24] Moreover, thinkers blamed this excessive production of history on accelerated specialization among the disciplines, which undermined whatever coherence they may have once commanded.[25] The problem confronting historical practice was the loss of a stable ground, provoked by a modernity dedicated to the ever-changing new, with its inability to capture a coherent and unwavering representation. At the heart of this crisis was the perception that the speed of change, embodied in the developmental imperative, required a historical practice capable of providing a steadfast image free from the erosion of unconstrained change and the negativity of relativism. This task was assigned to a new philosophy of world history, which, it was believed, could overcome a crisis-ridden modernity dominated by frenzied development and social abstraction by returning to the concrete "real life" that could realize a Japanese modernity. In this scenario, the sought-after concreteness fused the old received practices and the new. Inverting quantitative measures into qualitative difference (culture and quality for economic materiality and the advantage and accident of time) had been common sense among imperializing countries since the nineteenth century, including "latecomers" like Japan; it also encouraged, if not camouflaged, the unevenness that had been common among modern societies of the industrial West. While colonizers forcibly inflicted this perspective on their colonies, in Japan, the importation of foreign, material culture (especially U.S. culture in the 1920s) merely ratified the perception that emulating these exemplars meant that those societies had already overcome the stigma of uneven development. In the 1930s, Marxists and progressives expressed anxiety over visible signs of unevenness. Even conservative folklorists like Yanagita Kunio warned against the growing separation between countryside and city, wherein the former was constantly making sacrifices to the latter. Yanagita saw this domestic relationship as a sign of an internal time lag that replicated the larger relationship between colony and metropole.

Cultural theorists such as Kuki Shūzō worried about excessive uncritical imitation of foreign cultures, whereas liberal publicists such as Hasegawa Nyozekan and scholars such as Imanaka Tsugimaro were convinced that Japan's economic backwardness would lead to fascism. Both Hasegawa and Imanaka drew comparisons with contemporary Italy to demonstrate the relationship between a weak economic base and fascism.[26] Hasegawa, along with other Marxists, believed that the Meiji Restoration of 1867 was as much a counterrevolution as an incipient bourgeois revolution yet perceived that their time lag differentiated Japan and Italy from the more "advanced" liberal democratic states in Europe and the United States precisely because it opened the way to fascism. Marxists such as Tosaka Jun saw the world crisis of capitalism exacerbating Japan's late-developing economy and confounding its liberal political capacity to resolve the issue. The equation between liberalism and fascism was perceived in both Germany (Herbert Marcuse) and Italy (Giovanni Gentile, Benito Mussolini) at the same time, and it was ultimately articulated in a cultural ideology that displaced economic unevenness with the idea of the folk as a unified, organic national community, to eliminate the conflict produced by clashing interests. In Tosaka's reckoning, this cultural ideology elevated the ideal of "restoration" (*fukko*), recalling the incomplete Restoration of 1867 (and Yamada Moritarō's analysis of capitalism's embodying feudal residues) and summoning archaic values to anchor the new folk community in an unchanging historical identity.[27] In this sense, fascism, which is always about values, exchanged one system of accumulated value—abstract labor—for another based on cultural form, seeking to replace abstraction with concreteness by integrating labor into a folk body and thus replacing economic—materiality—with culture—ideality. (Italian and German fascisms both used this tactic as well.) The importance of Tosaka's response lay in the observation that the Japanese were no longer living in real historical time but in the cyclic temporality of an ethnic-cosmic recurrence or an interiorized psychological and phenomenological time, enclosing subjectivity from the external, objective world and its political and economic structures, which both distanced and shielded the subject from the outside and induced acceptance of it as it was.[28]

Economist Yamada Moritarō, also a Marxist, further elaborated this connection between latecomer status and fascism in his powerful 1934 analysis titled *Nihon shihonshugi bunseki* (An analysis of Japanese capitalism), which supplied a paradigm for grasping the uneven development of capitalism in Japan since the late eighteenth century. Where Tosaka saw Japan's unevenness transmuted into a unifying cultural ideology that recommended restoring archaic elements from the past, Yamada focused attention on the "semifeudal" heritage that coexisted with modern capitalism. In doing so, he showed how Japan's temporally truncated capitalist development had been shaped by a mixture of practices from both older and more recent modes of production, a hybrid Japanese-style capitalism that diverged from established patterns in England and France. Rooted in the twentieth-century persistence of large pockets of "semifeudal residues of landholding" and their corresponding social relationships, Yamada's Japanese-style capitalism attested to an incomplete revolution promised by the Meiji Restoration and the failure of capitalism to adequately resolve its past and realize a completed modern order. Instead, Japan was left with a distorted copy that led to political absolutism—fascism.

Yamada's account may have resulted from a misreading of Marx and *Capital* in particular, and a misunderstanding of the meaning of "time lag," since he seems to have been driven by a desire to link contemporary political consequences to capitalism's failure to resolve its past. Faced with the unwelcome challenge of explaining the persistence of feudal residues and archaic remnants (a strategic substitute for the emperor to escape the notice of state censorship) of older modes of production, which stood against Japan's capitalist development, Yamada believed that the original promise of the Meiji Restoration was undermined by its own past. The result was not revolution but refeudalization, and a political absolutism that sharpened capitalism's contradictions and accelerated the passage of fascism at home and imperialism abroad.

Nevertheless, the idea of a Japanese-style capitalism paradoxically opened the way to acknowledging the importance of cultural difference and the risk of slipping into an exceptionalism that anticipated later calls to either overcome the modern or accept an alternative modernity. In fact, a symposium on the modern in 1942 pressed for the possibility of transforming unevenness from a symptom of failure into a sign of exceptional social endowment, to turn the defect of late growth into a distinct expression of modernity capable of retaining cultural residues alongside capitalism. Philosopher Miki Kiyoshi advised the promotion of this tactic on the eve of the Pacific War, when he proposed the retention of a "living culture" (*seikatsu bunka*) comprising constant interaction between old and new, instead of the 1920s concept of "cultural daily life" (*bunka seikatsu*) that emphasized consumption of modern commodities. In Miki's scheme, living culture would be the model for a new capitalist time and space for the "Orient"—the newly formed Greater East Asia Co-Prosperity Sphere.[29]

By contrast, Yamada's observations on the deformed nature of Japanese capitalism may have been an attempt to capture a positive image of irreducible uniqueness, strangely consistent with Marx's conviction that the remains of past modes of production inevitably accompany capitalism in the present. It is not clear if Yamada knew about Marx's late exchange of letters with Russian progressives like Vera Zasulich, in which he conceded the possibility that archaic remainders such as the Russian commune would gradually free themselves from the fetters of capitalism to promote production on a national scale. Yet, "precisely because it is contemporaneous with capitalist production, the rural commune may appropriate all its positive achievements without . . . frightful vicissitudes."[30] Marx, who had already acknowledged in *Capital* that he derived his sketch from the example of England's development but did not exclude other routes, was envisaging multiple possibilities that no longer required noncapitalist societies to replicate the European colonial model. Russia showed that it was possible to draw upon remnants of a prior mode of production to create a new register of formal subsumption, or bypass it. Yamada inched toward something similar when he named Japan's experience of development as Japanese-style capitalism, even though his analysis dwelled on the negative consequences of its contradictions rather than its new trajectory of development.

Ultimately, seeing through the ideological constraints thrown up by representing unevenness in the figure of a time lag that required societies on the colonial margin to catch up removes the division between the center and its periphery. Ironically, uneven forms were always more visible in the periphery than in the center, which could claim no exemption once the spell cast by the division was broken. According to Neil Larsen, the place of the periphery is where "capital concentrates its most extreme contradictions." While Larsen sees the boundary between the modern and its Other as more spatial than temporal, I believe that capitalism's capacity to produce uneven development and untimely, heterogeneous temporalities, which contrast most sharply in the periphery, expresses its contradictions in their most concentrated form. Larsen's "living emblems" are the great metropolitan centers of the Third World:

Mexico City, Manila, or São Paulo, "with its towering commercial and financial strongholds enclosed within a massive ring of pillaged human beings living within sight of modernity but yet beneath its plane."[31] But such spatial difference is marked by different temporalities, obliging residents of these cities to internalize untimeliness and navigate from one sector to another. Historical societies always display the overlay and structural coexistence of multiple modes of production, and even when one mode dominates over the others, the process of combining residues from earlier times persists, though these are assigned a dependent status to the new. Because the vestiges remain partially unassimilated to a dominant system, often assuming the appearance of revenants capable of reminding contemporaries of what has been lost and possessing the capacity for sudden, unscheduled surfacing, they can always challenge the principal mode of production and demand a space of their own, as Ernst Bloch observed in the rise of fascism in Germany during the 1930s.

Fredric Jameson named this configuration of combined residues a "cultural revolution": the moment when coexisting modes of production become visibly antagonistic, and determinations from different domains combine into a concentration of contradictions—an overdetermination—leading to what Louis Althusser described as "ruptural unity,"[32] the world of *zeitwidrig* (turmoil of temporalities). In late texts, Althusser aligned this synchronic nonsynchronism and its train of contradictions with the conjunctural event and its subsequent shift from static configuration (synchrony) to dynamic transformation and reconfiguration (diachrony). Jameson's "cultural revolution" was thus Althusser's "encounter."[33] In this connection, the image of China's 1919 Cultural Revolution and Mao Zedong's later imaging of a "culture of revolution" yielded a "revolutionary culture" and a new politics rooted in altered social relationships.

Though he did not actually address the unevenness introduced by capitalist colonial powers by backing off from its presence, Edward Said contemplated the unequal exchange of textual forms implicated in configuring the Orient and "dominating and having authority over it" and unintentionally disclosed the spectacle of what clearly was before him but had escaped his vision: colonialism as a vast terrain of unsynchronic synchrony stemming from the reproduction of capitalist accumulation.[34] This opening toward colonialism introduced the specularity of unevenness, constituting its sign and defining its relationship to the industrial states of Euro-America. It was precisely this experience among the so-called late developers—colonies and societies on the periphery— that allowed the "enfeebled center" of the West to recognize the temporal immanence of unevenness and its existence in our own backyard.

According to Jameson, late capitalism has witnessed the steady disappearance of the "local": "Expressions of the marginally uneven and unevenly developed issuing from a recent experience of capitalism are often more intense and powerful, more . . . deeply meaningful than anything the enfeebled center still finds itself able to say."[35] We now recognize that Japan, China, India, and countries in Latin America are capable of seeing what once had been concealed as the condition of the self-arrogation of centrality by industrial societies of Euro-America. Hence the spectacle of backwardness is no reflection of degraded archaic remainders or even failed past resolutions, but it signifies an "integral part of the way modern society" is constituted and "reproduces itself, or . . . as evidence of perverse forms of progress." For historians of Brazil, in agreement with Roberto Schwarz, and latecomers such as China, India, and Japan, this perspective empowers a "deprovincializ[ing]" that "inscribe[s] these once peripheral regimes on the present." Though once denied entry, they are now placed within the current global configuration, which had previously "seemed to distance [them] from it and confine [them] to irrelevance."[36]

While the era when area studies found its vocation has now passed, we still live in the same world of capital accumulation, albeit more advanced and globally hegemonic. Under the ferocious figure of neoliberalism, the world is no less free from the appearance of unevenness and the untimely. Societies once consigned to an underdeveloped, backward periphery have become "distant folkloric remnants."[37] There should be little disagreement over the proposition that neoliberalism found its momentum by promoting the law of uneven development and accelerating it as a global capitalist project (now that development has vanished from the post–Cold War scene), itself indifferent to the older division of center and periphery and capable of reproducing new forms of untimeliness on a scale hitherto unimagined. So much so that it is easy to romanticize the return of regionalisms and the offer of delinking.

In this regard, James Scott's *The Art of Not Being Governed* is instructive. Scott concentrates on the area from the Central Highlands of Vietnam to the northeastern corner of India—what has been known as the "Southeast Asian mainland massif."[38] Scott's conception of the region, which he calls "Zomia," differs from the Japanese construction of an East Asian Co-Prosperity Sphere, which was supposed to integrate the economies and polities of East and Southeast Asia into an imperial unity. Until its inception, the Greater East Asia Co-Prosperity Sphere had no history, being born of a metaphysical idea, and the political force of Japan's imperial aspirations determined its geographic dimensions. Zomia's history has created the "largest remaining region of the world whose people have not yet been fully incorporated into nation-states," though this history is even now passing into memory.[39] Scott is convinced that, until recently, self-governing communities constituted the rule rather than exception in human history. The highland peoples he writes about are "runaway, fugitive, maroon communities . . . who have been fleeing the oppression of state-making projects" in the lowlands, what he calls the "shatter zones."[40] Scott is, I believe, right to concentrate on those peoples and areas that were either excluded by the state or escaped from its enclosing propensities. In his reckoning, Zomia is marked not by the political unity demanded by a state apparatus but by "comparable patterns of diverse hill agriculture, dispersal and mobility, and rough egalitarianism, which . . . includes a relatively higher status for women than in the valleys."[41] In some respects, it resembles the world of untimeliness until it was enclosed by capitalism and a discourse of "civilization."

Scott's bold attempt to figure a region reveals the silhouette of a different area studies agenda, based on what he calls "riotous heterogeneity." This singular combination of history (now passing) and geography provides unity without requiring belonging to either nation or state; instead, it is a region capable of manifesting its difference. In this sense, Zomia resembles Bakhtin's conception of a chronotope that manages to configure the space-time relationship under specific historical circumstances. As a concept, "Zomia marks an attempt to explore a new genre of 'area' studies, in which the justification for designating the area has nothing to do with national boundaries (for example Laos) or strategic conceptions (for example, Southeast Asia) but is rather based on certain ecological regularities and structural relationships that do not hesitate to cross national frontiers. If we have our way, the examples of 'Zomia studies' will inspire others to follow the experiment elsewhere."[42] Like the everyday of a modernizing society, with its coexisting temporalities and possibility of multiple histories, Zomia opens up the promise, and indeed necessity, of crossing national borders and the prospect of envisaging comparative study of the political implications of the effort to resist enclosure by the nation-state. Politics and history appear at the juncture where discordant times intersect.[43]

The historicity of unevenness justified practices designed to prevent underdevelopment in any other direction than what models of capitalist achievement prescribed. What the Japanese memory of underdevelopment discloses was the drive, whether Marxian or bourgeois, to free capitalist modernization from carceral categories such as mimicry and emulation, by recognizing the utility of combining practices from past and present to show their claims to both equivalence and difference. In the charge of backwardness, something is advanced, just as the claim to being "advanced" produces backwardness. But difference here becomes a temporal tense. For, the past is never finished with because of its incessant unpredictability in the present, while the present plays out its drama in the garb of the old. If anything, Japan's historical accounting of the modern has dramatized the moments of rupture produced by capitalism, and the resulting constant collision of heterogeneous temporalities appearing in the figure of the noncontemporaneous contemporary have been inverted into what they are not. Rather than classifying the collisions as common moments of noncontemporaneity, they are judged as examples of time lag and assigned to a developmental trajectory characterized by permanent catch-up. These temporalities are presented as instances of culture talking about itself—and increasingly to itself—a reservoir of autonomous real value—the domain of Asian values—that encourages a romance with a cultural dominant by substituting spatial countenance for temporally prompted change.

What gets lost in this exchange is the world of *zeitwidrig*, nonlinearity, noncontemporaneity, a sudden discord created by capitalism's unrelenting propensity for producing "combined and uneven development." Daniel Bensaïd advised that history

> knows no one-way streets—whether longitudinally, following the sequence of centuries; or in cross-section, when one society lives the life of another in thought, while the latter acts out the thought of the former, without philosophy and history, economics and politics, ever achieving reconciliation in the tranquil harmony of some simple "correspondence." Construed as "backwardness" in relation to an imaginary temporal norm, anachronism ends up imposing itself not as a residual anomaly, but as an essential attribute of the present. Noncontemporaneity is not reducible to the immaterial unevenness of its moments. It is also their combined development in a novel historical space-time.[44]

If we recognize these mixed temporalities as heterogeneous to one another and articulate this relationship, we open the perspective of a genuinely "noncontemporary representation of historical development," capable of leading to comparative studies and realizing the original aspiration of area studies, which has always shown its capacity to lose its way.[45]

Notes

My thanks to the producers of the prescient 1968 Cuban film *Memories of Underdevelopment*, and apologies for using the title in a different way. Thanks also to Kristin Ross, Tani Barlow, Rey Chow, and Hyun Ok Park for the help they gave me on this essay.

1. Fredric Jameson proposes that cultural studies, at least in the United States, constituted a "desire," which, among its many ambitions, was the yearning to succeed Marxism and replace it. Before the formation of cultural studies, area studies laid claim to the desire to be an integrative discipline, bringing together several established disciplines to study regions of the world (usually outside Euro-America), and to the aspiration to replace Marxian models of conflict and social change for peaceful modernization makeovers based on a "normative" social science that emphasized the centrality of core values (consensus). Fredric Jameson, "On 'Cultural Studies,'" in *The Ideologies of Theory* (New York: Verso, 2008), 598–635.
2. Peter Osborne, *The Politics of Time* (London: Verso, 1995), 196.

3. Stavros Tombazos, *Le temps dans l'analyse économique: Les catégories du temps dans le "Le capital"* (Paris: Cahier des saisons, 1994).

4. Louis Althusser, *Philosophy of the Encounter*, ed. François Matheron and Oliver Corpet, trans. G. M. Goshgarian (London: Verso, 2006), 188, 196.

5. Harry Harootunian, *History's Disquiet* (New York: Columbia University Press, 2000), 25–58.

6. There is ample literature on the relationship between "modernization theory" and the practice of policy, which inevitably displaces or simply ignores the epistemological basis of the "theorization." For the former, see Michael E. Latham, *Modernization as Ideology: American Social Science and "Nation Building" in the Kennedy Era* (Chapel Hill: University of North Carolina Press, 2000). For the latter, see Harry D. Harootunian, *The Empire's New Clothes: Paradigm Lost, and Regained* (Chicago: Prickly Paradigm Press, distributed by the University of Chicago Press, 2004).

7. John Kraniauskas, "Difference Against Development: Spiritual Accumulation and the Politics of Freedom," in "Problems of Comparability/Possibilities for Comparative Studies," ed. H. Harootunian and H. O. Park, special issue, *boundary 2*, 32, no. 2 (2005): 68.

8. Kraniauskas, "Difference Against Development," 68.

9. I am indebted to Alain Badiou's writings for this following section, especially his *Ethics*, trans. Peter Hallward (New York: Verso, 2002), 18–29.

10. Margaret Hillenbrand, "Communitarianism, or, How to Build East Asian Theory," *Postcolonial Studies* 13, no. 4 (2010): 317–34.

11. Leela Gandhi, *Postcolonial Theory* (New York: Columbia University Press, 1998), 5–17.

12. This is essentially the argument of Badiou, whereby ethics becomes the "ultimate name of the religious, as such," inasmuch as the Other is related to the "authority of the Altogether-Other" (*Ethics*, 25).

13. Badiou, *Ethics*, 22.

14. Badiou, *Ethics*, 23–23.

15. Badiou, *Ethics*, 27.

16. Badiou, *Ethics*, 24.

17. James Scott, *The Art of Not Being Governed* (New Haven, Conn.: Yale University Press, 2009).

18. Gilles Deleuze, *Difference and Repetition*, trans. Paul Patton (New York: Columbia University Press, 1994), 71.

19. G. W. F. Hegel, *Lectures on the Philosophy of World History: Introduction*, trans. H. B. Nisbet (Cambridge: Cambridge University Press, 1975), 145.

20. Yamada Moritarō, *Nihon shihonshugi bunseki* (Tokyo: Iwanami shoten, 1934), 173–215.

21. Johannes Fabian, *Time and the Other* (New York: Columbia University Press, 1983), 6.

22. This is the argument in Fabian, *Time and the Other*, 155, and the formulations of Ernst Bloch's earlier work on "synchronic nonsynchronisms" (*Ungleichzeitigkeit*), in *The Heritage of Our Times*, trans. Neville and Stephen Plaice (Berkeley: University of California Press, 1990), 39–185.

23. Wendy Matsumura, "Becoming Okinawan: Japanese Capitalism and Changing Representations of Okinawa" (PhD diss., New York University, 2010).

24. Koyama Iwao, *Sekaishi no tetsugaku* (Tokyo: Kobushi shobō, 2001), 418–20.

25. The symposium on overcoming modernity devoted one section to the problem of specialization. See Harry Harootunian, *Overcome by Modernity: History, Culture, and Community in Interwar Japan* (Princeton, N.J.: Princeton University Press, 2000), 65–94.

26. See Hasegawa Nyozekan, *Nihon fashizumu hihan* (Tokyo: Ōhata shoten, 1932); see also Reto Hoffman, "The Fascist Reflection: Japan and Italy, 1919–1950" (PhD diss., Columbia University, 2010), 174–79; on Imanaka Tsugimaro, see Kevin M. Doak, "Fascism Seen and Unseen: Fascism as a Problem of Representation," in *The Culture of Japanese Fascism*, ed. Alan Tansman (Durham, N.C.: Duke University Press, 2009), 31–55, and Richard Torrance, "The People's Library: The Spirit of Prose Literature versus Fascism," in Tansman, *Culture*, 58–59.

27. Tosaka Jun, *Nihon ideorogīron* (Tokyo: Iwanami bunko, 1977), 172–85.

28. Tosaka Jun, *Tosaka Jun zenshū*, 5 vols. (Tokyo: Keisō shobō, 1978), 3:101.

29. On Miki, see Harootunian, *Overcome by Modernity*, 358–99.

30. Teodor Shanin, ed., *Late Marx and the Russian Road* (New York: Monthly Review Press, 1983), 106.

31. Neil Larsen, *Modernism and Hegemony* (Minneapolis: University of Minnesota Press, 1990), xxxv.

32. Fredric Jameson, *The Political Unconscious* (Ithaca, N.Y.: Cornell University Press, 1981), 95.

33. See Jameson, *The Political Unconscious*, 97–98n74, where Jameson sees Bloch's conception of nonsynchronism as a fulfillment of Marx's program (in Karl Marx, *Grundrisse: Foundation of the Critique of Political Economy*, trans. Martin Nicolaus [London: Pelican, 1973]) for dialectical knowledge "of rising from the abstract to the concrete."

34. Harry Harootunian, "Conjunctural Traces: Said's 'Inventory,'" *Critical Inquiry* 31, no. 2 (2005): 442.

35. Fredric Jameson, *The Geopolitical Aesthetic: Cinema and Space in the World System* (Bloomington: Indiana University Press, 1992), 155.

36. Roberto Schwarz, *A Master on the Periphery of Capitalism: Machado de Assis*, trans. John Gledson (Durham, N.C.: Duke University Press: 2002), 3.

37. Scott, *Not Being Governed*, 324.

38. Scott, *Not Being Governed*, ix.

39. Scott, *Not Being Governed*, ix.

40. Scott, *Not Being Governed*, ix–x.

41. Scott, *Not Being Governed*, 19.

42. Scott, *Not Being Governed*, 26.

43. Daniel Bensaïd, *Marx for Our Times: Adventures and Misadventures of a Critique*, trans. Gregory Elliott (New York: Verso, 2009), 22, 27.

44. Bensaïd, *Marx for Our Times*, 24.

45. Bensaïd, *Marx for Our Times*, 22.

PART II

CULTURAL FORM AND POLITICAL WITHDRAWAL

Tokugawa Japan

CHAPTER 3

CULTURAL POLITICS IN TOKUGAWA JAPAN

The Tokugawa "Society of the Spectacle"

Buyō Inshi,[1] the pseudonymous author of a Tokugawa-period (1603–1867) history entitled *Seji kemmonroku* (1816), complained early in the nineteenth century that the spectacle of popular culture that had apparently enthralled people of the city of Edo (present-day Tokyo) imperiled both the rule of the Tokugawa house, which had administered the realm since the seventeenth century, and the quality of moral life which the "floating world" (*ukiyo*) had thrown into disarray. *Ukiyo* was the term used to describe pleasure and entertainment, "society" and the "world"; it carried a sense of instability. Like a number of thoughtful observers who worried about the prospect of play—which the great city offered in almost excessive abundance—and who warned of worse things to come if the surplus was not contained, Buyō was responding to the proliferation of social groups and classes that constituted the city's vast population at the end of the eighteenth century, its virtual differentiation of new occupational constituencies and the expansion of a division of labor serving the interests of play. His account of contemporary history covers a time span from the late eighteenth to the early nineteenth century and concentrates on a variety of social groups which, in an earlier time, would have existed either on the margins of both society and consciousness or simply not have been present at all. In his catalog, there were samurai of all ranks, peasants who had obviously violated proscriptions that earlier had been promoted to keep cultivators in the countryside, shrine and temple priests plying their "dubious" nostrums, public litigants, pleasure quarter prostitutes, doctors, fortune-tellers, merchants, artisans, entertainers of all kinds, Kabuki actors, members of the pariah class (*eta*; *hinin*), and so forth. Buyō's description of city life, which composes a coherent world of social relationships, discloses the persistence of both spectacle and diversity, even though it is precisely these signs that cause him so much anxiety. The existence of such a vast army of occupational groupings attested to how differentiation and, hence, difference itself had seized hold of the daily life of Edo, altering and even undermining the received order of things. What seemed to bother Buyō most, as well as many others, was the recognition that endless social differentiation was now contributing to the dissolution of the natural divisions of society that had always privileged mental over manual labor, empowering the holders of the former to rule because of their possession of proper moral knowledge and the latter to "follow because they do not know," as Aizawa Seishisai (1781–1863) explained in his *Shinron* (1825).[2]

The fundamental division of labor separating intellectual and manual labor authorized the organization of society into precise and fixed categories such as samurai, peasantry, artisan, and merchant. People were to occupy these categories involuntarily and perform specific duties invested with the necessity of moral imperative throughout their lives. Under the circumstances of social proliferation, the fixed relationships between high and low, mental and manual labor would begin to blur. Proliferating diversification and differentiation of social relationships, especially in the larger cities, began to exceed the received fixed categories of social status. The sign of this slippage was stamped in the observable quest for private and personal interest which, according to Buyō, people everywhere were encouraged to pursue in open disregard for the natural duties associated with their status. "Standards have been lost," he announced, and "financial interest has now become the basis of life"; moral duty and obligation have been thrown to the wind; "the four estates, high and low, esteemed and despised, are now determined according to the accumulation of wealth and fortune."[3] The blurring of boundaries between the "esteemed" and the "despised," ruler and ruled, has become so great that natural standards differentiating groups since the beginning of the Tokugawa period have vanished, he continued. Contemporary custom (*sesō*) has undermined fixed relationships and the patterns of conduct expected of people in each rank. "When looking at contemporary custom, passion and madness have thrown things into disorder. The Way of Principle [*dōri*] seems to have disappeared. The struggle between gain and loss goes on strongly, without government sanction. Today, all people are either rich or poor."[4] So stricken was Buyō by contemporary failure that he was no longer able to endure either seeing what occurred or hearing about it.

Buyō's denunciation of contemporary woes left no group unscathed. The cause of the malaise, he asserted, was the unchecked spread of money, the increasing valorization of wealth and luxury and its consequences for fixed social relationships. The samurai, who had once nobly served as the example for all to follow as models of loyal devotion and duty, had now been replaced by merchants, businessmen, brokers, and moneylenders. Instead of received norms, Buyō noted, new standards have been erected everywhere to encourage people to "plan for profit and seek personal pleasures." In the scramble for profit, feudal lords [daimyō] constantly appropriated the stipends of their retainers, who were already hard-pressed to make ends meet, in order to finance their own quest for pleasure in Edo. "Virtue and benevolence have been lost through treachery," he wrote, and the loss has resulted in loosening the relationship of lord and retainer and separating obligation from duty. Lords have fallen into a cycle of habitual borrowing from brokers and been forced to seize the stipends of their retainers to repay their own debts. The effect of this cycle of debt, expropriation, and repayment has trickled down to the lower orders. Ultimately, those who originally had been servants left the lord's compounds to become rōnin or merchants and artisans, owners of brothels, restaurants, teashops, shipping agents, and entertainers. Hence, the "dignity of the lord" has been depleted, he said, while the conduct of the retainers and servants has become more disrespectful. While noting that service to the military households had been debased to the pursuit of personal pleasure, Buyō also condemned peasants for having ceased to work, leaving their fields for pleasure, like members of the military estate. As the fields empty out and production decreases yearly, the idlers swell the size of the cities.[5]

If Buyō's record of contemporary custom inadvertently represented Edo as the site of a dynamic spectacle taking place before him, a veritable explosion of new cultural forms and practices, it also reminds us of an earlier decorum deriving from the fear of excess and private impulse or passion, as it was called, which it sought to extinguish as a danger to civilized moral life. Much of Buyō's history rings with the hoary clamor of seventeenth-century neo-Confucian moralists, who worried incessantly about the production of disruption and disorder when people were encouraged to leave the path of public morality for a life of private interest. Echoing early Tokugawa moralists, who sought to explain the reasons for the one hundred years of civil disobedience, struggle, and fragmentation that preceded the new Tokugawa regime and supplied it with moral purpose, Buyō warned that a "politics that has made one's own interest first as its vocation . . . abandons the Way of Tranquilizing the people to concentrate on the development of the person. . . . It is fixated only on the glorification and honor of the body . . . and favors wine and women in order to make luxury a norm."[6] Owing to the temptations of private and selfish desire, people everywhere have embraced "abusive habits," he continued. Desire wreaks disorder upon the realm, turning people away from their natural duties and work to produce a surplus of differences which society can no longer contain. Forgetting their place in society and their moral obligations, people occupy different roles, competing with each other to gain advantage and accumulate wealth.

Buyō's dim vision of contemporary culture was shared by others, even though they might not always support the solution he advocated, a return to an earlier age and its morality. What all could agree upon, however, was the recognition of an immense cultural and social transformation in Tokugawa life, which they were able to grasp only in its effects, its parts, but not as a total phenomenon. Buyō's contemporary Shiba Kōkan (1747–1818), the artist and student of Dutch Learning, proposed that "after the continuation of a long-standing administration, men will favor beauty and extensive luxury. But luxury is not only in being luxurious. Like the approaching of years, which is never seen by the eye, one does not know they have grown old. There are people who do not know that they are simply being luxurious."[7] Shiba was undoubtedly correct to portray the incidence of widespread luxury as something deeper and more complex that could not easily be grasped by the eye but required knowledge and understanding to explain its causes. But whereas Buyō looked to a distant past for solutions, Shiba, a painter already familiar with Western conceptions of perspective and principles of composition, looked toward a new and as yet unenvisaged future.

If the antiquity Buyō sought to reinstate in the early nineteenth century was both remote and idealized, it was nonetheless vastly different from his present. Late Tokugawa writers regularly called attention to the contemporary situation, in which, they asserted, samurai had become involved in the pursuit of luxury to the extent that it conformed to the "ordinary state of things among townsmen today."[8] Complaining vigorously that contemporary townsmen were being instructed in the arts, as had been the aristocratic courtiers of antiquity, who performed Noh and the tea ceremony and engaged in the poetic composition of linked verse (renga), that merchants had now acquired the artifacts that previously only daimyo "took pleasure in," where price determined value when earlier it was taste and pleasure, Buyō spoke for many when he declared that commoners were acting impudently in the present.[9] The spread of an aristocratic style and the apparent democratization of taste among those who could afford leisure and luxury meant that the daimyo and the "esteemed" classes no longer possessed those emblems that attested to the intangibility of superior character. Like "name," taste could be bought, style purchased, as commodities. For critics, the prevalence of luxury meant consumption that struck at the heart of the idea of a natural order that had constituted the basis of Tokugawa legitimacy, premised upon the primacy of agricultural production and a morality that demanded strict economics in behavior and that depended upon the announcement of sumptuary rules to remind people of this imperative.

Inventing the Past

It was too late for moralists to restore the earlier world they sought, a world that was represented as having been brought out of civil chaos. Later writers and thinkers fearful of the specter of disorder and fragmentation looked back to the early Tokugawa period, with its virtuous leaders who had ended a century of civil strife and established the conditions for a protracted peace and prosperity. While it is true that the Tokugawa coalition, led by Ieyasu (1543–1616), succeeded in the early seventeenth century in establishing control over contending lords and leagues and, hence, bringing an end to the turmoil of a realm at war with itself throughout the sixteenth century, the representation of this achievement was rooted in claims of moral legitimacy and sanctions derived from the idea of a Heavenly Way (*tendō*), a key concept in the Confucian philosophic arsenal. During the preceding century of conflict, when territorial lords fought each other for land and supremacy, there had probably been a dialectical relationship between political events and the way the world was apprehended. Events seemed to move aimlessly and randomly and were, in time, represented as expressions of individual effort, self-interest and private impulse flying in the face of precedent and justified as legitimate because they reflected the particular. This version of the world, in which the individual self-interest—private passion (*ninjō*), denounced by Buddhists—prevailed was gradually seen as existing in a time of disorder and civil anarchy. By the early seventeenth century, when the first three Tokugawa shoguns had managed to establish hegemony, a new conception of social order was busily being constructed by neo-Confucian philosophers who sought to reshape the human order into a microcosm of nature. In short, civil war and unrelieved divisiveness ultimately led to both a process of consolidation accomplished by the Tokugawa house and the configuration of a view of social order that located the source of disorder and disharmony in unbridled private passion or feeling and selfishness which, as recent history had demonstrated, led only to particularism, fragmentation, and endless competition and division. This new conception of society emphasized the identity of the whole, expressed in terms like heaven (*ten*), realm or universe (*tenka*), public interest and the public world (*kugai*), over its constitutive parts; it was dramatized by an early Tokugawa appropriation of neo-Confucianism[10] and its metaphysical system, which promised to provide a cosmic paradigm of perfect order. By establishing nature or the cosmos as the model for society, the Tokugawa believed they had found a way to totalize the dispersed parts of the political realm—autonomous and semi-independent feudal domains—according to a principle of hierarchical organization.

In the early seventeenth century, Tokugawa Ieyasu had ended the civil anarchy that had prevailed for over a century. To prevent further fragmentation and continuing competition for land among feudal lords, he and his successors embarked upon a program to erect a system of order which, while it might still retain the semiautonomy of the domains, sought to impose a central authority from Edo, the Tokugawa castle town. This system entailed a conception of hegemony by presuming the authority of the Tokugawa over the domains, even as it permitted the continued existence of feudal houses. It consisted of a series of arrangements designed to prevent the formation of coalitions and leagues that might challenge Tokugawa hegemony. As a result, Tokugawa "legislation" sought to establish rules and regulations capable of governing the decisive aspects of daimyo life: lords were forbidden to have more than one castle and were required to receive permission from Edo to do any additional construction or repairs; they were obliged to send their families to Edo as hostages when they remained at home; marriages required prior authorization from the Tokugawa; and Christianity was proscribed and the islands closed off from foreign contact by the middle of the seventeenth century. Domains were rearranged, so that lords who had not originally been allied with the Tokugawa were invariably surrounded by houses of proven loyalty. In time, domainal reorganization led to the elimination of several houses. Finally, a rather elaborate system of surveillance was instituted to guard against sedition. Throughout the eighteenth and nineteenth centuries the Tokugawa issued countless regulations concerning the conduct of Kabuki actors, costumes, and business procedures, as well as proscriptions against certain kinds of illustrative and printed matter, forms of censorship that were unevenly administered against artists and writers like Santō Kyōden[11] (1761–1816), who was manacled for a time after being charged with publishing lewd verbal fictions. This form of moralizing was particularly distinct at times when the regime sought to implement reforms that might arrest excessive consumption and indebtedness among samurai and lords, as well as enforce greater moral economies by appealing to sumptuary edicts reminding people of their duties.

The Tokugawa represented their rule as an imaginary unity that had banished the spectacles of difference, division, and private interest, as well as the specter of social indeterminacy that the civil wars had revealed. Neo-Confucianism attempted to address the concern that the basis for social order had disappeared. As a philosophy, it privileged representation and presented the world as a systematic totality in which the parts cohered because of something called principle (ri). Its purpose was to represent society as a world free from conflict. Once neo-Confucianism was employed ideologically, it functioned to dissimulate the effects of the temporal division that had scarred the political terrain of the sixteenth century; it assimilated the question of social determinacy to a normative conception of nature and proposed that society merely reflected the harmony and order found throughout the cosmos. In this way, society was now made to appear as a natural unity, in which the various parts were organized hierarchically, as in nature, to constitute a seamless whole. This scheme also sought to make all things appear as resemblances of each other, despite their place in the natural hierarchy, because all things were informed by principle. The differences that naturally existed signified only that some people were morally superior to others and were thus empowered to rule, just as some species were higher in nature than others, some stars nearer, and so forth. Neo-Confucians were fond of saying that even the smallest forms of life, such as blades of grass, revealed the nature of all things in the universe because they were informed by principle. But regardless of where a person stood in the social hierarchy, each had to perform morally; their conduct had to exemplify ethics, which meant that they had to recognize their role in the pecking order and prosecute their duties accordingly. In theory, the rulership represented an exemplum of perfect moral conduct that the ruled were enjoined to emulate. In practice this meant that if one was born a peasant, he or she had to remain one throughout life and not aspire to any other status.

The neo-Confucian conception of society established a division of labor based on the primacy of the head over the hand, mental over manual labor. At the top of this social ranking system were the warriors, who early were made to appear as sage-teachers, instructing (i.e., leading) the people. Next came the peasantry, who provided the realm's source of production and its livelihood. (Since this vision of society presumed the existence of a natural economy, agricultural production and the peasant producer were assigned an important role in the representational scheme. Early in the regime, fear of both the loss of agricultural productivity and the peasant producer were assigned an important role in the representational scheme. Early in the regime, fear of both the loss of agricultural productivity and massive social disorder persuaded the Tokugawa authorities to literally reinvent the village community of small cultivators tied to the land by moral proscriptions against leaving the countryside.) After peasants came artisans and priests. At the bottom of the social ladder were the merchants, who, in this catalog, were seen as unproductive (and unnecessary to a natural economy) and the source of desire.

What neo-Confucianism promised to eliminate in Tokugawa Japan was the spectacle of private interest—the destructive powers of passion and desire that inevitably produced differences and conflict. In its own rather starchy ethic, it sought to turn Japanese society away from the political divisiveness that had plagued the sixteenth century and to remove its cultural analogue, exemplified by the word/concept *kabuki*, which in the late fifteenth and early sixteenth codes meant to "lean" or "tilt" and called attention to outlandish and playful behavior, often unusual debauchery and perversity. As a historical trope, *kabuki* invariably referred to the behavior of regional lords who not only acted out of self interest, consciously opposing precedent, but also ornamented their political rule with the trappings of a rococo culture often indistinguishable from their political conduct.[12] What this experience seemed to produce was a fear that culture itself would determine the content of politics. The will to cultural monumentality and the apotheosizing of a heroism larger than life were often identified with political claims appealing to heaven and linking the domainal realm to the universe.

It should not be supposed that this particular vision was followed uniformly throughout Japanese society. By the end of the seventeenth and the beginning of the early eighteenth century, there were already signs in cities like Osaka and Edo that life was being lived differently from the way prescribed by neo-Confucian moral texts. Peace and prosperity, especially for merchants who supplied goods and commodities, who controlled distribution and exchange, changed the tempo of life. Instead of the harsh, spare, and even dour forecast of life envisioned by the neo-Confucians, people were talking about passion and feeling as essential to human nature; instead of hard work, people in the cities were attracted to the good life and the burgeoning pleasure quarters, entertainment and the consumption of commodities.

In the eighteenth country, Edo became the hub of a world not yet imagined and imaged, even though it was being lived, a place where new social groups were appearing to meet the diversification of goods and services demanded by a growing urban population and where an enormous amount of boundary crossings were taking place among merchants, artisans, samurai, and even peasants quartered in the city's environs. Despite serving as the political nerve center of the Tokugawa control system, Edo's very political function provided the occasion for a massive transformation of the city into a cultural space that constantly recoded vertical relationships into horizontal groupings. This transformation was undoubtedly fueled by the demographic expansion of the city (which reached a plateau by the end of the century), caused by the system of alternate hostages (*sankin kōtai*), which brought daimyo families and their retinues to Edo on a regular basis, their needs as residents having to be met by an army of service workers, suppliers, producers, and so forth. Yet this cultural space offered the possibility for fostering both play as a leisure-time activity (or indeed as a serious vocation) and the sanctions for transgressing fixed boundaries and blurring roles. It was precisely this fluidity of social boundaries, the absence of fixity, that prompted writers like Buyō and Shiba to denounce a culture devoted to expenditure, extravagance, luxury, and surplus consumption. Nothing was more threatening to fixed class positions than the endless erosions inflicted by samurai and peasants who sought to imitate the cultural styles of townsmen, or townsmen who used their wealth to flout both social and political convention. Samurai, as popular verbal fictions testified, frequently fared badly in the new cash and commodity culture, inspiring earlier thinkers like Ogyū Sorai[13] (1666–1728) to observe that living in the cities was like residing in an inn where one needed money for all transactions. In order to deal with the unending prospect of reduced stipends or cyclic expropriations by debt-ridden daimyo—along with the fluctuations in the exchange rate for rice and the rising standards of living and inflationary pressures—samurai were often forced to sell armor, swords, and other valuables at the usurious rates of pawnbrokers and rent space in dormitories when they were off duty in Edo.[14] At the end of the eighteenth century, scores of critics were commenting that most samurai had lost their military skills and knowledge of weapons through infrequent practice but had acquired vast expertise in securing credit and loans.[15] Increased use of cash and new patterns of consumption made it increasingly difficult to distinguish between the various classes and status groupings.

What this emerging cultural space posed for the Tokugawa was a failure to control discourse and maintain the power of their own social imaginary over the experience of a lived existence that increasingly demanded accountability in representation. Even the most conservative critics of contemporary custom called attention to this apparent gap between lived existence and the expectations of a social imaginary produced in an earlier time to legitimate Tokugawa political rule, even as they, like Buyō, sought to return to a past arcadia. Yet it was too late for a simple return—too much like searching for noon at two o'clock, as the French saying goes. This disjunction challenged received determinations concerning what could be said and understood, as well as what it was possible to be; it struck at the heart of an arrangement that had insisted that the ruled would act according to the positions they involuntarily occupied in order to repetitively reproduce a specific social formation. In the eighteenth century, the opposition of ruler and ruled was beginning to exhaust its productivity and lose its capacity to sustain a vision of the political that could continue to constrain the complexity and plurality of the social urban environment. The new cultural space—the place of play, luxury, and expenditure—began to present itself as a vast spectacle of social surplus juxtaposed to the "rational" and organized structures of the Tokugawa order as imagined by neo-Confucianism. Social surplus spilled over status lines and destabilized fixed meanings by fostering play and plural identities. Where this cultural space collided with the Tokugawa government was not so much in the attempt of the former to curb the latter, a new "popular" culture. Rather, what provoked action were signs that people were not behaving as they were supposed to and that the productivity of the natural economic order was being challenged and undermined by new sources of wealth and an economy devoted to consumption, play, and undisciplined expenditure—leisure, laziness, and loss. The new cultural practice, recalling a time before the Tokugawa, was prior to and determinant of political form. If the fifteenth and sixteenth centuries revealed a rococo culture marked by "tilting," outlandish behavior, the late eighteenth century became known for a culture steeped in difference and eccentricity, heroized by figures like Hiraga Gennai, author of the eccentric text *On Farting* (*Hōhiron*) (1729–1779), disposed to the strange, the curious, the eccentric, (*ki*), the different, uncommon, and foreign and the fearful picture of a politics not yet envisioned. In response to signs of a culture of difference, Tokugawa authorities appealed to reforms calling for a reinstatement of a traditional moral order twice during the course of the eighteenth century and once in the 1840s. The eighteenth-century reforms of Matsudaira Sadanobu (1758–1829) not only sought to reinforce strict moral economies but also aimed to check what increasingly was being called "heterodox studies." Yet shogunal reforms, usually calling for belt tightening and trying to induce people to return to a more simple way of life, were less concerned with getting to the root of the problem, the new cultural space, than reaffirming the older representational scheme based upon the paradigm of nature.

Imagining the Daily Life

At the heart of this vast cultural transformation, prompting official response to some of its effects only, was the installation of a new conception of the daily life centered in the cities, a "living existence" as Marx put it elsewhere, that privileged not the head or mental labor but the hand or manual labor—that is, the body in its multiple activities. But the emphasis on manual labor did not lead immediately into a celebration of play but rather marked the place where serious play became possible. Play derived from the accumulation of wealth among townsmen and the need to express the force of a libidinal economy by those who could afford the means to fuel expenditure in a society constrained by a restricted economy. This shift implied a new conception of society and stemmed from the production of practical knowledge rooted in the daily life of the cities, a knowledge best understood by those who lived it. Possessing such knowledge empowered its holders to make decisions affecting the quality of their lives, to speak on such matters, and to master a history that they themselves made through their own activity. Ultimately, and only later, the new cultural space constituted a terrain on which it was possible to realign the political economy and the libidinal economy, work and consumption. Yet the appearance of a culture devoted to the daily life, work, and consumption showed also that ordinary folk, the ruled, possessed a specialized knowledge that had remained marginal to the official discourse and outside the great themes of moral life necessitated by the division between mental and manual labor. Nowhere was this more apparent than in cities like Edo and Osaka, which offered the occasions for ceaseless mobility, boundary crossings, the flow of travelers in and out of the environs, freedom from fixed positions—what the social thinker and political economist Kaiho Seiryō (1755–1817) described as the "gaze that disconnects and separates,"[16] the incessant exchange of goods and services.

Nowhere was this better signified than in the production of new forms of representation in verbal fiction and woodblock illustration that made this daily life its constant subject. Inasmuch as writing and illustrating were used to supplement each other, verbal fictions and woodblock illustrations shared a common ground. In some instances the writer illustrated his own fictions. Santō Kyōden was a prolific producer of fictions and often illustrated his own texts. Sometimes he would advertise his tobacco shop in his books. Yet text and illustration shared a common function, which was to provide a glimpse of a daily life that lay beneath the surface of things, objects and custom. The production of these forms was situated in a context that already favored different perspectives, which invariably apprehended the world as divided between surface appearances and what lay behind them. After the Kansei Reforms of 1790, *bakufu* (shogunate) officials also presumed the existence of a double perspective and invariably sought to prevent writers and illustrators from penetrating the surface to disclose glimpses of the true nature of contemporary customs. Writers and illustrators were often driven to develop doubling strategies that might allow them to appear to be tallying around the contours of the surface, looking closely at what was immediately before them, when they were really offering the representation of another dimension. More often than not illustrators like Utamaro (1754–1806) simply risked violating shogunal proscriptions on the chance that the authorities would not call attention to their productions which, in the case of his portrayal of the warlord Toyotomi Hideyoshi (1537–1598) (*Mashiba Hisayoshi*, which was a disguised portrayal of Hideyoshi), plainly went against censorship laws and earned for him punishment by manacling. Writers like Santō Kyōden, fully aware of the proscriptions against certain genres (e.g., *sharebon*), constantly wrote books extolling official moral pieties while continuing to produce texts like *Nishiki no ura*, which clearly lampooned Confucian values that promised that the "good are rewarded and the bad punished." Yet it was the repositioning of the body, as an instrument of consumption, play, sexuality, anatomical study, travel, pilgrimages, work, and even prayer that dominated the new culture of the cities and showed, time and again, how often it could be used for diverse reasons and still not exhaust its productivity in representation. More important, the body could be used for launching, quite inadvertently, counterideologies, since by centering it and its virtually inexhaustible power for representation that a "political unconscious" managed to disrupt the smooth functioning of the dominant ideology. The operation of this political unconscious and its capacity for disruption was already apparent in Tokugawa efforts to reinforce the moral economy in reform edicts, in the regular announcement of sumptuary legislation, and in the rather uneven efforts to impose censorship on writers of verbal fictions and woodblock illustrators of erotica.

So much of this literature and art concentrated on placing the body in an urban landscape, depicting scenes of consumption and entertainment, the circumstances of a lived material life, such as daily life as experienced in the bathhouses and barbershops, and travel along the main roads between Edo and Osaka for pleasure, pilgrimage, or even adventure. But all these scenes were held together by the fact that they centered on the body as the inexhaustible consumer of the city's diverse offerings and commodities, captured by the imagination of writers and illustrators who, more often than not, saw themselves as artisans working for a living.

Despite Tokugawa proscriptions aimed at discouraging unproductive activities, people flocked to the cities, which became the primary scene of this new cultural terrain. Ōta Nampō (1749–1823), a poet and litterateur, wrote in 1820 the following "mad poem" (kyōka), whereby he characterized Japan's three principal cities largely in terms of things and commodities: "Kyoto is water, greens, women, dyed goods, special needle shops, temples, tofu, eels, mushrooms; Osaka is ships and bridges, castles, walking straw sandals, sake, turnips, guilds, brothels, stone; Edo is salmon, bonito, daimyo mansions, sardines, priestesses, the color purple, winter onions, large white radishes."[17] Writers never tired of comparing the three cities as sites of consumption and pleasure, yet Ōta's classification fixed obvious associations: Kyoto was the center of the traditional arts and skills, beautiful and aristocratic women, religion; Osaka, a long-standing commercial center described commonly as the "merchant of the realm," signified canals and rivers, a network of navigation and the transporting of goods in small boats, and the guilds that managed distribution and exchange; and Edo summoned the image of political power, symbolized by permanent mansions housing families and retainers of domainal lords who left them as hostages. Yet the poem imbricated these characteristics with consumption, good things to eat, entertainment, and pleasure.

A character in Kyakushoku yōroku, by the Kabuki playwright Nishizawa Ippū (1665–1735), describes Edo as a city whose "feeling" (kimochi) is less than half of Kyoto's because there is no control over the production of shoddy goods, which people "see only with the white of their eyes."[18] Nishizawa explained that Edoites are so eager to consume that they never take time to inspect the quality of goods. Despite the inevitable elevation of Kyoto by writers like Nishizawa as the place of "elegant manners," the writer of historical romances Takizawa Bakin (1767–1845) was probably closer to the truth when he proposed that "in Edo, people learned how to live."[19] Kaiho Seiryō, comparing Osaka and Edo, observed that money was used differently in the two cities: in Osaka it is rarely spent but recycled back into the making and selling of goods, which increases profit; but "in Edo, people are like children, fools, beginners, undisciplined in the spending of money."[20] "Edo is the land of splendor," rhapsodized the humorist Shikitei Samba (1776–1822), "and without it there would be no place to sell things."[21] Samba worried that the city's most cherished product, the Edokko, "Edo kid," born and bred in the city, would not have been able to exist without the city. Recognizing that the entire realm depended upon the city, Samba called Edo "Mr. Prosperity" and advised that all must set their eyes on the city.

Accordingly, Edo was seen as the "standard of the realm" by most writers, not simply because it represented the center of political power but because of its wealth. Kaiho Seiryō noted that the city constituted a magnet, drawing in vast numbers of people from the countryside. "The city," he wrote, "rears people in an exclusive outlook which looks down upon those who live elsewhere as provincials."[22] Moreover, he continued, the Edo townsmen have been coerced by the samurai who also live in the city. Recognition of this fact has driven merchants and artisans to find refuge in an exclusive culture of their own. Writers everywhere acknowledged that townsmen had assumed responsibility for samurai consumption in the city, for providing all the goods and services that made it possible for lords, their families, and retainers to exist in Edo. Few failed to note the irony of a politically and socially privileged class depending upon social inferiors for their daily livelihood. Townsmen also reveled in the irony and developed a critical consciousness that irreverently exploded in billingsgates and catcalls that regularly ridiculed samurai by calling attention to their miserable financial status and the necessity of leading penurious lives or their efforts to impose social control on the daily life. Kaiho, as a student of the new political economy, had declared that " buying and selling things was the principle of the world" and nothing to laugh at, and dramatized the importance of commercial wealth, which authorities consistently failed to grasp, and consumption, even though he did not always admire the Edokko, who typified the city's lifestyles. In fact, he denounced Edo custom as wasteful, profligate, and excessively luxurious, yet his observations disclosed a recognition of the vast power played by the accumulation of commercial wealth. What Kaiho perceived was the power to spend and to waste, the power of luxury to determine expenditure and a kind of loss that constantly defied the logic of a natural economy. Indeed, the culture of luxury noted by social critics began to reveal, in vague outline, not simply the formation of political economy but more importantly the challenge of a general economy of expenditure against the restricted economy of mere production. What appeared in eighteenth-century Edo was surplus, money to waste, glorious expenditure that increasingly displaced political authority altogether to the accumulation of wealth and extravagance. It also allowed those who worked and produced to displace their lowly status onto their daily life. Yet this incidence of wealth and expenditure should not be seen as merely the sign of an emerging bourgeoisie, who would, according to the law of political economy, reinvest wealth on the expectation of a return. This kind of productive use of wealth would have been consistent with Tokugawa political pieties. Rather, what the new cultural practices were showing was the underproductive expenditure of excess based upon the body's endless needs, the apparent imposition of a dangerous libidinal economy, not utilitarian consumption, and this recognition revealed the shape of a social order far more troubling to the Tokugawa than merely the appearance of a commercial economy.

As mentioned, the principal sign of this displacement was the Edokko, a playboy whose style concentrated on play and consumption. The Edo kid, usually a commoner, both of whose parents had been born in the city, constituted about 10 percent of the population. Where the Edo kid differed from other varieties of playboys and dandies, such as the *tsū*, who was known for his possession of an elusive style called *iki*, was not so much in the enactment of a certain style of living but in his cockiness, his willingness to make life into play and consumption and identify those practices with the daily existence. Money passed through his hands like water. A contemporary *senryū* (short poem) advised that "to have failed to be born an Edo kid, one is forced to only accumulate money."[23] The Edo kid was often portrayed as one who looks down upon those who merely accumulate by selling, say, fish; the Edo kid never expects to keep his money overnight but rather to spend it the day he receives it. The writer Santō Kyōden stated in his fiction *Tsūgen sōmagaki*[24] (1787) that poetic ditties regularly praised the lifestyle of the Edo kid. The consumption of the Edokko, his talent for play and expenditure, became the subject of countless narratives and defined the contours of this new cultural space devoted to play and excess. This was not, as supposed, a fugitive space or even a sublimation. It represented an assertiveness, fluidity, self-possession, and aggressive confidence unexpected from members of a socially inferior class.

The wealth that fueled consumption and play derived principally from large brokerages that exchanged rice stipends for cash. By 1800 there were ninety-six such houses (*okuramae fudasashi*). "Today," complained Buyō Inshi, "there are ninety-six brokerages. Indeed, the personal fortunes of innumerable upper-ranking samurai and their house servants have fallen into the hands of these ninety-six men. . . . They loan money out according to the status of the borrowers and recover interest amounting to half the stipend. . . . They display rudeness, commit violations against the military houses freely, and collect excessively large profits. These ninety-six houses spend their lives in luxury and hoarded wealth."[25] Wealth permitted brokers and credit lenders to live in a style steeped in the signs of money and lavish expenditure. Among the acknowledged eighteen great players more than ten were from the ranks of brokerage houses.

The lifestyle of the wealthy, and even the not so wealthy, was based upon the conviction that money was to be used for extravagance. The possession of money bought the right of surplus expenditure and conferred upon its holder a different kind of social identity. Even after the Kansei Reforms of 1790, which sought to curb the expenditure of excess, play, and luxury would still continue to attract writers and illustrators as the subject of their narratives and illustrations. Among brokers who were also players the best known was Ōguchiya Jiheigyo (a late eighteenth-century figure), who, it has been said, served as a model for the Kabuki hero Sukeroku. Tales of Ōguchiya's talent for expenditure report that when he cruised the Yoshiwara district (a well-known Edo pleasure quarter) he wore an edged, crested kimono of black silk, carried a sword in a sharkskin sheath and a pill box, and walked on clogs made from the wood of the paulownia tree in foot gloves made of gold-threaded material. His presence constituted a spectacle by itself, inevitably commanding the attention of all. Once he entered through the great gate marking off the district from the rest of the city, women who worked in the teahouses gathered on both sides of the street and cheered, "There goes Mr. Deity of Good Fortune."[26] The contemporary account that recorded this spectacle, the *Okuramae bakamonogatari* (Foolish tales of brokers), condemned Ōguchiya for having "spread foolishness everywhere he went."[27] Ōguchiya's apparent passion for cleanliness drove him to even greater heights of excessive expenditure. It was reported that after visiting the toilet he would pour generous amounts of salt on a large plate and wash his hands in it. His daily use of salt amounted to a yearly total equivalent to thirty-five pounds of rice!

The *tsū* was a specialist in the knowledge of pleasure who knew how to navigate the pleasure quarter. What some contemporary critics condemned as foolishness, others saw as meaningful. Like the dandy described by Baudelaire nearly a century later in France, the player signified an area of activity, independence, and autonomy. But the player had to have money in order to demonstrate that spending it wastefully showed it had no instrumental meaning: one needed money to demonstrate that having it meant nothing. Santō Kyōden proposed in the *Yoshiwara yōji* that "success or failure in the pleasure quarter depends upon how much one spends money. Unless one spends a great deal of money, he will not be able to enter the realm of paradise."[28]

The Culture of Play

In late Tokugawa life, play had complex associations. Before the Tokugawa period, it was usually associated, according to the historian Amino Yoshihiko, with the place of unconnectedness (*muen*). Such places were usually temple courtyards, where women could find refuge from husbands and households and children could play without being disturbed. The playing of the *tsū* in pleasure quarters resembled this scene of child's play unconnected to the world of power; it signaled a form of "breaking connections" (*engiri*) with the world of politics.[29]

Yet play entailed acquiring a detailed knowledge of its rules, a thorough grasping of the varieties of playful activities and a complete understanding of the spatial terrain of the pleasure quarters. In this sense, play was not really separate from life and often attempted to displace the political economy with the bodily requirements of a libidinal economy. Physically, the area of play was a defined enclosure, separated from the rest of the city, the places of power and work; it had its own rules of conduct, codes of dress and discourse. If the game was to be played expertly, it demanded serious and intense absorption. Nothing profitable could be derived from it. To play well, one had to have style, which usually required knowing how to present oneself, in clothing, manner and demeanor, speech; in erotic games one must never fall in love, since this would mean that playing was still connected to the world.

Based on the display of emotionality when it was disallowed, a classification system was constructed to distinguish real players from mere semiplayers (*han-katsu*) and rustics (*yabo*). Santō Kyōden often poked fun at those men who hopelessly fell in love, comparing their fate to that of a worm. The player knew custom and was familiar with all aspects of play; what distinguished him from either the semiplayer, who could never achieve the higher status, or the rube, who could, was that he was a watcher of other people's play, a bystander and even a voyeur, an ethnographer of playful customs in places like the Yoshiwara or Fukagawa districts. In fact, much of the verbal fiction produced in the late eighteenth century show how the player spent as much of his time observing and recording the activities of those who tried unsuccessfully, as did Enjirō in Kyōden's *Edo umare uwaki no kabayaki*, to represent themselves as genuine players. In this regard, the ethnographic reporting of custom in Edo verbal fictions and woodblock illustrations, invariably aiming to disclose daily life in the cities, resembled comparable efforts by nativists like Hirata Atsutane (1776–1843) and his rural followers to record beliefs, daily practices, and forms of work and prayer in the countryside. But whereas writers and illustrators of city life were concerned with showing those material customs related to excess and expenditure, Hirata and other nativists sought to dramatize the necessity of disciplining the body for work and religious devotion, in fact eliding them, in order to move society back to a new kind of restricted economy.

The rube, by contrast, was unprepared to make his way in the pleasure quarter. He lacked both money and knowledge. Samurai, in this regard, were often portrayed as rustics but rarely as great players, whose mark of character was their ability to make the crucial differentiation between a dandy and a rube. For writers like Kyōden, being a genuine *tsūjin* was like being a sage. The real player understood the limits of "proper" behavior and knew when to stop, unlike the poor wretches who were destined to remain semiplayers the rest of their lives. Kyōden's Enjirō dramatizes the pitfalls of being a semiplayer who lacks character. He showed an early talent for breaking all the rules of the pleasure quarter, he attempted to commit suicide for love, he tattooed his body and spent entirely too much time trying to be recognized as a player.[30] Another example of a rube is a character from Kyōden's *Shigeshige chiwa* (1799), a braggart who walks with his chest thrust outward so that "people will take notice of his splendid outfit," his hair is dressed in a topknot whose stem is a "bit longer than usual," he drinks "according to the style of tea ceremony" when it is not called for, and, when he sits and smokes, he blows "smoke from his nose and mouth like an incense burner in the shape of a lion's head."[31]

Hence, the role of the dandy was ethnographic but judgmental, to unmask fraud, what lay below surface impressions, and to call attention to the humor disclosed by misconduct. Just as "playful writing" (*gesaku*) exempted the author from serious connection with his product and even occasioned disengagement, so the player/dandy was distanced as a knowing bystander who ridiculed the very object he reported since it too was not serious. Underlying play, of course, was custom, habit, the common world of things, and the recognized importance of trying to link people's political and libidinal economics together: conduct, food, homes, pleasure, speech, daily routine, drinking and eating, sexuality, bathhouses and barbershops. But by concentrating on custom, as such, play also called attention to the centrality of the body and the daily world it inhabited through its ceaseless activities. In representing this world of custom, writers and illustrators merged textuality and illustrating, as if each constituted simply a different way of telling a story. The function of illustrations, which often concentrated on depicting a crucial scene in the narrative or a play, both facilitated and contributed to the reaching of an ever-expanding readership. In some cases, illustrations were used to tell their own stories, as in triptychs or narrative series; in other cases they were used to advertise products, teahouses, plays, and so forth. Throughout the productions of illustrators like Sharaku (active late eighteenth century) and Utamaro, the world of the townsman and the pleasure quarters are portrayed in graphic detail, as if to suggest a metonymical relationship between what they chose to represent and the larger world. Hence, Sharaku portrayed actors in their roles and men in their offices, while Utamaro and Utagawa Kunisada (1786–1864) drew upon the pleasure quarters and its denizens, especially its women, and presented them not as idealized beauties (as had earlier woodblock artists) but as human beings possessing individualistic characteristics, just as writers sought to present detailed descriptions of dress, speech, and character. Many of these illustrators also depicted parts of the body, the head, the nape of the neck, breasts, partial torsos, often entangled in seemingly impossible positions. Some showed sexual activity involving a threesome (a male, a younger male, and a woman, a favorite combination in Tokugawa Japan), as in Okumura Masanobu's (1686–1764) *shunga*, or a seminaked woman fondling her lover's penis. But what this detail disclosed was the easy transaction between writing and illustrating, since both modes shared the same subject matter, demonstrating not simply the close collaboration between writer and illustrator and their interchangeability but also the centrality of custom and daily life. In many of the verbal fictions produced by writers like Samba or Jippensha Ikku (1765–1831), author of the *Tōkaidōchū hizakurige*, a serialized travelogue of two picaresque characters, we have examples of the pursuit of custom expanding from the pleasure quarters of the world of the streets, the barbershops, bathhouses, inns along the Tōkaidō (the main road connecting Edo and Osaka) and so forth. What these fictions reveal is a self-referential world, inasmuch as their narratives are constituted less of plot and more of people speaking in a colloquial tongue. Many of the more comic verbal compositions drew heavily upon the street language, forms of traditional storytelling—usually ending with a joke or wordplay—Chinese archetypes, and even historical episodes scaled down to satisfy a popular readership, such as a triptych portraying a scene from Ryūtei Tanehiko's (1783–1842) *Nise Murasaki inaka Genji*, a fiction that resituated *The Tale of Genji* in a later feudal period. In 1842, Tanehiko was condemned for having written such a book because it was seen by domainal authorities during the Tempō Reforms as unbecoming a samurai. Yet allegations circulated that the fiction was a thinly disguised account of the shogunal court of Tokugawa Ienari (1773–1841), known for his profligate lifestyle.[32]

What writers and illustrators produced (on demand) and reproduced was the world of things, familiar objects from daily life, repositioning them in such a way as to make them appear strange. The raw material of verbal fictions and woodblock illustrations was found in the process of habituation encouraged by the routines of daily life; artistic creation consisted in the making unfamiliar of the overly familiar, the usual, so as to inculcate a new, fresh, even childlike vision in the reader and viewer. The purpose of so much of the writer's and illustrator's art was to restructure the ordinary world of things, customs, and received perception so that readers could actually see and grasp the world rather than merely recognizing it numbly. This was the meaning of the phrase *ana no ugachi*, which was used to articulate the purpose of many verbal fictions. The idea referred not simply to point of view, as such, but rather to the capacity of the writer to "penetrate the hole," to understand what lay below the surface of things and custom that the masses could only recognize but not actually grasp. The real thrust of this concept was both to show the centrality of what people had taken for granted and to make them aware that the very world they inhabited offered new possibilities of meaning they had not even imagined. In this way, *ana no ugachi* performed as a hermeneutic technique, focusing on the immediate surface of everyday life to access what lay below that animated its rhythms and produced meanings. What it appeared to suggest is the silhouette of a new figure of the social that resembled a palimpsest constituted of a depth of layers below the surface. Contemporaries increasingly saw the "hole" (*ana*) as either habit (*kuse*) or custom or deportment (*fū*) and often went to great lengths to classify the range and variety of things that such terms included.[33] Tamenaga Shunsui (1790–1843), the writer of *Shunshoku umegoyomi*, a widely read "book of feeling, often resorted to this particular concept to dramatize affect that was not always explicitly visible on the surface of things."[34] Ultimately, the operation involved penetration (which carried with it the sexual association) of those customs that constituted society. The hole that writers penetrated might reveal the shape of a whole, a different conception of society that invariably ran counter to the expectations of Tokugawa authorities. Yet it was a world that already announced the principles of a new general economy, against the constraints of a restricted economy of production and steeped in the gargantuan joys of the flesh and the expenditure of excess.

"Bodymatters"

Bodily imagery in verbal and woodblock representations signified a different kind of social reality with an inverted scale of priorities for the Edo townsman.[35] It was an order that had as its head the genitalia or anus and its heart the stomach.[36] Often, verbal fictions described the body, with its mouth and arms, as a devouring totality; in both writing and woodblock prints humans appeared as bodies who related to the world through their orifices rather than through the exercise of public duties demanded by fixed social status and disciplined intention. Moreover, the body's needs were never satisfied and never completed; people continued to eat, drink, speak endlessly about the world they inhabited, make love, and evacuate ceaselessly without any prospect of an end. In this regard, the needs of the body were consistent with the demands of a libidinal economy that drove wealthy townsmen to excessive expenditure—as if potlatching their lives was the only guarantee against a return. To portray the infinite details involved in partying, with its random arrangement of empty cups, vomit, and half-filled bottles the morning after, or to pay close attention to foods, eating, and the accompanying conversations, or to supply information and knowledge of the pleasure quarters and the inns along the post roads— all recognizable as appropriate subjects (not simply objects) for presentation rather than representation—dramatized a world of activity and things that no longer referred to anything outside it. People were now made to see mundane activities they took for granted in a new and quite strange light. Tokugawa verbal fiction and woodblock illustrations enforced a new awareness of a world that people had habitually placed in the background by repositioning it in the foreground of represented experience. In this way, these art forms enhanced and signified a lived existence by expanding an awareness of it by those who lived it. But, more importantly, the culture that sanctioned such practices offered radically different alternatives to the world of public and official ideology. To the demands of the Heavenly Way (*tendō*), often satirized by writers, it provided a space for play, laughter, and passion and learning in anatomical representation, a veritable people's utopia, an arcadia of flesh, joy, and excess experienced by the body, a ceaseless delight that came from endless consumption and the discharge of waste.[37] In this way, late Tokugawa fiction and prints appropriated the common and customary to work on the dominant ideology. The idea was to make it strange and unfamiliar and to recast the somber requirements of official expectation within the floating world of play. By using immediate experience as its subject and making people aware of their daily lives and surroundings, writers and printmakers were able to transform the quotidian experience into a system of knowledge that even the most common could possess and master. The result of these cultural practices was to make the body into a text and reading and seeing into acts of consuming knowledge. And yet this emphasis on the body in writing and illustrating also attested to a conception of humanity whose very difference with the abstract image of Tokugawa officialdom posed a threat of incalculable proportions to the public order.

While Tokugawa authorities sought to curb excess by legislating against it and censoring perpetrators among the artisans who wrote and made prints, the real dangers of this new culture space were defined both by a number of critics who denounced excess and expenditure as a threat to maintaining a stable public order based on production and a number of discourses that saw in the pursuit of private pleasures a fragmentation of interests that blinded people to the necessity of collective purpose. What ensued throughout the last decades of the Tokugawa period was the pursuit by a number of discourses dedicated to finding the tangible and sensuous offered by the daily life as opposed to the abstract and discredited presumptions of a moral order based upon a differentiation between mental and manual labor. An important effect of these new discourses was the effort to discipline the body, to turn it away from private pleasure toward some instrumental purpose that would both satisfy new social relationships in production and instill the proper mental attitude so as to induce people to have their activities correspond to certain mutual intentions. But what these moves hoped to achieve, above all else, was to offset the baneful influence of received arrangements that insisted on separating mental from manual with the more recent customs in which the body performed and played to excess. These new cultural practices sought to reimagine the body as an instrument of work, prayer, mutual assistance, and, ultimately, political devotion that was envisaged only after the Meiji Restoration of 1868. Only after the Meiji Restoration and the modernist transformation of Japanese society did the state finally disciplinize the body for work and political loyalty by applying to the general population a bodily regime that was realized first in the construction of a modern military establishment.[38]

Notes

1. Buyō Inshi (dates unknown) is the pseudonym of an Edo samurai, probably a master-less retainer (*rōnin*), who wrote a long account of contemporary conditions in the late eighteenth and early nineteenth centuries. The work is a veritable compendium of customs that prevailed in Edo and represents a stinging condemnation of the changes that had altered life there. In many ways, Buyō's critique gives definition to the carni-valistic image of spectacle that best describes life in the great city and discloses how distant it was from the ideals of an earlier age, when martial values and discipline prevailed.

2. Aizawa Seishisai was a principal theorist of what came to be known as Mitogaku (Mito learning), named after the Mito domain. His major essay, the *Shinron*, was written in response to the appearance of foreign ships in Japanese waters and the threat they posed to Tokugawa seclusion policies. The work is a synthesis of neo-Confucian and native elements seeking to uphold the basic cultural values of the Japanese that the Tokugawa were pledged to preserve. While it reaffirmed the received order in its legitimacy, it also opened the way for a reconsideration of the role of the emperor. The work was read and discussed widely by younger samurai in the late Tokugawa period, who were bent on ridding Japan of the foreign threat and reforming the social order.

3. For Buyō's writings, I have used Buyō Inshi, *Seji kemmonroku*, in *Nihon shomin sei-katsu shiryō shūsei* (Tokyo: Misuzu shobō, 1969), vol. 8. I have also consulted Aoki Michio, *Tempō sōdōki* (Tokyo: Sanseidō, 1979), 1–9, and Sugiura Mimpei, *Ishin zenya no bungaku* (Tokyo: Iwanami shoten, 1967), 23–46.

4. Buyō, *Seji kemmonroku*, 643.

5. Buyō, *Seji kemmonroku*, 653.

6. Buyō, *Seji kemmonroku*, 656.

7. Shiba Kōkan, an independent scholar of what was known as Dutch Learning, which invariably involved astronomy, geography, and anatomy, was also an important painter who began to experiment with Western theories of perspective. This quote, which is from his *Shumparō hikki*, an account of a trip he took to the south and west, is taken from Naramoto Tatsuya, "Chōnin jitsuryoku," in *Kokumin no rekishi* (Tokyo: Chūko bunko, 2005), 17:38.

8. Naramoto, "Chōnin jitsuryoku," 40.

9. Naramoto, "Chōnin jitsuryoku," 40; see also Buyō, *Seji kemmonroku*, 653.

10. Neo-Confucianism had been developed in China in the Song period (twelfth and thirteenth centuries) in response to Buddhism and its powerful theory of the cosmos. In the process, Confucian elements were supplemented with Buddhist metaphysics. As a philosophy, it was brought to Japan by Zen monks in the fourteenth and fifteenth centuries and was used increasingly to explain the kind of social order that might avoid civil war and chaos.

11. Santō Kyōden, a prolific writer of verbal fictions for popular consumption, was also an illustrator. Kyōden was subjected to official censorship for having written a text on a proscribed subject.

12. The idea of *kabuki* as a historical trope is taken from Hayashiya Tatsusaburō, ed. *Bakumatsu bunka no kenkyū* (Tokyo: Iwanami shoten, 1978), 3–39.

13. Ogyū Sorai, one of the most original Tokugawa thinkers, rejected neo-Confucianism for a "return" to the most ancient texts of China's sages. Sorai was a perceptive observer of the transformation taking place between city and countryside and feared that if it continued samurai would be impoverished. To this end, he called for a policy that would return samurai to the land as managers.

14. Marius B. Jansen, "Japan in the Early Nineteenth Century," in *The Cambridge History of Japan, Volume 5: The Nineteenth Century*, ed. Marius B. Jansen (Cambridge: Cambridge University Press, 2008), 63.

15. Jansen, "Japan," 63–64.

16. Hiraishi Naoaki, "Kaiho Seiryō no shisōzō," *Shisō* 677 (November 1989): 52–53.

17. Kitajima Masamoto, *Bakuhansei no kumon*, vol. 18 of *Nihon no rekishi* (Tokyo: Chūō kōronsha, 1967), 261.

18. Kitajima, *Bakuhansei no kumon*, 262.

19. Naramoto, "Chōnin jitsuryoku," 50.

20. Kitajima, *Bakuhansei no kumon*, 262.

21. *Nihon koten bungaku zenshū* (Tokyo: Shōgakkan, 1970), 47:296.

22. Naramoto, "Chōnin jitsuryoku," 52.

23. Naramoto, "Chōnin jitsuryoku," 53.

24. Nakamura Yukihiko and Nishiyama Matsunosuke, eds., *Bunka ryōran*, vol. 8 of *Nihon bungaku no rekishi* (Tokyo: Kadokawa shoten, 1967), 19.

25. Buyō Inshi, *Seji kemmonroku*, quoted in Naramoto, "Chōnin jitsuryoku," 53–54.

26. Naramoto, "Chōnin jitsuryoku," 54–55.

27. Naramoto, "Chōnin jitsuryoku," 54–55.

28. Jo Nobuko Martin, "Santō Kyōden and His Sharebon" (PhD diss., University of Chicago, 1979), 107.

29. Amino Yoshihiko, *Muen, kugai, raku* (Tokyo: Heibonsha, 1978).

30. Martin, "Santō Kyōden," 117.

31. Martin, "Santō Kyōden," 120.

32. Donald Keene, *World Within Walls: Japanese Literature of the Pre-modern Era, 1600–1867* (New York: Holt, Rinehart and Winston, 1976), 434.

33. Nakamura and Nishiyama, *Bunka ryōran*, 60.

34. Mizuno Tadashi, *Edo shōsetsu ronsō* (Tokyo: Chūō kōronsha, 1974), 17.

35. The title of this section is taken from an essay by Ann Jefferson, "Bodymatters: Self and Other in Bakhtin, Sartre and Barthes," in *Bakhtin and Cultural Theory*, ed. Ken Hirschkop and David Shepherd (Manchester, UK: Manchester University Press, 2002), 201–28.

36. This sentiment is from Bakhtin, but the wording is from Tony Bennett, *Formalism and Marxism* (New York: Routledge, 1979), 84–85.

37. Bennett, *Formalism and Marxism*, 85.

38. I am indebted to Professor Takashi Fujitani for making this link between the disciplinizing of a modern military establishment in the Meiji period and its reapplication among the general populace.

CHAPTER 4

LATE TOKUGAWA CULTURE AND THOUGHT

Japanese historiography has conventionally located the beginning of the end of the Tokugawa (*bakumatsu*) in the decade of the 1830s, when the regime and the several domains embarked on a series of reforms aimed at arresting economic failure and restoring public confidence. Historians who have concentrated on making sense of the signs of financial failure point to the implementation of the Tempō Reforms as recognition of a gathering crisis. Some have established the revolt of Ōshio Heihachirō in Osaka in 1837 as the turning point in Tokugawa history. But regardless of the many opinions concerning the beginning of the end, most discussions of the end of the shogunate have used economic signs, political events, or a combination of both as criteria for periodization. Yet to establish the beginning of the end in the 1830s obliges us to accept a concomitant assumption that cultural events constitute a second order of activity; one that avoids organizing the world in terms of a base-superstructure dyad but still sees culture and ideas as determined by material forces. Culture is then made to appear as a dependent variable of economic and political processes, and the observer is diverted from recognizing that the production of culture may in fact possess a logic of its own, one that seeks to resolve problems belonging to an entirely different class of events and facts.

If we regard culture as something more than a pale reflection of changes detected earlier in the material realm, we will be persuaded to propose that the special culture of late Tokugawa culture did not begin in the 1830s, or even later, but probably in the late eighteenth century or the early 1800s.[1] Sometime in the

1830s there appeared a historic conjuncture between new forms of self-understanding, which constitute the content of culture, and the critical political and economic events that began to jar the viability of the *bakufu-han* system. The realization that the order was losing viability may well have been possible only after the formulation of new forms of self-understanding and the establishment of new modalities of relating things to one another.

An essay by Professor Hayashiya Tatsusaburō offers the possibility of using the *bakumatsu* as a metaphor or historical trope.[2] By constructing a model of *bakumatsu*, which draws on the common experiences of the late years of the Kamakura, Muromachi, and Tokugawa shogunates, Hayashiya has identified a number of conditions shared by the three and the cultural means whereby contemporaries sought to represent their own sense of an ending and recognized that they were living through a time of profound change. His metaphor thus tries to bring together political, social, economic, diplomatic, and cultural developments. In all three cases the dissolution of the political order was accompanied by a displacement of the authority of the military estates and wider participation in a broader arena of struggle. This explanation presupposes a theory of "crisis" that ultimately is expressed in the occurrence of a "rebellion." Hayashiya noted vast social changes in the wake of this political event that signify transformations in the structure of values and norms, swiftly followed by the development of equally important economic forces, such as shifts in patterns of landholding, the circulation of currency, and new forms of exchange and foreign and domestic trade. Finally, Hayashiya links to this the emergent cultural styles that characterize and shape the social, political, and economic transformations. These new styles were symbolized by terms like *basara* in the Kamakura period, *kabuki* in late Muromachi times, and *ki* and *i* in the Tokugawa. *Basara* referred to love of the gaudy and ornate and the self-indulgent and unauthorized behavior with which some warrior leaders set the example for their peers; *kabuki* meant "to lean" or "to tilt" and called forth the outlandish and playful, often associated with debauchery and perversity; and in late Tokugawa, *ki* invoked the strange, curious, and eccentric, whereas *i* signaled the different, uncommon, and foreign. Thus in each *bakumatsu* the prevailing attitudes were inscribed in style and conduct previously signified as different and nonnormative, even unthinkable and unimaginable.

It is important to recognize that these new styles were not reflections of more basic material forces. Rather, the real function of this metaphor is to establish a different relationship between material conditions and symbolic or cultural representation. The historical trope allows us to glimpse a unified world, a universe in which discontinuous realities are somehow bonded and intertwined with one another, thereby suggesting a network of relationships among things that first seem remote. The trope manages to establish a momentary reconciliation between the material and spiritual world without assigning priority to one or the other and persuades us to acknowledge disparate elements as equivalents in relationships whereby each determines and is determined by the other. It is as if the interaction resembled a form of dialectical traffic that permits a transaction between the language of social change and cultural form.[3] Such an approach to late Tokugawa culture helps us read the content of the socioeconomic macrocosm, the massive substance of the "real," in terms of form and representation that appear as significations of it. *Bakumatsu* represents a rhetorical figure, a form in time, ordering a specific reality, but precisely at that moment when the most disparate facts order themselves around a model that will later offer "meaning."

In the late Tokugawa period we can note a confluence between the content of real, transforming productive processes and the construction of new cultural forms that promised to make sense of what was occurring in social life. Yet the relationship between the effort to meet the consequences of newer productive forces and social relationships and the attempts to stabilize meaning between politics and culture had less to do with a simple reflection from one "base" to the "superstructure" than with the operation of mediations. The massive transformations in the social process were translated into the cultural sphere, and this placed great strains on the social image of Tokugawa Japan and its conception of cultural praxis.[4] The polity was called on to meet the contradictory demands of stabilizing conditions of private accumulation while responding to requests for social welfare. A search for meaning and self-understanding in a changed environment was expressed in calls for benevolence and greater political participation at a time when urban expansion and cultural participation required new definitions. New forms of cultural production accompanying the expansion of cities collectively signified what we may call, from playful literature (*gesaku*), the "culture of play." By the end of the eighteenth century this had exceeded the limits of its own formal constraints to reveal in vague outline the possibility of constructing a social imagination vastly different from the one authorized by the Tokugawa. The culture of play then turned into a play of culture committed to finding stable and permanent forms that might best accommodate new demands and expectations by reconstituting the whole.

At the core of this cultural development was the search for new and different forms of knowledge and the search for ways to implement them. The explosion of new forms of knowledge in late Tokugawa Japan was increasingly difficult to assimilate to the categories of the existing political system. What occurred in the late eighteenth century was the recognition, first in the cities but soon exported to the countryside, that the opposition of ruler-ruled and external-internal had exhausted its productivity and was incapable of constructing a vision of the political that could accommodate the complexity and plurality of the social urban environment. The physical and demographic expansion of urban sites like Edo, Osaka, Kyoto, and Nagoya, not to mention lesser castle

towns functioning as regional market centers, and the resulting differentiation of social and cultural life were presented as a spectacle of social surplus
juxtaposed to the "rational" and organized structures of the Tokugawa "order"
imagined by Confucian ideologues. According to Hayashiya this perception
was proclaimed in the calls like Yoshida Shōin's for the "different" and the
strange.[5] It was inscribed in countless practices associated with the new culture
of play, and it called into question the suppositions of a political ideology rooted
in the logic of similitude.[6] That logic neatly divided the political and hence the
cultural spheres between the rulers, who possessed mental powers, and the
ruled, who labored manually. The former were supposed to know, and the latter
were enjoined to follow. The social identity of the ruled was fixed in a closed,
hierarchic chain, resembling elements in a stable structure that reflected the
order found in nature. Yet the material expansion of Edo as the hub of a world
not yet imagined made it possible to challenge these fixed identities through
the proliferation of different subject positions. The multiplication of needs and
the differentiation of services contributed to the city's expansion and to the
concomitant blurring of fixed distinctions between ruler and ruled.[7]

At the heart of the culture of play was a system of signification that recognized that the fixed boundaries and social identities established to guide people had become increasingly uncertain as society grew larger and more complex. The new systems of meaning agreed that social space and differentiation
of positions invalidated most earlier distinctions. With the observation that
people who resided in the cities acquired multiple identities, the culture of play
produced a threat to the social identity of society. When, for example, the
Tokugawa authorities laid down the proscription of heterodoxy in the late eighteenth century, they were recognizing the threat to social identity that the new
cultural forms were beginning to pose. But even Matsudaira Sadanobu, who
promoted the prohibitions, acknowledged that "principle" and "reading books"
fell short of grasping the "passions of the times" and equipping the ruled with
proper instruments to prosecute their managerial duties.[8] What his edict disclosed was thus an acknowledgment of social surplus that seemed to elude the
conventional forms of representing the social in the fixed dichotomy of ruler-
ruled. His call for the promotion of men of talent and ability through the social
formation still took for granted the received political divisions. Ironically, the
edict contributed to the problem of surplus and difference rather than to its
solution, by encouraging the development and sponsorship of new skills in science, medicine, and Japanese and Western studies that promised to supply the
leadership with practical techniques to grasp the "passion of the times."

If late eighteenth-century Japan appeared as a scene of social surplus and
blurred identities, its cultural praxis expressing play sought not only to displace
fixed boundaries representing the real but also to show how the real, the differentiated masses living in the cities required new modes of representation.

Play (*asobi*) referred to a form of subjectivity that existed outside the "four classes" that operated within the space of the "great peace," *taihei*.⁹ A sense of liberation, closely resembling the nonrelated, insubordinated autonomy associated with the free cities of the late Middle Ages in Japan, demanded freedom from fixed positions as a condition for endless movement, best expressed in excursion narratives and tales of travel.¹⁰ Yet the reference to movement evinced still another meaning associated with *asobi*, which was to authorize crossing established geographical and social boundaries. According to Kaiho Seiryō (1755–1817), the ideal of this playful subject was the "gaze that disconnects and separates" (*kirete hanaretaru moku*): once the spirit was separated from the "body," it would be possible to carry on "independent play."¹¹ As a *rōnin* (masterless samurai), Kaiho had abandoned fixed positions of status in order to "play" within the "great peace"; as a traveler he journeyed to more than thirty provinces in his lifetime. The conception of play held by intellectuals like Kaiho was invariably related to the production of "playful literature," the deliberate decadence of "mad poetry," comic verse, and an inordinate taste for the different and exotic. This type of autonomous individual liberated from the collectivity in some sense resembled the person who buys and sells commodities as a condition of commercial capitalism, but the relationship was less causal than homologous. On numerous occasions Kaiho expressed best what many contemporaries believed and acted upon when he proclaimed that it was human nature for the self to love the body. He saw a world of universal principles dominated by substantiality—that is, things and bodies interacting with each other. In this arrangement, thing or object (*mono*) was increasingly identified with commodity (*shiromono*) and each person functioned as both buyer and seller. Rules that now constituted the social related more to calculation and self-interest than to moral imperatives of status, and they were mandated by the exchange of commodities.

Late Tokugawa cultural practice seemed to converge upon the body, making public what hitherto had remained private, whether in eating, drinking, speaking, bedding down with either a man or a woman, or relieving oneself, and often led to gargantuan indulgences coming from the joys of the flesh. Despite the variety of forms of verbal fiction that proliferated in the late eighteenth century to meet the rapid diversification of tastes, pleasures, and demands for greater "consumption," the content of playful culture invariably focused on the activities of the body. This concern for the autonomy of the body, expressed in Kaiho's "independent spirit" of movement, constituted the subject matter of most of verbal fiction and woodblock illustrations. One of the distinguishing features of the culture of play was its tendency to juxtapose a part, whether limb, organ, face, or body itself, to a larger entity, not as a substitute for the whole but, rather, as an adequate alternative to it. To dismiss the whole in this way was clearly to discount it. Centering on the body and its activities emphasized

the physical and the manual; by the same token it called into question the superiority of mental over manual skills on which the older distinction between
ruler-ruled, external-internal, and public-private had rested its authority.
Finally, the emphasis on the body as the maker and consumer of things put daily
life in the forefront and valued the things that composed it. Late eighteenth-
century Japan was a time when, recalling Marx, "the frames of the old *orbis
terrarum* had been broken" and "only now . . . was the earth opened up . . . ,"
when the search began to find ways to link real history, the daily life, to the
space of the real earth.[12]

What the verbal fictions of the culture play first disclosed was a new form of
time and its relationship to earthly space. This resulted in individualizing personal and everyday occasions, separating them from the time of collective life
identified with the social whole, precisely at that moment when there appeared
one scale for measuring the events of a personal life and another for historical
events. When Hirata Atsutane sought to figure a narrative that would recount
the tale of the folk collectivity, he was reacting to a culture that had already
divided time into separate units and differentiated the plots of personal life—
love, marriage, travel—from the occasions of history. In texts that provided the
plot of "history" and the private plots of individuals, interaction between the
two levels took place only at certain points—battles, the ascension or death of
an emperor, transgressions—and then ended as they proceeded on their separate ways. Although political economists sought to reapprehend the relationship between the life of nature and that of humans in order to retain the category
of nature, and nativists tried to naturalize culture in an effort to restore it to a
place of primacy, the two were increasingly uncoupled under the new regime.
Now the various events making up daily life—food, drink, copulation, birth,
death—were denatured and separated from the conception of a whole and
integrated life to become aspects of a personal life. Existence became com-
partmentalized and specialized.

Hence the life narrated in late Tokugawa fiction is presented as individual
and separate sequences and personal fate. The social formation was being differentiated into classes, groups, and specialized constituencies, each conforming
to functional scales of value and each possessing its own logic of development. The activities of daily life that concentrated on bodily performance lost
their link to common labor and a common social whole; instead, they became
private and petty matters on which writers reported as though through a peephole.[13] Contemporaries increasingly saw that peephole as habit or custom and
deportment and went to great lengths to classify its range and variety. And yet
to discover and categorize it so also presumed a conception of the whole, of society itself, even though the *gesaku* writers consistently apprehended personal
affairs as mere particularities that implied no conception of a larger whole or
meaning.[14] The impulse to "pierce" the crust of custom necessitated paying close

attention to detail. More often than not, tactility, rather than a discernible story line, was figured as the plot of the narrative and usually told the tale that the author wished to pierce. The absence of any real story in many "narratives" in favor of continuous dialogue about the interaction of things attests less to a diminution of literary standards than to their being in contest. These literary productions of the culture of play managed to convey a sharp dissatisfaction with conventions of narrative closure. Writers seemed convinced that failure to attend to the way that things were arranged, people were dressed, and foods were presented risked losing any chance to penetrate the surface of affairs. Readers were required to recognize differing levels of meaning in order to plumb hidden intentions below the surface. By making the familiar objects that inhabited daily life seem "strange," they persuaded readers to believe that they had been living in a hole, and not the whole, a rut whose very surroundings had obscured a recognition of the way that things really were. The texts (*kokkeibon*, "amusing books") of Shikitei Samba (1776–1822) and Jippensha Ikku (1765–1831) offered an endless stream of snapshots of the most mundane, familiar, and trivial activities that townsmen encountered in their daily life and on the road. But by rearranging them so that they appeared unfamiliar, by forcing readers to look at activities that they performed habitually and objects that they took for granted, writers could jar them into seeing custom in a new and different light. Laughter was recognition of the familiar made to appear strange and even alien. The world of Ikku's Tōkaidō travelers is peopled by characters who, when they are not about to seduce a maid or slip out of an inn without paying the bill, are preoccupied with farting, soiled loincloths, and a round of trivial involvement. The conversations that Samba records in barbershop and bathhouse relate to the most mundane affairs in the daily life of readers who now see and hear themselves speaking. Both writers emphasize the details and particularity of life in conversation or movement, such as eating, bathing, drinking, burping, and farting, in which the readers recognized their quotidian existence. Even in the more solemn historical romances of Bakin or the books of emotion (*ninjōbon*) which were preoccupied with the trials of love, the effect was to confront the reader with the familiar in an entirely different context. Bakin's explorations into the grotesque and fantastic in the well-known *Nansō Satomi hakkenden*, for example, concern a dog who performs a meritorious act of loyalty and then demands the reward, which happens to be the daughter of his feudal lord. And Ryūtei Tanehiko's *Nise Murasaki inaka Genji monogatari* recalls the Genji story in a different historical setting and projects contemporary custom and speech into the fifteenth century. At another level it still remained the world of the shogun Ienari, now identified with a familiar exemplar of corruption in the past.

Although the focus on the body as a maker and consumer of things emphasized the parts, it ultimately drew attention to the idea of a whole and a conceptualization of the social order, but in terms that were new and different from the officially sanctioned version. Bodily imagery in both verbal and illustrated texts signified a different kind of social reality with an inverted scale of priorities for the Edo townsmen. It was an order that had as its head the genitalia or anus and as its heart the stomach. Often, verbal fictions described the body, with its mouth and arms as a devouring, consuming totality; humans appeared as bodies that related to the world through their orifices rather than through public duties demanded by fixed social status and disciplined intention. Moreover, the body's needs were never satisfied and never completed; people continued to eat, drink, speak, make love, and evacuate ceaselessly without any prospect of an end. To portray the infinite details involved in partying, with its random arrangement of empty cups, vomit, and half-filled bottles the morning after, or to pay close attention to foods, eating, and the accompanying conversation—all recognizable as appropriate subjects (not objects) for representation—dramatized a world of activity and things that no longer referred to anything outside it. Tokugawa verbal fiction and woodblock illustrations enforced a new awareness of a world that people had habitually placed in the background by repositioning it in the foreground of represented experience. It also offered human alternatives to the world of public or official ideology. To the demands of the Heavenly Way (*tendō*), often satirized by writers, it provided space for play, laughter, and passion in anatomical representation, a veritable people's utopia, an arcadia of flesh, joy, and pain experienced by the body, a ceaseless delight that came from endless consumption and to the discharge of waste. In this regard, late Tokugawa fiction appropriated the common and customary to work on the dominant ideology in order to make it appear unfamiliar and to recast the somber requirements of official expectation within the world of play. By using immediate experience as its subject and making people aware of their daily lives and surroundings, writers were able to transform the quotidian experience into a system of knowledge that even the most common could possess and master. In this way, verbal fiction and the illustrator's art made the body into a text and reading an act of consuming knowledge.

Finally, the mass readership of late Tokugawa times was far more interested in identifying and recognizing contemporary custom than in retrieving ethical lessons from a history that, according to one authority, probably assaulted their sensibilities.[15] Early nineteenth-century writers like Samba and Tamenaga Shunsui, for example, wrote with an eye for details and nuances of contemporary life among the different quarters of Edo. Their production of *gesaku* helped define the conception of a coherent social world signifying changing conditions propelled by the constant interaction of humans, making and consuming, even though it consistently opposed the part to the whole. The early nineteenth-century Kabuki playwright Tsuruya Namboku portrayed what he called a "world" (*sekai*) bounded by "living custom" (*kizewa*). But Tsuruya's world, often darkened by violence, bloodshed, and conflict, was still nothing more than a reminder that social life was the stage on which contemporaries acted out their encounter with custom. This increasing identification of the culture of play and the world of theater with society—life following art—was noted by contemporaries who could agree that "its plot resembles the puppet theater" and that "its world is like the Kabuki."[16] There were contemporary moralists and thinkers like Buyō Inshi (dates unknown) and Shiba Kōkan (1747–1818) who alerted their contemporaries to the dangers inherent in conceptions of society grounded in play and enjoyment inspired by the world of theater. This new social criticism brought about a conceptualization of the whole, called *seken* or *seji*, that was able to accommodate the differentiation and fragmentation of life proclaimed by the culture of play. Whether such critics were openly opposed to contemporary social life (Buyō Inshi), saw in laughter a problem and not its solution (Hirata Atsutane), or envisaged a new set of arrangements conforming to the changes that had taken place since the middle of the eighteenth century (Shiba Kōkan), they believed that the culture of play had exhausted its productivity and imperiled the prospect of maintaining a stable public order. All seemed to agree on the necessity of restoring a conception of the social whole to counteract the baneful effects of the progressive particularization and privatization of life, but it was more difficult to reach a consensus on how the whole should be reconstituted. What concerned the critics most was the way that "custom" was generating new combinations of social relationships and eroding the older guarantees of solidarity. Buyō Inshi charged that the changes noted in his narrative of contemporary history (*Seji kemmonroku*, 1816) would inevitably undermine the political order by persuading people to turn away from their public duties for the private pleasures of the body.[17] Shiba Kōkan's *Shumparō hikki* (1818), a lasting testament to contemporary changes in its recording of an excursion to the south, condemned the widespread prevalence of private desire as evidence less of moral bankruptcy than of insufficient knowledge, which made unknowing people vulnerable to the temptations of self-indulgence.[18] Nobody would deny that changes in society had uncoupled the fixed relationship between culture as self-understanding and political purpose. Yet the resolution of the crisis, many believed, required a systematic effort to reconstitute society's self-understanding in such a way as to make it possible again to realign the various parts with a whole capable of instituting public order. Critics like Buyō Inshi looked to the seventeenth century and to the even more remote past to find models for the present, whereas others, like Shiba, trained their sights elsewhere and began to envisage new possibilities for the eventual reunion of politics and culture.

The specific grievance that agitated many critics was that the relentless pursuit of private desire fed the process of fragmenting interests and blinded people to the necessity of collective purpose. Everywhere people seemed to be turning inward to satisfy private desires and human needs. Yet such behavior constituted a public act, for self-understanding came to mean self-indulgence. The crisis of self-identity underscored the need to find new forms of knowing and understanding that could offer meaning in the new social environment without compromising the chance for order and stability. Any reconsideration of knowledge would have to account for the vast transformations that had taken place in Japanese society since the middle of the eighteenth century, transformations that had been noisily announced by the culture of play: the discovery and valorization of daily life, the common world of things and objects, the particularity of experience, the dehistoricization of the present, the ceaseless obsession with the body, and the possibility of constituting subjects for knowledge. What ensued in the late Tokugawa period was a play of culture, which entailed finding the means to represent stable forms of identity and meaning in discourse and a coherent voice. Although social critics like Buyō Inshi and Shiba Kōkan grasped the importance of knowledge for a resolution of the crisis of identity, they differed widely over its content. Predictably, Buyō called for a return to proper moral knowledge as a sure antidote to the "bad knowledge" of townsmen, but this meant excluding commoners as knowers in order to recast them in the role of the ruled and make the present look like the past again. By contrast, from his study of Western painting, Shiba favored a concept of empirical investigation based on the plurality of perspectives in viewing an object in order to open the way for new principles of the organization of knowledge and society. Shiba's promotion of perspective offered the prospect of making knowledge accessible to any group or person.[19]

What this play of culture inspired was a broad search for new forms of knowledge adequate to explain to certain groups the spectacle of surplus and why the social image of the past no longer applied to the early nineteenth century. Once these new forms of knowledge were structured, they would be able to authorize the establishment of cultural constituencies and the representation of interests and claims that had hitherto not been granted entry into official discourse. Yet almost simultaneously these new configurations sought to find political forms consistent with the content of culture that they wished to designate. The play of culture differed significantly from the culture of play in just this capacity to envisage stable or permanent political forms consonant with the new cultural constituencies. This coupling of culture and politics was mandated, and even accelerated, by the apparently rapid deterioration of domestic order and the appearance everywhere of events that seemed to signify the inevitability of decline. Catastrophic events like violent and unseasonable rains throughout the Kanto area and elsewhere, earthquakes in Echigo and Dewa (1833), urban "trashings" (*uchikowashi*), and widespread peasant rebellions were taken as signs of uncontrollable and unmanageable disintegration. Prevailing political forms seemed inadequate to prevent disorder and to provide assistance, relief, tranquility, and the semblance of safety to needy peasants. It was within this framework that the foreign intrusion, which had already begun at the turn of the century, was added as one more sign confirming the generally held belief that the realm was doomed. Thus whereas groups sought to represent knowledge of themselves in the will to form discourses, the new discourses invariably sought correspondences between culture and politics. A good deal of this activity was poured into efforts to stem disorder and to provide relief, security, and assistance. Virtually all the new discourses of the late Tokugawa period— Mitogaku (Mito learning), national learning, Western learning, and the new religions—tried to unite a conception of culture with politics. This impulse is surely reflected in the Mito identification of ceremony and polity, in nativist conceptions of *matsurigoto* (government as ceremony), the emphasis of the new religions on a community of believers free from hierarchy, and Western learning's formulations of science and morality. Moreover, when these new discourses spoke to vital issues of order and security, relief and assistance, equality and fairness, they were pressing not only a claim to represent interests constituted as knowledge but also the right to speak on questions directly affecting their constituencies. Gradually their "businesses," their interest, became society's business, just as their conception of culture and political organization became a substitute for the social formation as a whole. The claim of right to participate in and resolve problems of common concern, which meant survival, order, and defense, became the condition for creating a public realm in late Tokugawa society.

The new claims were often rooted in questions of productivity and security. When they were, groups were inadvertently led to challenge the authority of Tokugawa society, whether it was invested in the shogunal arrangement of power or in principles of a natural order of legitimacy. Such acts invariably resulted in defection from the center, the Tokugawa polity, at a time when authorities were finding it difficult to meet their own responsibilities and satisfy demands for "order" and "relief." Such withdrawals to the periphery were usually prompted by the conviction that if the Tokugawa structure could not live up to its obligations, then the groups would have to take care of themselves. Thus what appeared from the 1830s onward was a progressive retreat from the center to the periphery, not as explicit acts of revolutionary sedition but as an expression of diminishing confidence in the system's ability to fulfill its moral duties. The new cultural disciplines provided justification for groups to perform for themselves tasks that the Tokugawa polity was now unable to perform. This required the formation of voluntary associations, some of which ultimately flew in the face of a conception of a natural order that defined groups according to their natural and expected function. The occasion for this massive impulse to secede was provided by the way that contemporary history was grasped by those who acted to arm themselves with self-definition. The move to emphasize the production of wealth, the centrality of daily affairs, the importance of the communal unity for nativist thought and new religions, and the widespread concern of all groups with aid and relief, mutual assistance, equality in the distribution of resources, along with talent, ability, and utility did not so much "reflect" the conditions of *bakumatsu* as "interpret" such facts and events. Ultimately all these new cultural discourses sought to merge with power that knowledge based on principles of inclusion and exclusion of both objects and people. To appeal to new forms of knowledge that different groups could know meant talking about different conceptions of power. Each of these groups saw itself and its response to contemporary problems as a solution to the social, and imagined that the part that it represented was a substitute for the unenvisaged whole. The proper kind of knowledge, it was believed, would lead to a solution of the problems agitating society. All assumed that a decision on one part would disclose the shape of the whole. Hence Mito turned to the primacy of the autonomous domain sanctioned by the national polity (*kokutai*); *kokugaku* (national learning) concentrated on the self-sufficient village authenticated by its relation to the primal creation deities; *yōgaku* (Western learning) celebrated a crude form of the mercantilist state, propelled by virtue and science, and the new religions announced the establishment of new forms of sacred communalism in their effort to give permanence to a conception of epiphany and the liminal moment.

All these new discourses were formulated in the early nineteenth century. All aimed to understand the world anew and lessen its problems by offering solutions. Yet they contributed as much to *bakumatsu* problems as they did to their resolution. They all were generated by a will to knowledge that masked more fundamental considerations of power. Every manifestation of how the new discourse sought to fix rules of formation and discipline disclosed an accompanying and almost obligatory concern for the foundations of knowledge and learning. Every discussion of the status of knowledge and learning inevitably raised questions concerning the identity of the knowers and what should be known.

Good Doctrine and Governance

The problem of defining cultural context and finding an adequate political form for it was engaged first by a generation of samurai intellectuals from the Mito domain (Fujita Yūkoku, his son Tōko, Aizawa Seishisai, Toyoda Tenkō, the daimyo Tokugawa Nariaki) and their spiritual associates, Ōhashi Totsuan, Yoshida Shōin, and Maki Izumi. As early as the late eighteenth century, Mito writers began to search systematically for ways to enunciate a program of

practical discipline and education. Mito had long been the center of an ambitious historiographical project, the *Dai Nihon shi*, a lightning rod for serious-
minded philosophic speculation in the neo-Confucian mode. But there was
a difference, if not a break, in intellectual continuity, between the meditations
of the so-called early Mito scholars and the discourse of the latter Mito
school.[20] Whereas the early Mito writers clung closely to a rather formal neo-
Confucianism, the later thinkers selected a syncretic position that mixed parts
of neo-Confucianism, nativist religious, and mythic elements to produce a
comprehensive statement very different in structure and purpose from what
had gone before. Politically, Mito was one of the three collateral houses of the
Tokugawa family and thus occupied a relatively privileged position near the
center of power. But in economic terms, Mito, like so many domains in the late
eighteenth and early nineteenth centuries, encountered problems that seemed
to resist conventional solutions. Fujita Yūkoku (1774–1826), a middle-ranking
retainer named to the Mito historiographical bureau, called attention to the
diminishing domainal financial resources and the consequences for people
and government. His student Aizawa Seishisai (1781–1863) later specified the
cause of the contemporary "crisis" when he proposed that it had stemmed
from the decision to move the samurai off the land into towns and the consequent growth of the use of money and the dependence on the market. Mito
writers were especially concerned with the economic impact of these changes on
the ruling class, which had incurred deep indebtedness to meet daily expenses,
as they adopted luxurious lifestyles inspired by the pursuit of private interests.
What worried the critics was the way these changes seemed to have affected
agricultural productivity and contributed to the growing power of merchants
and moneylenders who benefited from the samurai's need for cash.[21] Yet they
were no less sensitive to the recurrence of famines and other natural disasters
that undermined agricultural production. Both samurai and peasants suffered
from the hardships caused by such events. Taxes were relatively high in Mito,
Yūkoku noted in his *Kannō wakumon*, and the population had decreased
steadily since the middle years of the century.

These developments were not unique or even exceptional for the times, but
the Mito writers interpreted them as signs of impending disintegration. Yūkoku
complained that fondness for money and usury had already led to a number of
disrupting abuses in the domain. The most serious by far in his inventory was
the growing frequency of peasant rebellions. Here, he advised the leadership
to take stock of its responsibilities to rule "virtuously." Instead of relying on laws
and ordinances, always a sign of slackening control, it was necessary to promote
a leadership skilled in the art of governance. In the context of the late eighteenth
century, what this meant was a redefinition of virtue into practicality, and the
training of administrators who would be able to understand the requirements of the times. Years later, Aizawa expressed grave misgivings regarding

the invasion of gamblers and idlers into Mito and saw their presence as a man-ifestation of moral decay. He concluded that such unwanted guests had been permitted to enter the domain because of administrative laxity and ignorance concerning the way they could corrupt village morals and encourage peasants to abandon work for drink, gambling, and expensive foods. Underlying this was the belief that ordinary people naturally loved profit and were eager to pursue private interest whenever they were given the slightest opportunity. Aizawa also feared the influence of new religions like the Fuji cult (Fujikō), which had recently established itself in Mito and was beginning to recruit large numbers of followers among the peasantry.[22] But he reserved his harshest judg-ment for Christianity, a "cruel and unjust religion," which won over the minds of ignorant people and diverted them from the path of moral rectitude.

The Mito writers were convinced that the problems threatening domain integrity resulted from inadequate leadership. If the masses lost their way, it was because the managerial class had abdicated its responsibilities to provide moral examples.[23] Fujita Tōko (1806–1855) lamented that the way of loyalty and filiality had disappeared. Order could be restored by clarifying these princi-ples once more and redirecting the rulers to govern the realm properly. Yet, he noted, this would require an understanding of the part and the whole, between the leader and the people, the domain and the realm.

The sanction for the Mito effort to resolve the contemporary crisis lay in the reunification of learning and doctrine. Writers like Fujita Yūkoku argued the necessity of knowing how to rectify names (*seimeiron*) and straightening the arrangement of duties so that name would correspond to responsibility (*meibunron*). In the rectification of names he saw the general problem of social decay as a failure of representation in language. In this Yūkoku shared the assumptions of an eighteenth-century discourse that had already drawn atten-tion to the problematic relation between words and the things they were sup-posed to denote. Because names and status no longer conformed to reality, it seemed imperative to realign name to truth.[24] A realignment along these lines made possible by language itself promised to retrieve the archetypical way of loyalty and filiality. According to Yūkoku, "In the realm, there are lords and retainers, and there are the upper and lower orders. If the designations of lords and retainers are not corrected, the division between the aristocratic and non-aristocratic classes will blur, and distinctions between the upper and lower orders will vanish. The strong will come to despise the weak and the masses will be thrown into confusion and disorder."[25]

His son Tōko went even further when, following the lead of the contempo-rary nativists, he noted that even though in ancient times the Way had no name by which it was known, everybody naturally knew and understood its requirements. Although writing did not exist in that remote age, the meaning of the Way was conveyed through song and poetry (a point made earlier by

Kamo Mabuchi in the *Kokuikō*), in manner, custom, deportment, education, and government. Yet when the effort was finally made to express the Way in written texts, its "true and original nature suffered."[26] Both writers believed that rescuing the Way in language in their times was the supreme duty of leadership and the first principle of education. The Mito conception of the Way differed from the more established neo-Confucian view of the conviction that the Way could not be found in nature but only through human effort, a proposal they shared with the eighteenth-century philosopher Ogyū Sorai. Victor Koschmann has argued, in this connection, that "representation . . . means precisely the objectification of the 'natural' state (the Way of heaven, unity between Heaven and Earth) through some form of 'unnatural' (linguistic, instrumental, demonstrative) action. The object to be represented through human mediation is Heaven itself, not a temporary arrangement."[27]

By calling attention to the operation of rectification and designation, the Mito writers were able to demonstrate the primacy of the domain as an adequate space for the realization of the necessary alignments. Much of their formulation was powered by a strategy that reduced the parts to an essential and original whole, to the primal origins of the realm as expressed in the term *kokutai* (national polity or body). *Kokutai* was identified as the whole for which the parts stood. For the Mito writers, the concept represented the indissoluble link between status and loyal behavior (*chūkō no michi*) and the corresponding network of designations and duties. It was their intention to show how the realignment of name and duty could again be implemented in the domain and how, in fact, the appeal to *kokutai* mandated the resuscitation of the domain along such lines. To argue in this fashion was to propose that a morally reconstituted domain serve as a substitute for the whole. This was surely the meaning of Yūkoku's enunciation, in his *Seimeiron*, of the vertical ties of loyalty that stretched from the emperor down through the lower orders. But it is also evident that the linchpin in this hierarchical chain was the domainal lord. "How can we strengthen the rectification of duties and designation," Yūkoku asked rhetorically, "How is the country of the *bakufu* to be governed today?. . . At the top we live under the heavenly descendants, and at the bottom we are tended by the various lords."[28]

With this strategy, the Mito writers were in a position to interpret the events they encountered in the early nineteenth century and make reality appear less problematic. They moved along a rather broad arc whose terminal points were marked by a profound distrust of the people and a moral sense of benevolence and compassion for them. Among the recurring anxieties expressed in their writings, none seemed more urgent and frightening than the prospect of imminent mass disorder in a countryside affected by foreign intrusion and, by implication, the incapacity of the Tokugawa *bakufu* to stem the swelling threat of mass civil disorder. The growing incidence of peasant rebellions since the late eighteenth century, they believed, related to the disabled status of the domain itself and reflected a widespread agreement that the general administrative machinery no longer functioned properly. The Mito writers regularly complained that the shogunate had departed from its earlier role as the largest domain among equals to pursue policies deliberately designed to undermine the military and financial autonomy of its peers. By the end of the eighteenth century it was clear that these policies had made the domains more dependent on the *bakufu*. Resolving the domains' declining status required persuading the *bakufu* to accept a less exalted position in the arrangement of authority. But this move was prefigured by the Mito insistence on rectifying names, duties, and designations as a necessary condition for the moral realignment of the system. If the *bakufu* fulfilled the expectations associated with its name, it would cease acting in a self-interested manner.

Once the relationship between shogunate and domains was rectified, it would be possible to turn to the problem of the ruled. People can be governed, Aizawa announced, only when rulers rely on the Way of loyalty and filiality. This proposition was not based simply on a dim view of human nature—most members of the managerial class in Tokugawa Japan held that as an article of faith—but on a more complex conviction that because an agricultural population was necessary to the survival and welfare of order, it must be made to acknowledge its duty to produce as a moral trust. This was also what Fujita Yūkoku had meant when he proposed that "people are the basis of the realm. If they constitute a firm foundation, then the realm will also be stable."[29] Aizawa, who constantly referred to the people in uncomplimentary terms, believed that because they were predictably disorderly and forever prevented from acquiring the niceties of virtue, they were capable only of being led. But leading the people meant making sure they produced. "People properly should rely . . . on rules; they should not know them."[30]

Under the sanction of this conception of privilege, the Mito writers directed their rhetoric toward explaining the reasons that the people were "naturally" excluded from having knowledge and why they had to be ruled, which meant work. If the ordinary folk were left to their own devices and were not persuaded to perform their proper duties, Aizawa explained, they would act like children and pursue profit, pleasure, and personal luxury at every opportunity. The possession of knowledge entitled a few to rule and required the many to follow. Neither the exercise of coercion nor the accumulation of wealth was equivalent to knowledge as conditions for rulership. Those who "should not know" must always depend on the informed guidance of those who "know." This conception of knowing and knowers prompted the Mito writers to look harshly on all religions organized to enlist the people, because their doctrines invariably promoted forms of nonexclusionary knowledge accessible to all. Fujita Tōko declared rather excitedly in his commentary on the establishment of an academy in Mito (*Kōdōkanki jutsugi*) that heretical doctrines continue to "delude the people" and "bewilder the world." As a result, he discerned a causal relationship between the slackening of belief in the true Way and the dissolution of ties and dependence, currently reflected in the incidence of peasant uprisings. Yet he was convinced that these disturbances were only manifestations of new forms of knowledge that actually confused and confounded the people to embark on a course of disorderly conduct.

Hence, the Mito writers viewed disturbances as expressions of private interest encouraged by new opportunities for the pursuit of self-indulgence and new religious doctrines promising rewards to all. To offset such threats they recommended the establishment of a regime devoted to benevolence and compassion and advised the leadership to "love" and "revere" the people. Once love and reverence were actualized in concrete measures, they believed, the fears of the managerial class would diminish, and the incidence of "unhappiness" in the countryside would disappear. Despite Aizawa's scarcely concealed contempt for "mean people," he remarked that "loving the people" required hard commitments from the leadership. He believed with his teacher Yūkoku, who had earlier called for a program promoting people's welfare, in "assisting the weak and restraining the strong, fostering the old and loving the young, prohibiting laziness and idleness."[31] He sided with Tokugawa Nariaki, who, upon becoming lord of Mito in 1829, announced the promise of a reform reflecting the leadership's duty to love and provide care for the people. "Virtue is the root," Nariaki declared, "commodities the branch"; a virtuous leadership cannot "avoid bestowing blessings on the people."

The issue that the Mito writers sought to resolve was how to increase productivity and exercise greater control. The "good teachings" of etiquette and civilization, which Aizawa believed only the leadership could know, were guarantees of permanent order and wealth. By equating the status ethic and its proper discrimination throughout the domain with "loving the people," the Mito thinkers could argue that if leadership "bestowed proper blessings upon the people," the realm would administer itself. Yet if the rulers abandoned "good doctrine," the people would, according to Tōko, "avoid political laws as one avoids an enemy. Their yearning will be like that of a child for a mother's affection." When people are not under total control, Tōko noted, recalling Ōshio's recent rebellion in Osaka in 1837, they will resemble a "product that first putrefies and then gives way to worms and maggots. People who are heretical are similar to those who are ill. Men who govern the sick will first promote their health; men who expel heresy will first cultivate the Great Way." Nariaki and later observers continued to assert that if the "peasantry bears a grudge or resents the upper class, it will not stand in awe of them." Control required providing assistance which, in this context, referred to restoring order in the Mito domain. "If we succeed in exhausting our intentions day and night to return the blessings, we will be able to sympathize with all our hearts." But control, through the blessing of conferring assistance and relief, required returning people to the land and increasing their productive labor. Earlier, Fujita Yūkoku had outlined a program for "enriching the domain" in *Kannō wakumon*, and in the late 1830s Nariaki and Tōko worked out a comprehensive land policy that included a land survey, a realignment of tax quotas, greater efforts for empathy to draw peasants and local officials more closely together, a study of new agricultural techniques, and, not least important, a recall of samurai from Edo back to Mito. This last plank, which announced the domain's intention to withdraw from the center for a reliance on its resources in the periphery, was more than enough to disturb large numbers of retainers who had become accustomed to city life.

The lord of Mito thought that the times were ripe for a "restoration of the domain" (*kokka o chūkōshi*) in the 1830s and a "renovation of custom for the unification of all." The purpose of the economic and educational reforms Nariaki announced in the late 1830s was to halt the fragmentation of social life that had spread throughout the domain. Fragmentation referred to "evil customs," and its elimination required economic and educational renovation. Aizawa had already indicated in *Shinron* (1825) that as loyalty and filiality become one, "the education of the people and the refinement of custom is accomplished without a word being spoken. Thus, there is no essential difference between government and the indoctrination of the people."[32] This sense of unification, realized through identifying teaching and doctrine, became the special task of the academy in Mito, the Kōdōkan, whose task was to instruct samurai and commoners (through a network of village schools) in how to "refine custom" and reinstate proper morality. Tōko's commentary emphasized this sense of union in neat slogans designed to remove differences to reach the underlying similitude of all things: "the unification of Shinto and Confucianism," "the inseparability of loyalty and filiality," "*sonnō jōi*" (revering the emperor, expelling the barbarian, a term first coined in the proclamation establishing the school; it meant renovating the domestic system in order to be able to withstand external interference), "the union of military arts and civilian skills," and the "indivisibility of learning and practice." The purpose of the school was to reunify doctrine and government, which had become distinct in the course of the long peace. Duties and designation had to be reunited and custom brought into line with morality.

Following Yūkoku and Aizawa, Nariaki used language that called attention to the basis, as against the unessential. The solution to the contemporary problem was to return to essentials. This meant reapplying the classic injunction of the "great learning," "The base of the realm is the family; the foundation of the family is moral discipline," to the domain itself. In tightening moral relationships the domain was required to embark on far-reaching reforms in "custom" and "military preparedness." Aizawa observed in *Shinron* that a long peace had resulted in extravagant customs, indulgent lords, and the "bitterness of the poor," and Nariaki noted in his *Kokushiden* that "with a tranquil realm we can never forget about rebellion . . . we have forgotten about the thick blessings that have been bestowed by peace today . . . and we have been concerned only with being well fed and well clad. The samurai have become effeminate and resemble a body that contracts illness through exposure to cold, wind, or heat. They are idlers and wastrels among the four classes."[33]

In this way the Mito discourse came to see in the domainal space the only prospect for a genuine restoration. Toyoda Tenkō, in an essay composed along restorationist lines in 1833, wrote that even though the "ancients wrote that 'a restoration is always difficult to accomplish,' it must be even more difficult to do so today."[34] Yet he was convinced that the time and place were right. The ancients had linked the achievement of a restoration to the successful termination of a rebellion, but Tenkō saw the recent decline of the domain as equivalent to embarking on the difficult task. The logic for this conception of restoration had been powerfully articulated by Yūkoku in the late eighteenth century and was eloquently restated by Aizawa, who saw in the moment an opportunity that comes only once in a thousand years. Aizawa's proposals were propelled by his belief that the *bakufu* had willfully followed a policy of self-interest, in which the base had been strengthened at cost to the branches.[35] Aizawa charged that this represented a distortion of Ieyasu's original intention. Ieyasu had strengthened the center and weakened the periphery in order to head off rebellion and anarchy. He had done this by assembling the warriors in the cities, where their stipends were weakened, and by sheltering the people from a military presence.[36] "The military were lessened, and the masses were made into fools." But Aizawa believed that the time had now come to reverse this policy and to strengthen both the base as well as the ends by "nourishing" and "strengthening" the lords.[37] If the lords were permitted to play the role originally designated to them by the emperor, Yūkoku had asserted earlier, they could turn to the task of rectifying their own domains. Though he acknowledged the overlordship of the Tokugawa shogun, Aizawa wrote in the *Tekii hen* that there was a reciprocal relationship between lord and subject. The vertical relationships outlined by Yūkoku thus gained new force in the context of domain reform in the formulations of Aizawa and Nariaki. The shogun should assist the court and govern the realm, just as local leaders should support the emperor and obey the *bakufu*'s decrees in their provinces. But "the people who obey the commands of the daimyo are in effect obeying the decrees of the Bakufu."[38] Because the *bakufu* was limited by the court, it had not absolute authority over the Mito domain. What this meant for Mito ideologues was the elevation of the domain and the virtual reversal of the base-ends metaphor.

The intellectual sanction for this new edifice envisaged in the Mito discourse was the identification of the whole in a mystical body called *kokutai*.

Elaboration of this seminal idea was provided chiefly by Aizawa in his *Shin-ron*. This construct was universal and absolute, but it could mobilize the rich tradition of Japanese mythohistory. "The heavenly ancestors introduced the way of the gods and they have established doctrine; by clarifying loyalty and filial piety they began human history. These duties were ultimately transferred to the first sovereign and they have since served the great foundation of the state. The emperor joined these divine ordinances to his own body."[39]

Just as the emperor looked up to the virtue of the heavenly descendants, Aizawa continued, so the people received in their bodies the heart of their ancestors and respected and served the emperor for an eternity. When the emperor receives the will of their ancestors, there can be no change in history. Similarly, the emperor himself, worshipping his ancestor the sun goddess, has realized the principle of filial piety and reveals this obligation to the people. Because the principle of loyalty and filiality had existed without needing to be articulated, daily practice—the practice of the body—signified the inseparability of worship, ceremony, and governance.

Such an ideal had always been represented in ritual. In the first book of the *Shinron*, Aizawa discussed how ancient rulers displayed filiality by carrying out worship at ancestral tombs and in performing the solemn ceremonies and rites.[40] The most important of these rituals was the *daijōsai*, the great food-offering ritual performed by each new emperor at the time of the first harvest after his succession. The rite consisted of offering new grain to the sun goddess (Amaterasu), but the significance of the ritual was its reiteration of archetypal themes such as the divine creation of the land and the benevolence of Amaterasu toward her people. Aizawa noted that in the actual ritual, subject and sovereign experience the presence of Amaterasu and ultimately "feel like descendants of the gods." For a moment, history is frozen; past flows into present; and the great principles of loyalty and filiality—dramatized by the exchange between sovereign, who presents the divine progenitor with riches she has made possible, and her subjects, who must return the "blessings"—are represented as timeless and universal norms. By invoking the example of this great ritual, Aizawa was able to show how mere history, a record of changing circumstances, differed from timeless truths reaching back to mythical origins. The *daijōsai* annuls history; the primal moment restores to each participant presence and self-identity. The ceremony should unify sovereign, subject, and descendants and thus dissolve the division between governance and worship. "If the whole country reveres the heavenly deities, then all will know how to respect the emperor." If civilization in Japan was to withstand the erosion of history, it was important for the people to know how to express respect as represented in ritual. The present was the appointed time, a unique opportunity, Aizawa said, "to inform the people of this principle and purify the public spirit." When this great enterprise had been accomplished, "past will be united to present," sovereign to people.

In this manner the essential national body, a mystical whole signifying origins and continual presence, validated the domain's claim to restore the great principles of loyalty and filiality. For the Mito writers, the ideal *kokutai* functioned at several levels. It represented the whole to which the parts—the domains—could relate; it also provided the sanction for the domain, pledged to reinstate the timeless principles, to act as a substitute for the whole. *Kokutai* served to remind every generation of the essential beginnings from which all things had come and to which all things are reduced. This is surely what the Mito writers meant when they advised contemporaries "not to forget about the basis" and to "return the blessing to its origins." What could be more essential than the body of the realm, however shapeless, vague, and mystical, the *karada* (body) of the *kuni* (country)? "What is this body of the country?" Aizawa asked, and he answered, "If countries do not have a body, it cannot be made by men. If a country has no body, how can it be a nation?"[41] Aizawa envisaged this body as a form that distinguished the idea of a unified realm from chaos. It was his purpose to link the sense of the whole to a new political space represented by the autonomous domain. His actual proposals for reform were unexceptional and echoed Yūkoku's earlier suggestions and Nariaki's later measures. Yet they confirmed the belief in the inseparability of representation and action, learning and practice.

Changes in contemporary history altered the character of the Mito discourse. This is not to say that the Mito writers changed their minds about the veracity of their vision but only to suggest the possibility of varying emphases within the discourse. Whereas in the 1840s Mito rhetoric was pressed into service to reconstitute the domain through a series of reforms, in the 1850s and 1860s, as the area of political space widened, the reformist impulse came to address national issues and to advocate direct action. Whereas the earlier goals aimed at rebuilding the domain without necessarily affecting the *bakufu*, the later course of action made the destruction of the shogunate a condition for realizing domainal autonomy. The generation of samurai intellectuals who had been attracted to the Mito discourse in the Tempō period, not to mention the retainers of the domain itself, turned gradually to representing the ideals in the form of direct action calling for a restoration of imperial authority and the destruction of the *bakufu*. Mito retainers themselves had taken matters into their hands in 1860 when they participated in the assassination of the shogunal counselor Ii Naosuke. Four years later the domain was torn apart by civil war. Yet the theoretical justification for extending representation to include direct action was provided by thinker-activists like Yoshida Shōin, Ōhashi Totsuan, and Maki Izumi. The general outline of this Mito theory of action was propelled by the recognition that in the new political arena of the 1850s, especially after the opening of the country (1854) and the subsequent signing of commercial treaties with Western nations, the *bakufu* no longer possessed either the authority or the will to speak for the nation as a whole. Such authority resided with the emperor, as the Mito writers had proposed earlier in their discussion of vertical relationships, and it was he who must now lead directly in the great accomplishment of renovation.

Yoshida Shōin (1830–1859), a specialist in military instruction in the Chōshū domain, saw the signing of the commercial treaties as the opportunity to dramatize the failure of the *bakufu*. What hc demanded of the shogunate was a domestic order that could withstand foreign contact. He recognized that the *bakufu* had succumbed to the treaties out of indecision and fear. But the new treaties affected the nation as a whole, not simply the shogunate or the domains. "If problems arise in the territory of the shogun," he wrote at the time, "they must be handled by the shogun; if in the domain of the lord, by the lord."[42] This was fully consistent with the Mito arrangement of authority and its corresponding definition of jurisdiction. The problems facing Japan in 1856–1857 were not restricted to the shogun or indeed the lord but involved both because they now related to the security of the imperial land itself. It was the emperor, not the shogun, who had the right to make authoritative decisions concerning foreign demands, because the crisis imperiled all of Japan. "This affair [the signing of the treaties] arose from within the territory of the emperor." Hence, the shogunate had shown not only weakness but had actually committed treason by committing an act of lèse-majesté.

The *bakufu* had acted willfully and "privately" by agreeing to treaty negotiations. Yoshida proposed that its officials be punished and the institution dismantled for ignoring an imperial decree calling for the immediate expulsion of foreigners. The *bakufu* had committed a crime of unprecedented magnitude: "It has abjured heaven and earth, angered all the deities. . . . It has nourished a national crisis today and bequeathed national shame to future generations. . . . If the imperial decree is honored, the realm will be following the Way. To destroy a traitor is an act of loyalty." To this end Yoshida, in his last years (he was a casualty of the Ansei purge of 1859), worked out a program that would best fulfill the requirements of direct action and loyal behavior. He called for a rising of "grassroots" heroes, appealing principally to the samurai and independent villagers, willing to leave their homes and perform what he called meritorious deeds. "If there is no rising of independent patriots, there will be no prosperity. How will these unaffiliated men reinstate the saintly emperor and wise lords? Men who follow my aims and are of my domain must follow this rising. Through the unauthorized power of the rising, small men will be excluded, evil men will be thrown out, and correct and able lords will be able to gain their place."[43]

Yoshida's call for an organization of grassroots patriots willing to act directly was also the subject of Ōhashi Totsuan's (1816–1862) meditation concerning the contemporary situation. Ōhashi, who came from the small domain of

Utsunomiya, affiliated with Mito, was contemplating the possibility for direct action at the same time that Yoshida was seeking to call his own followers to arms against the *bakufu*. Ōhashi was more consistently committed to classic neo-Confucian arguments concerning the importance of differentiation between civilization and the barbarism represented by the West. Yet this philosophic conservatism merely elaborated Mito's ideas on expulsionism (*jōiron*). Ōhashi's thinking on restoration first favored removing incompetents from high shogunal offices. This effort to rob the *bakufu* of its top leadership (favored by Yoshida as well) showed the later restorationists how to dramatize the issue of able leadership and also how to paralyze the *bakufu*. The failure of this tactic later encouraged others to consider raising a small army for an imperial campaign against the shogunate, something that was first suggested by the Satsuma retainer Arima Shinshichi (in 1862) and tried by Maki Izumi a year later. Ōhashi's most explicit statement on restoration appears in a work he completed in 1861 called *Seiken kaifuku hisaku* (A secret policy for a restoration of political authority). The work was written in response to the *bakufu*'s attempt of 1860 to unite court and shogunate by securing Princess Kazu no Miya as the consort of the shogun. His plan sought to extend the culturalism of his earlier writings.

> Since the coming of the foreigner and the expansion of commerce, the Bakufu's position has not been good; it has carried temporizing to extremes, and the arrogance of the barbarians has been rampant. . . . Bakufu officials are afraid of them. . . . Even though only one barbarian was permitted to enter in the beginning, now several have pushed their way in. . . . Although trade is not yet three years old, the rising prices of commodities, the exhaustion of domainal resources, and the impoverishment of the lower classes must be viewed as disasters.[44]

Ōhashi was also convinced that the *bakufu* had systematically undermined the "brave and loyal samurai" of "courageous domains." The only solution, he reasoned, was a call to arms under the "banner of an imperial decree." Like Yoshida, Ōhashi believed that the decision to take Japan out of the hands of the barbarians belonged to the imperial court. Hence, he declared, all people, out of love of the emperor, lay waiting for the "august movement of the court. . . . As with the booming clap of a thunderous voice, once an imperial decree is promulgated all men must act, since all will be inspired. It will be like the collapse of a dam holding back a lake." Ōhashi believed that the *bakufu* had violated the strictures of *meibun* and had acted out of contempt of the court. He was convinced that nine of every ten men were alienated from the Tokugawa exercise of power. "The people of the realm," he urged, "must abandon the Tokugawa before it is too late, deepen their devotion to the imperial court, and move toward a revival of the emperor's power. The time must not be lost."

Ultimately Ōhashi's views on restoration melded into the organization of a small group of plotters—grassroots heroes, recruited from Mito and Utsunomiya, willing to execute a plan to assassinate the shogunal counselor Andō Nobumasa. The plot was carried out in 1862 and is known as the Sakashitamon incident. Ōhashi saw the assassination as the occasion for both a rising of patriots and the promulgation of an imperial decree condemning the *bakufu*. Although he played no direct role in the attempted murder (Andō was wounded), he was willing to accept responsibility for his part in its planning.

The failure of Ōhashi's theory of restoration prompted a shift to the second method, that of raising an army of loyalists prepared to embark on an imperial campaign. This method was developed chiefly by the Kurume priest Maki Izumi (1813–1864), an enthusiastic follower of the Mito discourse. The locus of activity also shifted from Edo to Kyoto, the site of the imperial court and the emperor. Whereas Ōhashi stressed the more formal neo-Confucian elements in the Mito discourse, Maki, owing to his Shinto education, emphasized the native mythohistorical dimensions of the discourse. Maki was also critical of the meditative and quietistic tendencies of neo-Confucianism, which he felt contained little sense or practicality. Neo-Confucianism, like Zen, was too abstract to use in understanding the contemporary situation. It was his intent to replace passivity, meditation, and self-cultivation with direct action. Maki also plunged into national politics in the early 1860s after spending years in house imprisonment for activities in the Kurume domain. Almost immediately, he began to develop a theory of an imperial restoration to arrest the "unceremonial" behavior of the barbarians and to punish the "effeminacy" of the wavering *bakufu*. He was convinced that it was the court's duty to seize the initiative and to act. This was the moment, he wrote in 1861, to encourage the emperor to promulgate an expulsionist policy that would announce the restoration of imperial authority. In a letter to a Kyoto courtier, Maki outlined the way to accomplish a restoration: (1) select talented men for positions of political responsibility, (2) reward men who act for the court with status, and (3) preserve the "great polity of the realm" by "returning to the prosperity of antiquity." Here, Maki brought together two themes—*kokutai* and the heavenly ordinance, both familiar conceptions within the Mito discourse, and pressed them into the task of formulating a new theory of emperor. To see the emperor armed with the moral authority of heaven and the divinity of the national ancestors and personalized by history (a tactic that the Mito writers failed to promote) became the condition for Maki's call for restoration. His theory sought to actualize the Mito conception of representation by calling up the historical characteristics of ancient emperors (although Mito merely summoned the principle, not the principal, of imperial authority) and rescuing the sovereign from his seat "beyond the clouds," as he put it, in order to liberate him from court concealment and return him to the world of politics. He believed that this conception of the emperor, now conforming to hard, concrete elements derived from actual history, corresponded to the requirements of contemporary political reality more closely than to the bland and abstract image envisaged by the neo-Confucians.[45]

Maki saw the present as the moment in which to implement what he called, in his *Kei-i gusetsu*, a "great enterprise." He later translated the "great enterprise" into an "imperial campaign" against the *bakufu*. The idea of such an "imperial campaign," pledged to bringing about a restoration, was authorized by historical examples. Emperors in the past had satisfied heaven's requirements to act. "Jimmu Tennō had erected the great feudal system, established the teachings of Shinto, and unified the public spirit. . . . Temmu Tennō expanded the skills in a hundred ways. He planned for the central administration, swept away abuses in the court, established a prefectural system." Ancient imperial precedents showed contemporaries that current conditions necessitated a comparable response, what Maki called the "labor of the august Imperial Body." But completing this act in the present demanded commitment and heroism. In 1860 and 1861 Maki conceived of a plan to organize an imperial campaign aimed at overthrowing the *bakufu*. In an essay called the "Record of a Great Dream" he argued that the time had arrived for the emperor to exercise direct authority by issuing an edict branding the shogun a traitor and usurper. The edict would also call for an imperial campaign led personally by the emperor from a new base of operations established in the Hakone mountains. There, the emperor would take up residence and assemble shogunal officials for punishment. Next, he would summon the young shogun Iemochi and demand from him the return of former imperial possessions. Finally, the emperor would enter Edo and seize the shogun's castle, which would become the new imperial capital, and issue a "proclamation announcing a great, new beginning." Because for Maki the whole purpose of the imperial campaign was to destroy the *bakufu*, he recommended a return to an antiquity before the shogun and military estates had appeared as a model for the present, even though he favored retaining the feudal order in form. As for the composition of the imperial campaign, the *Gikyo Sansaku* (1861) advised that the first principle had to be the recruitment of loyal lords. Beyond appealing to feudal lords, Maki also looked to enlisting small guerrilla groups composed of samurai and upper-ranking peasants capable of carrying out lightning-like action. In the end, Maki, together with men from Chōshū, tried to bring about an imperial restoration in 1864 at the Imperial Palace in Kyoto. It was a desperate plan, and it failed. But Maki's concept for restoration was to become a rehearsal for a real and successful performance in 1868. In Maki, the Mito discourse, which had begun with Confucian statecraft for domain reform, had gone on to provide the validation of Shinto mythology for the organization of efforts for nationwide reforms and emperor-central revolution.

The Restoration of Worship and Work

Just as the Mito discourse interpreted contemporary reality in order to establish the "real" and the "appropriate" as justification for the autonomous domain, so the nativists (*kokugakusha*) advanced a theory of the self-sufficient village as the substituted part for the unenvisaged whole. The nativists operated under similar constraints but sought, in contrast with Mito, to represent a different social constituency selected from the rural rich, such as the upper and middle peasantry and village leaders. They also proceeded from the assumption that the vast changes in the content of culture necessitated finding a political form adequate to the transformation. Like the Mito discourse, nativism originated at an earlier time in the late seventeenth century and initially concentrated on resuscitating the landmarks of the Japanese literary and aesthetic tradition. National studies represented an effort to structure what we might call native knowledge and matured under the guidance of scholars like Kamo Mabuchi (1697–1769) and Motoori Norinaga (1730–1801) in the eighteenth century. Toward the end of his life Motoori began to show sensitivity to contemporary conditions and recommended ways of averting social failure. Although he was the most gifted and original practitioner of *kokugaku*, a man whose range of interest was truly prodigious, it was one of his self-styled students, Hirata Atsutane (1776–1843), who virtually transformed the nativist discourse in the late eighteenth and early nineteenth centuries into a discipline of knowledge addressed to specific interests.

This transformation resulted in a radical shift from poetic studies (which were carried on by Motoori's adopted son and successor, Motoori Ōhira) to practical religiosity and a preoccupation with daily affairs. Under Hirata's reformulation, nativism left the cities, where people like Motoori had lectured to wealthy townsmen and samurai, for the countryside, where the message was appropriated and even altered by the rural rich as a response and a solution to the apparent incompetency of the control system to provide security against disorder and assistance to the general peasantry. The immediate target of the peasants' discontent was invariably the village leadership and the rural rich. Thus nativism, as it became a discourse representing the leading elements in the countryside, constituted a break with its original purpose and character. This is not to say that Hirata and his followers abandoned their original tenets. Hirata had started his career as a conventional student of *kokugaku*, and his earliest writings in this idiom concentrated on poetry and aesthetics. Early in the nineteenth century he broke with the main line of *kokugaku* and began to emphasize a different position, but he was still very much dependent on earlier formulators like Kamo Mabuchi and Motoori Norinaga. Hirata tended to give weight and emphasis to ideas and elements in nativist thought that had, in earlier studies, remained recessive. The result was a new mapping of nativism and a plotting of its structure of thought to make it appear different. Hirata's mapping was virtually transformed into a new discipline, the study of the Japanese spirit (*yamatogokoro no gakumon*), whose subject would now be the "ancient Way" (*kodōron*) rather than language and poetry. Later followers like Ōkuni Takamasa (1792–1871) reshaped these new formulations into a systematic field of knowledge that Ōkuni called "basic studies" (*hongaku*) or into a unified doctrine that Yano Gendō (1823–1887) referred to as "the study of basic doctrine" (*honkyōgaku*).

Adopted into a family of doctors, Hirata Atsutane appeared on the scene in the late eighteenth century and opened a school in Edo. He claimed to have studied with Motoori, but there is no record that he did. Almost immediately he became known as an outspoken critic of contemporary custom and urban mores. Intemperate to a fault, excitable but self-possessed, Hirata's special targets were scholars of all stripes, but especially Confucians (*bunjin*), whom he identified with writers of verbal fiction, and vulgar Shintoists. In his discussions on the practice of worship (*Tamadasuki*, 1828) he struck hard against contemporary preoccupations with poetic parody, wordplay, and *gesaku* fiction. Thus although he excoriated writers of verbal fiction for confusing people, his own concerns aimed at providing the ordinary folk with more useful instruction. Ordinary people served as both the subject of his lectures and the audience or object. He talked to them about themselves and their daily lives. Texts like the *Ibuki oroshi* and the *Tamadasuki* employed the language of daily speech, often the same idiom found in *gesaku*, and projected a vernacular voice studded with references to both the "ordinary person" (*bonjin*) and to things constituting their world. Yet it was precisely this juxtaposition between the "ordinary" and "extraordinary" (emphasized by Motoori in his discussions of aesthetic sensibility) that Hirata hoped to dramatize in his denunciations of contemporary scholars, poets, and writers. To underline this stance, he rejected the status of scholar for himself, as if by doing so he was cementing his ties to an audience of ordinary street people. "This humble person hates scholars. . . . The scholars of Edo do not devote themselves to bringing people together. Still, the ordinary people are not nauseating. Because it is good to assemble people together, I am fond of this kind of association. If you ask a commoner, he will speak, but ordinarily he does not like [to listen to] a scholarly tale."

Hirata boasted that there were many like himself among the ordinary folk, who simply did not consider themselves as scholars.[46] Specifically, "scholars are noisy fellows who explain the Way. Such people as Confucians, Buddhists, Taoists, Shintoists, and intuitionists broaden a bad list indefinitely." Scholars feared obeying the "sincerity of august national concern" and avoid "emphasizing the court" in their studies. In the end, Hirata added, they poisoned the people's intention and neglected the emperor. "Even though there is an

abundance of men in society who study, what fools they all are!" The reason
for this "habit" was that there were simply too many men "who despise the
eye and respect the ear." It was far better to study the "words and sayings of
men who are nearby, men of our country, rather than the sayings of foreigners
or only the deeds expressed by ancient men." Hirata's criticism sought to
show that arcane knowledge monopolized by scholars had no relevance to
large numbers of people; the immediate was more useful than the mediate,
and knowledge of what was "nearby" was prior to what was distant, remote,
and foreign.

If Hirata left no doubt of his dislike for contemporary scholars who knew
nothing about the present, he saw himself as a man devoted to studying the
"true Way" and as one who possessed "extensive knowledge of the truth."[47] He
believed that despite the army of erudite scholars inhabiting Edo, most were
addicted to the good life, the arcane, and the strange. They all were essentially
ignorant of the real goals by which ordinary people lived. His own lectures were
first directed to reaching townsmen, but by the 1830s, the rural population.
"Men of high rank have leisure time to read a great many books and thus the
means to guide people; men of medium rank do not have the time to look at
books and do not possess the means to guide people." Yet the ruled must be
offered assistance and the opportunity to hear about the Way, as it was as relevant to those who might not be able to read well as to those who did have leisure time. "I would exchange one man who reads books for one who listens,"
he announced to his audience, "for those who hear the Way have realized a
greater achievement than those who have reached it through reading."[48] Clearly
Hirata was claiming the necessity of offering representation of a different kind
of knowledge to the merely ordinary—those to whom Motoori had referred as
ideal but rarely had specified or tried to reach. Hirata's tactic for creating a discourse designed for the ordinary person resulted in a shift to discussing the
"ancient way" and showing that its content was no different from that of daily
life. "Great Japan," he said, "is the original country of all countries; it is the
ancestral country. From this standpoint the august lineage of our emperor has
been transmitted successively and rests with the great sovereign of all nations.
The regulations of all the countries are commanded and controlled by this sovereign." The *bakufu* and the managerial class were obliged to satisfy the "spirit
of Japan," which came to mean fulfilling the "august obligation to the spirit of
Tokugawa Ieyasu" by "serving" and "studying antiquity."

The immediate purpose of Hirata's thought was to allay popular fears concerning death and to provide consolation to the people. He believed that the
popular mind had become confused by fashionable explanations that made
people susceptible to the temptations of licentious and private behavior. It was
for this reason, after the 1790s, that he apparently turned his attention to the
lives of the ordinary folk. Yet it would be incomplete to say that his only goal

was to pacify the present. By centering on ordinary folk in discourse, Hirata provided a powerful warrant for independent action.[49]

Hirata's aim to offer consolation to ordinary folk involved a comprehensive strategy demonstrating the connection between all things and establishing a genealogy for that kinship. Connectedness showed family resemblances, and family resemblances revealed the relationship of all things, past and present, owing to the common and creative powers of the creation deities (*musubi no kami*). By promising unhappy contemporaries the prospect of consolation, Hirata and his followers resorted to a systematic classification capable of representing the relationship of all things. His own favored mode of relating was expressed in cosmological speculation (already pursued by a number of late eighteenth-century thinkers) which presumed to explain why it was impossible for the spirits of people to migrate after death to the dreaded and foul world of permanent pollution (*yomi*). The purpose of this form of speculation was to provide comfort to the large numbers of ordinary folk who, Hirata believed, feared death and consequently expressed their anxieties and unhappiness in activities such as peasant rebellions, escape to the cities, and self-indulgence in the privatized pleasures of the culture of play. Hirata's explanation (articulated in *Tama no mihashira*, 1818) was rooted in a fundamental division between "visible things" (*arawanigoto*) and "matters concealed and mysterious" (*kamigoto*). Although this classification between the seen and the unseen had been initially authorized by the *Nihon shoki*, it now demanded apprehending phenomena as being related in the modality of the part-whole relationship, which permitted reducing one thing to function as a substitute for another. Nativists were able to make this move because they believed that both realms were ultimately produced by the creation deities. Yet they valued the world of "hidden things" more than the visible world of the living and made the latter dependent on the actions of the former. Because the invisible realm had been originally identified with the kami's (deities) affairs, it was natural to see it as the source of the phenomenal world of living things. But by linking the visible to the invisible in this way and bonding conduct in the former to judgment in the latter, Hirata and his rural followers were able to offer representation and even meaning to the life of groups who had remained outside or on the margins of official discourse. Judgment of performance based on an assessment of morally informed behavior usually meant work and productive labor. Each individual was obliged to perform according to the endowment (set) bestowed on him at birth by the heavenly deities. Whatever one did in life was important and necessary.

Hirata's elaborate cosmology did more than simply enjoin the ruled, the ordinary folk whom he now called by the antique name *aohitokusa*, to fall into line and work hard.[50] The significant result of his reformulation of the relationship between divine intention and human purpose was to transform what hitherto had been regarded as an object into a knowing and performing subject. Accordingly, the ordinary folk now occupied a position of autonomy through the valorization of their quotidian life and the productivity of their daily labor. By arguing that the living inhabited the invisible world where the spirits and deities resided, Hirata was able to demonstrate the existence of a ceaseless transaction between creation and custom. Even though each realm was considered separate from the other, they were nonetheless similar in all decisive aspects, as the living were descendants of the spirits and deities. If creation was initially the work of the gods, it was maintained by humans who continuously created to fulfill their divine obligation of repaying the blessings of the gods. The two primal creation deities established the connection of the two realms at the beginning of heaven and earth.[51] For thinkers like Hirata, the conception of *musubi*, creativity and productivity, established the divisions, the classes of events and things, inner and outer affairs, human and sacred, visible and invisible, yet such categories attested to the integrated wholeness of life and its continuation from one generation to the next. The archetypal example of the creation deities making the cosmos continued to manifest its "necessity" down to the present in manifold ways: the procreation of the species, the production of goods, and the constant reproduction of the conditions of human community. *Musubi* also denoted linkages, the act of binding things together, and union, an observation made by Ōkuni Takamasa that served as the leading principle in the formulation of the theory of harmony (*wagō*).

Above all else, the most explicit sign for the continuing activity of the creation deities was agricultural work. Work constituted the guarantee that the creation would be reproduced in every generation and appeared as the bond holding the community together. Here, nativists offered it as an alternative to securing social solidarity, fully as effective as mere political obedience because it was associated with the sacred. In this way Hirata and his followers succeeded in shifting the emphasis from performing specific behavior-satisfying norms to the essence of life activity itself, work, now authenticated by the archetypal event of creation, as the measure of all real conduct in the visible realm. By altering an argument based on abstract principles governing power relationships to valorize concrete and practical mundane activities, the nativists had found a way to highlight the means of social reproduction and its realization as the content of discursive knowledge.

In rural Japan this nativist intervention had great consequences. The hidden world, once the domain of the gods, now became synonymous with the departed ancestors of the living. This identification between the hidden and the space occupied by the spirits of the living increasingly served to encourage folk religious practices emphasizing guardian deities, tutelary beliefs, and clan gods. Yet it also induced the community to concentrate on its own centrality in the great narrative of creation and the reproduction in custom. In texts like the *Tamadasuki* and the starchy enjoinment to daily worship, Hirata outlined in some detail the way that the most mundane forms of daily life interacted with worship and how the lives and activities of ordinary people represented a religious moment. Summoning daily life to such a discourse and linking it to worship and religious observances made archaism (*kodōron*) meaningful to wider audiences in rural Japan. To be sure, Hirata imagined these mundane activities as living examples of the archaic precedent and authoritative proof that no real disjunction separated the present from the preclass, folkic past. In his exposition the ancient Way, once identified with sincerity and ethics in poetry and theater, forfeited its privileged status to the ordinary folk living in the present. When peasant leaders who had passed through Hirata's school juxtaposed this concentration on the unity of work and worship, life and labor with their perception of rural unease, it appeared to offer a solution to unrelieved fragmentation, divisiveness, and the threat of decreasing productivity, as well as conferring a form of representation on their leadership. By rescuing the ordinary folk from the margins of official discourse, *kokugaku* could enforce a community of interests among the upper and lower peasantry and overcome the apparent ambiguity stalking the relationship between the village leaders and their followers.

That link was provided by the status of the ancestors and the centrality accorded to the village deities in binding the various parts of the village into a whole. Together, they constituted a world of relationships more real and fundamental than those found in the visible realm of public power. For the flow of ties, transactions, and traffic between the hidden world of the ancestors and tutelary deities and the visible realm of work and social relations disclosed a commonality of interest and purpose that transcended ascribed status and mundane ethical duties. The logic for this connection between work and worship in the rural setting was plainly prescribed by Hirata's systematization of ancestor respect within the larger framework of folkic religious practices. In these lectures, he was able to link people with their ancestors and the creation deities, explain the central importance of the clan deities (*ujigami*) and tutelary gods (*ubusuna no kami*), and show why the creation deities were so vital to the agricultural project. These explanations also became elements in the formation of a theory of village rehabilitation and self-strengthening. By identifying increased productivity and agricultural labor with religious devotion, by making work itself into a form of worship repaying the blessings of the gods, and by projecting a theory of consolation that promised immortality to the spirits and certain return to the invisible realms after death, Hirata and his followers were able to strike deeply responsive chords in the villages of the late Tokugawa period and present the prospect of resolving the problems of the countryside and reconstituting life anew along different lines.

The most obvious contact with village life was provided by the creation deities and the necessity to continue agricultural work. A variety of writers like

Satō Nobuhiro (1769–1850) and Mutobe Yoshika (1798–1863) pursued this connection further by showing how wealth originated in agricultural production
and how rural life corresponded to cosmic categories. Hirata had already, in
the *Tamadasuki*, established the necessary linkages among the creation deities,
the ancestors, and the households (*ie*) as indispensable to reproducing the social
means of existence. He argued that the spirits of the dead inhabited the same
place as the living and that they fixed the essential similarity between the invisible and visible realms. In an afterword to his inventory of daily prayers, Hirata
noted that it was as important to make observances to one's ancestors as it was
to other deities. Men who carried out household duties properly were also
obliged to pray to the deities of the *ie* and to the shelf reserved for the ancestors. One should also worship the various clan deities and the deities of
occupations.[52]

If the household represented the most basic and essential unit in Hirata's
conception of the invisible world, then the village defined its outermost limits.
Village, household, spirits (ancestors), and distant deities reaching back to the
creation gods constituted a series of concentric rings, one within the other,
linked by kinship. As Hirata's prayers to the ancestors called for protection and
good fortune of the household, so his invocation to the tutelary gods and guardian deities served to secure protection and prosperity for the village community. "Grant all protection to this village [*sato*]," the prayer intoned, "Before the
great tutelary deities we offer prudent respect. Protect the village day and night,
and grant it prosperity."[53] Hirata related these village shrines to the hidden
realm. "Regional spirits [*kunitamashii*] and the tutelary deities have been
directed to share the administration of the realm among themselves and to
assist Ōkuninushi no Kami, whose basis of rule is concealed governance."
Authority was manifest in the tutelary shrines of the various locales. While the
deities conferred protection and prosperity, a thankful community should offer
prayer, supplication, and hard work. Prayer and work meant the difference
between continued wholeness (order) and fragmentation and decreased productivity (disorder). Indeed, in Hirata's thinking it was natural to move from
formal religious observance to more enduring forms of gratitude, work. This
identification of worship and work was refined by others, but it is clear that
Hirata figured work as another way of talking about worship. His conception
of work was rooted in a concern for repaying the blessings of the kami. This
meant returning trust to the deities who had bestowed benefits. This trust, as
he pointed out, meant both the land that produced food and the material from
which clothing and shelter were made.

This sense of a powerful, hidden realm directing the fortunes of the living
represented a structural similarity with the world of the household and rural
community. It was a world symbolized by the authority of the tutelary shrines
(which themselves represented a manifestation of the invisible world) and hence

the place of the village, hidden, powerless in the realm of public authority, but nevertheless vibrant with "real" activity. Here the nativists, who, like the Mito writers, turned away from Edo, pitted a horizontal realm, close to nature and origins, against the vertical world of the Tokugawa *daikan*, daimyo, shogun, and even emperor. The hidden world of the village, deities, ancestors, and descendants was more "real" than was the visible world of power and consumption. Without the sanction of the hidden world, the idea of an autonomous village would not have been possible. At its most fundamental level, the world envisaged by the nativists was one of linkages and kin relationships. It was a realm where microcosm, the household and the village, served as a substitute for the macrocosm, the so-called national soil (*kunitsuchi*), where the emperor as a living deity met the tutelary deities and the ancestors administered by Ōkuninushi and where the vertical claim of public authority collided with the horizontal claims of village life.

In its rural appropriation, *kokugaku* sanctioned the elevation of the village as a substitute for the whole, just as Mito had projected the domain for the totality. The argument for an autonomous and self-sufficient village, removed from the centers of power, relied on people recognizing their duty to return the "blessings" to the creation deities from whom all things literally flowed. This meant replicating the archetypal act of creation through agricultural work and reproduction. Judgment and final authority lay in the hidden realm administered by Ōkuninushi no Kami, not the "living deity" who was the emperor. Duty was described as a form of stewardship that, as stated earlier, referred to the actual event in which the creation gods gave something to the other deities, the imperial descendants, and the land itself as a trust. Trust required repaying the divine gift with work. Late Tokugawa *kokugakusha* like Miyauchi Yoshinaga (1789–1843), Miyao (or Miyahiro) Sadao (1797–1858), and Hirayama Chūeimon (dates unknown) (all priests or village leaders) saw the idea of entrustment as the means to emphasize the central importance of agricultural life. It was in this context that Miyao, a Shimosa village leader, argued that the realm was founded on agriculture and that the village was the appropriate instrument for organizing people to work together in the countryside. Others saw the village and the household as one and the same. Miyauchi responded to what he believed were signs of fragmentation in rural life as an example of neglecting the imperial doctrine imparted by the two creation deities. Evidence appeared everywhere in "rebellion," "disorder," and "wastage," which Miyauchi attributed to improper leadership. Theoreticians like Ōkuni coupled this notion of proper village leadership with the idea of an administration pledged to taking care of the people (*buiku*). All agreed that *kokugaku* was a method for solving problems in the countryside. Even a high-ranking samurai nativist scholar like Ikuta Yorozu (1801–1837) (who followed the route of rebellion) believed that peasant disturbances would cease if good doctrine and leadership were administered to the villages. Such a method was dramatized in the formulation of a conception of relief and assistance (used also by the new religious groups) that would program stewardship. In the end, stewardship or entrustment became the grounds for village self-sufficiency and the justification for secession from the center.[54]

According to the rural nativists, all of this would be possible if proper knowledge were available. Miyauchi, for example, saw knowledge as the proper definition of the boundaries of order, whereby all persons knew what they were required to do and what was sufficient for their livelihood. When people violated established boundaries, they invited disaster. "If one does not extend [through work] the boundaries imposed by the heavenly deities, one will surely neglect his productive duties and be impatient toward them. . . . In the end it destroys the household and is the source of disaster."[55] Miyauchi's *Tōyamabiko* (1834) is sensitive to the frequency of rebellions and disorder, and the text's apparent purpose was to understand their causes in order to arrest their occurrence. The question Miyauchi asked was how not to forget what one was supposed to do. Selfishness undoubtedly turned people away from the established divisions and tempted them to excess. Excess transcended boundaries and could lead only to unhappiness and ruin. Those who had "exceeded their own boundaries," neglecting "household duties," had gone beyond "endeavoring" and had ceased to work. Working for the household brought order; work out of that context meant disorder. Such duty represented "entrustment" from one's parents and beyond them from ancestors and deities. Following the lead of Hirata, Miyauchi enjoined people not only to work but also to worship the ancestral deities and pray at the tutelary shrines. Like other rural nativists, he tried to remind contemporaries that because people had become so habituated to the uses of money, they had forgotten the source of wealth. "Treasure" (*takara*) was the word that many nativists used to designate the peasants (*hyakushō*), and by that they meant people working in the fields. Such people reflected a blessing of the gods, whereas offenders of divine injunctions, men who committed polluting acts (*tsumibito*), resembled "annoying pests" who gathered together to destroy the household. Such concerns led Miyauchi to examine the function of tutelary shrines as a focus for life, work, and worship, with a constant reminder of the necessity to "repay the blessings" of continued good fortune.

So powerful was this impulse to restructure village solidarity around the tutelary shrine that it became the basis of a nationwide movement in the 1840s. Another Shinto priest, Mutobe Yoshika, devoted his major texts to elucidating the connection between such shrines and the two creation deities. In his cosmological *Ken'yūjun kōron*, he proposed that the creation deities responsible for the procreation of humans were indistinguishable from the gods associated with the tutelary shrines. "These . . . deities reside in their *gun, ken, mura*, native place [*furusato*], and it is decreed that their ordinances are to be regulated by the tutelary gods."[56] Elsewhere he argued that the division according to fixed boundaries and deities representing various regions in the country meant that each place had its own tutelary god. The purpose of these deities, he declared, was that they informed people regularly of the "secret governance" of procreation and its administration. "In these places people daily grasp in their lives both the spirit of activity and calm from . . . the shrines."[57] Although the invisible government was not seen by mortals, it was manifest symbolically in the precincts of the shrines. They represented a bonding between the invisible realm and the visible and a guarantee of the continuing presence of the former in the world of the living. "The shrines of tutelary deities are very important," Mutobe wrote in the *Ubusunashako*. "Because that is the case, we must first offer daily prayer to these deities; next we should make regular visits to these shrines."[58] When such devotion and respect were carried out faithfully, there would be a guarantee of prosperity and abundance. Guided by this conviction, Mutobe was prompted in the 1840s to call for the establishment of a countrywide movement pledged to worship the tutelary deities.

Whereas writers like Miyauchi and Mutobe were shrine priests who emphasized the importance of worship, Miyao Sadao, who described himself as a "potato-digging village official," stressed the primary role of the village official. Yet his concerns for leadership and work reflected another way of talking about worship and respect and stressing the importance of making the village a self-sufficient economic and political unit. By advising peasants to understand and preserve the "commands of the *nanushi*, which are no different from the public ordinances [of the lord]," Miyao was envisaging the role of village leadership (in the manner of Mito writers writing about domainal leadership) as a substitute for the entrustment represented by the emperor, shogun, and daimyo, not as a challenge to officially constituted authority. His intention was merely to recognize that within the jurisdiction of the village, officials "must make the administration of the peasantry their chief duty." Most rural nativists acknowledged that the village, especially in bad years, would have to take responsibility for the extension of relief and assistance. This idea had been promoted earlier by agricultural writers of such differing persuasions as Ninomiya Sontoku and Ōhara Yūgaku. But assistance and relief, real necessities for village survival in the hardship years of the 1830s and 1840s, also underscored the primacy of collective purpose over private interest. It was seen as a method whereby the village, following the model of the household, would rely on its resources and its own efforts to reproduce the necessities of social life and thereby achieve a sense of the whole. This preoccupation with relief and mutual assistance, leading to the achievement of village autonomy and self-sufficiency, logically drew attention to the quality of local leadership. Promoting policies of strict economy meant urging the peasants to increase productivity for the sake of the village community as a whole under the informed guidance of agricultural sages, usually village officials, elders, and local notables (*meibōka*), instead of simply tightening their belts. Yet such leaders—Ninomiya, Ōhara, and rural nativists like Miyao believed—had to possess the right kind of knowledge of rural affairs in order to validate their authority.

For the rural nativists, knowledge meant "knowing about the kami." But to "know" about the kami meant also knowing about the ordinary folk. In other words, knowledge of the customary life of ordinary people was equivalent to knowledge of the deities, and vice versa. Village leaders were obliged to know both the divine intent of the gods and the conditions of daily existence that might satisfy the purpose of creation. Miyao described his own appointment as a divine trust that bound him—and all officials—to the duty of promoting self-sufficiency and economic self-reliance. This formulation concerning the identity of divine and human knowledge represented a transformation of an idea introduced earlier by Hirata. Whereas Ōkuni Takamasa catalyzed the formula into a discipline of learning in the 1850s, the rural nativists had already made its "content" a criterion for proper and authoritative leadership. Miyao in his *Kokueki honron* advised that the wealthy of the region properly instruct the people into the way of the kami. He shared with thinkers like Ninomiya and Ōhira the conviction that people had to be inculcated with the spirit of the work by showing them how their daily life related to a world larger than mere day-to-day subsistence and the paying of taxes. This meant teaching them about the necessity of producing children to increase the labor force and to ease the financial burden on the rural populations.[59] By the same token, village leaders must attend to famines, natural disasters, and the general well-being of the community. "Uneconomical policies," he asserted, "result in shame for the village, and the shame of the village becomes the shame of the lord."[60] Improper leadership always revealed a lack of knowledge and lack of piety before the deities. What Miyao feared most was the ever-present threat of conflict and division within the village. Its officials should promote harmony and "guide ignorant peasants." Their trust to administer well was even greater in hard times because they had "replaced the *daikan*." "During times of bad harvests," Miyao stated, "one cannot rely on the assistance of the regional lords and officials. One helps oneself with one's own savings and effort. One must understand that one should not bother or depend on the leaders in bad times."[61] To say this was to recognize that local autonomy and authority prevailed in the countryside.

Suzuki Shigetane (1812–1863), an independent student at the Hirata school and a casualty in the loyalist explosions of the 1860s, gave even sharper expression to this identification of trust and knowledge and the stewardship of local leadership. In *Engishiki norito kōgi* (1848) he presented the idea that officials do not differ from the emperor inasmuch as they are obliged to offer "mutual help

and assistance in the great august policy . . . to preserve the household enterprises given by the gods and make substance for food, clothing, and shelter."[62]
Suzuki was referring to the rural elite assigned to administer the communities
under their jurisdiction. Although he accepted a division within society, he was
convinced that each sector exercised a sacred trust to fulfill the divine obligations "to make things for other people in hard times." His student Katsura
Takashige (1816–1871), a village leader in Niigata, constructed an argument
whereby Suzuki's conception of "making the *kunitsuchi* habitable for the people" was enlisted to promote the primacy of village administration. In fact, writers like Suzuki and Katsura simply spoke of the village as if it were the larger
realm (*kunitsuchi*). In *Yotsugigusa tsumiwake* (1848), Katsura envisaged the village as the equivalent or adequate political form for the realm as a whole and
local leaders as exemplars for peasants. This should require no reliance on coercive measures, laws, or ordinances, as trust bound ruler to ruled. Such trust
was conveyed to the people through "preaching" and "exhortations" from elders
and superiors. He explained how this was to be done: "First, depend on the
Great August intention [heart] which deepens and widens the kami learning
of the people. . . . This learning is transmitted from court officials [priests] who
have made their own intention identical with the Great August Heart, down to
regional lords, county officials, village chiefs, and headmen, to the peasantry.
The peasants also receive and transmit this intention to each household in the
learning of the deities."[63]

The systemization of *kokugaku* into a discipline of knowledge was completed by Ōkuni Takamasa, who sought to show how "learning about the
kami" amounted to "learning about the ordinary folk." The term, he believed,
referred to the realm itself. In the age of the gods, he wrote in *Hongaku kyoyō*,
there had been three instances of entrustment, and two in the age of men. The
first of these was from the heavenly deities to Izanami and Izanagi; the second
from Izanami and Izanagi to Amaterasu (the formation of the moon and sun);
the third was Amaterasu's entrustment to the imperial ancestor Ninigi no
Mikoto.[64] For the human world, the two great grants were to Sukunabikona
and Ōkuninushi to solidify the realm and to make it habitable. Here was the
basis for a theory meant for local leaders searching for the authority to establish
an arrangement of mutual assistance and relief in the interest of a productive
and harmonious life, as well as the larger sanction for a restoration of antiquity. At the mythic level, this link was forged in the example of the grant to
Ōkuninushi to render and restore the national soil to human cultivation and
habitation, and at the historical level it appeared in demands for the local leadership and peasantry to live up to this trust.

Ōkuni structured these trusts and obligations within the framework of a discipline. He associated knowledge of the gods with knowledge of the ordinary
folk, without whom the creation would be meaningless and "talk about ruling

the realm useless." One must always view the times from the perspective of the ordinary people. No real distinction could be made between the customs of the gods and those of ordinary people. In *Yamatogokoro* (1848) Ōkuni wrote that the human species was divided into two categories. The Chinese called these two categories "great" and "small" men, but in Japan it had been the learning of the gods and the customs of the ordinary people. "When one learns about the deities, then even the small person will become a lord and great man, and when the lord and great man learns about the *aoihitogusa*, they will become as ordinary people."[65] A knowledge of origins (*moto*) thereby taught that the official was the base, and one's body, the ends. Together, they formed a reciprocal relationship. Yet in recent times, he continued, the ordinary people had reversed the order of things and had begun to consider their "bodies as the base." To do so resulted in pursuing pleasure and neglecting household duties. Moreover, this habit had affected the lords as well. Ōkuni warned the lower classes against imitating upper-class habits and advised them to "learn well the customs of the deities." He worried most about conflict and disharmony, division and fragmentation. Even though men had different faces and appearances, they were fundamentally the same because they were human.[66] Owing to divine intention, all humans were linked to one another by "mutual concern." When people conformed to this intention, times were good, but when they went against it, disaster ensued.

"The deeds of the gods join base to ends." Actualizing divine intention in practice resulted in the organization of a human community. But the ends of human activity represented the making of products from the natural material of the land granted by the gods. If the "customs of the ordinary people" (work, mutual assistance, relief) were successfully reunited with the customs of the gods, as specified in the ancient texts, then the true meaning of a harmonious union would be recovered and made manifest in the present. Indeed, the customs of the gods were equivalent to the "desires of the deities." The human impulse to help others expressed the desire and deeds of the gods. If the identification of godly deeds and human nature constituted the core of Ōkuni's thinking about politics, the installation of a harmonious community, wherein all were united by mutual assistance, became the form he envisaged for it as a displacement for contemporary institutions and administration. Because this form of human community existed before the establishment of all historical political structures and ordinances but had been forgotten in time, the present generation was appointed to restore it from memory to resolve the contemporary "crisis."

The *kokugaku* conception of work and mutual assistance was brought to completion by another rural writer from the Shimosa region, Suzuki Masayuki (1837–1871). Suzuki's central text, written just before the Restoration, was the *Tsukisakaki*, which tried to demonstrate that work was fundamental to life and that activity and performance represented the fulfillment of the cosmic plan. He attributed the "generation of all living things" first to the primal creation gods and then to the ancestral spirits. The spirits, he believed, were actually kami who had formerly been humans. The meaning of creation was, therefore, related to the "generation of life." Since the beginning of time, all "have endeavored similarly for the enterprise of generating life." Such an enterprise prevented conflict and disharmony. Excesses everywhere, Suzuki noted, could be avoided if people pursued the completion of virtue by working to generate life. Yet the generating of life bespoke mutual assistance, much in the manner that it had been conceptualized by Ōkuni Takamasa. "To work by and for oneself," Suzuki wrote, "will, in general, fail to bring about an accomplishment" of the great enterprise.[67] Like many nativists, Suzuki appealed to the body as a model, not to specify never-ending pleasures but to represent the unity symbolized by household and village. The eyes see, he declared, the ears hear, the mouth speaks, the hands hold, and the feet move; each part relies on "mutuality" in order for the whole—the body—to operate. Suzuki then projected this metaphor to describe people working together as the key to realizing the great enterprise. If any part fails to assist the other, the body will collapse into dysfunction, just as neglect of reciprocity in work will terminate the "generation of life" and plunge the realm into disorder.

Suzuki was convinced that destruction of the work ethic would drive the realm into riot and rebellion, forcing people to turn against one another and transforming Japan into the image of China. Ultimate responsibility for the interruption of life-generating activity, however, belonged to the lords, and not to village officials. Lords obstructed and often prevented people from performing work. Suzuki went further than most nativists to portray the disruption and discontinuity between ruler and ruled and showed how kokugaku, in creating a discourse centering on the producer—the ruled—would hold the leadership responsible for interfering in activities necessary to the continuation of life. The lord, like the parent, provided the conditions for life-giving activity; the land constituted the basis of this activity. But although this arrangement reflected a positive good, it could also turn into evil. Work and productivity could be misused by the lord for private and selfish purposes. Private desire drove the realm into a "deep valley." Higher loyalties to the land and to the deities should be repaid with life-generating work. Suzuki's explanation of private desire rested on the conviction that confusion was caused by "evil doctrines." It was necessary to "jettison the evil and mistaken doctrines of foreign countries [China] and return to the original intention . . . to cast off contemporary abusive customs in order to study the ancient minds." In his last, post-Restoration text on local government, Suzuki pointed to the village as the crucible for carrying on life-generating activity and an autonomous administration as the surest defense of proper doctrine.

Religions of Relief

Commenting on the contemporary religious situation, the author of *Seji kem-monroku* roared, "In today's society, the representatives of Shinto and Buddhism resemble national traitors. All the kami have ascended to heaven; the Buddhas have left for the Western Paradise; and all present and other worlds have fallen into disuse. Providence and retribution have been exhausted. All the Buddhist priests have fallen into hell and have ended [their mission] by becoming sinners."

Buyō Inshi's astringent condemnation of religious life in the Bunka-Bunsei era, like his sweeping renunciation of social life, may have been hyperbolic, but it signified a general playing out of older, more established religious forms at a time when people were beginning to search for new kinds of meaning and faith. Hirata Atsutane was already in the streets of Edo denouncing the vulgar Shintoists, the deceiving Buddhists, and the "stinking Confucianists." Provincial life was beginning to show renewed interest in more basic, nativist forms of religious practice. In the spring of 1830 large numbers of people from several areas of Japan streamed toward the Grand Shrine at Ise. This mass movement, numbering in the hundreds of thousands, was the most recent of periodic pilgrimages to the shrine of Amaterasu. The pilgrimage disintegrated into disorder and violence. It had no disciplined structure (although many groups were organized as *kō* for this explicit purpose), and it is not clear who its leaders were. But people were prompted to leave their households and villages—men, women, even children—to make the long and often perilous trek to Ise. The greater portion of pilgrims were from the lower classes, and even though they were proscribed from making the visitation, they nonetheless felt compelled to leave their work, families, children, parents, wives, and husbands to make the journey to Ise. Some writers proposed that the pilgrimages represented an enlargement of the late Tokugawa impulse for travel. If it is true that the pilgrim experienced momentary release, freedom, or even a sense of unconnectedness while traveling on the road, the pilgrimage was nonetheless religious or political in its intensity. Travel, propelled by religious zeal, offered temporary release from the harsh uncertainties of everyday life, the very same life that *kokugaku* scholars had made the centerpiece of their new discipline of learning. It also heightened awareness of the power that large groups could command. "We have stimulated an earthquake and unleashed the august virtue of the Grand Shrine; the heart moves Japan. We have unleashed the august good omen in the pilgrimage, and it is called an earthquake; the heart moves the country of Japan," so announced a contemporary riddle.[68] The pilgrimage of 1830 also dramatized questions of social surplus, fragmentation, poverty, and the prospect of even greater disorder. People went on such pilgrimages for many reasons. Some even had a good time, but many were driven by hopes of divine relief, assistance, and the desire for good fortune. The experience signified both a new religious zeal and a concomitant search for new forms of community. It also disclosed what had become disturbing and disquieting about the tenor of life for large numbers of ordinary people.

It was in this context of a massive search for divine assistance and relief, and the quest for new forms of communitarian and voluntary association, that a number of new religious groups appeared in the late Tokugawa decades. Along with the establishment of new, syncretic religious organizations, some older sects, like the *nembutsu* sects and Fujikō, also underwent renewal and revitalization. But it is important to note that the new religions, like Mitogaku and *kokugaku*, represented a departure from past and more established religious forms that, many believed, had been played out. Like other discourses in the late Tokugawa period, the new religious message reflected the operation of a strategy that sanctioned bringing together older ideas, elements, and practices into new combinations. Organizationally the new groups like Tenri, Konkō, Kurozumi, and Maruyama sought to realize the promise of voluntary association (as against the involuntary association demanded by "nature") and horizontal relations by reconstituting themselves as autonomous communities. These new religions recruited their followers from the broad stratum of society but appealed largely to the lower classes. Their recruitment signified both the attempt of the people to represent themselves in a discourse, by centering themselves and their lives as its subject, and a criticism of Tokugawa social conditions. In this connection Professor Yasumaru Yoshio has written, "In order to criticize society as a whole from the standpoint of popular thought, which tended to make humility, submission, and authoritarianism as its substantive element, a great leap was necessary. The mediation that made this leap possible took on a . . . character that was, in many cases, religious. The new popular religions offered an ideal . . . that transcended the authority of the contemporary feudal system."[69]

Like *kokugaku*, many of the new religions were disposed to blend elements of myth with contemporary history as a means to create new forms of expression and interpretation. Moreover, they were often driven by the same impulse to ascertain the "real." Their solution, which led to even more radical secessions, disclosed an obsession with autonomy and the desire to remove their followers from the contagions of contemporary history and the corruption of the center. The most extreme example of this obsession was the *yonaoshi* (world renewal) movements and *ee ja nai ka* (ain't it grand?) outbursts of the last years of the Tokugawa period, whose constituencies were usually the same people against whom both Mito and *kokugaku* sought to find protection by granting relief and assistance. Recalling the intentionality informing both Mito discourse and nativism, the new religions consistently projected an unpolitical stance in the promotion of new programs and new relationships based on different conceptions of knowledge, even though their activities resulted in political consequences. Adherents to these sects often saw themselves as providing pockets of productivity and relief in a context of scarcity and unrelieved hardship, rather than as challenging the established world of politics and public authority. But when they sought to eliminate the divisiveness of politics by dissolving the collectivity into autonomous religious communities, they instead contributed to the very political fragmentation that they were seeking to displace. In the move to establish the principle of autonomy and wholeness, in which they apparently saw neither, the new religions withdrew from the center and offered their own interpretation of contemporary history by rejecting it. At the periphery, they believed that they would find a place sufficiently removed from the corrosions of temporality to establish new political forms growing out of the content of culture. An apprehension of the world in this manner was equivalent to changing it in order to secure the necessary communal arrangements that conformed to the new forms of knowledge and conceptions of human nature. Nowhere was this commitment to acting and changing the world expressed in greater extremity than in those groups yearning for "world renewal" (*yonaoshi*).

If the new religions strove to recapture an original experience of wholeness, they also believed that the horizontal relationships that their belief authenticated came before the vertical ties demanded by the "discrimination of names" and the Tokugawa status system. This was their most distinctive and dangerous contribution to the general discussion in late Tokugawa society. All looked to the establishment of a genuine human order organized along horizontal relationships devoted to realizing equality. By the same token the new religions showed sensitivity to the way that distinctions caused social inequality. Consequently they announced their determination to find forms of organization calculated to diminish the reliance on hierarchy. The form favored by most recalled the traditional *kō*, groups of believers in which every member served as an equal partner, which characterized the groups participating in the *okage-mairi* (i.e., Isekō) and merchant investment societies.[70] Under the sanction of an egalitarian organization, the new religions projected an image of relief, mutual assistance to all followers, and even reform of existing structures by calling for the equitable distribution of land and resources. At the heart of their programs was the valorization of daily life and its importance for maintaining the solidarity of community. Although their organizational principle emphasized human connectedness (the brethren) and the necessity of working and living together in mutual reciprocity as a solution to the fragmentation of more established social units that had taken place with the commercialization of the countryside, it also made equality the condition for sustaining community.[71] The new religions sought to console the spiritually and materially poor who occupied the lowest rungs of the social scale of Tokugawa Japan. In their understanding of the times, people who were "poor" were also "unhappy," and only association and mutual cooperation could alleviate that state.

What enabled the new religions to interpret contemporary reality in this way and to claim interest in the poor and unhappy was a special conception of knowledge and of learning. They all substituted faith and belief in the powers of deity for conventional sources of solace. Faith and belief appeared to be comparatively rational, as the new religions made an effort to discourage believers from relying on superstition and traditional magical practices.[72] In parting from the more structured sects of Buddhism in which Tokugawa regulations had required villagers to register, they also represented a direct search for new forms of knowledge and belief, often promising health and happiness, that met the needs of daily life. In this they could be related also to the focus on utility that characterized Mito and *kokugaku* thought. Thus Konkōkyō proposed that "learning [*gakumon*], without belief, never assists people," whereas the founder of Tenri, Nakayama Miki, advised her believers that only faith could enable people to know the exalted state and secure relief from contemporary suffering and hardships. Kurozumi Munetada, founder of the Kurozumi sect, constantly admonished his followers to stop "worrying about the Way" in order to "know and transmit the virtue of Amaterasu to people of the times."

It is important to note that many of the new religions originated in localities where newer commercial arrangements were in the process of disturbing older modes of production and social relationships and where economic distress seemed to be the most severe. In large part this observation describes the frequency and distribution of peasant rebellions as well and suggests why the new sects often ended up recruiting the same kind of people who were willing to join rural jacqueries. Owing to the regional nature of economic hardship, many of the new religions enlisted local nativistic practices and traditions to familiarize their messages when recruiting a followership. Yet it is undeniably true that many struck deep roots in regional and village religious practices associated with Shinto and shamanism and that they derived their authority from a broadened base of shrine Shinto and religious conventions related to agricultural life.[73] But the appropriation of older, local practices frequently betrayed the limited appeal of such groups and revealed the intimate relationship between regional hardship and the construction of consoling ideologies, even though many of these religions projected a universal message.

In general, these sects promoted doctrines calling for the regime of relief everywhere, according to the blessings of a single and all-powerful kami who represented a first principle (or principal), whether it was Amaterasu Ōmikami of Nyorai and Kurozumi, Tenri Ōmikami of Tenri, Tenchikane of Konkōkyō, Mount Fuji of Fuji *kō*, or Moto no Oyagami of Maruyama *kō*. Such deities supplied authority for claims promising to offer relief and assistance and contrasted dramatically with the rather discredited obligations of the feudal order to provide benevolence and aid in times of need. It is also true that nativists assigned a comparable role to the creation deities and to the tutelary shrines, even though they emphasized the human capacity for self-help. In many instances, these all-powerful gods were seen as creators of the cosmos and progenitors of the human species. And the reliance on a reliever who bore striking resemblance to the Buddhist Miroku (Maitreya) or simply to one who possessed kami character explained to the poor and the beleaguered the necessity for help and assistance among humans and why it was absent in their time. The effectiveness of this explanation often depended on the powers of the founder of a sect to demonstrate the efficacy of his or her knowledge and charismatic powers. Unlike nativism, which often diminished the powers of the person for the spirit of the word (*kotodama*), the new religions relied principally on performance to validate the message. Part of this reliance on the performative act stemmed from a distrust for conventional forms of knowledge based on the primacy of words and abstractions, yet part of it was undoubtedly inspired by the emphasis on the body and on the importance of its movements, whether in play or in physical work, in late Tokugawa thought. What appears important is the emphasis on the performative powers of the body and its kinship with manual rather than mental activity. This projection, of course, reflected the primacy of daily life. It is, in any case, this factor that accounts for the difficulty in dissociating the religious career of the founders from the discourse that they helped construct and in separating actual demonstration and action from verbal utterance. Frequently, the performance model of the founder became a text for the followers to read, as a source for correct knowledge, just as the body served as a text in verbal fiction.

The founder's performance depended on a successful appropriation of elements from shamanistic practice related to kami possession and healing spiritual powers. Many of the new religions resorted to the convention of identifying the founder of the sect as a "living kami" (*ikigami*), a designation that the nativists reserved for the emperor. The act of describing the founder as a living god, mediating between the primal voice and the followers and supplying his or her body as a vessel to convey the deity's wishes to the faithful, added authenticity to the autonomous doctrine that each was trying to articulate. The process whereby in most cases this new persona was realized began with the founder's illness (later interpreted as time spent with the primal deity), followed by divine intervention and speedy recovery, which led to a change in personality, which in turn bore fruit in miraculous cures among the local inhabitants and was accompanied by periodic trances to reinforce the new charisma. The ritualization of the founder's life into a drama of living kami undoubtedly served the same purpose as the Mito celebration of the timeless presence represented by the *daijōsai* and the nativist enshrinement of tutelary worship as a technique for securing continuous contact with the creation deities and the work of Ōkuninushi no Kami.

To explain a world based on knowledge that only initiates could know (closely resembling *kokugaku*'s valorization of the activities of daily life) risked provoking conflict with the authority system, which had its own claims to a privileged knowledge entitling certain people to rule and its stated responsibility to provide benevolence. Even so, some of the new religions, like Tenri and Maruyama, developed doctrines announcing "world renewal" in the present and the beginning of a new heaven on earth. So powerful was the appeal of this ideal that by the end of the epoch, world-renewing rebellions and *ee ja nai ka* disturbances in cities like Kyoto and Osaka were proclaiming their cause in slogans of relief and assistance to the people. Despite the world-renewal project, such revolutionary utopianism usually drew attention to this-worldly temporal orientations. All the sects, including the revitalized *nembutsu* organizations like the *myōkōninden*, spoke of "extreme happiness in this world" and underscored the necessity to find contemporary answers to prayers requesting the kami to eliminate struggle and "correct illness and disease." Tenri insisted on making a "fresh start beyond death" and enjoined its followers to concentrate on their daily lives without fear or anxiety concerning their fate after death. Underlying this attitude was the conviction that humans, not nature, were the standard of action or behavior, just as the present, rather than some remote and transcendent sanctuary in the future or elsewhere, was the place for carrying out the duties of the daily life. Here again is a close resemblance to the claims of late Tokugawa verbal fiction and woodblock illustrations with its own elevation of human subjectivity as the maker of society and custom. In the case of the new religions, primacy of the human, regardless of status, was intimately related to the process of becoming a kami. Doctrines like Konkō and Tenri, for example, joined humans to the deities by employing such familistic metaphors as "children of the kami" or "family of the deities." Yet such reference to the divine merely reinforced the essential kinship that it was believed all humans shared, regardless of status, class, sex, or even race. To be human meant promoting programs of relief and assistance to all folk, whose destitute and often impoverished lives constituted the touchstone for recruitment into the new religions. Konkōkyō constantly dramatized the importance of "men who assist other men" as the major criterion of being human, whereas Nakayama Miki exhorted her followers to "never forget other men"—not just people of abundance, the rural rich, merchants, and managers, but the diligent and nameless people about whom official discourse had been silent, who now inhabited the "bottom of the valley" (*tanizoku*). Social division itself, it was held, set people against one another and created the circumstances of conflict and struggle between the rich and the needy. The purpose of programs pledged to relieving the poor was a radical presumption of the equality of all individuals and between the sexes and the promise to redistribute wealth and land. Behind this call was the sustaining power of human love for others and a dangerously optimistic belief in the essential goodness of human nature.

Among the late-Tokugawa religions the most representative sects, which also captured the largest followings, were Kurozumi, Tenri, and Konkōkyō. Kurozumi was the earliest and was founded by Kurozumi Munetada (1780–1850) in Okayama Prefecture. He was born in a village in Bizen, the son of a Shinto priest of Imamura Shrine, a guardian deity of Okayama Castle. His mother was the daughter of a priest. When Munetada was in his thirties, he contracted tuberculosis, after losing his parents who apparently also died of infectious disease, and was confined for a year and a half. His illness and confinement solidified his resolve to devote his efforts to securing assistance from the sun goddess for the ill, diseased, and downtrodden. It has been reported that he aspired to become a "living deity" and felt cheated because of the imminent threat of death, deciding that after death he would become a deity devoted to healing the ill. But Munetada survived and recovered after experiencing unity with Amaterasu while venerating the rising sun at the winter solstice. Upon recovering, he began a new ministry of cures, teaching his first followers the lesson he had learned about the sun and the benefaction and compassion of Amaterasu. Success led to disciples and the establishment of a formal organization.

Kurozumi's doctrine was based on conversion to the sun goddess. He advised people to know how to concentrate their devotion on the august virtue of Amaterasu; the light of the sun goddess had not changed for an eternity and wanted the "august intention of Amaterasu" and the people's intention to become united.[74] Like other founders, Kurozumi was convinced of the possibility of becoming identified with the deity. This devotion undoubtedly derived from his own religious background, but his focus on the singularity and superiority of the sun goddess also offered a way to overcome the claims associated with other deities prevalent among traditional agricultural believers. Hereafter relief and assistance were to be related to the saving powers of a single deity. In time such relief came to range from simple cures to the prolongation of life, abundance, having children, easy delivery, increased success in trades and business, bumper crops, and larger fishing catches, all things that would make life easier.[75] If Amaterasu were idealized as the sun and the source of life, then life itself would find meaning only within the confines of her powers. Hence Kurozumi advanced a conception of enclosure (found in other doctrines as well) bounded by belief and occupied by the faithful. In a letter he confessed that there "was no special way to relate this basic unity [between believer and sun goddess] outside this circle (O)."[76] This imagery of the circle was scattered throughout his writings and referred to an enchanted enclosure free from desire and misfortune. In the early 1840s he wrote,

The Way is easy to serve, even though we can see that some do not serve it easily. To serve this Way is to live in it. This Way, as I have repeatedly stated, is
Amaterasu Ōmikami. That is, it is the circular deity. As I have said before,
things should be entrusted to this circle. It is easy to leave things to this Way,
and it is very strange that people in China and Japan have not been aware of
this. They are perplexed by the name of the Way. Men who have been separated from the true Way are all under heaven. Not to be separated from the
true Way is the Way I have been talking about.[77]

If all things were done gratefully, the "august intention of Amaterasu Ōmikami"
would be satisfied.[78]

To explain the grace provided by the circular enclosure made it appropriate
to develop an idea of order faithful to its requirements. The central principle
lay in the deity's capacity to fulfill all requests. When individuals entrusted
themselves to the sun goddess's ordinances, they were immediately relieved of
evil. To enter the enclosure meant leaving the world of suffering and misfortune, and as the epoch came to a close, followers increasingly read that to mean
the Tokugawa social system. Kurozumi's message presupposed the power of the
deity to deliver people's requests. By locating all blessings in the sun goddess,
he was able to place his principal emphasis on the believers' faith in the deity
and their willingness to make the effort to improve conditions. Kurozumi held
that the unification of the believers' intention with that of Amaterasu meant
that people themselves had to show by faith and goodness they were deserving.
Failure to secure grace or blessing revealed only one's unworthiness and lack
of real faith. Next came the idea that all people were brothers and sisters. This,
too, resulted from the conception of a united intention. "When assisting," he
wrote in a poem, "there is life."[79] Life was accessible to all. Kurozumi believed
that all people were ultimately children of the sun goddess. "There are none who
do not give thanks sincerely; one truth is that all in the four seas are brothers."[80]
With the universalistic thrust of this idea, its immediate purpose was to stem
contemporary conflict and distrust. The idea promoted a powerful sense of
equality and sharing. Things are important, Kurozumi wrote, but they do not
constitute criteria by which to separate people between the esteemed and
despised. Neither life nor death, high nor low can separate people from one
another. In this connection Kurozumi sought to juxtapose the spirit of sun
(light and happiness) to the principle of darkness. According to Kano Masanao,
the dark, or *in* (yin), principle was the symbol for the peasants' circumstances;
it was precisely the association manifest in the status order that made the peasant low man in the hierarchy. "The august belief in the sun goddess (projecting the symbol of light—*yō* [yang])—increasingly dispels the spirit of darkness." If too much attention were devoted to darkness, to the exclusion of the
principle of light, it would ultimately lessen and destroy the spirit of light.

Kurozumi believed that a balance between the two would fulfill the expectation of a perfect and complete society, perhaps the circle he had drawn to dramatize the sacred space designated for believers. His conception of the social order was revealed in his meditations on the circle. For the circle, the sun, light, Amaterasu represented fullness, plenitude, presence, perfection—surely an attractive alternative when juxtaposed to the received arrangement of authority. Kurozumi saw the installation of this new age of the kami as a veritable Utopia glowing in the midst of progressive social darkness. "The age of the gods and of the present are one; they offer compassion to all at the end of the world."

More than Kurozumikyō, Tenri was implicated in the trials of the oppressed and conveyed the sense that the present constituted a time of crisis. It was founded by a peasant woman near Nara, Nakayama Miki (1798–1887), who was oppressed by her family and her husband and knew hardship, pain, and personal suffering. Miki's biographers have attributed her zeal for helping people to her personal experience. But Nakayama Miki also had a keen grasp of political realities; she was a sensitive recorder of the Tempō famine and an understanding witness of the *okagemairi* pilgrims who passed through her village on their way to Ise. The pilgrimage and the famine signified suffering for her and showed the necessity of finding ways to provide relief and assistance. As with Kurozumi Munetada, Miki's life unfolded as a series of cases of caring for the needy and the poor. Self-sacrifice, ascetic zeal, and a sense of injustice propelled her on her ministry. According to Carmen Blacker, Miki's ministry was marked by a number of important "tribulations" in which she was able to demonstrate her powers to heal the afflicted.[81] In time she was credited with the powers of a local shaman (*yamabushi*). In one session, when Miki was beginning to chant the incantatory spells, her face began to contort, and she fell into a trance. While still possessed by a deity she replied to a question that she was Ten no Shōgun, "the true and original god who has descended from Heaven to save mankind."[82] In the presence of her husband and others, the kami who had come to inhabit her body asked Miki to abandon her family to serve as the vehicle and messenger for the divine work of assistance. Should her husband refuse to comply, the deity threatened to cast the family under the pall of a curse. This trance lasted three days, and only after Miki's husband consented to the divine demand did Miki return to normal. She experienced subsequent signs of divine origin as part of her passage into a new state. The sudden fits of possession and her erratic behavior as a condition for her ministry led to ostracism and poverty, but her success in healing, especially with respect to painless childbirth, brought her followers and the beginnings of an organization.

Miki's transformation into a divine vehicle for relief began when, commanded to give up her possessions, she decided to distribute her family land. The act dramatized personal attachment to land and the belief that ownership itself was the source of all inequality. Because equal distribution under conditions of ownership is impossible to realize, true equality can be realized only through abject landlessness. Miki's behavior underscored her teaching that "one must fall into poverty." Poverty and relief from pain became the axis of her vision. This vision was further reinforced within the structure of a cosmological myth, derived from native myth, legend, and history. According to this, the world originated in a muddy ocean (the salty brine of *kokugaku*) inhabited by a variety of fish and serpents. Because the parent deities wished to create humans, they gave birth to myriads of people on the site of the Nakayama household in Japan. These grew to great size and died. After this, the deities had created birds and beasts and a variety of insects; these also died. All that was left were monkeys. From the monkeys, men and women were born; then heaven, earth, mountains, and plains were differentiated. Humans lived first in water for eons and eventually moved onto the land. It is interesting to compare this crudely evolutionary conception with Hirata's earlier assertion that all humans originated from the insect world.[83] Although such notions were indispensable to the peasant experience, steeped as it was in a firsthand involvement in the cycle of growth, they also showed how earlier concerns for natural history had become part of a prevailing consciousness. Moreover, such an evolutionary process demonstrated the common origins of equality among all people and validated Miki's articulation of a Utopian vision in her hymn *Mikagurauta* (1869).

This long text, written in Nara dialect, focused on increased agricultural productivity. "The intention of everybody in the world requires fields and lands,"[84] "if there are good fields, everybody in a row will be cleansed of desire,"[85] and it would be possible to increase the abundance of Yamato through the unlimited powers of the deities.[86] Miki also sang her expectations of social reformation: "Drumbeat, the New Year's dance begins / How wonderful; if we erect a structure for teaching / What prosperity! Revering the body and securing health / *yonaori*."[87] Related to the idea of "world renewal" was, of course, the ideal of mutual assistance which was the central theme of both the *Mikagurauta* and her instructions (*Ofudesaki*). The hymn opens with a celebration that all people will be one when they assist one another. Assistance will also confer the blessings of the spirit of light: "If one speaks the faith in the wider world, one and then two will be cleansed by helping each other." Assisting people will bring freedom and an eternal abode in the heart of the kami. Disturbances can be dispelled by recognizing the fundamental equality of all humans. "When one compares humans from the standpoint of the body," Miki wrote, "they all are the same, whether high or low." Once more, it should be noted, we encounter the metaphor of the body and its centering as subject, known by acting; it is the body, not status, that confirms humanity; not the trappings of civilization, but the blessings of the gods.

To neglect the ordinances of the kami and to fail to work for universal relief and assistance were to incur divine wrath. In order to ward off anger and forestall misfortune, repentance was necessary. In this context Miki pointed to the quality of late-Tokugawa leadership and its failure to deliver relief and help. She characterized the leadership as high mountains, remote and distant from the ordinary folk who dwelt in the valleys and in the real world. But the power of the kami was vastly stronger than the power of "those who are high and make the world's conditions as they are; will they know about the misfortunes of the deities?"[88] Indeed, she had no hesitation in calling attention to the "contrast in intention between the kami and those in high places." The false division between high and low constituted a sign of the way that things were and the conditions of life that had to be overcome. People would change, she was convinced, because humans were "the children of the gods" and possessed a good nature. Their problem was pride (*hokori*). Pride, for Miki, was the basic human evil and produced the "eight dusts"— desire, regret, sweetness, avarice, arrogance, hatred, rancor, and anger—qualities she associated with the powerful. The powerless were advised to trust themselves to the deity of world renewal, who held out for them the promise of a renovated moral life. How the gods were to bring about this idealized world was already prefigured in Miki's conception of assistance and relief. It was, as Yasumaru Yoshio explained it, the world vision of small cultivators and encompassed diligent and frugal peasants bound together in a community of cooperation.[89]

Konkōkyō was established by a peasant named Kawate Bunjirō (Konkō Daijin) (1814–1883) in Bitchū, also part of present-day Okayama Prefecture. Adopted into a rural family, Kawate, unlike Kurozumi and Nakayama, was deeply versed in agricultural affairs. The area was marked by commercialization and a subsequent decline of smallholding farmers. The founder experienced a long life punctuated by hardship and poverty, and this undoubtedly prompted his deep concerns for the unrelieved hardship among cultivators of the vicinity. The boundaries of his own thought were marked by his desire to secure relief from contemporary circumstances and a zeal for bringing about order and prosperity. His religiosity was early revealed in a decision to make the trek to Ise with fellow villagers during the Ise *okagemairi* of 1830. Several years later (1846) Kawate made still another pilgrimage to the Grand Shrine. His personal ministry was interrupted by bouts of illness, and it ultimately brought on a trance that disclosed to him his true identity as the brother of Konjin, one of the calendar gods of the yin-yang tradition observed in rural areas. In folk belief this deity was capable of inflicting great harm or abundant prosperity, depending on how he was worshipped. Kawate received the ordinances of this god into his body which, as with Nakayama Miki, became the instrument for the "august intelligence" (*oshirase*). Kawate also received permission from the deity to be called the "family Kane no Kami's lower leaves" and to take the divine appellation of "Bunji Daimyōjin."

Once Kawate, or as he now came to be called, Konkō Daijin, served as the vessel of Konjin's *oshirase*, the popular understanding of that kami was transformed. A figure that had been associated with curse and calamity became a kami of love who brought good fortune and abundance to those who followed his commandments. As the instructions of the kami proliferated and encouraged agricultural activity among believers, the cult spread.[90] In 1859 Konkō Daijin, on instructions from the kami, went into concealment. Empowered as a *daimyōjin*, Konkō Daijin now functioned as a living kami. Like Miki, he gave up all his possessions to demonstrate his faith in Tenchi Kane no Kami. His new organization coincided with the critical events of the pre-Restoration decade. In an environment charged with political struggle and shogunal failure, a saying went, "How many distressed *ujiko* [members] there are in society! But if the kami help, the people will be able to live."[91] Nine years before the Restoration, when he returned from his concealment, Kawate established a formal religious organization.

More than other founders, Konkō Daijin stressed the importance of knowledge in the form of the *oshirase*. This is not to say that other groups were not interested in the question of knowledge. But Kawate was more systematic about the kind of knowledge that his followers should possess. While he served as the agency to transmit divine knowledge, the revelations he made in response to specific problems were not sudden. He received instructions in a conscious state, not in the circumstances of a trance, but he alone was able to recall the content of the divine instructions and interpret them to others.[92] Sharing with the founders of the other sects a profound distrust of conventional knowledge, Kawate's central text for the faithful condemned learning (*gakumon*) as something that "consumes the body" and as the product of mere "cleverness" and contrivance.[93] He freely granted that he did not have much formal learning and was not very literate:

> Today's society is one of wisdom and knowledge. By permitting humans to become clever, we risk losing the virtue of the body. In this age the principal pollutant is desire. Let us be released from the use of the abacus. It is said that we are clever but have no skills. We show off our cleverness and rely on artifice. Let us separate ourselves from cleverness, contrivance, and wisdom. Let us depart from the assistance and customs of society. By leaving society, we will be able to entrust our body to the kami.[94]

Accordingly, acts of "listening" and "understanding" were supremely important. In the operation of listening and understanding, the body became the reservoir for intentionality and knowing similar to the way Konkō used his own body as agency for divinity. It was the action of the body, not the contrivances and ruses of mere knowledge extracted from books and conventional instruction, that promised to secure people relief from society's afflictions. The *Konkō Daijin rikai* reported that the founder disapproved of religious austerities and advised that "eating and drinking are important to the body."[95] The body required strength if it was to express its faith and belief by working and acting.

The knowledge valued by Konkō Daijin related to how people were to assist others. Like the other new religions, Konkō stressed relief and assistance for others as the condition for faith. No other kind of knowledge was required. Here again, this idea pertained to contemporary society and custom which had failed to provide relief to the distressed. Konkō Daijin constantly called on people to leave society, with all its contrivances and fragmenting propensities, and to entrust themselves to the kami, whose grace would manifest itself in people helping people. "Men, assisting men, are human."[96] Mutual help distinguished humans from other species and represented a special form of thanks to the kami. Just as the deities, at times of illness and disaster, offered assistance to humans, so humans should assist the needy in times of distress.

Such assistance was also based on the idea of human equality. Here Konkō proposed two interrelated notions: all people are members of the "family of the deity" (*kamisama no ujiko*), and they are capable of becoming deities themselves. Together they represented a new concept of community. "All under heaven," he advised, "are the *ujiko* of the deities of heaven and earth. There are no other kinds of men."[97] Because all were potentially *ujiko*, "one cannot look down on humans or befoul them." Closely associated with this sense of equality was the new status assigned to women. All the new religions elevated women to a status equivalent to men, and some, like Konkō, even tended to exalt them. "Women are the rice fields of the world," Konkō Daijin announced, and in the "teachings of the deities, if the rice fields are not fertilized and enriched, they will be of no value."[98] Life itself would not be possible. Hence Konkō proposed, employing familiar metaphors of samurai politics and power, that women were the *karō* (principal retainers) of the household; if there were no *karō*, there could be no castle. Thus women and peasants, precisely because they lacked access to the established disciplines of learning, became exemplars of what was truly human. Belief came from women; they were close to the deities. No doubt valuing women in this way stemmed from an idealized agricultural respect for productivity. Both Kurozumi and Tenri also showed real concern for women physiologically, especially with reference to problems and pain incurred at the time of childbirth.

Yet ultimately all people were capable of becoming godlike. "Deity and man," Kawate announced, "are the same. Whatever deity one worships, if he fails to correspond to the heart of man, he will not correspond to the heart of the kami; and if he fails to correspond to the heart of the deity, he will not conform to the heart of man."[99] Konkō Daijin wrote that as he had received the "august principle of yin [okage] to become a living deity, so you [anatagata] will receive the principle as well." A living kami was nothing more than someone doing the work of the deity in a human moment and was a status available to all. Hence he constantly played down his own exalted status as an intermediary and acknowledged personal "ignorance," as he was simply a man who "tills the soil and does not know anything." Irony notwithstanding, Konkō Daijin possessed the kind of knowledge necessary to make him and all followers living kami. The community of believers thus constituted a divine assembly, as "all receive their bodies from the kami of heaven and earth."[100]

In its elaboration of a new community of believers serving one another and withdrawn from official society, Konkō stressed, not least of all, the primacy of household work and agricultural cultivation. As he himself was a committed farmer, he paid close attention, as did the rural kokugakusha, to growing conditions and agricultural techniques. He was particularly interested in weather ("wind and rain" as he put it) but linked such conditions to the presence or absence of belief. He rejected the idea that a mere visit to the shrine would bring wind and rain at the right time. Proper conditions could be secured only if faith allowed the kami to enter one's body. Evidence of such faith was shown by attending to one's household duties. The believer's sense of joy, he noted, would make him feel obliged to tend to his household duties.[101]

Defense and Wealth

In the late Tokugawa period, Dutch studies, as it was first called, combined with eighteenth-century discussions on political economy (keisei saimin) to create the possibility of a new discourse. Dutch studies expressed an interest in the new sciences of medicine, anatomy and physiology, natural science, astronomy, physics, and geography. Political economy aimed at uncovering the sources of wealth. As it was formulated in the early nineteenth century, the new discourse first emphasized maritime defense and related science and technology and then moved on to discuss national wealth. The impulses underlying such a discourse was the increasing presence of foreigners who were searching for adventure, trade, and empire, and the domestic economic failures, which the Tempō Reforms were seeking to arrest. At the heart of this new discourse was a dissatisfaction, bordering on outright criticism, with the shogunal political arrangement and its evident incapacity to act decisively and effectively to find adequate sources of wealth for relieving the people (saimin).

Writers at the turn of the century had already alerted contemporaries to the foreign menace and the need for adequate coastal defense and a firm national policy. Discussions on defense turned on the question of adequate military technology, but any consideration of science and technology invariably raised the issue of political decision making. An early proponent, Kudō Heisuke (1734–1800), saw the installation of new maritime fortifications as the fundamental condition for a new policy. "The first aim in governing the realm," he wrote, "is to deepen the power of our country. To deepen the strength of the country, we have first to allow the wealth of foreign countries to enter Japan." Trade was an absolute necessity, as it generated the wealth that many came to recognize as the key to a proper defense. Kudō went on to advocate the opening of new lands like Hokkaido and the systematic search for gold, silver, and copper. Another contemporary, Hayashi Shihei (1738–1793), author of a famous geographic miscellany, *Sankoku tsūran zusetsu*, shared a similar view and was even more insistent about the merger of defense and the search for wealth. It was Honda Toshiaki (1744–1821) who first grasped in global terms the problem of wealth and formulated a coherent statement yoking wealth to defense: "Because Japan is a maritime nation, crossing the ocean, transport, and trade are the primary vocations of the realm. In governing with the power of only one domain, the national strength weakens increasingly. This weakness affects the peasantry, and it is a natural condition for them to yearly decrease their productivity."[102]

He was convinced that policy must reach beyond a single domain to represent and employ the resources of the whole. Trade and markets were also necessary. Once Japan was thrown into the global market network, it would have to compete with other countries in a struggle for scarce resources. Appearing as a good mercantilist, Honda was persuaded that the search for trade and markets was prompted by the domestic scarcity of goods, products, and natural resources. Yet it was in Japan's national interest to promote foreign trade if the realm was to survive and overcome chronic domestic difficulties. Honda noted that Japan differed from other, Western nations only in its scientific and technological inferiority, but he was convinced that the gap could be closed.[103]

More than any other political economist, Honda recognized the relationship between trade as a source of national wealth and Japan's technological backwardness. To rectify both, he proposed in an unpublished essay, "Keisei hissaku" (1798), four urgent priorities: (1) the systematic manufacturing of explosives for military and civil purposes; (2) the development of mining, as metals were the backbone of the nation's wealth; (3) the establishment of a national merchant marine that would enhance the national treasury by selling products abroad and help avoid domestic famines; and (4) the abrogation of seclusion for a policy of colonial enterprises in nearby territories.[104] Collectively, these proposals were meant to show that Japan had pursued an unnatural course that had led to an economic dead end. Isolation was anachronistic, territorial decentralization destructive to the national interest, and agricultural primacy was a fiction in view of Japan's maritime position. Japan should promote a policy directed toward the opening of trade in order to meet, rather than to be subdued by, the European thrust in Asia.[105]

Any consideration of defense and wealth entailed employing a new knowledge capable of developing military technology and finding new sources of wealth. When thoughtful men turned to this question, they embraced a form of inquiry that validated the investigation of first principles, but they were also mindful to balance the inherent formalism of first principles with a conception of historicism that accounted for changing circumstances. As did other contemporary discourses, Western learning used a strategy that required reducing things to origins in order to demonstrate how the principle of the past authorized changes in the present. Whereas Mito, *kokugaku*, and the new religions resorted to primal deities and archetypal events to specify first principles, Western studies referred to paradigmatic heroes in the remote past whose accomplishments reflected the conviction that each age demanded policies adequate to its requirements. The discourse on defense and wealth, owing to its commitment to defend the realm as a whole rather than as a domain or a region, inched toward abandoning feudalism for a conception of a larger political unity. Ultimately, the cultural content of the discourse came to suggest the political form of the early modern state to satisfy the imperatives of national wealth and defense. If other discourses searched for ways to deliver relief and assistance to the needy, the discussions on defense and wealth saw a mercantilist state as the form most able to realize this goal. Honda early perceived in the state the agency to supply such services when he observed that the "several European nations are kingdoms that provide assistance to people; it is a heavenly duty of the kingdom to relieve hunger and cold with trade, overseas transport, and passage."[106] The state that such writers came to conceptualize was more mercantilist than despotic or absolutist and was based on social labor and productivity, manufacturing, and trade. In this regard, it was also more ethical than merely political, which many writers identified with the privatism of the Tokugawa *bakufu*. Although the practitioners of this discourse, as good mercantilists, shied away from thinking about an equitable redistribution of national resources, as did the Mito writers, they displaced the egalitarian impulse by turning to merit, talent, and ability as criteria for recruitment and advancement. The demonstration of talent (*jinzai*) depended on the mastery of expert knowledge useful to the necessities of the day. The discourse on wealth and defense envisaged human subjectivity as the maker of custom and history and agreed that the human species, even though people held different stations in life, originated from a single source. Although Western studies rejected the existence of qualitative distinctions among people, it did believe that status derived from the acquisition and demonstration of useful knowledge, which constituted the only acceptable criterion of social and political preferment. But it also agreed with Mito that such knowledge was not available to all, even though it resisted making this conceit into a principle of preemptive closure. It is, furthermore, important to note that its followers frequently came from small and medium-sized domains, often *fudai* houses, and sometimes large merchant houses, men who were no doubt convinced that transforming the *bakufu* into a national organization devoted to promoting wealth and defense would save them as well.

The maturation of the discourse on wealth and defense occurred in 1830, with the establishment of the Shōshikai, two years after the famous Siebold Incident. Two of the members of this group had previously been Siebold's students. By resorting to examination of the foreign scientist as a "spy" and condemnation for his chief contact, Takahashi Kageyasu, the authorities had raised the stakes for anybody desiring to pursue the new knowledge independently. One of the casualties of the incident and a former student of Siebold's, Takano Chōei (1804–1850), remarked in the wake of the persecution that because of the *bakufu*'s policies, the "school of Western scholars was momentarily frightened, and Western studies began to decline."[107] As a result, organizing an independent study group in Edo years later constituted an act of calculated risk.

The Shōshikai's agenda was to explore new kinds of knowledge that promised to yield practical solutions to contemporary domestic and foreign problems; its heyday coincided with the Tempō famine, mounting peasant disturbances, violent urban uprisings, and Ōshio's Osaka rebellion. Writing years later in *Bansha sōyaku shoki*, Takano Chōei explained that the society aimed to supplement traditional samurai learning which, emphasizing elegance and ornamentation in expression rather than substance, prepared people for purely literary careers. He commented that this tradition "has not been useful for the relief of society" and recalled that when the group was founded, many believed it was necessary to "understand how to mend social abuses."

> Since 1833, famines have occurred among the lower classes in the cities and the countryside. One can only conjecture at what is happening in the countryside. In response, there have been expressions of regret, and many have produced books concerning relief and ruin. Because many of these [books] investigated specific conditions relating to political economy, several domains implemented policies [to rectify the conditions] and tended to question the nature of political affairs itself. But because the problems have become exceedingly complex and so difficult to resolve, we decided to establish the Shōshikai.[108]

In addition, news concerning the intention and appearance of foreign ships, though frequently incorrect, seemed to appear more frequently during the 1830s and was used increasingly by shogunal critics to justify their demands for new policies.[109] One such rumor circulating throughout Edo prompted Takano and Watanabe to question the *bakufu*'s expulsion policy. Takano's *Yume monogatari* (Tale of a dream, 1838) and Watanabe Kazan's report on foreign policy resulted in shogunal action leading to the dissolution of the society, imprisonment of its principal members, and Watanabe's eventual suicide. The incident became known as *bansha no goku*, or "the purge of barbarian scholars."[110]

It is important to note that the society, many of whose members had begun in Dutch studies with some proficiency in medicine, anatomy, and natural history, shifted its focus to investigating knowledge that might be put into the service of the country. Guiding this decision was the belief that appropriate policy could not be formulated unless it was informed by knowledge adequate to its objectives. This apparent coupling of knowledge and power was fully acknowledged by the society when it demonstrated how policies concerning famine relief drew attention to political conduct or when it made public the official insensitivity to questions relating to maritime navigation and defense. Yet it is important to add that the society's leading figures envisaged political criticism as an effect of a new conception of culture. Takano Chōei, for example, explained in his *Wasuregatami (Tori no nakune)* that it was possible to imagine changes in the content of culture and necessary to pursue a critical course if such changes were to be enacted. As evidence, he offered the example of his associate Watanabe Kazan, who had been transformed from the status of a high-ranking samurai noted for his literary and artistic interests into a serious and committed student of Western learning. Despite his considerable achievements in traditional disciplines, art, composition, and his exquisite sensibilities, Watanabe had changed, Takano reported, after observing places marked by disaster and famine in recent years.

What provoked Watanabe to make this cultural "sea change" was his search for reasons explaining contemporary hardship and disorder. The rich, he observed, seemed to get richer, while the poor slipped farther down the scale of poverty. Everywhere the poor were resorting to rebellion. "Because tumult has spread throughout the society for one reason or another," Takano wrote, "he [Watanabe], impelled by a grieving heart, began excerpting selections from Dutch books on the *kokutai* of all countries and political affairs and circumstances revealing social conditions and the way people felt." Next, he had turned to examining the pros and cons of contemporary affairs, writing essays on the issues of the day and discussing these matters with other thoughtful men. "Even though he had studied the way of old, he had become a person whose doubts could no longer be concealed."[111] In place of the traditional learning that served him so well before but that now fell short of providing an understanding of contemporary conditions, he sought to substitute science and technology. Watanabe himself confessed as much in a letter in 1840 to Maki Sadachika in which he asserted that no division existed between the Way and the reality of custom.[112]

Watanabe's views on Western culture confirmed the efficacy of this new content. Western learning represented a new orientation, he believed, and thus required new methods to achieve it. In *Gekizetsu wakumon*, he complained that the traditional discrimination between "civilized" and "barbarian" was bound to cause serious trouble for Japan in the future as it affected Western nations. Times changed, and the present could never be the same as the past. Men who apprehended the present from the standpoint of the past tried to anchor the *koto* (Japanese harp) to a support and were obliged to pull both harp and support when they moved. The learning of Tang China was inapplicable to Japan's current needs and resembled a "dream within a dream." Watanabe relied on the explanatory powers of historicism to explain that great changes have occurred since antiquity. Among these changes, one of the most important had been the Western use of "things" (in physics). Although he plainly recognized a differentiation between practicality and doctrine (morality) in the *Shinkiron*, he also acknowledged that each could assist the other and form a complementary relationship. When juxtaposing the "Way of the West" to the "Way of Japan," it might be supposed that they were different, but because both were informed by reason (*dōri*), they were ultimately one and the same. Study showed that what distinguished Western societies from Japan was their discovery and development and science and technology, not their favorable climates (as Honda Toshiaki had thought), rich lands, or even vast populations. Western superiority disclosed the difference between diligence and indolence. For Watanabe, diligence meant wisdom, knowledge, and effort. Western schools prospered in subjects like political studies, medicine, physics, and religion, whereas Chinese learning was moribund. "Because the Western barbarians have concentrated chiefly on physics, they have acquired detailed knowledge of the world and the four directions." Fearing the West, the Japanese "hear the thunder and block their ears. The greater evil is to shut one's eyes because one detests listening. It is our duty to investigate not only the principles of creation but also the principles of all things and opinions."[113] Technology, the application of scientific principles, as Watanabe understood them, was particularly important to this new endeavor, because it showed how to transform the physical landscape through methods of construction and excavation, to put up schools, hospitals, and poorhouses; technology pointed to the way that culture might be changed.

Watanabe's faith in the practical use of science and technology inspired specific proposals. The foreign question had become particularly irksome, and Japan was the only country that did not have a relationship with the West. As a result, Japan has come to resemble a "piece of meat left along the roadside. How can the attention of wolves and tigers be avoided?" Without proper knowledge, Japan's security had acquired all the "contentment of a frog in a pond."[114] Politics originated on the basis of what was considered reliable, whereas misfortune ushered in the smug assumption that nothing was wrong. Today, Japan existed only because of the happy accident of geography that offered protection by distance and the seas. But it was no longer possible to depend on what others had relied on in the past and to be consoled by solutions that had worked before. China, once a vast and powerful land, was already heaving under the impact of seaborne Western intrusions. Hence, the first task for Japanese was to abrogate the seclusion policy and then to embark on a program of maritime trade and defense.

Watanabe saw that the globe had become a competitive arena for struggle among nations, but Japanese leadership had failed to see that Japan would involuntarily be drawn into this contest. Tang learning had come to Japan in remote antiquity. Since that time empty studies had prospered continuously to divert men's minds from the real tasks at hand. The new learning demanded a commitment to preparing for the defense of Edo Bay. The *bakufu*'s failure to recognize the necessity for such preparations revealed an even more basic incapacity to grasp the power offered by Western knowledge. Not even the *bakufu*'s most reliable allies had yet been deployed to the region of the bay. Caustically, Watanabe described the situation as a sign of "domestic catastrophe" (*naikan*), rather than "external disaster" (*gaikan*): a failure of nerve rather than an outside threat.[115]

The threat of an invasion imperiling a defenseless Japan haunted Takano Chōei as well. Unlike Watanabe, Takano was a professional student and translator of Western learning and a leading proponent of the utility of the new learning. This interest in medicine fostered in the discourse on Western studies continued even after many of its adherents shifted their focus to questions concerning defense and military technology, and it represented an impulse comparable to the effort of relieving the ill and diseased found among the new religions. As a principal participant in the Shōshikai, Takano had begun in the 1830s to direct his own interest toward resolving the perceived disjunction between the domestic policy of feudal fragmentation and the question of national defense. Upon learning of a proposed visit of an English ship in the late 1830s, he drafted an essay to express his alarm at the probable rejection of such a probe. Takano charged in *Yume monogatari* that expelling the *Morrison* would be considered by the British as the act of a belligerent country that understood neither right nor wrong. The loss of virtue resulting from this action would result in untold disasters.[116] Years later, Yokoi Shōnan transformed this reading of national moral conduct in international affairs into a classic defense of trade and peaceful foreign relations against the noisy claims of xenophobic expulsionists.

While others joined the discussion on maritime defense in the early 1840s, the issue came to command serious attention by shogunal officials, who understood that a decision on defense meant a prior commitment to a different conception of knowledge. Even as Watanabe and Takano were trying to establish the outer boundaries of the discourse on defense, *bakufu* officials like Egawa Tarōzaemon and Torii Yōzō turned to formulating appropriate proposals for policy after making their inspections of Edo Bay. Egawa's views corresponded closely to those held by Watanabe, but Torii rejected any suggestion of entering into relations with countries like England. Torii (who has sometimes been portrayed as the archetype of malevolence) was not a simple witch hunter; his memorandum late in 1840 disclosed a keen awareness of weapons manufacture. But he also recognized that a new conception of the world was at the heart of the problem of defense. Unlike many contemporaries, he was not convinced of British technological superiority at this time and thought the English victory over China to be inconclusive. What distressed him about proposals calling for new measures of defense and the implementation of Western technology was that they were linked to a larger view of the world whose acceptance he rejected as vigorously as he denounced colonialism. Although the cannons used by the West performed efficiently, he wrote, and might be especially useful for coastal defense, in Japanese warfare there had been little utilization of weapons useful chiefly for a precision strike applied in places where large numbers of men were concentrated in close quarters.[117] This difference dramatized the profound distinction between Japanese and Western customs. The West planned only for the pursuit of profit, in contrast with a society intent on rites and rituals; it waged war to compete, rather than to defend morality. Owing to the disparity between these two social orders, it was inappropriate for the Japanese to have any faith in Western science and technology. What Torii implied was that any acceptance of Western technique necessarily meant adopting the culture that had produced it. Writers like Watanabe and Takano had already demonstrated that their interest in the West was not restricted merely to cannons but included the whole matrix of education and customs on which its culture was based. The dangers of a policy aimed at incorporating Western culture, Torii warned, were great. "The first principle of defense entails encouraging the strengthening of traditional military and civilian skills. At the same time, it is important to eliminate frivolous military discipline and esteem competence."[118]

In response to Torii's critique of the new Western learning, Egawa argued that Torii had deliberately misrepresented the nature of British activity in China and had misunderstood the knowledge they employed. Although wise planning always involved the study and mastery of military skills, it also included an evaluation of methods that were strange and effective. In accord with the ancient advice to "know the other in order to know oneself," it was imperative for the Japanese to learn as much as possible about the English before formulating a policy. When the Chinese were confronted by the British, they had no knowledge of the adversary they faced. How could they have devised a wise plan? China's failure and its subsequent defeat by the British reflected a reliance on empty theories and useless knowledge. Egawa was confident that importing cannons and other hardware would not constitute a faddish whim. It was common knowledge that Confucianism and Buddhism had been imported from abroad, and it was well known that there were many foreign products esteemed for their convenience and value. If such goods had a useful purpose, they were not fads. To favor trifling and useless toys might be a waste, but it was not whimsy to adopt useful items.

In the ensuing debate, the real problem clearly lay in the relationship between employing foreign military technology for defense and adopting the whole system of knowledge that produced it. Torii rightly considered this enabling knowledge as a threat to the legitimacy of the Tokugawa order, and he derived little solace from Egawa's thinly disguised effort to justify importing discrete items rather than the whole cultural matrix. Provoked less by charges of official incompetence (which he could easily acknowledge) than by the threat to Tokugawa claims to legitimacy, Torii recognized that the importation of military technology would inevitably lead to incorporating the enabling culture and jeopardizing the foundations of the traditional world order. His fears were systematized in classic manner by Ōhashi Totsuan years later in a last-ditch defense of the neo-Confucian conception of a natural order.

In the last decades of the Tokugawa era, the discourse on defense was transmuted into a coherent theory of cultural purpose capable of combining the claims of a traditional worldview with the principles of scientific discovery. This task was accomplished by Sakuma Shōzan (1811–1864) and Yokoi Shōnan. Although they were initially prompted by the project to find a fit between neo-Confucianism, however they understood it by this time, and Western learning, they contributed to reinforcing the primacy of the new knowledge as the fundamental condition for understanding the world and acting in it. Their effort to secure entry into the new knowledge through the agency of received philosophical idiom attests to the importance they assigned to finding a way of using both. Yet their ultimate solution was to lay the foundations for the subsequent dismissal of nature in favor of a history that was crucial to later Meiji efforts to establish a system of useful and instrumental knowledge.

The key to this vast transformation lay in Sakuma Shōzan's decision to recognize in Western knowledge a source of power as great as morality. Both Watanabe and Takano had taken steps in this direction, but neither of them went as far as to propose systematically the equivalence between two different forms of knowledge. The nature of international events in the late 1840s and 1850s had changed considerably, and the frequent appearance of Western ships in Japanese waters undoubtedly persuaded Sakuma to conclude that the world had come to represent a stage on which nations acted out their claims. If Japan failed to compete in this struggle for power, it would be eliminated. Accepting Western learning under these circumstances, "controlling the barbarians with their own methods," resolved the problem of acquiring the necessary strength and power to compete effectively in the coming contest. But power really referred to knowledge and its enabling cultural matrix. It was necessary to grasp the very principles that produced the techniques that now promised to protect the realm against Western colonialism. Without such principles, Sakuma warned, Japan was doomed.

It is important to note that Sakuma's commitment to study Western weaponry failed to follow the usual course of appraising neo-Confucian metaphysics first. During the 1830s he made two extended trips to Edo. On the first he studied with the prominent Confucian teacher Satō Issai (1772–1859), the mentor of many late-Tokugawa figures. His second trip coincided with the controversy over the alleged *Morrison* visit, shogunal punishment of Watanabe and Takano, news of the first Anglo-Chinese war, and the continuing debate over the defense of Edo Bay, a debate fueled by Takashima Shūhan's memorial calling for a new program of cannon casting. During his residence in Edo, Sakuma also witnessed at firsthand Mizuno Tadakuni's shogunal reforms, which included the appointment of Shōzan's lord, Sanada Yukitsura, to the post of naval defense. Sanada selected Sakuma as his adviser and commanded him to begin studying military technology. In response, Sakuma enrolled in Egawa Tarōzaemon's school. This sequence of events suggests that Sakuma did not enter into Western studies through neo-Confucianism, as if it constituted a logical extension of his philosophical position, but found himself involved in the immediate and practical problem of coastal defense and cannon casting, thanks to the initiative of his lord. The identification of power as a new element in global policies, and the urgency to define practical programs enabling Japan to compete, prompted him to think about the relationship between the claims of the new knowledge and neo-Confucianism, his own intellectual endowment. Sakuma's appraisal of neo-Confucianism proceeded from his encounter with the new knowledge.

Through his contact with Egawa, Sakuma learned of the imprisonment of members of the Shōshikai and secured knowledge of Watanabe Kazan's writings. His own thoughts concerning European kingship appear to be a replay of Watanabe's elaborate explanation of kings and their importance in the expansion of the state. Disappointed in Egawa, Sakuma soon left the school after deciding that it had nothing to offer comparable to the views articulated by Watanabe.

Following a lead forged first by Egawa, Sakuma argued that the promise of an investigative method (*kyūri*) had been smothered by excessive concern for textual studies and that the true meaning of "the investigation of things" had been lost. Since antiquity, the Japanese and Chinese had therefore been robbed of the fruits of investigation and had forfeited the means to build national power. He advised that it was essential to national survival to make the effort to know the enemy, even though such knowledge had been forestalled by cultural conceit and complacency. "The urgency for preparing to meet a foreign invasion does not begin just by knowing them [the foreigners]. The method by which you know them lies not just in exhausting their skills but in combining their learning with ours."[119] If they had large ships, Japan should construct large ships; if they had large guns, so should Japan. Sakuma warned against using outmoded and ancient methods that could not ensure victory. To use new technologies from the West was the condition for containing the foreigner. The expansion of the West and the war in China had shown that mere ethical propriety was no longer an adequate defense against colonization. By recognizing the centrality of power over morality alone, Sakuma distanced his discussion from the Mito discourse and made the crucial distinction between the opportunity of power and moral opportunity.[120] His recognition of power drove him to abandon a view that foreigners were mere barbarians who knew nothing of the niceties of morality and civilization.

And yet Sakuma's concern with power compelled him to minimize the substantive difference between Japanese and Western societies. He condemned the Chinese for having lost to the British because of their unwillingness to see foreigners as something more than barbarians who were no different from birds and beasts. To slight the great powers as barbarous, he wrote to his lord in 1849, "is a principle of great injury and small benefit to the state." Ultimately, he saw no incompatibility between "customs of the West and Japan's conventions." "When . . . foreign studies are carried on prosperously, the beautiful customs of our country will gradually change," but "if there is distrust and doubt, then they [foreign studies] will be impeded."[121] Received learning, like any learning, had to demonstrate its universality before its validity could be established. Attachment to rites and propriety should not be restricted to China and Japan alone. Knowledge knew no boundaries; nothing was foreign if it proved useful in preserving the independence of the realm.

Thus Sakuma viewed the new knowledge as a form of power. Knowledge of military technology guaranteed power, and its mastery was mandated by the "welfare of the state." Although this view originally restricted the adoption of Western learning to military matters, (trade, he still believed in 1843, would result in the importation of useless products), Sakuma was to change his mind. The positive inducement of Western scientific technique would result in the expansion of contact with other nations. If "strength" was the criterion, then any policy, including opening the country, would be justified if it led to the realization and completion of national power. This opinion marked Sakuma's thought after the Perry mission (1854) and the subsequent signing of commercial treaties. In the wake of these events, he began to advocate maritime travel and foreign trade. He considered the opening of trade between Japan and the outside world as a corollary to his conception of power. Military prowess needed a sustaining source of wealth, and trade was the only policy by which a small Japan could accumulate national power to strengthen its military capacity. In one of his last petitions (February 1862) Shōzan eloquently made the case for greater contact with the West. "The skills and techniques of foreign countries," he wrote, "especially the inventions of Newton and Copernicus and the discoveries of Columbus, have progressed long distances and extended to things like physics, geography, shipbuilding, cannon casting, and the construction of fortifications." From their prosperous study of the steam engine, the Europeans had navigated steam-driven ships at sea and steam-driven trains on land. Such accomplishments depended on exploring for resources at home: iron for railways and coal for foundries. "How can we enrich and strengthen the national power? We must deduce from the facts." In Japan, he continued, neither the *bakufu* nor the domains had made much of a start. "If, however, Japan exerts itself for the profit of trade, strengthens its national power, attends to preparing ships, casting cannons, and building warships, it will be able to resist any country. . . . Should we not unite with the great countries and formulate a plan?" Knowledge and superior technology, he believed, would lead to "mutual refinement" and "mutual growth."[122]

This argument rested on the conviction that countries such as Japan and China were inferior to the West in more than military ways. If Japan was to withstand the peril of the Western presence and preserve its independence, it would have to proceed from the basis of powerful knowledge and powerful learning. In the past the trouble had stemmed from the failure to identify the essence of useful learning. This perception was linked to Sakuma's understanding of the "investigation of principles." He now tried to restructure neo-Confucianism by rescuing an earlier tradition of philosophic monism and by superimposing the idea of *kyūri* on Western natural science. Rather than investigating to satisfy the needs of ethics, he emphasized grasping the "principle of things" in the natural, material world. What he proposed was a "correspondence" between Zhu Xi Confucianism, which he never rejected, and Western natural science. "The meaning of Zhu Xi's thought is to penetrate principle in conformity [with the needs of] the realm so as to increase knowledge. When the meaning of the Cheng-Zhu school corresponds to such things as the investigation of Western conditions, the explanations of those two teachers will correspond to the world. If we follow the meaning of the Cheng-Zhu school, even Western skills will become part of learning and knowledge and will not appear outside our framework."[123]

Sakuma saw no real conflict between neo-Confucian claims to knowledge and Western skills. If conflict appeared, it would have meant postulating two distinct cultures, a "we" and a "they," which were foreclosed by his conception of power and global struggle. In a letter to a friend, he stated that "there are not two principles of the universe residing in different places. The learning skills developed in the West are conducive to the learning of the sages."[124] And to the shogunal official Kawaji Toshiakira, he wrote that because the Western science of investigating principles conformed to the intention of the Cheng-Zhu school, their explanations should apply correspondingly elsewhere. In this reformulation of the traditional epistemology, Sakuma expanded the meaning of investigation to include measurement, proof, and evidence and concluded that they constituted the real bases of all learning, which was mathematics. All learning was cumulative, "refinement," as he put it. Because Sakuma saw no conflict or duality of principles but, rather, a correspondence, he was able to couple Eastern morality with Western science. His famous phrase in *Seiken roku*, bonding Eastern morality and Western science, was not an acknowledgment of a division but, rather, a recognition of particularistic manifestations of a universal science. Sakuma's view of knowledge as power and his construction of a scientific culture implied a conception of politics. At one level his constant admonition "to explore the five continents" for knowledge put Japan in a wider world. Greater knowledge of that world prompted him to accept what it could offer to bolster Japan's strength. Although he never went as far as Yokoi Shōnan did to recommend complete political and social reorganization, he was willing to alter his view of political possibility to adhere to the requirements of a scientifically based culture. Even though he willingly acknowledged that Japan was weaker than the Western nations, he added that such weakness was physical and material and demanded systematic correction. However good the "American political system was," he wrote, "it could not be carried out in Japan" because history inhibited such a transfer.[125] The acceptance of Western knowledge did not mean abandoning the moral way. Just as science was universal, so, too, was the morality of the five relationships. Western nations did not yet possess these truths. By retaining the idea of a natural order with its specific sense of politics, Sakuma was prevented from envisaging a larger social entity. Ethics always ruled the inner realm, whereas the outer, the world of politics and history, was changeable and could be served only after making a proper investigation of contemporary conditions. Although the idea of a prior natural order militated against actually substituting society for nature, Sakuma's commitment to science resulted in consequences for the Tokugawa social imagination that he could not have foreseen.

Contemporary events required new attitudes. Japan was facing an emergency. "However important the rules of the past have been," Sakuma announced, "they have to be replaced because of the hardships they have brought." He was referring here to seclusion; it was natural to "reform the august laws that have been erected for the realm," as "it is a moral principle of Japan and China to follow ordinary law and procedures in ordinary times, and emergency measures in time of emergency."[126] His advice to abandon "old standards" (remarkably similar to Watanabe's earlier plaint) foresaw the possibility of a new political form. He imagined something higher than the "dignity of the Tokugawa house" and the court itself and pointed to what he called the "welfare of the realm" as a principle of legitimation. From this point he constructed an image of a nation-state, no doubt derived from his observations of Western countries, devoted to defending the wider realm and not just protecting the Tokugawa family. Sakuma, like many contemporaries, saw in Western knowledge the promise of immediate relief and assistance. The solution was a national community (*tenka kokka*) that could compete with comparable nations "throughout the five continents." Ultimately, he proposed the establishment of some sort of comity of nations, whereby each country would retain a uniqueness insofar as it would not disturb the continuation of harmonious relations. The "divine land" would become the Japanese state, and Japan would earn for itself a place among the nations of the world through the exercise of the "correct principles of civilization." This conviction led him to propose internal reforms. These fell short of total reorganization, but the core of his program was rooted in the recognition that proper and able leadership preceded all other considerations. Although he retained the imperial office, he identified its occupants with national kings like Peter the Great and Napoléon. Here, Sakuma came close to earlier views that had linked national strength to the power of kings who could lead their countries to power and wealth.

The intervention of Yokoi Shōnan (1809–1868) in the discourse on wealth and defense resulted in refashioning this conception of king and country into a theory of political formation that favored the mercantilist state. If Yokoi shared a discursive world with Sakuma and Hashimoto Sanai, his predecessor in Fukui *han*, he differed significantly from these two thinker-activists in crucial areas of experience and study. Sakuma and Hashimoto had immersed themselves in the study of foreign languages and rudimentary science, but Yokoi had had only the slightest exposure to these disciplines. Yokoi was more deeply committed to a traditional Confucian metaphysic, and his examination of its claims derived from an internal struggle with its philosophical propositions rather than an awareness of a national crisis. Like Hashimoto, Yokoi served as an adviser to the lord of Fukui, Matsudaira Yoshinaga (Shungaku), who was himself a prominent figure operating at the center of national politics during the late 1850s and early 1860s.

Yokoi's philosophic differences with Sakuma are instructive and help explain the decision to denature the social as a condition for establishing a modern state in Japan. Whereas Sakuma envisaged the act of investigating principle as a form of natural science and even tried to reinterpret the scientific discipline as inquiry based on a rational and empirical method, Yokoi, closer to a received metaphysic, grasped the investigation of principle and the concomitant "examination of things" (*kakubutsu*) as the vital connection between "true intention" and a "correct heart."[127] As a result, Sakuma moved toward an "investigation of the natural world," whereas Yokoi rejected any tendency that sought to "make morality a small consideration and imprudent and to transform knowledge into extensive reading and memorization." This attitude toward knowledge would lead only to "vulgar Confucianism" and "mere uselessness." In actuality, the investigation of principle and the examination of things referred to grasping the "physics of daily use." Despite Sakuma's decision to couple *kyūri* with empirical investigative methods, he was never able to overcome the dilemma of studying a primary natural order with the techniques of a natural science. Undoubtedly Sakuma recognized that the two categories of nature differed substantively, even as he tried to bring them together in an impossible synthesis. But Yokoi, who declared his fidelity to the true tradition by summoning the exemplar of the three dynasties and the ancient sages, found a transcendent way valid for all times and places. At the heart of his discovery was a reconstituted conception of the social now free from the responsibility of mirroring nature, which he believed conformed to the experience of the archetypal sages of antiquity, Yao and Shun. Their great achievement, Yokoi proposed, was to construct a viable social and political order adequate to the needs of their time alone and thereby to bequeath to future generations the universality of this particular experience, not a timeless arrangement of authority. In this manner, the universalism of the ancient precedent liberated Yokoi from the Song conceit of defending the idea of a static natural order as if it constituted a norm for all times to come. Even though Sakuma came close to making this move by positing his conception of universalistic principles, he failed to follow through on its consequences. By contrast, Yokoi explored the possibilities inherent in the universalizing of the ancient precedent and went on to conceptualize a new social image for Tokugawa Japan based on the production of wealth and the deployment of power.

Yokoi shared Sakuma's conviction concerning the relationships between knowledge and power. Early in his career, he drew attention to what he called the "vulgar learning of the useless" which he discerned in the contemporary practice to separate forms of knowing from political affairs. The essence of learning required disciplining the self for governance. If men failed to understand the site on which the ancients inaugurated their own project, they would inevitably become "slaves of antiquity." In Yokoi's thinking, the logic that identified knowledge with politics was provided by a commitment to understanding the practical details and necessities of daily life. That life itself exemplified the great lesson of antiquity and validated the very historicism authorizing men in each generation to change and to prepare for new requirements. Scholars of later generations, especially since Song times, had missed grasping the importance of daily use because they had been consumed by efforts to understand books: "When thinking about how one should study Zhu Xi today, you must think about how Zhu Xi himself studied. Without doing so, you will become a complete slave of Zhu Xi when you take to reading books. When one thinks about composing a poem and how it should become, you have to consider the kind of things that Du Fu studied, which means going back to the Han, Wei, and Six Dynasties."

Underlying this approach was the deeper conviction that texts are constituted and subsequently implicated in the very time they have been produced. But their identity is not fixed for all times to come. Active thinking, not blind acceptance of established precedents and morally irrelevant pieties, must become the essential condition for all learning seeking the mastery of principle. Yet Yokoi recognized that the decision to abandon old precedents and cast off ancient abuses would not necessarily lead to an understanding of the "physics of the daily" unless it were accompanied by the proper intention, sincerity, and honesty, a kind of good faith motivating thoughtful men to investigate themselves first. Writing to a colleague, Yokoi asserted that despite living in a universe that is the proper place for "our thinking, our minds have not yet investigated the various things we encounter and penetrated their principle." When one practiced sincerity and relied on "daily experiences, then one will have movement or the exercise of minds."[128] Self-examination prompted by sincerity invariably demands an investigation of the outer world and, accordingly, distinguishes between the act of merely knowing and genuinely understanding.

By constantly exercising the mind, men would reach a "true understanding of the governing principles that are brought out from thought." The Song theorists, Yokoi complained, remained mired in the pursuit of mere knowing and wrote learnedly about the act of investigation but never understood it as a technique for "improving the welfare of the people."[129] In their hands, the examination of things and the investigation of principle, *kakubutsu kyūri*, served as an instrument for speculation and never as a tool for grasping the external world in its constant flux and inducing men to make the appropriate responses. Under the sanction of this conception of knowledge and understanding, there could be little room for the idea of a timeless and fixed natural order.

"The conditions of past and present are different," Yokoi announced in his discussions with Inoue Kowashi at Nuyama, when he was under house arrest, "and although today and yesterday correspond to principle, they are not the same." Here, following the historicist impulse of eighteenth-century political economism, he differentiated principle (*ri*) from conditions (*sei*).[130]

Principle consistently guided men during times of change and enabled them to grasp the reality of circumstances in order to devise appropriate courses of action. Compelling men to overcome the temptations of an inactive subjectivism, the idea of sincerity would motivate them to know their times and to "assist nature's work," which now meant political administration or what the classic of the *Great Learning* called "outward pacification." In this discussion, Yokoi revealed his own conception of political form. If a culture was ethical, as he surely believed, informed by sincere intent, "good faith," prompting men to meet changing conditions head-on, then its form should also be ethical. Practical action undertaken to confront the challenge of changing conditions must always aim to actualize benevolence, which in the context of late-Tokugawa times had become widely synonymous with the "public interest." What Yokoi was to imagine as the nation-state was principally an ethical space in which rulers pursued the public interest by serving the people's welfare. In this way, he realigned the conduct of political affairs with the larger conception of an ethical imperative. Behind this reformulation of place and purpose were the classic formulae that the "realm belongs to the public" and the "people are the base of the realm." "If there are no people," Yokoi asked rhetorically, "how would it be possible to erect a realm? But if there is a realm, it must serve the people who make it up." In an 1860 text, *Kokuze sanron*, Yokoi specified this conviction by calling attention to the Tokugawa failure. The Tokugawa household had acted as despots, he explained, demanding financial support from the several regions even when resources were scarce, thereby embarking on a "private management" that served only the "convenience of one family." Political doctrine alone never managed to tranquilize the realm by making people into children. "Perry was correct when he called this a nonpolitics." Real politics always assisted the people. "[For to] govern the realm means governing the people. The samurai are the instruments used to govern the realm. Even though it is fundamental to the way to teach filial piety, honesty, and loyalty to the samurai and the people, doctrine must also aim at bestowing wealth. . . . Wealth must be the most important task."[131]

Good leadership must always make sure that its conduct and policies conform to the public interest. Profit should exist only on behalf of the people. "The usefulness of benevolence . . . reaches men in the form of profit. . . . To abandon the self is to profit the people. The ideograph for profit is the name for unprincipled [action] when it is used privately. When one profits the people, its use is benevolent."[132] In these circumstances, the realm should encourage trade and maritime commercial relations in order to realize the requirements of the public interest.

According to the *Kokuze sanron*, agriculture remained the source of livelihood, even if it was only one aspect of it. Without the innumerable products that people needed for their daily use, life would be impossible. These products were obtained through exchange. Trade and the circulation of currency affected the whole country. Because such a system had not been put into practice, contemporary Japan was a comparatively poor country. As a result, every effort should be made to prepare for the development of a variety of products in several areas. But before this could be accomplished, there had to be a system of markets for the distribution of goods. A market system and the flow of currency would prevent stagnation by regulating the exchange and distribution of products. It would keep in check the activities in the economic realm. In fact, Yokoi's writings show a gradual shift of emphasis to the market over the national defense among Western enthusiasts once the opening of the country had made international relations possible. Yokoi chose the *han* (especially Fukui) as the unit in which the new economic arrangements should be implemented, but he also believed that the form of *fukoku kyōhei* could be extended to other domains because the "proper administration of one realm can be expanded to the whole country." On the national level, Yokoi, like Sakuma, supported the project of large domains striving to bring about a reconciliation between the court and the *bakufu* in the establishment of a new conciliar arrangement. The importance of his mercantilist program was that it could be applied to the broader national scene. At this time, Takasugi Shinsaku was already seeking to establish a comparable program in Chōshū, and Ōkubo Toshimichi was trying to transform Satsuma into a wealthy and powerful domain. Eventually, as Yokoi became committed to finding ways to account for the existence of plural interests, he drew his political model from the example of the United States.

Yokoi developed a coherent argument justifying claims for broader participation in issues relating to the welfare and security of society as a whole. The idea of "public discussion" (*kōgi yoron*) signified an effort to formalize this claim to speak about society's business. This arrangement meant that the *bakufu* should summon all talented men of the realm to Edo (because the "great urgency of the day is to confide in sincerity") "to bring together the able of the realm and its political affairs." This policy would "seek out the words of the people in the realm and transmit people's intention on benefit and injury, gains and losses."[133] Yokoi particularly envisaged the form of a unified structure that still allowed for the expression of domain interests, resembling most the American federal republic which he came to admire. He hoped to install a hedge against the divisiveness of the *bakuhan* system, which inevitably invited "private management," by resorting to the idea of public discussions that would equate ability with efficacy or utility, informed by expert and specialized knowledge, and mediated by an awareness of changing times and a concern for the people's will and feelings. He believed that he had found the appropriate means to express the Confucian imperative that made the private morality of the lord ("disciplining and cultivating oneself") equivalent to governing the realm in the public interest. Knowledge came to replace morality as the necessary criterion for leadership. This was revealed in his recommendation to Matsudaira Yoshinaga (Shungaku) of Echizen in 1862 which urged "the abandonment of the selfishness that the Tokugawa *bakufu* has shown since it acquired countrywide authority." It was the season to "reform the nonpolitics of the Tokugawa house" and to "govern the realm" in the interest of a larger public.

Cultural Practice and the Triumph of Political Centralization

Among late-Tokugawa writers and activists, none came closer than Yokoi Shōnan to grasping in the "current situation" the play of differences represented by new discourses, the destruction of received political identities, and the need to find a way to accommodate the plural claims that were being made in the explosive environment of the 1860s. Yokoi's "reading" of contemporary circumstances proposed a resolution of the problems of security and assistance that involved installing a hegemonic arrangement capable of stabilizing the political order while retaining the differing articulations. In fact, the conjuncture of discursive claims ultimately became the terrain for a new hegemonic political practice.

Since the turn of the century, the steady increase of discourses augmenting distinctly articulated practices presented the spectacle of a ceaseless play of what might be called cultural overdetermination,[134] a process whereby multiple causes and contradictions reappeared regularly in condensed form to shape an image of rupture and fragmented meaning. The new practices all announced the importance of "difference," which, since the late eighteenth century, had been associated with blurred social identities that demanded accommodation. The culture of play reflected an experience of fragmentation and division as the starting point of literary, artistic, and intellectual production. The collapse of a view that divided political space between ruler and ruled, the gradual dismissal of a meaningful cosmic order within which people occupied precise and determined places, and the replacement of this view by a self-defining conception of the subject combined to launch Japanese society on a constant search to reconstitute its lost unity. Each discourse, including Mito, acknowledged in its way the end of a simple division between ruler and ruled, which had authorized a hierarchic order accountable only to itself and directed by a metaphysic based on the paradigm of nature. Under the sanction of neo-Confucianism, the social body had been conceived as a fixed whole. As long as such a holistic mode of social imagination prevailed, politics would remain a mere repetition of the hierarchical social relations. What the several discursive "interpretations" disclosed was the recognition of the incessant need to find instruments for restructuring that society by identifying and articulating social relations. Each discourse revealed an overdetermination implied in annulling the contradiction among a growing number of differences, a plethora of meanings of the "social," and the difficulties encountered in any attempt to fix those differences as moments of a stable structure.

All the discourses proceeded from the presumption that the issues they sought to understand and speak to constituted society's business, not other people's business. Henceforth, questions relating to order, security, productivity, relief and assistance, the centrality of daily life, and the practical knowledge needed to reproduce social conditions of existence required a concept of the social capable of being mobilized for the realization of its goals. The creation of public opinion in late-Tokugawa discourse as a condition for considering issues vital to the collectivity made it possible to conceptualize a new political space. All the discourses shifted the terms of legitimation from cosmic and natural principles to the agency of human performance and productivity. In this they contributed their greatest challenge to the established Tokugawa order, whose claims rested first on metaphysical principles and only second on the instruments of production. Driven by a common impulse to overcome the division between ruler and ruled, the several discourses all sought to place daily life in the forefront of attention by emphasizing the tangible and sensuous against the abstract. As a result, all the discourses aimed at showing how knowledge derived from the daily life of a certain social constituency entitled its knowers to the power to make decisions affecting their lives. An effect of these new systems of knowledge was the disciplining of the body, whereby the proper mental attitude was made to correspond to certain mutual intentions, in order to offset the baneful influence of received arrangements that insisted on separating mental from manual and more recent customs in which the body played and performed, often to excess.

To make other people's business one's own required finding a different form of authority that would validate the act of centering on the activity of people who had hitherto been disenfranchised. Any discussion of politics or administration, as officially defined, among groups long considered ineligible because they lacked the proper knowledge risked danger; it also challenged the officials' claim to designate objects for political discourse. This move entailed displacing the center from politics to culture and rethinking the identity of social relations in areas of religion, science and technology, and economics in order to locate an arena capable of offering representation to such groups. By the same token the move to imagine a new arena of this sort permitted conceptualizing different political forms. Each one of the new discourses produced a vision of political form consistent with the social identity of the group that it wished to represent and that, it was believed, had emerged from the new content of culture. Mito emphasized the autonomous domain; the nativists projected the self-sufficient village; the new religions installed the sacred enclosure or community of believers; and the proponents of defense and wealth promoted the nation-state. Yet for the most part the institution of envisaging a stable system of "differences" had become overdetermined, was directed at solving the problem of the whole by substituting a part for it.

As a distinct process of articulation, the several discourses tried to move away from the center to a periphery, or envisaged a plurality of centers by creating a larger public space as a forum for discussing issues that affected society as a whole. This signaled both the dissolution of a politics in which the division of identities between ruler and ruled had been fixed for all time and a transition toward a new situation characterized by unstable political spaces, in which the very identity of the contesting forces was submitted to constant shifts and calls for redefinition. In the late Tokugawa period the discursive field was dominated by a plurality of practices that presupposed the incomplete and open character of the social. This signified challenging closure and finding a form of mediation between the general need to stabilize order and promote productivity and a local demand to guarantee the preservation of the various social identities produced by the will to discourse. Only the presence of a vast area of semiautonomous, heterogeneous, and unevenly developed discourses and the possibility of conflict made possible the terrain for a hegemonic practice competent to satisfy both order and difference. For many who belonged to the new discourses, the Restoration vaguely promised the possibility of accomplishing a hegemonic formation committed to stabilizing the social and preserving interests and fixed identities. Yet the existence of these various claims to interest and projections of social identity would soon become the problem, not the solution.

In a sense, the initial stage of the Meiji Restoration, or, as it was called, *ōsei fukko*, appeared at the moment when many believed it was necessary to find a form that would contain and even represent the various interests that undermined Tokugawa control. It should be noted that each of the movements discussed, in its efforts to discredit the center and replace it with centers, supplied its own conception of political restoration: Mito had already announced the goals of *chūkō* (restoration); nativism lodged its appeal in an "adherence to foundations" (*moto ni tsuku*); the new religions epiphanized their image of a new order in calls for "world renewal"; and proponents of wealth and defense sought in some sort of conciliar arrangement (*dai kakkyo*) a way of rearranging the constellation of political forces that existed in the 1860s. Nor least important, all could easily support a restoration symbolized by the emperor and court that promised nothing more binding than a return to the age of Jimmu Tennō, a "washing away of all old abuses" and a search for new knowledge throughout the world. Here, for a brief moment, was the necessary fit between the forces that combined to bring down the Tokugawa and a hegemonic political structure that promised to reinstate order and security and to distribute relief while preserving regional autonomy. Uncertain as to its future goals, *ōsei fukko* could project the image of a hegemony willing to take into account the interests of all groups by presupposing a certain equilibrium among the various forces. So powerful was the appeal of an *ōsei fukko* in 1867 that writers like Suzuki Masayuki were encouraged to declare (significantly in a *chōka*, an archaic long poem), "Even the despised people will not be lacking / The emperor [*ōgimi*], hidden in the shade like a night flower, will flourish increasingly / Everyone will rejoice in the prosperity of the august age."[135] This sentiment seemed to be shared widely throughout society, and people everywhere saw in the Restoration, albeit momentarily, a representation of their own hopes and aspirations.

Yet before long, other voices were beginning to condemn the Restoration as a deception and a death blow to their most cherished ideals. In Yano Gendō's short, elegiac lament for the vanished glories of Kashiwara and the promise of returning to its golden age, all that was left by 1880 was a "dream that will never be."[136] Almost immediately after *ōsei fukko*, the prospect for a hegemonic formation of the Restoration polity disappeared in the construction of a modern bureaucratic state—the Go-Ishin—pledged to eliminating precisely the fragmentation, difference, and overdetermination that had defeated the Tokugawa system of control. The reorganization of an ensemble of bureaucratic administrative functions arranged by criteria of efficiency and rationality after 1870 aimed at removing the very antagonisms that had surfaced in the discursive articulations of late Tokugawa and that were necessary for the installation of a hegemonic order. The very conditions that produced new political subjects demanding order, relief, assistance, security, and the subsequent withdrawals from the center now constituted a problem that many believed had to be resolved. The contest down to the 1890s consisted of an opposition between proponents of discursive practices insisting on preserving a measure of autonomy, usually expressed in movements calling for local control, and a new leadership committed to the rational centralization of power and the elimination of all articulations requesting the reinstatement of a hegemonic arrangement in a genuinely constitutional policy.[137] This is not to say that the Meiji Restoration successfully terminated the several discourses. Mito had already taken itself out of the political field as a result of a destructive civil war in the early 1860s, even though the later Meiji government appropriated parts of its program. Through the support of courtiers like Iwakura Tomomi, nativism briefly sought to control the course of events in 1867 and 1868 by proposing the implementation of a new restorationist polity based on ancient models, but it was too late for the construction of an order more religious and mythic than political and more self-consciously archaic and agricultural than modern and industrial. As a discourse, it was dissembled into a state-controlled sect promoting the worship of Ōkuni no Nushi, the god housed in Izumo Shrine. Later it was transformed into a Japanese science of ethnology that once again was formulated to forestall the power of the new bureaucratic state. The new religions continued a checkered course of withdrawals, staging confrontations with the state, recruiting larger numbers of followers, and generating newer and more radical communities like Maruyamakyō and Ōmotokyō. Finally, the older discourse on defense and wealth continued its own efforts to curb the centralization of the Meiji state by trying to give substance to ideas of broader political participation and local autonomy, ending with a systematic attempt to "civilize" and "enlighten" Japanese society in the 1870s and 1880s as the condition for a permanent moral and rational order.

Yet the Meiji state, as it was completed in the 1890s, was also a solution to the *bakumatsu* problems that have been addressed. It was precisely the loss of control in late-Tokugawa decades that catalyzed a contest over how the center, and hence the whole, was to be reconstituted. Fear of the continuing failure to arrest the disorder—first in the countryside and the cities—and of the inability to meet the foreign threat, plus the clear need to put an end to centrifugal forces set in motion by secessions and withdrawals, served to impel a search for more effective ways to restructure society. In this restructuring, the struggle was seen increasingly as one between authority and community, between the effort of various groups to attend to society's business and the belief that that business was too important to leave to the public. The modern state managed to exclude surplus social meaning, by fixing the identity of the public interest in its quest for order and security while relegating communitarian claims to the margins of otherness. It should be recalled that all the late-Tokugawa discourses projected an image of assistance and relief, even when, as in Mito, that image was an ambiguous mix of loving and caring for the people while treating them as dependent children. But the Meiji leaders recognized that politics must determine the content of culture, rather than the reverse, and felt that social identities must be made to comply with the necessity of the state because an opposite course would have encouraged a continuous generation of new subjectivities and divisive antagonisms. Once the state had arrogated to itself the modes of cultural production, it was possible to remove culture from play and employ it as an ideological instrument to depoliticize the masses. That act required reducing the polyphonic discourses of the late Tokugawa, with their many voices speaking about the same things, to the single voice of an authoritative discourse.

Notes

1. This is certainly the argument of Naramoto Tatsuya, *Nihon kinsei no shisō to bunka* (Tokyo: Iwanami shoten, 1978), 65–214; Maruyama Masao, *Nihon seiji shisōshi kenkyū* (Tokyo: Tōkyō daigaku shuppankai, 1953); and the more recent essay by Sugi Hitoshi, "Kaseiki no shakai to bunka," in *Tempōki no seiji to shakai*, ed. Aoki Michio and Yamada Tadao, Kōza Nihon kinseishi 6 (Tokyo: Yūhikaku, 1981), 17–70.
2. Hayashiya Tatsusaburō, ed., *Bakumatsu bunka no kenkyū* (Tokyo: Iwanami shoten, 1978).
3. Fredric Jameson suggests this conception of conjuncture in *Marxism and Form* (Princeton, N.J.: Princeton University Press, 1971), 3–59.
4. The idea of a social imaginary was advanced by Cornelius Castoriadis, *L'institution imaginaire de la société* (Paris: Seuil, 1975), and Claude Lefort, *Les formes de l'histoire: Essais d'anthropologie politique* (Paris: Gallimard, 1978). The concept of a social imaginary, as used by these writers, refers not to a specular image submitted to reflection but, rather, to the indeterminate ways in which society organizes the production of

material goods and the reproduction of its members. The domain of the social imaginary therefore conforms not to the fact that humans must have resources to survive and reproduce but to the variety of ways in which they are able to do so, which builds on but surpasses the basic material conditions of life. It is the way that a society seeks, through forms of signification, to endow itself with an identity different from those of other societies and from chaos.

5. The term "social surplus" is my reading, not Professor Hayashiya's, of the sociopolitical scene.

6. On the logic of similitude, see H. D. Harootunian, "Ideology as Conflict," in *Conflict in Modern Japanese History*, ed. Tetsuo Najita and J. Victor Koschmann (Princeton, N.J.: Princeton University Press, 1982), 25–61.

7. Hayashiya Tatsusaburō, *Kasei bunka no kenkyū* (Tokyo: Iwanami shoten, 1976), 19–42.

8. Hayashiya, *Kasei bunka no kenkyū*, 43–80, 343–95.

9. Hiraishi Naoaki, "Kaiho Seiryō no shisōzō," *Shisō* 677 (November 1980): 52.

10. The argument is made by Amino Yoshihiko, *Muen, kugai, raku* (Tokyo: Heibonsha, 1978).

11. Hiraishi, "Kaiho Seiryō no shisōzō," 52–53.

12. This quotation is from M. M. Bakhtin, *The Dialogic Imagination*, ed. Michael Holquist, trans. Caryl Emerson and Michael Holquist (Austin: University of Texas Press, 1981), 206.

13. Nakamura Yukihiko and Nishiyama Matsunosuke, eds., *Bunka ryōran*, vol. 8 of *Nihon bungaku no rekishi* (Tokyo: Kadokawa shoten, 1967), 60; see also Mizuno Tadashi, *Edo shōsetsu ronsō* (Tokyo: Chūō kōronsha, 1974), 17, and Nakamura Yukihiko, *Gesaku-ron* (Tokyo: Kadokawa shoten, 1966), 137.

14. Nakamura, *Gesakuron*, 137.

15. Sugiura Mimpei, *Ishin zenya no bungaku* (Tokyo: Iwanami shoten, 1967), 3–22.

16. Quoted in Maeda Ichirō, ed., *Kōza Nihon bunkashi* (Tokyo: Misuzu shobō, 1971), 6:121.

17. Buyō Inshi, *Seji kemmonroku*, in *Nihon shomin seikatsu shiryō shūsei* (Tokyo: Misuzu shobō, 1969), 8:656. See also Aoki Michio, *Tempō sōdōki* (Tokyo: Sanseidō, 1979), 1–9, for a useful account of Buyō's jeremiad, as well as Sugiura, *Ishin zenya no bungaku*, 23–46.

18. Shiba Kōkan, *Shumparō hikki*, in *Nihon zuihitsu hikki* (Tokyo: Yoshikawa kōbunkan, 1936), 1:404, 435.

19. Shiba, *Shumparō hikki*, 444; Numata Jirō, Matsumura Akira, and Satō Shōsuke, eds., *Yōgaku 1*, vol. 64 of *Nihon shisō taikei* (Tokyo: Iwanami shoten, 1976), 449, 484–85.

20. Bitō Masahide, "Mito no tokushitsu," in *Mitogaku*, ed. Imai Usaburō, Seya Yoshihiko, and Bitō Masahide, vol. 53 of *Nihon shisō taikei* (Tokyo: Iwanami shoten, 1973), 561. Hereafter cited as *Mitogaku*.

21. J. Victor Koschmann, "Discourse in Action: Representational Politics in the Late Tokugawa Period" (PhD diss., University of Chicago, 1980), 30, later published as *The Mito Ideology: Discourse, Reform, and Insurrection in Late Tokugawa Japan, 1790–1864* (Berkeley: University of California Press, 1987).

22. *Shinron*, in *Mitogaku*, 105. *Shinron* has been translated by Bob Tadashi Wakabayashi in *Anti-Foreignism and Western Learning in Early-Modern Japan* (Cambridge, Mass.: Harvard University Asia Center, 1986).

23. Koschmann, "Discourse in Action," 34.

24. *Seimeiron*, in *Mitogaku*, 10.

25. Takasu Yoshijirō, ed., *Mitogaku taikei* (Tokyo: Mitogaku taikei kankōkai, 1941), 3:382.

26. Koschmann, "Discourse in Action," 52.
27. Koschmann, "Discourse in Action," 61.
28. Takasu, *Mitogaku taikei*, 3:388.
29. Takasu, *Mitogaku taikei*, 3:179.
30. *Shinron*, in *Mitogaku*, 147.
31. Takasu, *Mitogaku taikei*, 3:179.
32. *Shinron*, in *Mitogaku*, 56.
33. *Kokushiden*, in *Mitogaku*, 211.
34. "Chūkō shinsho," in *Mitogaku*, 197.
35. *Shinron*, in *Mitogaku*, 73.
36. *Shinron*, in *Mitogaku*, 73–74.
37. *Shinron*, in *Mitogaku*, 78.
38. Koschmann, "Discourse in Action," 171; see also Masao Maruyama, *Studies in the Intellectual History of Tokugawa Japan*, trans. Mikiso Hane (Princeton, N.J.: Princeton University Press, 1974), 305.
39. Koschmann, "Discourse in Action," 79.
40. *Shinron*, in *Mitogaku*, 81.
41. *Shinron*, in *Mitogaku*, 69.
42. Quoted in H. D. Harootunian, *Toward Restoration* (Berkeley: University of California Press, 1970), 219.
43. Harootunian, *Toward Restoration*, 237.
44. Harootunian, *Toward Restoration*, 270.
45. Matsumoto Sannosuke, *Tennōsei kokka to seiji shisō* (Tokyo: Miraisha, 1969), 72–82.
46. Haga Noboru, "Edo no bunka," in Hayashiya, *Kasei bunka*, 183.
47. Haga, "Edo no bunka," 184.
48. Hirata Atsutane, *Ibuki oroshi*, in *Hirata Atsutane zenshū*, ed. Muromatsu Iwao (Tokyo: Hakubunkan, 1912), 1:2. Hereafter cited as *Ibuki oroshi*.
49. Despite Hirata's apparent valorization of the ordinary folk, many contemporaries would have agreed with the writer Bakin's assessment that Hirata was less concerned with commoners than he was with self-aggrandizement.
50. This is the argument of Matsumoto Sannosuke, *Kokugaku seiji shisō no kenkyū* (Osaka: Yūhikaku, 1957). Following Maruyama's interpretation of nativism as an irrational prop capable of eliciting voluntary submission of the ruled to the emperor, Matsumoto shows how *kokugaku* was made to serve the ideology of the managerial class.
51. Tahara Tsuguo et al., eds., *Hirata Atsutane, Ban Nobutomo, Ōkuni Takamasa*, vol. 50 of *Nihon shisō taikei* (Tokyo: Iwanami shoten, 1973), 18.
52. Hirata Atsutane Zenshū Kankōkai, ed., *Shinshū Hirata Atsutane zenshū* (Tokyo: Meicho shuppan, 1977), 6:4–19.
53. Hirata Atsutane Zenshū Kankōkai, *Hirata Atsutane zenshū*, 217.
54. The idea of a self-sufficient village "movement" was developed by Haga Noboru in several essays and books but notably in "Bakumatsu henkakuki ni okeru kokugakusha no undō to ronri," in *Kokugaku undō no shisō*, ed. Haga Noboru and Matsumoto Sannosuke, vol. 51 of *Nihon shisō taikei* (Tokyo: Iwanami shoten, 1971), 675–84.
55. Haga, "Bakumatsu henkakuki," 333.
56. Mutobe Yoshika, "Ken'yūjun kōron," in *Shintō sōsho*, ed. Nakajima Hiromatsu (Tokyo, 1897), 3:2–3.
57. Mutobe, "Ken'yūjun kōron," 3.
58. Haga, "Bakumatsu henkakuki," 229.
59. Haga, "Bakumatsu henkakuki," 293.

60. Miyao Sadao, "Minka yōjutsu," in *Kinsei jikata keizai shiryō*, ed. Ono Takeo (Tokyo: Yoshikawa kōbunkan, 1954), 5:317.
61. Miyao, "Minka yōjutsu," 304.
62. Suzuki Shigetane, *Engishiki norito kōgi* (Tokyo: Kokusho kankōkai, 1978), 13–14.
63. Katsura Takashige, *Yotsugigusa tsumiwake* (Niigata, 1884) (pages are unnumbered).
64. Tahara et al., *Hirata Atsutane*, 408–9.
65. Nomura Denshirō, ed., *Ōkuni Takamasa zenshū* (Tokyo: Yūkōsha, 1937–1939), 3:18, 43.
66. Nomura, *Ōkuni Takamasa zenshū*, 5:32.
67. Suzuki Masayuki, *Tsukisakaki*, in *Hirata Atsutane*, ed. Sagara Tōru, vol. 24 of *Nihon no meicho* (Tokyo: Chūō kōronsha, 1972), 387.
68. Quoted in Fujitani Toshio, *Okagemairi to ee ja nai ka* (Tokyo: Iwanami shoten, 1968), 168–69.
69. Yasumaru Yoshio, *Nihon kindaika to minshū shisō* (Tokyo: Aoki shoten, 1974), 90.
70. Murakami Shigeyoshi, *Kinsei minshū shūkyō no kenkyū* (Tokyo: Hōzōkan, 1977), 21.
71. Yasumaru, *Nihon kindaika*, 18.
72. Kano Masanao, *Shihonshugi keiseiki no chitsujo ishiki* (Tokyo: Chikuma shobō, 1969), 138.
73. Miyata Noboru, "Nōson no fukkō undō to minshū shūkyō no tenkai," in *Iwanami kōza, Nihon rekishi*, vol. 13 (*kinsei 5*) (Tokyo: Iwanami shoten, 1977), 209–45.
74. Kano, *Shihonshugi*, 138. See also Helen Hardacre, *Kurozumikyō and the New Religions of Japan* (Princeton, N.J.: Princeton University Press, 1986).
75. Kano, *Shihonshugi*, 139.
76. Kano, *Shihonshugi*, 140; see also Murakami Shigeyoshi and Yasumaru Yoshio, eds., *Minshū shūkyō to shisō*, vol. 67 of *Nihon shisō taikei* (Tokyo: Iwanami shoten, 1971), 130.
77. Murakami and Yasumaru, *Minshū shūkyō*, 115.
78. Kano, *Shihonshugi*, 114.
79. Kano, *Shihonshugi*, 102.
80. Kano, *Shihonshugi*, 116.
81. Carmen Blacker, "Millenarian Aspects of the New Religions in Japan," in *Tradition and Modernization in Japanese Culture*, ed. Donald Shively (Princeton, N.J.: Princeton University Press, 1971), 574–76.
82. Blacker, "Millenarian Aspects," 575.
83. See Kano, *Shihonshugi*, 147–48, for an account of the Tenri mythology.
84. Murakami and Yasumaru, *Minshū shūkyō*, 184.
85. Murakami and Yasumaru, *Minshū shūkyō*, 185.
86. Murakami and Yasumaru, *Minshū shūkyō*, 181.
87. Murakami and Yasumaru, *Minshū shūkyō*, 181.
88. Yasumaru, *Nihon kindaika*, 83.
89. Yasumaru, *Nihon kindaika*, 83.
90. Murakami, *Kinsei minshū*, 177.
91. Murakami, *Kinsei minshū*, 179.
92. Seto Mikio, "Minshū no shūkyō ishiki to henkaku no enerugī," in *Henkakuki no shūkyō*, ed. Maruyama Teruo (Tokyo: Gendai jānarizumu shuppankai, 1972), 67.
93. Murakami and Yasumaru, *Minshū shūkyō*, 364.
94. Murakami and Yasumaru, *Minshū shūkyō*, 376.
95. Murakami and Yasumaru, *Minshū shūkyō*, 400, 404.
96. Murakami and Yasumaru, *Minshū shūkyō*, 420.
97. Murakami and Yasumaru, *Minshū shūkyō*, 401.

98. Murakami and Yasumaru, *Minshū shūkyō*, 416.

99. Murakami and Yasumaru, *Minshū shūkyō*, 416

100. Murakami and Yasumaru, *Minshū shūkyō*, 416

101. Murakami and Yasumaru, *Minshū shūkyō*, 366.

102. Quoted in Maeda Ichirō, ed., *Kōza Nihon bunkashi* (Tokyo: San'ichi shobō, 1963), 6:58.

103. Tetsuo Najita, "Structure and Content in Tokugawa Thinking" (unpublished manuscript), 54.

104. Najita, "Structure and Content," 54–55; see Donald Keene, *The Japanese Discovery of Europe* (Stanford, Calif.: Stanford University Press, 1969), for a partial translation of "Keisei hissaku."

105. Najita, "Structure and Content," 60.

106. Maeda, *Kōza Nihon bunkashi*, 6:59.

107. Kitajima Masamoto, *Bakuhansei no kumon*, vol. 18 of *Nihon no rekishi* (Tokyo: Chūō kōronsha, 1966), 367.

108. Satō Shōsuke, Uete Michiari, and Yamaguchi Muneyuki, eds., *Watanabe Kazan, Takano Chōei, Sakuma Shōzan, Yokoi Shōnan, Hashimoto Sanai*, vol. 55 of *Nihon shisō taikei* (Tokyo: Iwanami shoten, 1971), 190.

109. Satō et al., *Watanabe Kazan*, 192, 193.

110. The novelist Ishikawa Jun wrote a moving account of this complex and concerned intellectual: *Watanabe Kazan* (Tokyo: Chikuma shobō, 1964). Marius B. Jansen, "*Rangaku* and Westernization," *Modern Asian Studies* 18, no. 4 (1984): 541–53, also describes this early Westernizing impulse, based on a survey of the recent secondary literature.

111. Satō et al., *Watanabe Kazan*, 179–80.

112. Satō et al., *Watanabe Kazan*, 123.

113. Satō et al., *Watanabe Kazan*, 78.

114. Satō et al., *Watanabe Kazan*, 69, 72.

115. Satō Shōsuke, *Yōgakushi no kenkyū* (Tokyo: Chūō kōronsha, 1964), 168.

116. Satō et al., *Watanabe Kazan*, 168–69.

117. Sugiura Mimpei, ed., *Kirishitan, Rangakushū*, vol. 16 of *Nihon no shisō* (Tokyo: Chikuma shobō, 1970), 353.

118. Sugiura, *Kirishitan, Rangakushū*, 354.

119. Shinano Kyōikukai, ed., *Shōzan zenshū* (Nagano: Shinano Mainichi shimbunsha, 1922), 1:128.

120. Uete Michiari, *Nihon kindai shisō keisei* (Tokyo: Iwanami shoten, 1974), 39–40.

121. Shinano Kyōikukai, *Shōzan zenshū*, 2:710.

122. Satō et al., *Watanabe Kazan*, 322–23.

123. Shinano Kyōikukai, *Shōzan zenshū*, 2:549–51.

124. Miyamoto Chū, *Sakuma Shōzan* (Tokyo: Iwanami shoten, 1932), 53.

125. Uete, *Nihon kindai shisō keisei*, 61.

126. Shinano Kyōikukai, *Shōzan zenshū*, 1:98–99.

127. Uete, *Nihon kindai shisō keisei*, 83.

128. Uete, *Nihon kindai shisō keisei*, 83.

129. Yamazaki Masashige, ed., *Yokoi Shōnan ikō* (Tokyo: Meiji shoin, 1942), 922.

130. Satō et al., *Watanabe Kazan*, 506.

131. Satō et al., *Watanabe Kazan*, 444. *Kokuze sanron* is translated by D. Y. Miyauchi in *Monumenta Nipponica* 23, no. 1/2 (1968): 156–86.

132. Satō et al., *Watanabe Kazan*, 504.

133. Uete, *Nihon kindai shisō keisei*, 83.

134. The term "overdetermination" has a venerable genealogy that, for our purposes, goes back to Sigmund Freud's *Interpretation of Dreams*, in which he applied the concept to describe the process when a dream's elements appear to have been represented in dream thoughts many times over. I am using "overdetermination" to refer to the presence of plural discursive representations during the late Tokugawa period, whereby the same elements appear time and again in different form. In brief, those elements (fear of disorder, concern for productivity, anxiety over questions of security, the idea of community free from fragmentation, new concepts of authority and legitimacy, and the like) that seem to have the most numerous and strongest supports acquire the right of entry into the content of discourses.

135. Itō Shirō, *Suzuki Masayuki no kenkyū* (Tokyo: Aoki shoten, 1972), 287–88.

136. This quotation from Yano's poem is from Hirose Tamotsu, ed., *Origuchi Shinobu shū* (Tokyo: Chikuma shobō, 1975), 386.

137. The terms of this contest between *center* and *periphery* are documented in Michio Umegaki, *After the Restoration: The Beginning of Japan's Modern State* (New York: New York University Press, 1988), while the proponents of the localist inflection have been romanticized in Irokawa Daikichi, *The Culture of the Meiji Period*, ed. Marius B. Jansen (Princeton, N.J.: Princeton University Press, 1985).

PART III

PATHWAYS TO MODERNITY'S PRESENT AND THE ENDURING EVERYDAY

CHAPTER 5

SHADOWING HISTORY

National Narratives and the Persistence of the Everyday

Everyday life, policed and mystified by every means, is a sort of reservation for good natives who keep modern society running without understanding it—this society with its rapid growth of technological powers and forced expansion of its market. History—the transformation of reality cannot presently be used in everyday life because the people of everyday life are the product of history over which they have no control.

Guy DeBord

The issue this essay wishes to address is how history, as encoded in historiography of history writing, is actually based upon its capacity to conceal, disguise, and indeed suppress the everyday. This is especially true when you consider that most history is really driven by the nation-state and that far from envisaging a history free or rescued from the nation, most history writing ends up reinforcing it. In other words, history's primary vocation has been to displace the constant danger posed by the surplus of everyday life, to overcome its apparent "trivia," "banalities," and untidiness in order to find an encompassing register that will fix meaning. With Hegel, narrative was given the role of supplying the maximal unity by which to grasp the meaning of history. What immediately got privileged was, of course, the nation-state in the making of world-historical events and ultimately class, subjects who can claim world-historical agency. By the same measure, the surplus or messy residues of modern life, especially its immensely staggering complexities, its endless incompletions and repetitions—all irreducible—are repressed or in some instances the microcosmic is sometimes mobilized to reinforce macrocosmic meaning. (This has frequently been called history from below and what Germans have called *Alltagsgeschichte*.) What I would like to do is explore the category of everydayness, ushered in with the masses and the appearance of the subaltern, as a minimal unity that provides its own principle of historical temporality that easily challenges the practice of history writing as we know it.

Past Presents/Present Pasts

One of the interesting recurrences throughout Asia during the interwar period was not simply the evident material transformation of societies under the impact of capitalism and colonialism but also the way these societies came to understand this modernizing and modernist experience. Owing either to the accelerated destruction of long-standing received cultures of reference inflicted by the implementation of new modes of production and the introduction of commodity consumption or, in some instances, to enforced colonial domination which, in cities like Shanghai or Bombay, dramatized the incongruence of politics and culture, the common response was to find an optic through which to account for the experience of a phenomenal present, as such, rather than resort to the "knowledge" offered by a historical representation of the past. In this fateful encounter—experienced, I believe, more intensely in societies like Japan, which came late to capitalist modernization, or India and China (not to forget Africa and Latin America), which had it forced upon them through the violent agency of colonization than their Euro-American counterparts—the spectacle of the present, condensed and accelerated, took precedence over the past and history's knowledge. Often the rate of change inflicted by the forces of capitalism and colonialism was so rapid and fierce that not even the immediate past was accessible to historical consciousness, prompting Fanon's observation of the brutal destruction of "systems of reference . . . matched by sacking cultural patterns . . . values are flaunted, crushed emptied" (1970, 33, 41). This is not say that societies in Asia were not interested in historical representation. But when history in these places was written to bridge the great "epistemic violence" caused by capitalism and colonialism, it was invariably bonded to the nation form, if there was one, or the idea of the nation yet to come after the demise of colonialism, thus replicating established historiographical practice in Euro-America. As in the industrialized world of the interwar period, the Asian periphery especially, and I suspect parts of Africa and

Latin America, identified history and its narrative with the story of a particular group or folk and the heroic formation of the nation-state. If history writing served to catalyze, if not sanctify, the new nation form in the nineteenth century, nation and narrative increasingly functioned to unify diverse populations and to secure the guarantee of civil order through the often fictive agency of common identity and the more or less voluntary assent of the people to work and die for one's country. This particular lesson was learned early by Japanese, who happily escaped foreign domination only to become colonizers, to achieve nationhood before colonized and semicolonized societies like India and China. With India, its peoples were seen as subjects of the Crown—albeit second-class ones—who were enlisted to work for the Raj and fight Great Britain's enemies. When, at the time of World War II, the anticolonial Indian National Army was formed and threw in its lot with the Japanese, its adherents were instantly branded as traitors. Yet even in these colonial sites, the nation constituted the principal category for historical representation. So powerful was this association that the Indonesian nationalist Soetomo spoke of the nation's history in his *Autobiography* long before there was one (Anderson 1998, Harootunian 1999).

However, after World War I—and a first phase of "globalization" that transported capitalism and commodity consumption to Asia, Africa, and Latin American—the problem was how best to account for (and represent) what was occurring in the present, not what had happened in the past. This entailed forging a present of one's own that would become a past in place of a practice in which another's past dominated the present. The experience of capitalist penetration under the sign of modernization and a new temporality called "modernity" meant that the lived reality of the everyday by the masses was different from the nation and its narrative telling people how to fulfill its requirements for national subjectivity and citizenship. If the nation composed a narrative of enactment by the people, the everyday of the masses wrote a vastly different history of its own. The immense upheavals that sent mass migrations from the countryside to the new industrial sites of the cities prompted a growing awareness of a different life in kind among those national subjects who entered new labor markets and the world of commodity consumption. The perception of this transformation was registered early by thinkers throughout the emerging capitalist world in places like Germany, France, Japan, Brazil, and then later in India and China, who began to examine the specific texture of the everyday lived by the urban classes—especially workers—and the consequences of commodity culture. With the Bolshevik Revolution this new everyday began, for the first time, to make possible the envisaging of history in such a way as to foreground the present—the now—in contrast to the past of national narratives that ultimately implied an identity with both present and future. The effect of this emphasis on the present was to disclose the recognition of the existence of different temporalities between history (especially "national history") and the everyday, where the former looked to an indeterminate past leading to the present and capable of both shaping the future and securing the identity of each moment (periodization and stages in a trajectory), while the latter saw in the present a break with all antecedents and thus a new way to envision the relationship between the present and the past. By the same measure, this new perspective resulted in rehierarchizing the event and reordering the relationship between the significant and insignificant by showing that what now counted as a force of disruption and change was no longer the large-scale happenings but the micro-occurrences of the everyday. (This strategy was not only later promoted by the Situationists in the 1960s but also put into brilliant documentary practice by filmmakers like Imamura Shōhei in his memorable *History of Postwar Japan as Told by a Barmaid*.) It is in this sense that the everyday, marking a different kind of historicity, shadowed the narrative of national history and the putative movement of world historicality, just as Asia, Africa, and even Latin America existed in the eclipse cast by Euro-America but whose very negativity enabled the claims of universality associated with History. The turn to the everyday meant fixing on the present and was not simply seen as the site of punctual events but rather as the location of a durational moment and its subsequent ontologization. It is this relationship I would like to explore further in order to see if there is some way we can restore to historical practice the everyday which, according to phenomenology since Husserl, has constituted the kernel of the historical world and designated the identity of the *Lebenswelt* as the sign of historicality itself. In pursuit of this program, I will first consider how, momentarily, the idea of everyday life appeared as the basis of history in Hegel and subsequently was abandoned for the more expansive conceptualization of world history that fixed the primacy of the nation-state as the sign of true historicity. This notion was subsequently reinforced by the further development of the nation-state in nineteenth-century Europe, especially, and its vocation for capitalist accumulation that not only demanded of new national subjects unwavering willingness to sacrifice their lives but also, as a penultimate service, to work for it. The organization of work time closely matched the progressive sequentiality that figured the national narrative and seemed to have inspired its smooth and seamless linearity. In this way, the capitalist nation-state reduced different, coexisting temporalities lived by diverse groups within different realms of the social formation to constitute variations of segmented and cumulative time that opened the door to a historical consciousness rooted in evolutionary and progressive plotlines. This sense of historicity was challenged in the twentieth century by the formation of mass society in new industrial sites whose lived experience in the present—making their own history—collided politically with the claims of the national narrative, just as their privileging of the everyday or now time clashed with the temporal presumptions of a completed national past. I will end this examination of how everydayness supplied new principles for a history of the present and produced the forms appropriate to it by reconsidering its meaning for the current practice of cultural studies.

Historicizing the Everyday

According to Kracauer, writing in his last book, *History: The Last Things Before the Last*, there was a moment in the early nineteenth century when history and the everyday encountered each other through the mediation of photography. He recalls how, in 1840, Friedrich von Raumer's contemporary histories were "praised for resembling daguerreotypes" in that they captured the "fleeting shadows of the present" on the wing (Kracauer 1995, 58). Kracauer was concerned with drawing out a shared structure of history and the everyday, which he called the *Lebenswelt*, since "camera reality" paralleled "historical reality," as both were amorphously "patterned" on the "half-cooked state of our everyday world." (It is important to recognize that this coupling of history and everyday sealed by photography actually contradicted an earlier view Kracauer had proposed in *The Mass Ornament* that argued for their difference and separation.) In this new kinship, he discerned, nevertheless, the contingent nature of the material, random events, "transient and unforeseeable encounters" (1995, 58). However, history, especially national history in the nineteenth century, was never seen as the locus of contingent events but rather as the arena of purposefulness and destiny. From this perspective, it is safe to say that the contingent was associated with the precinct of the "half-cooked state" of the everyday. While Kracauer acknowledged how photography invariably precluded any chance for achieving completion, he failed to recognize that historical reconstruction always (until recently) aspired to completeness since it was about a past that was long over. Only the isolated traces of a long national history could be caught in the photographic lens. The present, the site of the everyday, could never claim completion until it became past, while the past was over and done with, ready to be definitively reconstructed. Although this separation between a completed past and an incomplete present partially explains why photography and history prematurely ended what might have become a productive relationship for both, Kracauer seemed more interested in liberating the "lifeworld" from its relationship to philosophy (and science) and realigning it with history, with which it supposedly shared a structure. By contrast, we know that Benjamin saw in photography a model for history, but one built on images signifying the now time of everyday life that recognizes in the concept (*Begriff*) of history proposed in the *Theses on the Concept of History* an interchangeability between the operation of how thought seeks to bring history within the grasp of a concept and the camera's ceaseless fixation on a moment of history

(Benjamin 1999; see also Cadava 1997, xviii). In his quest for a materialist historiography, Benjamin was convinced that there could be no thinking about history without at the same time thinking about photography.

Yet the separation between a completed past and an incomplete present had already been accomplished earlier by Hegel. In the *Aesthetics*, Hegel early identified the everyday with what he called the "prose of the world."[1] For Hegel, the prose of the world was concretized in the endlessly multifarious activities of the everyday. "This is the prose of the world," he wrote, "as it appears to the consciousness both of the individual himself and of others: a world of finitude and mutability, of entanglements in the relative, of the pressure of necessity from which no individual is in a position to withdraw" (Hegel 1975, 150). Everydayness constitutes both the temporality and the unity of the prose of the world. It is the present in which intersubjective relations are carried out, pointing to a future on whose path the past—the history of each individual based on a priori experiences—acts as a steady guide. At this moment in Hegel's thinking, history would thus be conceived as the multiplicity of individual experiences, an inexhaustible tableau of actions and events, and its subject matter would seek to comprehend the entirety of the human condition itself. (While no actual history ever came close to approaching this truly global ideal, a trace of this aspiration is still visible in Balzac's monumental desire to map the world of early nineteenth-century France.) Nothing would be excluded from this history of the human condition, no culture, class, ethnic group would be ineligible. Yet not too long after Hegel abandoned this breathtakingly heroic task to comprehend and represent the totality of human experience, he decided to narrow the compass and reidentify history with the nation-state, transmuting the prose of the world into Spirit's unfolding in world history. By discerning in history the patterning of Providence and the itinerary of Spirit's unfolding plan, Hegel not only linked significant eventfulness to a "higher necessity" but also banished (apparently as insignificant) entire cultures and continents from the achievement of historicality. It is ironic to observe that, more than a century afterward, the world of the excluded that had once been eliminated from History turned to the everyday, as if it were the return of the repressed, to mark the historicity of its experience with the modern present and perhaps rescue the promise of Hegel's original vision of an all-encompassing history of the human condition. With this move, it was able to call into question the universalistic claims of History's narrative at the same time it began to supply the resources for envisioning, especially among the colonized, new political projects for the future. In fact, the appeal to the everyday was to become the primary method to rehistoricize the present.

The Hegelian model of evolutionary development is too well known to recount in any detail. But what is important about it is the recognition that Spirit moves through stages as it "actualizes" itself and that each actualization is expressed in the form of a national spirit that progressively, and I should add purposefully, acquired knowledge of the "movement of its own activity . . . and frees its consciousness from natural immediacy" (Guha 2002, 26). Along Spirit's route, "nations" have achieved partial actualization in emancipating themselves from nature and consciously affirming such freedom, only to stall and become stranded in permanent "standstill." The development of the state— revealing the fullness and completion of Spirit's self-consciousness—fulfils the vocation of freedom and thus finds for a people a place in world history— that is, history itself now differentiated from prehistory. We know, of course, Hegel's Oriental World—China and India, especially—failed the test and remained fettered to nature's immediacy and far from the realization of true freedom. By the same token, these "nations," or as he called them "forms of nations," were destined to become "people without history." Marx's "Asiatic mode of production" and Weber's confident identification of rationality in a specific religio-cultural endowment later merely reinforced the great divide Hegel's providential plan had produced. Both, moreover, were persuaded that Asia—and presumably the rest of the world outside Euro-America—could free itself from the lockstep and rejoin History through agencies of capitalism and scientific rationality. The Japanese folklorist Yanagita Kunio, commenting on H. G. Wells's *The Outline of History, Being a Plain History of Life and Mankind* (1919), observed how whole continents like Africa and entire peoples had simply vanished from the screen of world history. History, the world historical thus came to mean only those "nations" which had, as in Europe, managed to develop a state—thus sealing the kinship between history and historiography and the category of the nation-state as its true object and "rational content." Hence, the nation-state became the principal vocation of history since it was history that recorded the development of the state (a theory of development we have not yet overcome) as Spirit's self-objectification and the content of historical writing. It was precisely this totalizing identity between reason, history, and nation-state that eliminated the space of the everyday, or, at the very least, consigned it to the domain of contingency. Consequentially, the everyday was reduced to the status of either a repressed remainder or ethnographic atemporality—to those aspects of life that had not yet been assimilated to the nation form or which, somehow, had been able to resist its hegemonizing templates of behavior and conduct. (In Durkheimian social theory, nation-state was replaced by the category of society based on organic solidarity and the capacity of the division of labor to ultimately find a place for everybody.) Kracauer, it is important to recall, wanted to show both the linkage of photography and history, whose promise had not been realized, and history and the "life-world," whose necessary mismatch he failed to grasp. However, historians early rejected the partnership of history and photography by dismissing the latter as mere "reproduction" of the immediate, despite the Rankean dictum to see "how things actually are."

Instead, they saw in history the form of "reconstruction" and even representation of the "nature of things," much like a painting, according to one prominent historian (Kracauer 1995, 51). Above all else, history was concerned with the past of the nation rather than the experience of the present—how the nation came into existence—whereas photography and the everyday it captured in its particularity were too fastened to the present and rooted in an indeterminate temporality not yet completed. Because the past was completed, it was the time and place history had been made, whereas the present could only reaffirm its identity with it and recall its exemplars by designating places of memory but not remake it. It would have to wait for the moment it became past, itself requiring a distancing operation, which would have made it past and eligible for historical status. Owing to the process of commodification, this distancing would eventually be objectified in the collective temporalization of events, by distinguishing between a "then" and the "now" (Feather 2000, 134). Commodification would further result in placing other times beyond the grasp of a frozen and seemingly endless present. Ultimately, the past would have to find permanent expression in the reformulation of national history as heritage. In fact, it was Benjamin who observed how history in its historicist inflection transmuted the phenomena of the past into enduring manifestations of their value as "heritage" and "cultural treasures" for the nation. It was this distrust of historicism that, in part, induced him to turn the "focus of historiography away from narrative forms of historical totalization to montage," from story to image, quotation, anecdote (Osborne 1995, 115). Japanese, on their part, not only envisaged and implemented the project of national history to eternalize the accomplishment of nationhood but also established a classification system in the 1930s that organized and designated artifacts from the past as "national treasures," "cultural property," and ranked artisans/artists who were still working as "living national treasures." There were even attempts to assimilate the everyday into "living culture" (*seikatsu bunka*) founded on the survival of vestiges now configured as "heritage." The importance of this valorization of national history into heritage (long before the British turned to it after World War II) is the identity of a distancing trope that demanded forgetting not only the role of the present in historical memory but also everything in the past which continues to resist transmission as national heritage (Osborne 1995, 140). Yet it is important to recall that one of the principal purposes of national history and its reliance on narrative form was to not only flatten out time, literally reducing temporality to a timeless space, but also to remove all those sediments from different pasts that if engaged in the present would prevent a closure of the future. It is interesting to recognize, in this connection, the parallelism between national narratives and dominant narratives of modernity.

In the nineteenth century, the everyday and the now, according to Bakhtin, thus left the domain of history writing and historical knowledge to become the content of the realist novel—inadvertently yoking experience to the task of fiction and opening the way to overcome the authoritative univocal narrative of national history for polyvocal enunciations signifying different plots, plural political perspectives, and differing temporalities. The everyday, thus, was increasingly seen as the place where events were transformed into a mass article through the process of commodification and instantaneous transmission that made possible the repeated experiencing of the image-event. It was the act of recognizing reproducibility that prompted people like Benjamin to conclude that experience was being removed from both traditional and spatial determinations, resembling most the commodity form. By contrast, the events that continued to configure historiography could only be recalled and remembered but not experienced. Benjamin saw these "recurrences" as the sign of a repressed history, its watermark, perhaps, the repeated production of the image that constituted for him the fundamental event of modernity. This is why he famously proposed in *On the Concept of History* (thesis no. 5) that the "true picture of the past flits by" and can only be "seized as an image which flashes up at the instant it can be recognized and is never seen again."

By proposing that in modern times nation-state and history formed an original alliance, a vocation for each other, I am not implying that such an arrangement excluded other kinds of historical representation. The dramatic example of Jacob Burckhardt discloses the possibility of envisaging a different kind of history not constrained by the nation form. I am suggesting that the form of the nation-state constituted the primary category through which historical writing "reconstructed" the past for the present. Its content usually concentrated on the origin and development of a specific group or people and their realization of a state entitling them to occupy a place in world history. It is interesting to recall how Japanese thinkers in the late 1930s saw the coming of a war with the West as an affirmation of the Japanese state's "world-historical mission." The task of the national history was to recuperate this achievement of the past in the present in order for the nation-state to accomplish the principal goals of unity, wealth, and power. Historical practice meant discovering a "timeless truth" of the nation's past, a fixed "eternal image of the past." When we look at the later refractions of nationhood in Asia, we see the replication of this model, despite differences of time, place, and political circumstances, and the repetitive appeal to pastness intimately linked to the creation of national subjects who at an abstract level collectively shared a common identity that was intended to secure the prospect of unity and social order to be realized in their willingness to work and die for the nation. The hyphenated nation often approximated the commodity form itself, inasmuch as its mystical and spiritual side remained concealed yet was unfailingly recruited to interpolate subjects to work and sacrifice themselves. The constitution of people as subjects, emblematized by appeals to race, language, and timeless national culture, were employed as the forms through which to objectify the hidden spiritual and mystical side of the nation that accompanied the continuous creation of the past. A subject for the nation also worked, at least initially, to displace or subsume subject positions demanded by the new division of labor. In this regard, Chatterjee reminds us that the national dichotomization of inner and outer aimed to shift national subjectivity away from bourgeois liberal notions of universal humanity to forms of particularity and difference—to the recognition of the "national community as against other communities" (Chatterjee 1993, 75). In other words, nation formation always presupposed a principle of inclusion and exclusion, based upon a presupposed givenness, for its effectiveness and sought through abstract emblems of identity to unify, if not actually homogenize, a population into a fictive ethnos. While this impulse was directed to penetrate and permeate daily life through the staging of punctual rituals, ceremonies, holidays, fixing places of national memory, etc., it rarely succeeded in completely assimilating the everyday to its protocols. Even in the daily life of workers and colonial labor, especially migrants to the metropolis like Koreans in Japan, who constituted a virtual Industrial Reserve Army ready for capital bonded to the insecurities of day-work, there were still areas in the lived experience that were capable of resisting assimilation to the structures of domination. This was especially the case in the twentieth century with massive industrialization and the formation of mass society, persuading Weber to entrust state bureaucracy with the task of "dominating everyday life," which meant eliminating precisely the excess or surplus that remained unassimilated. In this regard, the everyday appeared as a repressed and irreducible remainder of the nation-state, what was leftover, surplus, which, in the eyes of Japanese, Chinese, and Indian observers in the interwar period, came to constitute the zone of noneveryday life. What seems clear is that the domain of everyday life possessed its own complex mix of temporalities (Mariátegui's prescient sense of what we might today call mixed temporalities in Peru) and routines that often clashed with national time and behavioral expectation.

Investment in the nation form promised a solution to the problem of smoothing out or leveling the ground of society for the accomplishment of capital accumulation and its continuous reproduction, that is to say removing the fetters to its installation and implementation, even though the necessity to create unevenness was inscribed in the social formation of the new nation-states. Hence, it was the desire of nation-states, everywhere, to present the picture or image of an even, unblemished surface, capable of concealing its enabling conditions of existence. Yet this effort to secure a smooth surface, hiding nothing, and polish the rough edges of unevenness in order to achieve unity, common sense through shared identity, coherence was powerfully mediated by received temporal and spatial matrices deriving from earlier modes of production (Poulantzas

2000, 104). The new meanings of territory and history were reinscribed in more fundamental changes underlying the conceptual matrices of space and time whose rhythms were now regulated by significant shifts in the mode of production. A new spatial configuration fixed boundaries between inside and outside, within which the reproduction of capital was able to take place. The state thus acted to monopolize the organization of social space in such a way as to materialize its various apparatuses—army, schools, central bureaucracy, penal system—and patterned, in turn, the subjects over whom it exercised power. While this space split the labor process into capitalist units of production and reproduction, the uneven development of capitalism in its spatialized dimension was actually coterminous with this "discontinuous morphology" (Poulantzas 2000, 104). In other words, the state was embedded in a spatial matrix implied by the labor process and ultimately in the circulation of commodities and consumption. Because of this arrangement, production, especially as it was augmented by machine power and the factory system, entailed further segmenting, serializing, and dividing a cumulative and irreversible time. This practice stood in marked contrast to received premodern conceptions of temporality that were usually considered as reversible. The nation-state's objective was thus to master time in such a way as to secure a standard single and homogeneous measure—clock time—capable of reducing the different, coexisting temporalities lived by diverse groups within different domains of the social formation by acknowledging a distance between each. For the first time, then, the temporal matrix of the capitalist nation-state mapped out the particular moments as different temporalities and construed them as variations of segmented and cumulative time. These different temporalities, in turn, were totalized into a procession of moments following one another that would make way for the construction of modes of historical consciousness rooted in narratives of evolutionary and progressive plotlines (Poulantzas 2000, 111, 113). With relentless linearity, each moment led to and produced the next to represent yet a further move in an irreversible series. The awareness of this linear movement provided a perspective for envisaging a before and after, a then and now—differentiating the present from what preceded it and comes after. Here, in any case, was a model for national history and the construction of a continuist and totalizing narrative capable of explaining how the folk—in time and space—had managed to create the nation-state and how the history of this achievement revealed a progressive unfolding which materialized or objectified the fusion of idea and reason. The combining of spatial and temporal matrices of capitalism disclosed how spatial unevenness of diverse spheres of the social formation and the respective coexistence of different temporalities constituted a function whose relationship between history (time) and space (territory) was articulated by the nation-state. The modern nation form supplied the occasion for the interaction of these matrices to produce a "historicity of territory" and a "territorialization of a history," both the calling and the content of the national narrative (Poulantzas 2000, 114).

Quotidianizing the Present

While the task of the national narrative was to concretize the link between history and territory, and to exceptionalize the particular story that had been carried out by the folk, this did not mean that the idea of the national was able to reach and permeate the space-time matrices of everyday life. If the national culture failed to become the end point of everyday life but only its "ground" that would continuously be reworked and recoded, it was also the case that everydayness was expected to lift itself up to the dignity of the nation (and thus reason). In other words, everyday life was supposed to be colonized by the national idea, yet it too often escaped this colonizing impulse to exist as a remaindered excess outside its reason. Even though the spatial and temporal matrices of the capitalist nation-state were supposed to be articulated through the forms of everyday life, to perform the national narrative, so to speak, it—everydayness—invariably resisted this assimilative process to become an other to the form of historical representation. The presumed subsumption—more formal than real—of the everyday to the consensus producing demands of the nation and national identity was never complete. In a sense, it was the emphasis on the nation's pastness, rather than its present, and its meaning for the future, and the necessity to homogenize time that provided the everyday with both the identity of social space—the world—and the temporality of the now to remake life in the twentieth century.

The reemergence of the everyday as an active concept demanding political, social, and cultural transformation occurred in the twentieth-century conjuncture whose coordinates were marked by the Bolshevik Revolution and the accelerated and technological modernization during and after World War I. If the Russian Revolution unveiled the power of the masses to determine, momentarily, their own everyday for the first time in history, the unprecedented move to capital industries, massive urbanization, and the subsequent production of consumer commodities and the global expansion of capitalism signaled the figuration of a new kind of mass society. By the same measure, the new everyday itself was transformed, in turn, under the impact of fascism and Stalinism in the 1930s. Accompanying this profound change in the social topography—one the nation-state form was hardly prepared to meet—was the formation of a new hermeneutic which, with thinkers like Georg Simmel, sought to concretize philosophic understanding by constituting metropolitan life and its complex of social interactions into an object of inquiry. Under the impact of social and economic transformation, the everyday was thus "denaturalized" into a domain of common experience whose hidden significance, as Freud proposed at the outset of the century in *The Psychopathology of Everyday Life*, was already manifest in the countless slips and mistakes encountered in daily speech. At the same time it was also seen as the spatial and temporal location of social contradictions, as perceived by Georg Lukács, signified by the "reified reproduction of immediacy" (Roberts 1999, 17). In 1920s Japan, the thinker Tosaka Jun called for the "quotidianization of philosophy" and turned to examining both custom—a code for the commodity form—as a symptom that concealed lived history and the practice of journalism that reinforced the reified surface of daily life. Throughout the interwar period the category of the everyday had become the ground of an analytic minimal unity. Moreover, it would be seen as the empirical place for staging social and cultural transformations seeking to reclaim it for the masses (Marxian Communism, non-Marxian socialism) or contain them (fascism). If, as proposed earlier, the image was envisaged as the central event of modernity (Benjamin), its locus was the everyday, now grounded in the commodity form. But its identification with the global expansion of capitalism and the virtual transformation of the older nation-state system into an expanded version consisting of new states, colonies, and semicolonies already challenged the received division between center and periphery. More importantly, it contributed to the further exhaustion of an excluding national narrative and its effort to historicize spatial unity and homogenize time. In conception and experience, the everyday dramatized both diversity and temporal unevenness within an immanent framework and the existence of a world that no longer was simply divided between Euro-America and its "shadow." It also began to offer the possibility of another kind of history that was capable of recognizing how the working masses had been able to separate the collective experience of the dominated from "religious and cultural fatalism" invariably employed by the ruling classes (Roberts 1999, 16). Hence, the appeal to the everyday would now mean accounting for the active relationship of custom and commodity and new forms of representation promised by technological invention and innovation. This implied not simply a change in the putative content of history and the addition of new social constituencies to the story as subunits of the national subject (simply filling out a consensual order). Rather, it promoted a change in form that would appeal to new verbal and visual devices. It would also lead to a reconsideration of the question of subjectivity and social agency itself resulting from the replacement of the folk by the collective power of the working masses, who saw in the everyday the "entangling pressures of necessity" Hegel observed a century earlier. While Lukács constructed a critique of everyday life in the figure of the "reified reproduction of the immediate," it was Walter Benjamin—in Europe—and Miki Kiyoshi in Japan who looked to the dissolution of art in the everyday and Tosaka Jun who saw in the day-to-day routines and frozen countenance of custom the necessity for representing them in their rehistoricization. However, it was a rehistoricization of what had been forgotten, despised, remaindered—in short the microscopic content of everyday life—now fused with what escapes the totalizations of reason and the nation-state. In fact, this effort to see the everyday as the site of rehistoricization, envisaged by a range of thinkers in the 1930s, referred to the observation that even though everyday life appeared as endless routine it was still marked by temporal unevenness. Under the achievement of a putatively smooth and even surface, different temporalities would manage to break through to emit significations of coexisting or coeval modes of production and class affiliation. It was the place where the constant braiding of different temporalities took place. Benjamin, who referred to these temporalities in the shape of an arabesque, was prepared to trade the smooth, even surface of historical continuity, what he called historicism, for a remembrance which modernity had made into a form of cultural unconscious. National history was nothing if not an abstracted continuity with the past, cast in the form of a natural and naturalizing chronology. The present, now constituting the temporality in which the momentous concurrence of the past in the present was occurring, signaled the great drama of unevenness, staged and sharpened by the specific location of societies, like Japan, China, India, and Brazil, which only recently had plunged into the process of capitalist modernization. What I am referring to is the role played by temporally rooted forms in the present and what Ernst Bloch identified as noncontemporaneous synchronisms, where past and present are not necessarily successive but simultaneously produced or coexist as uneven temporalities, just as the then and now of modernity are coeval, even though the former is invariably forgotten or repressed. In this drama of uneven temporalities—the contemporaneity of the noncontemporaneous—the past will be seen to break into and be gathered up in the seemingly eternal present in the form of memoration, often acting as a revenant or ghostly specter of the past bent on haunting and destabilizing the present, exacting its retribution for having been forgotten. The critical recovery of this memory from the surface of immediacy constituted an interruption—history as arrest—and provided both an occasion for reassessing the present's links to the past and thus the opportunity for historical experience. With this move, the everyday appears as a spectral precinct of time/space. The shadows of another life—sedimented temporal conditions—constantly act upon and are acted upon by the new. In this way, the now—Tosaka's *ima* or Benjamin's *jetzt*—could become the site for a qualitatively different experience of the now as a *historical* present. But this present would henceforth be grasped as a historical rather than simply a natural temporality, even though its very instantaneity made the everyday appear as nothing more than a static figure fusing nature and history into the image of atemporal eternity (Osborne 1995, 143).

(In a certain sense, this might conceivably be the only way to "experience" history since it is impossible to imagine how anybody could experience a national history that had already been made in the distant past, even by those who were presumably making it then, apart from declaring identity with it, what more properly has been called patriotism.) It was for this reason that Tosaka Jun argued that the everyday supplied the principles of historical temporality, even though nothing seemed to happen from one day to another.

The rejection of the identity of the everyday with immediate reality required the necessity to actualize the now for its repressed historical memories. The present actively conjuring up a past looms in sharp contrast to the national narrative that favored the past over the present or a social scheme that simply conflated the present with the way things are. It should be pointed out that while this interpretative strategy calling for actualization was supposed to serve the cause of social transformation, the everyday and the observable coexistence of different temporalities during the 1930s was often enlisted for other, less-progressive political agendas. Nothing better illustrates how the everyday embodied the symptoms of alienation, repressed revenants summoning a lost and forgotten past discounted by capitalist modernization and unfulfilled desire than those societies that either came late to capitalism or encountered it through the agency of colonization. Here, too, is a dramatic reminder of how the everyday structurally resembled the colony. In these societies, the constant concurrence of past in present was lived and experienced in the everyday which the national narrative had originally tried to eliminate by making the present continuous and identical with the past and the future. Throughout Asia in the 1930s, the everyday was often identified with an unchanging essential history, housing irreducible cultural characteristics or enduring folk custom. Both these perspectives converged on the projection of an eternal everydayness and its capacity to summon the real. In India, Gandhi utilized these resources to construct a non-Marxian communitarian movement aimed at enlisting the peasantry, who could recognize their everyday lives in its program. At the same time, Rabindranath Tagore, in one of his last essays, celebrated an enduring everydayness that had continued to escape imperial and national histories, the Japanese critic Kobayashi Hideo looked to literature, especially what he called the "classics of life," to show how a certain commonness characterized the everyday in contrast to history. Folklorists in both Japan and China punctually fastened onto unchanging custom lived and reproduced over the long duration as the surest sign of an eternal everyday. In our time, the historian Ranajit Guha has looked back to a form of common and unchanging everydayness, revealed by Tagore, as the alternative to a history founded on the nation-state (Guha 2002, 48–94). In other words, while some saw in the everyday the figure of incompletion and the occasion for remaking the world, others saw it as a completed reservoir of unchanging custom, irreducible experience, and timeless value. In both cases, we can see the discrowning of the narrative of nation-state. In other instances, the phenomenology of the everyday was (and still is) elided with ethnography, or some form of native ethnology, as a way of reducing the remainder to the object of observation and description, atemporalization, and dehistoricization. Yet all these appeals to an atemporal and unchanging everydayness too often raised the risk of slipping into or inviting appropriation by fascist calls for an auratic community and its authentic culture.

The opportunity for rehistoricization promised by the everyday was often indistinguishable from the new cultural practices made available by technology and consumption culture. Hence, the category of the everyday, which had appealed to realism (recast by thinkers like Lukács) as its epistemology, announced an unprecedented expansion of new cultural and representational forms supplied by new technologies, diverse artistic experimentation, film, photography, photomontage, documentaries, and novels depicting the experience of daily life and more that called attention to both a historical moment and the foregrounding of everyday life as the ground of history. In this inventory photography was able to renew its lease on history by serving as the quintessential technique and art capable of interrupting the seemingly atemporal present and calling a momentary pause to it in the interest of critically recovering objects and events from it and reconsidering their contemporary significance and relationship to its concealed past. This ground, therefore, referred not simply to how images were indexed according to whether or not they belonged to a "specific time" but rather how they "entered into the legibility" of that time, what Benjamin called the "now of a specific recognizability" that momentarily brought past and present, then and now together in a configuration best expressed in the form of the collage. The new forms through which the everyday found expression also began to mark the path through which everyday life sought to historicize its present. In this way, the documentary that played such an important role in Soviet culture of the 1920s sought to construct the category of the everyday, while the documentary narratives based on direct observation on the streets of Tokyo by Kon Wajirō chronicled how modern life was remaking the world at the level of everyday consumption patterns, gestures, ways of dressing, etc. (Kon called his practice "modernology" as against mere ethnographic reporting of the present urbanscape). At the same time, we can observe how new novelistic forms in Japan (the daily-life novels of Kikuchi Kan and the detective stories of Edogawa Rampo) and China (Zhang Henshui's *Shanghai Express*) were transcribing the textures and pace of urban life in serialized form in mass-circulating dailies; the increasing use of montage for narrative, whether photographic or verbal, indeed a cinema in Shanghai itself devoted to producing "vernaculization," performed both as the representational forms through which the masses were able to recognize themselves and the distractions of their everyday and the means that offered how best to imagine it as the place of constant remaking. Nakai Masakazu, an activist in the Japanese popular front in the 1930s, early recognized in the documentary the means to represent the real despite subsequent efforts to mediate its facticity. In his view, facticity, however fictionalized and recoded, is clearly still able to sustain its status as a recorder of fact as social reality, owing to the technology of reproduction. He also recognized in montage an entirely different kind of "narrative" signifying a difference of everyday life and its separation from the linear storytelling characterizing the feature films that captured spectators. But his most interesting innovation was to initiate a weekly magazine called *Doyōbi* (Saturday), which sought to vocalize and provide a voice to mass cultural aspiration. Through this newspaper, Nakai was convinced that the masses could give expression to their own everyday in such a way as to resist the encroachments of fascism and its desire to penetrate daily life. In colonial Korea, Ch'oe Myongik's short stories employed the technology of detail to explore the bourgeois self and its claims to autonomy, while Yi T'aejun, recalling Tagore and Kobayashi Hideo, imagined an Asian space outside commodity culture that still embodied the material past in the present.

In many ways, this promise of rehistoricization prompted by the appeal to everydayness was momentarily actualized in action discourses produced by colonial Marxisms in the wake of decolonization after World War II. While time and space do not allow for a full treatment of how colonial Marxisms moved beyond the static forms of Western Marxism and its culturalist lockstep, even the most cursory examination of early anticolonizers will remind us of the timefulness of their analyses and how a temporalizing present, embarked upon a new itinerary from a disabling past to reach future expectations, recognized a process whereby a nonlocational time generates imminent production through space to give it its "objective" givenness. Any reading of Césaire's "Discourse on Colonialism" will immediately recognize its moment and the world it speaks to and about. What characterizes Césaire's almost paradigmatic discourse is how deeply it is embedded in a specific spatiotemporality, suggesting further the relationship between the production of certain textual forms concerned with the labor of practice and organization and its capacity (desire?) to signify a specific project mediated by its durational present of everyday life in Martinique (Césaire 2000, 31–78). Césaire's text marks a significant departure from more conventional and received forms of Marxian analysis by situating its authority (if not authenticity) in the everyday, the lived experience and what it could offer for tactics, organization, and strategy. Similarly, Frantz Fanon moved uneasily between a ceaselessly dialectic tension attended by the immediate and specific moments of the colonial world—contingencies of a lived history, with all the socioeconomic structures it had created with the decolonization it had reprovoked and the desire to remember the "universally human," the formations of human commonness. In this regard, this oscillatory position is what marked the colonial Marxism of the 1950s and 1960s and undoubtedly derived from the colonial experience before World War II which had already been foreseen by writers and activists like M. N. Roy, José Carlos Mariátegui, C. L. R. James, Ho Chi Minh, and others. Yet to suggest this difference with a putative Western Marxism is to not saddle a new metaphysical necessity on a Marxism deeply devoted to assessing and seeking to engage the "current situation." With Fanon, it is true that he unmasked a fugitive universalism of Europe (like the Japanese Takeuchi Yoshimi) and its destruction of whole peoples everywhere. However, it is also the case that he was convinced that the lived political experiences of the colonial world would disclose a new conception of humanity he called "new humanism." Already in *Black Skin, White Masks*, Fanon prefigured a program based on the temporal present and its capacity to reveal the shape of a future (Fanon 1968, 134). In the *Wretched of the Earth* he underlined the importance of "examining" the conditions of the "colonial context" at "close quarters," that is, in its immediacy in order to make "intelligible" the nature of the domination in its spatial compartmentalization—a world locked in space, much like a prison—timeless, even though it is a temporal moment that will be succeeded, its nowness, that permits him to grasp it and see beyond it (Sekyi-Otu 1996, 16, 18). A broken world, whose culture of reference has been violently shattered through ambivalent and often self-destructive consequences of "spontaneity" leading to "self-repudiation" and "everyday, practical realism" replacing the "effusion" of the day before, it manages only to "substitute itself for the illusion of eternity" (Fanon 1968, 134). What must come forth is the work of "national culture" consisting of the "whole body of efforts made by a people and . . . through which that people has created itself and keeps itself in existence" (Fanon 1968, 232). Such a labor, Fanon announced, is neither a "delving into the past," as such, nor a folklore or "abstract populism" revealing the secret nature of people but actions attached to the "ever present reality of the people" that "prepares the ground where vigorous shoots are already springing up" (Fanon 1968, 253). If Fanon was riveted to the temporal immediacy of the now, Amílcar Cabral went a step further to define this arena as the "everyday." What Cabral meant by the scene of everydayness referred to a specific reality that signified History. "The colonialists usually say," he wrote, "that it was they who brought us into history: today we show that this is not so. They made us leave history, our history, to follow them, right at the back, to follow the progress of their history" (cited in Young 2001, 288). National liberation demands the rejection by all the people of their current social and economic circumstances. But it also requires acknowledging what had been taken away by the colonizers, "their land" and the "return of history." History, in this sense, meant the culture of everyday life, which constituted for Cabral "daily contact with the mass of people" (Cabral 1980, 145).

Finally, it is important to acknowledge how the everyday and its production of new forms of representation actually prefigured and supplied a different mapping of historical consciousness and history writing which, as Hayden White called for thirty years ago, were able to free themselves from the models of nineteenth-century art and science that held the former hostage to an unyielding formalism and the latter to a single truth—romantic art and positivist science—coextensive with the formation of the national narrative that employed the exemplars of both (White 1978, 27–50). However, White was, understandably, only partially correct in advising historians to look to newer models of art and science for imagining a different kind of history. What he overlooked was the crucial relationship between the form of the national narrative as the principal template for history's content and the temporality of the everyday, between the history of a specific national past—other people's past—and the rehistoricization of the present, a "knowledge" of the past and the "experience" and "memory" of the present, and a completed then and a forever incomplete now.

Epilogue: The Spatial Continent of Cultural Studies

In the post–World War II era, the everyday and its critique were momentarily refigured by thinkers like Lefebvre, Bachelard, Schutz, and Goffman. Fleetingly, they also provided the basis of what we might call Third World or colonial Marxisms, as distinct from a unitary "Western Marxism" locked in the immediacy of its geopolitical place and a constraining culturalism, now virtually museumified, which disclosed sensitive attention to uneven temporalities and unequal development to figure new strategies for liberation and political agendas in the wake of decolonization. In the industrial states of Euro-America, there were brief attempts to actualize the promise of social transformation prewar writers had once identified with everyday life. However, that possibility was rapidly eclipsed by the wave of modernization and the global expansion of consumption and commodity relations. Moreover, new forms of modernization inaugurated by the state invariably altered the relationship between the everyday and the nation to ultimately fuse consumption with national citizenship and subjectivity. Under these circumstances, the concern for the everyday eventually passed into the practice of social history and ethnographic reporting that expanded the boundaries of its content to include new social constituencies and its entailing range of eventfulness, all within national borders and the temporal framework of a "natural" and "naturalizing" chronology. In the United States especially, cultural studies overtook and even displaced the vocation of social history and ethnography by appropriating their exemplars in the cause of further dehierarchization and all-encompassing inclusion promised by the move to multiculturalism. Hence, everyday life was assigned the new task of recoding the signifying system of bourgeois culture (reflected in the work of de Certeau) to ultimately become a postcolonial discourse that "insinuates" the voice of the colonized other into the bourgeois text—its other half—to show how "imitation" and "mimicry" of the powerful signal resistance. Here, too, all objects—virtually everything, perhaps an exhausted attenuation of the "trivia," and "trash" Benjamin refused to "inventory" but wished only to "use"—are seen as potentially significant resources for possible resistance, aligning the practice of cultural studies itself with the "older history from below" at the same that it embraces self-referentiality and self-representation and the "free creativity of the enunciating subject" (Roberts 1999, 24). Above all else, the practice of cultural studies has come to be grounded in the supremacy of lived immediacy, "the creative powers of the consumer" inhabiting a timeless, spatial continent and what Rancière (1999) has called "postdemocracy," where everyday life is automatically expanded with the greater differentiation and proliferation of social subjects—identities—where nothing is left out, and where even the victims of modernity are finally assimilated to their proper place in the consensual community and thus accounted for.

References

Anderson, B. 1998. *The Specter of Comparisons: Nationalism, Southeast Asia and the World*. London: Verso.

Benjamin, W. 1999. "A Short History of Photography." In *Selected Writings, Volume 2*, ed. M. W. Jennings, 507–30. Cambridge, Mass.: Harvard University Press.

Cabral, A. 1980. *Unity and Struggle: Speeches and Writings*. Trans. M. Wolfers. London: Heinemann.

Cadava, E. 1997. *Words of Light*. Princeton, N.J.: Princeton University Press.

Césaire, A. 2000. *Discourse on Colonization*. New York: Monthly Review Press.

Chatterjee, P. 1993. *The Nation and Its Fragments*. Princeton, N.J.: Princeton University Press.

Fanon, F. 1968. *Black Skin, White Masks: The Experiences of a Black Man in a White World*. New York: Grove Press.

Feather, H. 2000. *Intersubjectivity and Contemporary Social Theory: The Everyday as Critique*. Brookfield, Vt.: Ashgate.

Guha, R. 2002. *History at the Limit of World-History*. New York: Columbia University Press.

Harootunian, H. 1999. "Ghostly Comparisons: Anderson's Telescope." *Diacritics* 29, no. 4 (Winter): 146–48.

Hegel, G. W. F. 1975. *Aesthetics*. Oxford: Clarendon Press.

Kracauer, S. 1995. *History: The Last Things Before the Last*. Princeton, N.J.: Weiner.

Osborne, P. 1995. *The Politics of Time*. London: Verso.

Poulantzas, N. 2000. *State, Power, Socialism*. London: Verso.

Rancière, J. 1999. *Disagreement*. Minneapolis: University of Minnesota Press.

Roberts, J. 1999. "Philosophizing the Everyday." *Radical Philosophy* 98 (November–December): 16–29.

Sekyi-Otu, A. 1996. *Fanon's Dialectic of Experience*. Cambridge, Mass.: Harvard University Press.

White, H. 1978. *Tropics of Discourse*. Baltimore, Md.: Johns Hopkins University Press.

Young, R. 2001. *Postcolonialism*. Oxford: Blackwell.

Note

1. My thanks to Ranajit Guha (2002, 20–21) for putting me onto Hegel's earlier appeal to the everyday. I have, however, moved in an entirely different direction from Guha's desire to fix experience in the site of an essentialized everyday, free from the corrosions of historical change. See also Hegel (1975, 149–50).

CHAPTER 6

OVERCOME BY MODERNITY

Fantasizing Everyday Life and the Discourse on the Social in Interwar Japan

If you live a daily life and it is all yours, and you come to own everything outside of your daily life besides and it is all yours, you naturally begin to explain. You naturally continue describing your daily life which is all yours, and you naturally begin to explain how you own everything besides. You naturally begin to explain that to yourself and you naturally begin to explain it to those living in your daily life who own it with you, everything outside, and you naturally explain it in a kind of way to some of those whom you own.

Gertrude Stein, *Lectures in America*

In July of 1942, a little more than six months after the Pearl Harbor raid, some of Japan's most prominent writers, thinkers, critics, and scholars gathered in the old imperial capital of Kyoto for two days of discussion on the theme of "overcoming the modern" (*kindai no chōkoku*) and the meaning of the war for its realization. The conference was sponsored by the Literary Society (Bungakukai), and its composition sought to represent the major intellectual-literary constituencies of the time, such as the Kyoto School of Philosophy, the Japan Romantic School, and members of the Literary Society. If urgency for calling such a meeting at this time was prompted by Japan's recent decision to wage war in the Pacific, the reasons governing the choice of a site were probably less clear, even though a dramatic tension was produced by juxtaposing the theme itself to the location of the ancient capital and sanctuary of Japan's cultural accomplishments before the coming of capitalism. According to the preamble delivered by one of the conference organizers, Kawakami Tetsutarō, the purpose of the discussion was not to definitively solve the problem of "overcoming the modern" but rather to explore the meaning of the war in view of the nation's modern experience. "Whether the conference is or is not successful," he declared, "I do not yet know. Still, that it was organized within an atmosphere of intellectual shuddering after the war had begun is a reality that cannot easily be disputed." Kawakami described best the problem when he noted that Japan's intellectuals had not yet "accounted" for the "blood of the Japanese that has truly motivated the original spirit of our intellectual life until recently and the rivalry of Western intelligence that has clumsily systematized our life in the present." Unavoidably, the conflict between the two must be a desperate and bloody one.

But the conflict he was referring to was not the war being waged outside, on the islands of the Pacific, but one that had been fought internally and continuously since the Meiji Restoration of 1868. The struggle was analogized to "war" as "peace" was to cultural submission. In the words of Kamei Katsuichirō, a member of the Japanese Romantics, "more to be feared than war was peace. . . . Rather a war among kings than the peace of slaves." Kamei saw the war as the culmination of a profound spiritual struggle that would finally rid Japan of the "sickness" of Westernization. "From the time we received the deathbed culture of the West called modernity," he wrote, "the deepest regions of the spirit have been violated . . . thought is permeated by this poison." The poison had spread so deeply that Japanese were now powerless to even "grasp the character of the enemy's unconscious—American and British—thought today." It had become a common sense, a kind of cultural conscious gripping the interwar Japanese intellectual generation, that even critics like Nakamura Mitsuo, another participant, acknowledged as second nature. "The war we are fighting today," Kamei concluded, "seeks to overthrow Anglo-American power externally, even as it serves internally as medical treatment for a [sick] spirit weakened by modernization."

The vast effort to overcome the modern had been seen throughout the 1930s as a solution to Japan's slavish reliance on Westernization; it was seen as the best defense against "homogenization" and "mechanization," as Kamei was to put it and promised to save the Japanese spirit by making the machine its "slave" rather than the reverse. Writers feared that the process of homogenization had been internalized to such an extent that, in Kamei's words, "it no longer appears as a self-evident symptom (of the current situation). Men have become its joyful sacrifice." How the modern has weakened and distorted "our spirit" was no different from the way disease attacks the body and lays it to waste. But like a life-endangering illness the "cure must be an equally powerful medicine." (It should be noted that the trope of disease and the appeal to a strong medicine to cure Japanese of the illness of sinophilia marked the critique of eighteenth-century nativist scholars.)

Yet the conference as an event, marking the war's world-historical meaning, would not have taken place without a prior history in which the experience of modernity—ceaseless eventfulness—clashed with the residual traces of received memory to put into question Japan's recent and rapid transformation. It is important to recognize that the event was seen as the means to call a moratorium on the eventfulness—the ceaseless historical change—which had marked Japan's modernity in the preceding two decades. The substance of the discussions in Kyoto recuperated all the major ideologemes that had been identified by a social discourse on modern daily life in the 1920s announcing the spectacle of endless consumption, fragmentation, and atomization and its secondary revision, a discourse on the social that sought to represent the image of a culture and community that was both whole and coherent and free from division. The idea of overcoming pointed to a restoration of cultural wholeness, finally rid of the fragmentation and alienation associated with everydayness, that would retrieve a secure identity sufficiently different from the West yet capable of rescuing the race from certain homogenization threatened by cultural colonization. A modernity that imitated the West appeared as a "historical sickness" and produced a surplus of history, an "excess of historical consciousness," as Kobayashi Hideo would describe it, which stifled intellectual creativity and cultural originality. As a result, Japan was forced to enlist its culture from the "vast storehouse of theatrical masks and costumes" that "Europe's past has become for it" (Nietzsche). Hence, the participants at the conference called for a program that might, in some way, eternalize the forces within culture and end the surplus of historical consciousness that had undermined art and imagination. What this required was the task of poeticizing everyday life in such a way as to construct a figure of culture that was both eternally fixed and outside of time, immune from the erosions of the passage of historical time. Such a strategy would lead to an "overcoming of history" and the stabilization of authentic values. By vocalizing the themes of the past two decades or more, the conference on modernity concentrated on the spectacle of unending change (the narrative of historical progress) and the specter of unrelieved uncertainty introduced by a dominant historical culture no longer anchored in fixed values but in fantasy and desire. The concern for historical surplus and cultural authenticity was the way discourse decoded the historical problem of the interwar period and the production of everydayness made possible by the massive transformation of the Japanese political economy at the time of World War I.

Historically, Japanese society was physically changed by the war and the move to heavier industrialization; during the decades of the 1920s and 1930s all the leading indices indicating heightened urbanization and the expansion of industrialization increased significantly and put Japan comparably and proximally close to societies like France, Germany, and Italy. In brief a discourse on everyday life and the modernist response to it appeared in a global historical conjuncture that would fix intersections where differing historical temporalities gathered to constitute a field of overdetermination. This historical conjuncture consisted of the shift to heavy industrialization prompted by the war and its subsequent peacetime transformation to commodity production, the persistence of semiaristocratic political classes rooted in the land despite the pace of capitalist modernization and the formation of a new class of industrialists—the so-called *zaikai*—until the outbreak of the war, and the challenges to it posed by new social constituencies demanding reform and revolution.[1] The Japanese experience of the interwar period inflected this global conjuncture and marked the place between a past that still coexisted with industrialization, an indeterminate present centered in the cities and dominated by new technologies, and, finally, an unenvisaged future. The coordinates of this conjuncture, manifest in a number of societies and Japan, then, was still a predominantly agrarian order with its semiaristocratic ruling class and an emergent capitalist system and incipient labor movement. If older cultural models associated with a still available past constituted a target for modernism, as it did in Europe and Japan, it also, and significantly, continued to supply an arsenal of resources that could be mobilized for protection against the ruin and reification caused by capitalist modernization and the centrality of the market which already had begun to serve as an organizing principle for new social relationships and a redefinition of daily life. Japanese modernism resisted the culture of capitalism and commodification—the regime of social abstraction—as it was being figured in a discourse on daily life in the 1920s that increasingly threatened to unleash a process of revolutionizing production, chronic civil strife, and social and economic uncertainty.

What the space of the expanding metropolitan sites produced was a social discourse of everydayness, often called *bunka seikatsu*, "cultural living," by contemporaries, that constantly announced, in mass media like popular magazines, newspapers, advertisements, and radio, the changes in material life introduced by new consumer products, and a conception of life vastly different from the rhythms of received practices; discourse continuously pointed to the succession of events, as the making of constant eventfulness became the principal commodity of newspapers and popular magazines, not to forget radio, and the fragmentation and destabilization of cultural forms. Yet this reflexive discourse provoked by the appearance and practice of new forms of everyday life was more important than the actual ubiquity of everydayness itself, since it pointed to a historical situation—something that was occurring in social practice and would continue to do so—and often prefigured and preceded the widespread establishment of commodity culture in Japan and its regime of new subjectivities and social relationships. More than reflecting a historical reality already in place in the 1920s it figured a fantasy life that demanded to be fulfilled. As such, this discourse on everydayness—what the Marxist philosopher Tosaka Jun named, at the time, the "quotidianization of thought" because he believed its message emanated from the lived experience of a new constituency called the "people" (*minshū*) and the "masses" (*taishū*)— was more futuristic and preparatory, fascinated but yet capable of prompting dread and anxiety. It was precisely this dread of mass culture and consumption (not to mention the specter of mass politics) and its promise to unhinge older, fixed social relationships and subjectivities that led to the formation of a secondary discourse on the social that aimed at representing the essence of society, by appealing to a timeless culture or figure of community, to perform a virtual poeticizing of everydayness in order to negate the divisions, fragmentation, and conflict that had instituted society in Japan. Both the left and the right participated in this secondary discourse on the social: Marxists sought to construct a conception of modernity rooted in an analysis of everyday life that would avoid reducing all historical epochs to capital yet might still be capable of retaining it as a moment in a historically larger process whose outcome was in the future. For conservatives, what Raymond Williams called "modernists against modernity," the task was to locate a space whose discovery would fulfill heroic cultural models outside history itself. This move entailed finding a refuge from what many perceived as an inauthentic social life of capitalism for a genuine authenticity capable of authorizing the establishment of a society without history within the heart of historical society, or, as Žižek was to describe it later, "capitalism without capitalism, or more familiarly fascism."[2]

For Japanese, modernity was speed, shock, and the spectacle of sensation. These qualities were often exaggeratedly symbolized in discourse as new subjectivities like the "modern girl," the "Marx boy," the "kissing girl," and the café waitress; it was conveyed by advertisements proclaiming new products like irons, phonographs, radios, labor-saving devices, Western-style skirts and trousers, new foods, the "culture house," etc., all promising "convenience," "utility," and "economies." All these commodities also pointed to the acquisition of new identities that traversed class, gender, and sexuality. In the post–World War I period the site of this explosion of everydayness was the metropolitan centers like Tokyo/Yokohama, Osaka/Kobe, and its primary constituencies were the masses who worked in the urban industries and consumed its products and played on its streets. In fact, the discourse on everydayness was really about life on the streets, where, as the urban ethnographer Kon Wajirō observed in countless studies conducted in the late 1920s and early 1930s, innumerable identities were being played out on every street corner and where people could assume different subject positions by the way they held and smoked cigarettes, dressed, walked, the choices of play and consumption they made in the Ginza. Life on the streets constantly externalized the power of desire and the way people enacted their innermost fantasies as if they were on a large and moving theater stage. In fact the term for "street"—*gaitō*—was coined in the 1920s and was immediately linked to the word employed to designate the people who came to colonize it and consume its offerings, *minshū*. For Japanese living in the cities during the 1920s, words like *gaitō* and *minshū* entered into that honored lexicon of commonly uttered buzzwords that were used everywhere in speech and the writing of the popular, mass media, called *ryūkōgo*, and came to be associated with dynamically progressive and fast-moving people on the streets, consuming new products and forms of entertainment. In Japan, no less than in industrializing societies like France, Germany, and Italy, as memory of the war receded, the heroism of production was being replaced by heroic consumption, which resulted not so much in a clash between newer and established values as a struggle of desire against values in general. The pleasures offered by a new consumption culture—the "philosophy of pleasure" (*goraku no tetsugaku*) recommended by the social critic Gonda Yasunosuke—and a social discourse defining everydayness may well have overdetermined and overstated the ubiquity of daily life as a widespread reality and concealed the observable fact that it was restricted to the urban middle class. But it must be recognized that it still attested to social practices and a lived history that would trouble critics searching for signs of social indeterminacy, fragmentation, and conflict. Many early recognized that in the power of desire to prompt endless consumption and to offset fixed values lay a challenge to settled relationships. Others were reminded of the unevenness of development between city and countryside and how the past still interacted with the present, how past, as William Faulkner once said, was not yet past. This everydayness, ready to explode into history and the rapid succession of events, was dramatized best by the appeal to American material culture and its cinematic representations prompting many writers to proclaim and denounce the 1920s as a time of "Americanization." Its hero was the overdetermined figure of the *modan gāru*—the modern girl—a combination of the Clara Bow flapper and women who had entered the new industrial workforce and realized for the first time autonomy and financial independence. Kawakami, at the time of the later conference on modernity, had called attention to this figure as "a laughable species" who imported the superficial culture of Americanization but fully recognized the threat it had already posed to received conceptions of social order.

It is interesting to note that the later discussants of modernity disparagingly looked back upon the mass culture of the 1920s as the time of Americanization, the film, and Fordism. Often they dismissed it as "hedonistic" and "crass" materialism, hopelessly superficial when contrasted to the historic culture of Europe, even though it had derived from it and had no other purpose than the circulation of commodities and the reproduction of consumption. Some saw in Americanization, as it was exported in film, a threat to the settled cultures of all societies, not just Japan. Contemporaries, like the Marxist critic Ōya Sōichi, condemned modern custom as superficial and diluted, while others noted its vitality and promise. As early as 1918 the influential opinion journal *Chūō kōron* ran a special issue on modernity that sought to identify the "symbolic currents of the new age" and found them in the "image of the automobile," the "movie pictures," and the "café." A decade later the playwright Kikuchi Kan declared that "true modernity, made in Japan, was just beginning," and proof of this lay in the appearance of what he called "new women and men" and the "birth of a new human being." In this historical conjuncture, Uchida Roan, a writer, reported that "after the war the cream of milk skimmed off in department stores and motion pictures was American capitalism," which he later described as an "essential something that had caught the public spirit."

For many writers, the film was the principal vehicle that conveyed the "textbook lessons for modern Japan." One writer was convinced that motion pictures had great cultural influence on Japanese society in general because "they imposed a Westernization of depth rather than one of the surface," recalling echoes of the novelist Natsume Sōseki's seething denunciation in 1916 of the surface culture of the West Japanese had hurriedly imported and threatened the country with the prospect of a nervous breakdown in the near future. But, now, according to another commentator, the people (*minshū*) might spend a lot of time laughing in movie houses, but he was sure that "they still understood well the thing called the West." "My favorite among the symbols of modernity," wrote the poet Satō Haruo, "is the motion pictures. When I reflect on them I feel duty bound to live in the present." And Kikuchi Kan confessed that "even though one watches continuously for four or five hours a day, one always does so cheerfully." He would gladly watch anything with a Western content rather than sit through a film dealing with Japan. American films, more than either Japanese or European imports, invariably relayed a culture of commodity consumption and the ever-persistent demands of desire. The film critic Tsumura Hideo observed that the American film had swept through Asia and reached the natives of the Dutch East Indies, Southeast Asia, not to forget the backlands of Kyushu and Shikoku. What counted for this sweeping success was both its presentation of a world of commodities—"cultural life"—and the observable fact that American films were "Westerns" and slapstick comedies that had little dialogue and could be easily understood.

The film was not just a sign of capitalism, because it was a leading industry exporting a product; it also displayed commodity culture produced by American capitalism and its principal subjects, modern men and women, their customs and daily life. In its capacity to deterritorialize, capitalism simply "undermined every fixed social identity" and produced innumerable new subject positions all challenging the fixity of received and traditional roles. Novelists like Tanizaki Jun'ichirō, Kawabata Yasunari, and especially the detective-story writer Edogawa Rampo explored new sexual identities and their consequences for settled social relationships. In discourse, "all seemed captivated by the modern girl and were drawn to her hairstyle, clothing, attitudes, facial and bodily movements, and her way of waltzing." The figure of the *modan gāru* was emblematized by the short skirt worn ten centimeters above the knees, Clara Bow haircut, lipstick and rouge, and appeared as a woman who "struts through the throngs" signifying both sexual and financial independence. An exaggerated image to be sure, but one which worked to dramatize the limits or extremities of new behavior and the excitement and danger it was capable of eliciting. Kikuchi Kan pointed to these "new women" as representatives of a new sexual awakening and declared that their appearance constituted the beginning of a true modernity in 1927. "Young women," he wrote, "have become unusually empowered at this time and they . . . are able to 'cross swords' with men in matters of love." Kikuchi, with others, was attesting to the prominence of these liberated and independent women in areas such as work and sexuality that had once been in the grip of the patriarchal system. Uchida Roan recognized the genuinely erotic behavior of the modern girl in her manner of "pouting" and "scowling" that "elicited widespread emulation." He also observed that it "would be difficult to understand the modern girl and boy without seeing American movies." While many recommended the film—the culture of images seen by the eye—as the route to grasping the new daily life, others saw how it could be understood concretely and holistically in newspapers and mass-circulation magazines and in new forms of popular music imported from the United States. Publications like *Modan Nippon* in its inaugural edition (October 1930) celebrated a litany of modern customs and images people would soon be seeing such as "flush toilets," "pavement," "Western clothes," "chairs," "apartments," "business suits," etc. Moreover, life would be more "sporty" and "speedy," "there would be more respect for women and a downgrading of men," and "people would be hearing more jazz," and "seeing more women's legs and breasts." Another edition of *Modan Nippon* and the Kōdansha popular magazine *King* praised the "Yankee spirit" and welcomed it and "American daily life" to Japan. Other publications reported on a culture of glimmering neon lights and the steady march of people from dance halls to jazz joints and crowds of people drinking hard in cafés and scurrying off in one-yen taxicabs on "broadened thoroughfares" constructed after the earthquake of 1923. Social discourse in magazines like *Shufu no tomo* described the new "culture houses" of salarymen, the appearance of nuclear families living in the cities, their household economies and outdoor recreation such as excursions to parks and miniature golf links and leisure time spent with the family milling through department stores stocked with affordable commodities like cameras, radios, irons, etc. The women's magazine *Fujin kōron* in the early 1930s ran transcripts of discussions in which Japan's most prominent male and female intellectuals assessed the status of the new cultural living. One particular discussion concentrated on the utility of the bed and bedroom in contrast to the tatami room and the futon. Opinion heavily favored the bed. The 1920s also saw a veritable explosion of a kids' culture consisting of new products targeting children such as phonograph records, toys like miniature trains and telescopes, and new candies produced by Meiji and Morinaga. Children even had their own magazine, which imitated the more popular women's journals like *Shufu no tomo* and *Josei*.

But because the social discourse on daily life was concerned with surface descriptions, literally advertising the establishment of a new reality, tracking and figuring it, it also began to reveal doubts about the consequences of this conquest of commodity culture and complain of the effects of unevenness and visible contradictions at about the time the army was occupying Manchuria. Aono Suekichi, a social critic, reported that salarymen in the early 1930s were beginning to show signs of "psychological unhappiness" because they could not satisfy their desire for consumption, and magazines like *King* tried to promote upbeat messages that sanitized "street life" in advertisements that extolled beauty, discussions advising ways to maintain healthy households, and living within one's means. Virtually every issue promised new knowledge and the virtues of what Kōdansha named "commonsense science" that reached a mass readership through direct mailing. One of the paradoxes of the period is how mass-circulation magazines dispersed an ideology of the recovered family and established social relationships yet continued to introduce new possibilities for consumption capable of eroding the bonds of social solidarity. What enthusiasm for modern custom conceded was the recognition that so many of the changes were restricted to urban areas and had not yet reached the countryside. The monthly *Ie no hikari* distributed widely throughout the countryside rarely advertised new products or offered articles describing the superiority of Western clothes and foods. Instead it provided information on the preparation of "joyful egg dishes for guests" and "how to make *shoyu* for household use." Other writers would point to the paucity of electricity in the villages as an index of economic and cultural inequality. Avoiding the glamorous side of woman's culture, it ran ads for "immediate employment" in jobs like "maids," "store clerks," "bus conductors," "inn maids," "factory labor," etc. Yamakawa Hitoshi in 1934 surveyed living conditions in the north (admittedly already affected by the world depression) and reported that most households did not possess even one futon to sleep on, while another critic, Ikuta Aoyama, dismissed modern men and women as a "parade of goblins that have no substance" and called for a termination of all further discussion of "Tokyo tastes and Ginza *gemütlich*." Researchers like the social gospel Christian Kagawa Toyohiko and Andō

Masayoshi demonstrated how modern life existed only in the cities and how it depended upon the countryside to fuel its pleasures. What Kagawa and Andō were referring to was the growing number of "revelers" in the cities and the café waitresses and prostitutes needed to service them. And at least one new religion, Hitonomichi Kyōdan, which rapidly recruited a wide membership, was organized to offer counseling to unhappy men and women and to emphasize the importance of "spousal harmony" as the work of the gods. While it offered the prospect of a stoicism of the spirit, less sex at home, it also promoted the possibility of realizing the good life in the customs and commodities of modern life because modern life required money. The magazine *Shufu no tomo* in 1931 addressed the issue of disharmony prompted by a dissatisfactory sexual life among couples and how it could be "injurious to nature." The magazine advised greater cooperation between couples, which meant that women should suppress their needs in the interest of saving the family. These frank discussions on modern sexuality conveyed a mixed or contradictory message that acknowledged a relationship between women's new status of liberation and an awareness of their own sexual needs at the same time that they counseled them to cooperate in the interest of preserving the family and affirming a patriarchal order that cared more for the male's needs.

What this surface discourse on daily life revealed was the historical role of "unequal development" in the subsequent production of a modernist discourse rather than the claims of High Modernism that capital unfolded evenly within the boundaries of a "universal ground."[3] It raised, albeit inadvertently, the spectacle of disunity, division, and difference, which it didn't know how to resolve. It conveyed this message of unevenness through juxtaposition and propinquity, and its image of an implied disunity collided with the consensual conviction upheld by the state that society must be made to show that no real divisions exist and that life corresponds perfectly to the very categories employed to provide the social unit with its representation of unity. This unity, as the discourse on daily life showed, was threatened by the separation of activities of social agents and the changeability of social relations; it could be restored only if the divisions, which have instituted society—capital and labor—are negated, concealed, or resolved in the future.[4]

This discussion on modern daily life ultimately produced a fold—a secondary discourse on the social—culminating in the wartime conference on overcoming modernity, devoted to displacing the doubts provoked by the perception of unevenness that challenged the metropolitan interpretation of its own experience as universal. Native ethnologists like Yanagita Kunio early recognized the presence of unequal development in the policy to sacrifice the countryside for the city, while the sociologist Takata Yasuma, a translator of Simmel and a proponent of interactionist social theory, declared his allegiance to *Gemeinschaft*, as he put it, and a reaffirmation of the principles of harmony and consensus as the essential form of social relationships in Japan. Takata's important essay "Class and the Third View of History," written in the late 1920s, proposed a conception of social order free from the fragmentations and conflict caused by class identity for a social arrangement rooted in received forms of cohesion and union (*ketsugō*). In folding back on the discourse on the daily, the new discourse on the social followed the lines of the instituting discourse, as if its task was to eliminate all those traces that threatened the image of unity.[5] In contrast to the discourse on the everyday life preoccupied with the surface and the present, it was a depth discourse that invariably searched for fixed essences beneath the visible covering of contemporary life and fastened on those visible traces that would reveal an existence prior to capitalism and modernity. The task it pursued was to construct a vast synchronic drama that because it was posited upon forgetting the instituting moment could not allow into it any diachronic reflection or reference. When Marxists turned to critique, they invariably projected an image of culture which, based on the existence of the everydayness of the present, would complete modernity in the future. Yet with both the left and the right the task was to overcome the division, disunity, and fragmentation which contemporary society was experiencing. This folding back and retracing ultimately made the discourse on the social ideological, inasmuch as its purpose was to remove, conceal divisions, naturalize historical relationships, and eternalize them and declare coherence by appealing to an essence outside time. Instead of attending to the place of production, it resorted to the production of place. The temporal process was incorporated into space. This discursive activity, split off from one derived from social practice, was less a simulation of the "real," as Marx, once believed, than a dissimulation of it.

If the discourse on everyday life constructed its figure from the metropolitan perspective and the desire of its middle class, its enthusiastic description of the glitter, glamour, and efficacy of urban life and the pleasures and excitements of street culture frequently concealed the reality of unevenness. While this unevenness was exposed primarily at the periphery, where the modern and its other met along a boundary that was both spatial and temporal, it was also easily recognizable and overdetermined in the difference between colonizer and colonized (upon returning to Japan in 1929 the philosopher Kuki Shūzō confessed that everywhere he looked there were signs showing how Tokyo had come to resemble a colony, "Like Singapore and Colombo") and the differential status between men and women even in the cities, the "people" (*minshū*) and the "masses" (*taishū*). Wherever this meeting took place, it often produced what Ernst Bloch elsewhere called "nonsynchronisms," a kind of "dissonance in modes of being" where people were found to occupy spaces marked by differing modes of production and temporalities that coexisted uneasily with capitalism in the "Now." While capitalism and social abstraction undoubtedly led to the more familiar modernist preoccupation with the aporias of representation, the recognition of unequal development problematized the question of social determinacy or the specter of indeterminacy—the principles on which society is founded—and how it might best be represented. The distrust for representation under capitalism invariably required the attempt to get outside it in order to think the concrete. It was the purpose of modernist discourse to revive the status of agency in the artwork, cultural artifact, social practice, or religious belief because it held the promise of a "prior grounding in a pure practice of representation, one that enjoys a grant of autonomy from the object."[6] What this entailed was a distrust of anything that was submitted to representation because it was already mediated by capitalist abstraction to constitute a kind of secondary revision that removed the object from immediate experience. Owing to the progressive and ceaseless change demanded by capitalism—its historical surplus—everything, as the saying goes, that is solid melts into air. Hence, the artwork, culture itself, was increasingly seen as the stand-in for the lost historical agency.[7] In this endeavor, modernism in Japan sought to replace the putative universal ground of capitalism as the source of all activity with the "seemingly concrete but historical indeterminate agency of the artwork."[8] Yet the issue was complicated by the recognition that capitalism had not developed evenly to produce a universal terrain but rather was progressing unevenly to problematize the question of a "ground" on which to construct a historical subject unified with its object, affirming it but denying it. What this resulted in was not only the acknowledgment that representation was a problem but more importantly the recognition that the split dividing historical subject and object caused by an uneven ground had to be mediated.[9] It was this problem that accounts for the effort of Japanese thinkers and writers to install in the present a moment of recall or recovered experience, a memory *of* rather than *from* a time before time, as the ethnologist Orikuchi might have put it, whether it was an aesthetic principle, a religious practice, communitarian ideal, or a cultural imaginary. In the writings of Yanagita Kunio we have the example of how the recognition of cultural unevenness— what he called *ai no bummei*—was not a temporary stage in an evolutionary narrative but a permanently entrenched condition which could be found throughout East Asia. His program sought, with others trying to account for the speed of modernization, to supply the figure of a palimpsestic imaginary where the earlier and essential layers of national life, in the form of custom, practice, and beliefs, were still able to shine through the modern overlays and provide a map for the present. The philosopher Watsuji Tetsurō, a former student of Martin Heidegger's, called this stratigraphic layering *jūōsei* and imagined history as a spatial stockpiling of strategic epochs in the itinerary of the spirit, each lying on top of the other. Yanagita appealed to the trope of a nonlinear history of custom by employing the descriptive imagery of a stalactitic formation that grows unobserved into the shape of an icicle. Others like Kuki looked to an essential experience such as *iki* that had reached its culmination in the late eighteenth century and was therefore prior to capitalism and free from Western metaphysics yet fully capable of anchoring the Japanese of the present, even though it called attention to a way of life of a particular past era. The native ethnologist Orikuchi Shinobu saw in folklore traces—what Yanagita had identified as living "vestiges"—of an originary figure of daily life that would recall another place of difference outside history and remind contemporaries of its production of enduring values such as "constancy," "eternity," and "absoluteness." But all of these were constructions that came into existence at the moment when older conceptions of life were beginning to disappear.

Thought and literature turned increasingly to locating a metaphorical space whose discovery would fulfill heroic models outside society itself. This move entailed finding a refuge from what many believed to be an inauthentic social life in which the processes of capitalist modernization were integrating people into larger and impersonal units of organization and greater dependence on them. What this discourse on the social revealed was an immense struggle to catch hold of an everydayness that always escapes because it lacks a true subject, to redefine daily life itself enduringly and give it a stable and fixed form and meaning in order to overcome an indeterminate public space—the streets— where culture was being lived and alienations, fetishisms, and reifications were producing their effects.[10] Under capitalism everyday life put into play the question of representation, which already was being seen as an abstraction of reality, and concrete experience which, somehow miraculously, had survived in vestiges and traces that had managed to escape the alienating constraints of representation. By rejecting an outer and objective world already in process of becoming reified, discourse began to identify the place of creativity which had produced enduring ethical and cultural values capable of fixing stable social relationships such as the family, village, and communal cooperative. In this transaction, the empirical was often abandoned to make place for an essentialized entity to occupy. As an interpretative mode aimed at unearthing the ground of authenticity, the new cultural discourse favored a hermeneutics that promised to probe beneath the surface and thereby unearth a fixed "existence"—a timeless everydayness—as imagined by native ethnologists, a paradigmatic moment revealing the genius of the race in a historical time/style (Kuki Shūzō), an eternal aesthetic or poetics (Tanizaki Jun'ichirō, Kobayashi Hideo, not to forget the Japanese Romantics), a spatially privileged climate and history free from change, authorizing an entirely different ethic of social relationships free from temporality (Watsuji Tetsurō), in the scene of speaking, (Tokieda Motoki) the countryside (Yanagita Kunio) or in the auratic experience of the "other place" (Orikuchi Shinobu). While Marxists and progressive thinkers rejected this method they nonetheless imagined the possibility of realizing a more evenly developed modern society which, through the exercise of critique, science, and rationality, would secure a genuine authenticity for the masses in the future based on the everydayness of industrial modernity and the masses. As late as 1941, the philosopher Miki Kiyoshi, who traveled an intellectual route from Marxism to phenomenology, sought to resolve the apparent fragmentations and divisions in daily life by uniting culture and lifehood. Miki appealed to an older Asian tradition that had always insisted upon the integration of culture into everyday life. "The philosophy of everyday life culture," he wrote, "starts from the basic idea that culture and daily life are unified, that daily life is culture."

If pursued from below one reaches culture, but if one begins with culture one reaches daily life. What Miki hoped to unify was a conception of "cultural life" (*bunka seikatsu*) that had marked the place of everydayness in the inter-war period with one derived from the actual experience of the social lifeworld of the people, yoking essence to a form of existence, poetics and history, without ever proposing a specific agenda. Yet we must read his proposal as a sign of the very fragmentation of everyday life and culture which the discourse on the social was seeking to resolve. Where he departed from so many of his contemporaries was in his belief that "living culture" was movement, making, transforming, not fixed, static, "things as they are," or simple negativity toward the given.

For most, the problem of the "real," then, was to find a stable ground of authentic experience and memory—the "lost home of literature" proclaimed by Kobayashi Hideo; the quest promised to be a "lonely journey," as imagined by the modernist novelist Yokomitsu Riichi, capable of unifying subject and object by reaching the genuinely concrete which the surplus of history and social abstraction were eliminating. Here, social discourse folded upon itself to become the domain of ideology masquerading as a discourse on the social that now aimed to represent the essence of society. Modernist discourse had to face the daunting task of simultaneously representing an order that would guarantee a natural determination with an articulation of existing social relationships yet conceal and dissimulate the effects of social and temporal division that had been produced to reestablish the "real." In the end, this effort to negate or conceal the social divisions that had instituted society in modern Japan gave way to a frenzied attempt to "overcome the modern" which was supposed to represent the first step in "constructing" what the poet Takamura Kōtarō was already celebrating as the "Great East Asian Family" in order to enlarge the basic social units that once had made Japanese life whole and integrated. If the discourse on the social and the conference on overcoming modernity sought to eternalize forces in a fixed "spirit," "essence," and "existence," it could only do so by dissolving the modern and appealing to myth and national aestheticism. But because modernity itself constituted a constant overcoming, Japanese found themselves facing the impossible task of temporally overcoming what was an overcoming. This dilemma could only remind them of the inevitable succession of historical phenomena, the excess of historical consciousness, and a common destiny that they would always remain overcome by modernity.

Yet it is important to call attention to the political implications of this discourse on the social that essentialized both the figure of a timeless community and culture. The strategy employed in projecting a conception of subjectivity that identified the people with the "folk" and society, history, and culture with nature, production with place, disclosed the immense stakes in upholding an imaginary in which subjects reproduced social relationships embedded in a timeless productive order that remained outside history. Tosaka Jun referred to this discourse as "archaism" and "restorationism" and believed that it failed to conceal the duplicity of its enabling conception of subjectivity and its antihistorical narrative in upholding the repetition of a timeless order. Ultimately he named it enduringly the "Japanese ideology." What he called for was the harder and politically more dangerous task of thinking history itself, which, as he observed, would clearly show the presence of a ready-made inventory of ideas that could already be found elsewhere, such as "crisis," "spiritual exhaustion," the call for spiritual and cultural renewal, communal intimacy steeped in myth, an eternally "abiding" folk that stood for a national subjectivity devoid of class, gender, or regional affiliation, the poeticizing of a timeless daily life, and the celebration of a national aesthetics signaled a systemic disorder that required understanding rather than ideological representations papering over social division.

In fact this discourse on the social, with its displacement of history by some version of a timeless national poetics, became in Japan, and wherever the fascist temperament gathered, the clarion of a general effort to bring about "renewal" and recover the originary spiritual start of a culture. In Japan, this quest took the form of an archaism yoked to the more modernist pursuit for a stable and authentic ground—shelteredness—which might animate the energy of spirit "weakened by the accidents of the itinerary" that was still of its own making. The purpose of this search was to uncover beneath those accidents of modern everyday life, which the critic Kobayashi Hideo identified with history itself, the contemporary regime of inauthenticity, an epic, an originary communal ethos, the organic growth of spirit or the Japanese ethnos, as Kuki Shūzō put it. This gesture constituted what it meant "to possess the meaning of history." But the possession also implied the realization of an infinite meaning, one that never exceeds itself, and which, even if it is somehow lost in the dross of contemporary inauthenticity, remains intact, ready to be recruited "to possess itself anew."

Notes

1. Perry Anderson, "Modernity and Revolution," in *Marxism and the Interpretation of Culture*, ed. Cary Nelson and Lawrence Grossberg (Champagne: University of Illinois Press, 1988), 318–26. The argument for a historical conjuncture is more fully developed in Arno J. Mayer, *The Persistence of the Old Regime* (New York: Pantheon, 1981).

2. Slavoj Žižek, *Tarrying with the Negative* (Durham, N.C.: Duke University Press, 1993), 216.
3. I am indebted to Neil Larsen, *Modernism and Hegemony* (Minneapolis: University of Minnesota Press, 1990), xxiv, for making this important connection between modernism and uneven development.
4. Claude Lefort, *The Political Forms of Modern Society* (Cambridge, Mass.: MIT Press, 1988), 149–51.
5. Lefort, *Political Forms*, 149–51.
6. Larsen, *Modernism and Hegemony*, xxiv.
7. Larsen, *Modernism and Hegemony*, xxiv.
8. Larsen, *Modernism and Hegemony*, xxiv.
9. Larsen, *Modernism and Hegemony*, xxiv.
10. Maurice Blanchot, "Everyday Speech," in "Everyday Life," ed. Alice Kaplan and Kristin Ross, special issue, *Yale French Studies* 73 (1987): 19.

CHAPTER 7

TIME, EVERYDAYNESS, AND THE SPECTER OF FASCISM

Tosaka Jun and Philosophy's New Vocation

Modernity's Time

In the interwar conjuncture (1918–1940) throughout the industrializing world of Euro-America, the Soviet Union, and Japan, and their colonial possessions, no philosophic concept proved more urgently demanding and less tractable to resolution than the question of time. By the same measure, no category of the social formation since the Bolshevik Revolution of 1918 loomed as importantly as the status of the everyday and its transformative powers to trouble the precinct of social theory. The Bolshevik Revolution dramatized the agency of the masses and their capacity to make and write their own history of the everyday at precisely the same moment capitalist modernization was installing consumer culture structured by the commodity form. What the everyday came to signify more than mere "dailyness" was the social space occupied by mass industrial workers denoting the site where the contradiction between value and social life was sharpest and the effort to overcome it most intense.

At the heart of this emergent configuration was the formation of new social space signifying the lived everyday in the expanding industrialized sites and new temporalities demanded by the establishment of the working day and capital accumulation, manifest in the coexistence of world standard time and countless local times, representing diverse forms of social existence and their pasts, people continued to live in the modern present. The nation-state, with its own national narrative and linear temporal trajectory, authorized calendars that fixed days of memory, observances, and duties that required repeating every year. This confrontation of temporalities, attesting to the immense unevenness people lived and negotiated daily, was frequently condensed into a competition of claims and even conflicts, especially in colonial domains and in the industrial cities that were already embodying the coexistence of different lived presents. These confrontations were often displaced in more general and formal discussions between the claims of experience and memory and historical knowledge which, in keeping with the new regimes of time shaped by science, led to establishing disciplines based on objective inquiry and the need to verify facticity over subjective intimations derived from sensory impressions. If experience proved to be only immediate, transitory, and memory temporally imprecise, history's knowledge could claim superior status owing to its correspondence to measurable time which constituted one of its principal assertions of empirical certainty. The competition between conflicting regimes of time was relayed through the categories of history and the everyday, knowledge and experience, and became one of the defining tropes of Japan's modernity in the interwar period. In the 1930s this discussion acquired a special urgency to resolve the conflict as history was identified increasingly with the nation-state and the everyday with a temporal reality that had not been entirely assimilated to it. The way to resolving this struggle turned toward rethinking through both the status of the historical and its temporality in order to counter the nation-state's monopolization of both. The implications of this intellectual shift required philosophy to acquire a new vocation devoted to the subject of the everyday, whereas its political connotations insisted on an open confrontation with fascism and its cultural ideology.

With capitalist modernization and urban industrialization, history became its own time, what Hegel earlier named "history, itself," as if it were now appointed to chart the momentous changes unleashed to measure their velocity toward the future. But this discovery of an autonomous historical time marked the appearance of an "internal time" which presupposed and incorporated a complex discussion on the status of temporality that generated a philosophic assault on both the domain of quantitative time and the ambition of the new science to measure all things objectively in order to classify them. What this critique revealed was a desire for a truer, qualitative time, ultimately expressed in knowledge derived from experience, removed from the external world of things. Despite its unease with the external world of scientific measurement, philosophic critique was as much directed at capitalism's commitment to quantitative and measurable time, abstract time, paradigmatically inscribed in the calculation of surplus value and labor time.

The familiar guideposts of this discussion were surely Henri Bergson, who probably inaugurated it; Georg Simmel, who explicitly linked the new urban metropolis to the interiorization of time; Georg Lukács, whose powerful critique politicized a philosophy devoted to the exemplars of science that were now made to disclose how social life had become objectified and reified; Edmund Husserl, who bracketed the external world to gain access to the state of pure, psychological experience; and Martin Heidegger, who temporalized existence and ontologized Being's "historiality." But what seemed to hold the diverse strands together was the effort to rescue the loss of qualitative time and to restore immediate subjective experience discounted by both science and capital as a form of knowledge, a lived time at the level of the everyday now removed from the structure of clock and calendar. This move was inflected in Japan, as well, with Nishida Kitarō's early *Zen no kenkyū* devoted to plumbing the precincts of "pure experience" underlying the everyday and absolutizing eternal values, Abe Jirō's solipsistic self, Watsuji Tetsurō's valorization of cultural form and other formulations which, regardless of place, would lead to internalization, dematerialization, and dehistoricization of time and the imposition of an everyday delegated to serve as the reservoir of interior, immediate experience no longer mediated by the external world of things. In Japan, this world was amplified by the *shi shōsetsu*, especially, the turn to a philosophy of cultural form free from historical determination and the figuration of a folkic everydayness whose countenance remained unchanged throughout time (Harootunian 2000, 202–357). What this particular convergence between a critique of quantitative time and the search for what Lukács identified as "a reality more real . . . than isolated facts and tendencies" (Lukács 1997, 18) produced was a conception of eternality (once the vocation of religion) offering the illusory promise with which to secure unity. Throughout the industrializing world of the 1920s and 1930s this impulse toward the idea of the eternal was manifest in the certainty of a continuing folkic community, as manifest in the eternal and unchanging everyday of Yanagita Kunio, and diverse forms of what Max Horkheimer had called "sublime self-deception" projected by idealist philosophy and its conviction in the transhistorical capacity of ideas and values (Horkheimer 2005, 14). Whereas in Japan the custodians of this metaphysical tradition were Nishida, Watsuji, Kuki Shūzō, and their followers, who provided the philosophical grounding for the virtual dematerialization of experience and the detemporalization of the everyday, it was Tosaka Jun who sought to restore to the everyday the rhythms of its uneven but coexisting temporalities and rematerialize the claims of cultural form.

Tosaka's Kyoto

It is interesting to note that Tosaka Jun was one of the principal philosophical adversaries of what in the interwar period was known as "Kyoto philosophy." The paradox of his commitment to putting into question with a penetrating critique the philosophic presuppositions of the Kyoto school, against such luminaries as Nishida Kitarō, Watsuji Tetsurō, Tanabe Hajime, and Miki Kiyoshi, lies in the obvious fact that he was a product of this intellectual tradition, a student of Nishida's and Tanabe's and intimate with many of its proponents like Nishitani Keiji. No greater tribute to both his brilliance and his decency as friend and the tragedy of his short life was offered than in the honest recollection of Tanabe Hajime, whose principal theorization on "species" (*shu*) Tosaka had sharply criticized.

> For me Tosaka Jun was in reality a friend difficult to forget. As is well known there was an intellectual opposition between him and myself. Not only did we meet and engage in mutually violent argumentation, from him I often received pointed criticism (printed in journals) that added fierce stimulation. But when meeting with him, he was unfailingly [*kiwamete*] friendly. Even though he was violently disputatious, he never left either improper ill feeling or feelings of estrangement. I had come to be the target of a left-wing attack, but in spite of the intellectual fury of Tosaka's assault, his way of presenting things was not simply . . . niggardly offensive dislike and indirectly cutting. On this point I could not but acknowledge a character in Tosaka that should be extraordinarily respected. . . . He did not have the common, indecisive nervousness [found] among men who present philosophy but [showed] a rarely seen manliness with generosity. Tosaka was a person who in reality had to be respected and revered as a man. Above all else, my grieving heart focuses on this point.
>
> (Tanabe 1976, 3–4)

Tanabe's grief was real enough, as was his conviction that Tosaka in the end was "a natural leader who was able to gather in his person the respect and reverence of people drawn by the charm of his character," a truly precocious human being.

The Kyoto aesthetician Nakai Masakazu also reported on Tosaka's disputatious but generous character. Nakai's non-Marxian socialism was probably closer to Tosaka's politics but his insistent neo-Kantianism too often clashed with his effort to read Marx's materialism through the same neo-Kantian optic. Despite the arguments they had while on long walks in Kyoto, the two were not as far apart as it seemed. Both shared an earlier socialization in neo-Kantian philosophy, which prompted Tosaka to move to considerations of science and its methods and Nakai to art and representation. What linked them together was a shared interest in the status of space and its structuring and enframing aptitudes. Both, moreover, were committed to Enlightenment ideals and the necessity of working for the dissemination of scientific knowledge among the masses: Tosaka with his abortive scheme to compile an encyclopedia for such purposes, and Nakai with his promotion of a weekly newspaper called *Doyōbi* for and by the masses. They also momentarily shared the politics of the popular front against fascism, willing to suspend their ideological differences (Tosaka's Marxism and Nakai s non-Marxian socialism).

Tosaka was born in Tokyo in 1900 and attended Seinan Lower School and Keisei Middle School and the elite First Higher School in Tokyo (Dai Ichikō). In 1924 he graduated from the philosophy faculty of Kyoto Imperial University and immediately volunteered for military service in a field artillery brigade stationed in Chiba Prefecture. He was discharged in the following year as a cadet. From roughly 1926 to 1931 he taught as an instructor in colleges in Kyoto and Kobe and in 1931 obtained a post at Hōsei University in Tokyo. The circumstances of this appointment resulted from Hōsei's decision to release Miki Kiyoshi, who apparently had earlier run afoul of the Peace Preservation Law. Tosaka's return to Tokyo was thus as Miki's successor, not a surprising move since he—Tosaka—had already been intellectually bonded to the elder Miki in Kyoto and his momentary but momentous embracing of Marxism after his study tour in Germany. During these early years in the Kyoto area, Tosaka wrote a number of articles based on his graduation thesis on space, as well as the seminal "On Scientific Method" and "The Logic of Ideology." He also began to move steadily away from neo-Kantianism toward Marxism. While still in Kyoto he became involved in a Marxism study group and became a member of the Proletarian Scientific Research Institute (1929) and was arrested as a sympathizer of the Communist Party.

The axis of his Marxian work on scientific method and ideology revolves around his seminal thesis on space. In 1927, for example, he produced an essay titled "Seikaku to shite no kūkan" (Space as characteristic), in which he first formulated the idea that space constituted a characteristic of nature at the same time that it presented a "dynamic confrontation" with it (Tosaka 2001, 295). He later refined this "confrontation" by re-presenting the dyad as a "dialectical" method and "object" in learning, guiding the "superiority of method" by way of a "solution of the problem." Once situated in the itinerary of a dialectical method (more Kantian than Hegelian), Tosaka moved rapidly to embrace materialism with the publication of *Ideorogī no ronrigaku* (1930), which developed further the role played by "object" and "method" and its final transformation into the categories of "position[ality]" and "problem" (Tosaka 2001, 295). Here, he concluded that the dialectical structure of "historical and social existence," founded on the predominance of the "problem" over "positionality," is grasped through a "reflecting on the theoretical structure of the characteristic logic." What Tosaka apparently aimed to elucidate was the ideological character of theory and logic. The subsequent drift to war and fascism, after the army's seizure of Manchuria in 1931, paralleled Tosaka's reorientation toward materialism (a move Tanabe associated with his talent for science rather than philosophy) and the establishment of the Society for the Study of Materialism (Yuibutsuron

Kenkyūkai), after the abolition of the Japan Communist Party. The "Society" was active until 1938, when it was shut down by the state, whose activities combined a sustained and (what seems now as an unparalleled) rigorous exposition of questions related to philosophic materialism and explicit antifascist activity and struggle at the cultural level. Its journal, *Studies in Materialism*, published seventy-four numbers, in addition to the *Yuibutsuron zenshū* (sixty-six volumes), to momentarily become the intense fulcrum of "enlightenment" thinking in a dark time of trouble. The intellectual excitement it generated was matched by penetrating political criticism in articles that invariably showed the telltale signs of state censorship. Tosaka, who was at the center of this intellectual whirlwind, directed his attentions on the one hand to envisaging a comprehensive theory of science (*Kagakuron*, 1935) and, on the other, to mounting a powerful assault on liberalism and capitalist cultural ideology under fascism (*Nihon ideorogīron*, 1935). At the same time, he opened up a critical front against fascism as it had permeated everyday life in the 1930s through the publication of works like *Shisō to fūzoku* (1936) and *Sekai no ittan to shite no Nippon* (1937) that sought to clarify the conditions of contemporary Japan. In this regard some of his most striking work addressed the logic of journalistic presentation and its unacknowledged reliance on hermeneutic philosophy (in newspapers and radio) and the representation of events. But it was precisely for this reason and the power of fascism that ultimately forced him to succumb, first in 1937 when he was prohibited from writing and then, a year later, when he and the group around him were arrested and found guilty for having violated the Peace Preservation Law. He was sentenced to three years of penal servitude for his leadership role. He was first incarcerated in the police prison in Suginami Ward and then later in 1944 sentenced to the Tokyo Penitentiary. A year later he was transferred to a facility in Nagano, to escape air raids. Tosaka died of malnutrition and impossibly cramped quarters after three months, on August 9, a week before the war ended. Unlike Antonio Gramsci, he was not permitted to have books, paper, or pen in his prison confinement. His friend and intellectual guide Miki Kiyoshi died in prison a month later, after the war's end.

The Separation of Art and Life

At the center of the philosophic quest for the "eternal" in the interwar period was the conviction that life had been severed from art and this dangerous separation prefigured a crisis of spirit—*seishin* (*Geist*)—which threatened the domain of culture and its dominance over everyday life. It should also be noted that culture had already been deployed to replace labor power and its capacity to create value. Specifically, this reflected the perception that culture—form— had once dominated everyday life but with the establishment of the system of bourgeois hegemony and the transformation of society into a vast social mechanism demanding the installation of an objective world determined by clock, calculation, and calendar—rational efficiency—everyday life fell sway to a new discipline devoted to producing objects, whereby all activity was subordinated to the routines of an industrial regime. Marx, of course, had seen this immense switch over in the nineteenth century in his observation of the objectification of social relations and the separation of worker from capital demanded by the sale of labor power for wages. Georg Simmel was one of the earliest to have recognized the growing distance between subject and object world in metropolitan life and sought to show how art—form—would remain impervious to life and history, "greater than life" (*Mehr-Leben*), as he described it in his writings on the philosophy of history and his last major text on historical time.

Continuing this precedent, his student Georg Lukács earlier made a heroic effort to return form to its privileged status, but when he turned toward Marxism he recoded the classic split between cultural form and everyday life by appealing to a theory of reification which demonstrated how worker's consciousness revealed the very divisions between subject and object worlds required by capitalist production. In a sense his effort to demonstrate the process of realizing subject-object identity in the proletariat echoed this earlier romantic impulse to reunite art—form—and life. In Japan, this concern for the role played by form and its direction of everyday life was revealed early in Nishida's texts that appealed to a realm of eternal values such as the good, true, and beauty, which subsequently was reinforced and expanded by a rigorous philosophic discourse that aimed to show the autonomy of art ("pure literature"), the eternality of form, not so much memory as "recollections of the present," and the identification of cultural essence—cultural value—that exceeded mere history—production—to constitute unchanging principles capable of stabilizing national life for all times and organizing everyday life according to their exemplars.

Early on, Tanizaki Jun'ichirō melancholically complained about the separation of art and life in *In'ei raisan*, but this culturalism and its efforts to control the present with the example of a completed and unchanging past became a modernist absolute in the decade of the 1930s and clashed with all those attempts, principally coming from Marxists, which sought to demonstrate how the present still reflected determinations of an older, absolutist order that now had to be surpassed. We can see in this struggle the silhouette of a more fundamental conflict of claims between the fixed spatial countenance upheld by culture (and its metabolizing of psychological time and experience) and the primacy of temporality and the pressure of the future on the present. The antagonism was over determining whether everydayness was a fixed space embodying the unchanging principles of national formation or rather a temporal unity constituted of repetitious routine on the surface but hiding the coexistence of immense contradictions produced by history that corresponded to uneven temporalities imminently ready to explode into difference. It was at this juncture that thinkers began to envisage a division between high culture and its dilution into mass consumption and align themselves with their respective claims and their political associations.

In response to this crisis of politics and culture, displacing the irreparable cleft between art and life, much of Tosaka's program in the 1930s drew upon a prior and firm grasp of a philosophy of science that had already absolutized the "scientific method" as the sole validation of verifiable knowledge. This meant dismissing claims to knowledge that had failed to satisfy the test of the natural and physical sciences, compelling a prevailing neo-Kantianism to resort to constructing a "science of spirit" that valorized subjective experience and promised to anchor knowability to a method based on the logic of culture rather than nature. Yet it was precisely this mimicking of natural science that condemned its metaphysics to inadvertently supporting (or supplementing) the very claims associated with an external world dominated by quantification, objectivity, and the rule of abstraction removed from considerations of common or collective social interest. With Tosaka, it is important to recognize that his thinking never went so far to the opposite extreme as to embrace metaphysics, even though he strove to address questions of knowledge science had left behind or had even discounted as unworthy forms of experience. Instead, Tosaka began with addressing the current situation and the corresponding political observation of how the emergence of fascism had relied on seizing the advantage offered by exploiting the separation between the unbridled development of capitalist economy and human needs which liberalism had always overlooked and undoubtedly sanctioned, as it still does in its new avatar. By the same measure he correctly saw how liberalism's penchant for plural interests had openly invited precisely those ideological dangers implicated in a metaphysics of ideal cultural forms (sculpted by its hermeneutic method devoted to meaning) and their entitlement to eternality. At the heart of this cultural turn was the role played by the subject whose experience created enduring forms.

In this way, Tosaka was able to detect in fascism a constitutive partnership of economics and culture that resulted in displacing a concern for social and human needs, allowing him, like Horkheimer at the same historical moment, to identify its claims as the true and legitimate heir of liberalism. Tosaka consistently endeavored to explain how what was happening in Japan during his short lifetime was actually no different from what was occurring elsewhere in the capitalist world. While acknowledging that fascism would invariably acquire different content mediated by local historical and cultural conditions, he was, nonetheless, persuaded that its appearance was not simply linked to the moment, as such, but rather to the epoch of capital, regardless of how advanced or delayed, and would remain indelibly inscribed in its interstice. It was the ghost in the machine. But the ghost was no metaphor.

Fascism, it should be recalled, eschewed all forms of political representation calling for a moratorium on them, in the interest of saving capitalism from itself, by eliminating the excesses of civil society and the spectacle of social (class) conflict. At the same time, fascism had successfully managed to transmute the subject of class into a communal or collective subject of the folk who created enduring cultural forms by rearticulating ideological components like the democratic national popular. In this way fascism actually appeared to banish precisely those aspects of liberalism that could solidify the people at the same time as it removed them from conflict-producing identities.

In his time, Tosaka recognized the relationship between a capitalist imperial chain and its diverse national links (*ikkan*) with Japan as simply a connecting rod in the formation of the sequence in a global network. Moreover, he recognized the importance of the role played by ideology (rather than merely economics) in the configuration of this imperial chain and its relationship to uneven development. This was the principal purpose of his book on the Japan ideology which raised not simply the question of the manifest content fascism aimed to project (Japanism, Asianism, archaism) but also the mystery of its latent form itself and how it behaved like the commodity (Tosaka 1977, 3:215–18). In *Shisō to fūzoku* he explained how "thought is able to acquire the [visage] of bodily reality in society by grasping the form of custom," which conceals its presence. Custom's "special characteristic," he observed, resembles the "skin of society" and thought is buried deeply within it (Tosaka 1977, 4:271).

We must, I believe, pay close attention to this privileging of form, as against simply content like social structure or organization, as an obvious conjugation of the value form that had already constituted global capital's self-mediating ground of the social to provide the filter through which to grasp the world. Such a move enables us to recognize the structuring capacity of the social formation by the value or commodity form, with its enormous aptitude for supplying a matrix empowering the production of all other forms of the "fetishistic inversion." In Tosaka's conception of fascism, the inversion took the form of thought which lay beneath its bodily representation in timeless custom and which worked to conceal the historical conditions of its own production, much like the commodity obscured the scandal of surplus value in order to enable unequal exchange between capital and labor and affirm its claim to second nature. Hence the invocation of custom commanded subservience for no other reason than its own that would lead to the fetishistic disavowal of knowledge: "I know . . . but all the same." In Japan, the emperor—not the system (*tennōsei*) ruling in his name—has signified this imperative, as he still does, and satisfies an arrangement that conforms precisely to Tosaka's conception of custom functioning to conceal the mystery of its form.

Everydayness and "History's Mystery"

Nowhere was the aporetic relationship between the surface appearance of phenomena and what lay beneath or behind better illustrated than in Tosaka's meditations on custom and the everyday. In the case of the former, there is formal appearance, which claims a timelessness made possible by the repression of the historical conditions of its productions; with the latter, the specularity of routinized repetition of daily life, where today promises to look like yesterday and tomorrow but which, like custom, manages to mask its historicality, what Tosaka called its "actuality." Both custom and everyday intermingle incessantly to present the figure of an interchangeable and interactive countenance. Yet both played the role of stand-ins for the commodity form which had already permeated the recesses of daily life and to whose "behavior" custom was now being assimilated. In Tosaka's reckoning, the commodity form was the socially structuring agent of society's relationships, whose condition of effectivity demanded the effacement of signs of historical production and time. What interested him most, and perhaps disclosed an unacknowledged residue of Kyoto philosophical idealism, was the conviction that surface phenomena—appearance—required investigations for traces of earlier forms of social custom and socialization received from the past. Pure phenomena merely called attention to an unevenness between the immediate presence of custom in the present, claiming the authority of timeless morality, and the vanished past that inaugurally produced it, between what now presupposed externality and a historicized interiority. In this connection, Tosaka summoned the example of Thomas Carlyle's *Sartor Resartus*, which had put into question the relationship between outer clothing and the "concealed body," between the mundane world and philosophy, which "is less in view than daily clothing" (Tosaka 1977, 4:272–73). The relationship between clothing, and what it hid, which Carlyle had failed to make a principle of philosophic speculation, constituted a trope that juxtaposed the everyday world of appearances and what its surface concealed. But Tosaka was quick to assert that clothing, by the same measure, changes over time to represent a historical index, even though it has come to resemble timeless custom because of the inattentiveness of philosophic idealism and its quest for "pure reason." In a sense, Tosaka was pointing to the "other" in the repetition of the same, what Gilles Deleuze, elsewhere, referred to as the "secret." "The most profound repetition: it alone provides the principle of the other one, the reason for the blockage of concepts. In this domain, as in

Sartor Resartus, it is the masked, the disguised, or the costumed which turns out to be the truth of the uncovered" (Deleuze 1994, 24, 70–71). For Tosaka, the model for this form of masking was custom itself, standing in for the commodity, which disguises its repetition by constantly appealing to the new as difference (even though it is the same). But it is only through its manifest repetition that the commodity is able to call attention to what is not apparently visible in appearance, its underside, so to speak, which is the side of its production, its having been made in a determinate moment and by specified labor power now lost to time. This difference is already prefigured by the commodity's (or custom's) unveiled outside and its unseen inside.

Because Tosaka had designated the quotidian and its materiality as philosophy's vocation, he was able to claim the everyday in the present as the proper category of philosophic reflection. Its materiality demanded an abandonment of diverse forms of transcendental speculation, which invariably bracketed both its empirical and historical dimensions. This move away from reflection founded on the passage of time, a philosophic intervention that always comes too late (like Hegel's owl of Minerva) meant engaging the immediacy of the phenomenal present filled with unrealized meaning capable of giving direction to history. What this entailed was acknowledging the present itself as the site in which time is deployed and the connection of successive instants into one another to constitute the lived everyday. People associate the everyday with a variety of things, he wrote, but rarely envisage it as a problematic principle (Tosaka 1977, 3:95). It is simply taken for granted like habit. What is overlooked is how the everyday is related to the "structures of history" and its capacity to illuminate the principle informing the historical. The identification of everydayness with history meant returning to the question of time and historical temporality. To grasp history's time, Tosaka reasoned, requires investigating the existence of the principle of everydayness, whose contours will reveal the hidden recesses of history's precinct. Why the everyday was so important is that it housed the principle of historical time and no longer needed to rely on temporal markers derived from outside history. If history was its own time, as Tosaka insisted, now liberated from borrowing from a phenomenological time of consciousness and natural science, with its presumption of "homogeneous time" that is constantly "minced," divided, or a pure temporality ultimately promoting an eternal time or an "eternal recurrence," it is the principle of everydayness, which, because it is the same as the "principle of presentness," constitutes the habitat of historical time (Tosaka 1977, 3:96–98).

It was, thus, at the level of the everyday where Tosaka perceived the structuring force of the commodity form—custom—in shaping both the experience of the present and lived reality of the "masses" and the moment of "possibility" (*kanōsei*) for realizing difference vested in the capacity of everydayness to break loose from ceaseless daily routine. "In the principle of the day to day," he wrote, "in the constant repetition of the same act, even though it is a different day, in the common activity of drinking tea, in the absolute inevitability of the principle of the everyday—in these things resides the crystallized kernel of historical time, here lies the secret of history" (Tosaka 1977, 3:101). Tosaka located this "secret" in the existence of character, which referred to politics mediated by social relationships and the "material forces of production," which qualitatively stamps its imprint upon experience to create history's difference, its "heterogeneity," as he put it (Tosaka 1977, 3:98–99). By the same token, he advised that "character" differs from individuality.

In an era when other voices were stridently appealing to the largeness of Japan's "world-historical mission," Tosaka's designation of the everyday—the smallest unity of modern society—underscored the importance of temporality and the time of the present and how it—the everyday—is always momentarily poised to write its own history because it was history itself. As a minimal temporal unity, the everyday was still able to preserve the kernel of history since it was here (and now) that history was lived and where it changed rather than in the individual and its consciousness as "recorded" in narratives reflecting the unfolding of historical consciousness.

Here, it is important to contrast Tosaka's conceptualization of historical time to Miki Kiyoshi's "philosophy of history" rooted in narrative progression and thus based on a conception of time borrowed from outside history. With Tosaka, history is rooted in a perspective that follows the movement of one day to another, exemplified in a parallelism that held that just as one person is a member of a class, a single day is a day in world history (Tosaka 1977, 3:102). For this reason, Tosaka was encouraged to propose the everyday as philosophy's true vocation and recommend a return to its materiality as a necessary countermove to offset the baneful effects of metaphysics and its appeal to the transcendent and eternal. Even though philosophy had begun to turn to the question of everydayness, Nishida, like Husserl, had made the bracketing of the outside world a condition for figuring it. With the production of literature, especially the process of novelization expressed in formalizing the *shōsetsu*, we can observe the first attempts to focus content almost wholly on the experience of the new everydayness as it was being lived as a solitary, individual existence in the interwar period. Virtually everywhere one turns it is possible to see that the subject of the *shōsetsu* was invariably embedded in the details of the present, the everyday life of the moment, the now time of experience. This sense of presentness—the now—Tosaka's *ima*—was so prepossessing that writers like Tokuda Shūsei, who concentrated on the vital division of city and countryside, employed prolepsis in order to secure the effect of a future that has already happened in the narrator's present (Fujii 1993, 151–96).

The important question for Tosaka is why historical time had become such a compelling question in the present. Aware of a prior philosophic discourse focused on the status of time, he was convinced of the necessity of rescuing historical knowledge from both scientific dismissal and metaphysical (and idealist) transcendentalism. The motive prompting this preoccupation was the recognition of the "reality people were living in this historical time." In other words, the problem for him was the present and the imperative to see how it is situated in "our historical time." The sense of vision that comes from the presentness of today, from the character of the now, "constructs an independent order of values." More importantly, it is not permissible to "measure the value system embedded in the reality of today with the categories of tomorrow" (Tosaka 1977, 3:102). The present announced its kinship with a period's "character" (*seikaku*), invariably a political marker, and thus called attention to a relationship between part and whole. The work of today must be done today, as tomorrow's work corresponds to tomorrow's necessity (Tosaka 1977, 3:101). From this observation, Tosaka was convinced he had found the proper "law of perspective" for planning work since the present determines what must and can be done before and what comes later (Tosaka 1977, 3:102).

What Tosaka was proposing was a conception of the historical present (echoing Miki Kiyoshi) that would effectively replace the domination of phenomenological time based on consciousness, a borrowed time, so to speak, enlisted from the domain of experience, as such, with one founded on the lived reality of a bodily temporality, since life, living, always takes place in the present. In this way, the present, containing the "kernel of the crystal," embodied the condensed meaning of historical time: it was both the site of "necessity" and "flexibility," encapsulated in the "today" and made "visible" in now-time (Tosaka 1977, 3:101). A today that epitomized the present and shared with it the concealed principle of historical understanding constituted the "everyday."

If, as Tosaka believed, the present appears as the "time of our life," a timeless duration of endless routine and repetition necessitated by work the everyday also furnished the location of "history's mystery." Here was an obvious appeal to the model of the commodity form (custom), whose mysterious form managed to conceal from view the principle of historical production whereby labor as value was transmuted into the operation of surplus value that now appeared as natural and timeless. A deeply embedded, nonhistorical everyday life—what Marx referred to as the "religion of the everyday"—thus housed the kernel of history that now demanded to be drawn out. The present stands apart from the past precisely because it constitutes an accent of historical time as a whole and shows itself as an "intense" condensation of its totality. In fact, the present shows itself as the "kernel of the crystal," now seeking to convey the association of Marx's description of the commodity form, and is capable of disclosing the secret of a prior, hidden history remaining in concealment. The reason for this, Tosaka explained, lies in the fact that the "solidity of history is congealed in these places." In fact, he saw the present manifestly miniaturized in the today (*konnichi*) and showing its shape in the "now" (*ima*). Hence, the present, reminding contemporaries of the "realm of necessity," must be the starting point for rehistoricization and actualization, the site of planning and organization of what comes before and what follows. Yet in spite of the regularity of routine, common experiences, and the same thing happening every day, Tosaka insisted on separating one day from another, distinguishing each day from another, while recognizing their inescapable dailyness, because the everyday still "housed the . . . kernel of historical time in such things" and disclosed the mystery of time's difference.

What made the everyday so crucial in Tosaka's consideration was the recognition that for most people it was the site of work, which never waits, because they must work today in fear that tomorrow may be worse if they do not. The present is always today and history must always be practical, the time and place of praxis, as well, capable of realizing "possibility" but not utopian anticipation and expectation (Tosaka 1977, 3:103). In Tosaka's theorization, historical time was compelled to conform to an order that permitted no exchanging of today for tomorrow or yesterday. Unless this mixing is avoided, he warned, the present will be confused with a possibility belonging elsewhere and forfeit the promise of "actualization" in the now (*ima*). Again, Tosaka's complaint targeted a formal theory impelled by the law of noncontradiction that would not tolerate the spectacle of nonidentity and difference and insisted on arranging (mediating) things by lining them up on the same plane in a linear series. In its place, he proposed a configuration that distributed things among other levels, rather than constraining them to a singular, linear plane that would open the way for possibility and difference capable of exceeding fixed identity and the rule of sameness.

The argument was based on a logic that presumed that even though a thing with one identity existed on one level, it was still possible for it to become something else and acquire another identity once transposed to another level. Implied in this equation was the possibility of envisaging differing but coexisting rhythms of time within the same social space, which would account for the possibility of different identifications. It was reinscription in a different register. Allowing for at least two levels of lived reality invalidated the law of noncontradiction and its indentitarian impulse and introduced into the everyday the multidimensionality of time and space (Tosaka 1977, 3:103). What, for me, seems particularly important in this new configuration is how the everyday now signaled the intersection of coexisting but different temporalities requiring an accounting (resembling the concourse of different speeds and velocities in the physical world not visible to the naked eye) rather than merely a single temporal linearity claiming sameness and simple repetition. With this perspective it would become possible for the everyday to produce a history that is never completed or closed.

But even in Tosaka's time, others were already working to eternalize the everyday and demonstrate its completion and place it beyond the bounds of history and time. This was particularly true of folklorists, who had already eschewed history and the historical for an unchanging everyday existence (*seikatsu*), a folkic narrative lived enduringly by the fold condensed in the residue of surviving customs and religious practices providing the anchor of authentic life. The impulse was also observable in the "static history" of Kobayashi Hideo, who envisaged an endless everyday as an alternative to historical narrative, what he designated as historical excess, Marxian and non-Marxian.

The content of Kobayashi's conceptualization of the everyday was based on a sense of commonness inscribed in the literary classics and religious art of Japan and available to every age as a guide to living in the present and living as if present were past. In Kobayashi's reckoning, the social experience produced by modernity demanded a form of involuntary forgetting that required repressing a truer history submerged in the humus of contemporary, commodified materiality. This quest for resuscitating a truer history resembles the operation of recollecting a past that had become uncanny, strange, and consisted of the continuity of "commonness" in the historical and cultural unconscious of the folk.

In one sense Kobayashi shared with Tosaka a desire to unveil what lay hidden. But whereas Tosaka was concerned with revealing the mysterious side of commodity form—that is, its missing history and the contradictions it sheltered—Kobayashi departed from his contemporary by figuring a scenario capable of distancing or removing the everyday from history itself for the recovery of a timeless heritage. Its aim was to invert a history of political economy that revealed how work created value into one where value—cultural value—produces life. When asked during the symposium on the overcoming of modernity how he was able to perceive the Unchanging in the movement of a changeable history, he replied that time was not development. To grasp history not as time-bound determination but as a timeless classic meant understanding the position of the artist in the continuum of creativity. Hence, the act of appreciating a classic, even for the ordinary person, is found "in the experience of the everyday" (Kawakami and Takeuchi 1979, 231).

The effort to deprive the everyday of a politics of time and the possibility of actualization in the present drew the attention of Tosaka's friend Miki Kiyoshi. For a moment Miki tried to devise a Marxian philosophical anthropology in the 1930s that might incorporate the everyday and contain its "possibility." But in the end he turned to envisioning an all-encompassing philosophical history that tried desperately, and failed to bring together Hegel's earlier (in the *Aesthetics*) recommendations for a total history based on the everyday and his subsequent decision to lodge reason and history in the fully formed nation-state. Where Miki sought to depart from Tosaka's powerful intervention was in his effort to yoke the everyday (which he also saw as the "grounding" of history) to the mission of world history. What this meant was emplotting the everyday *within* the framework of world history signifying the status of an achieved nation-state. But he could only accomplish this conjuration by taking on the additional risk of making the everyday complicit in Japan's vocation of fascism at home and imperialism abroad in Asia. The aporetic nature of this problem between everydayness and world history (the calling and domain of the nation-state) was manifest in the desire to fuse differing temporalities that would bring the now of everyday existence into alignment with the more abstract principle of Japan's world-historical mission. In many ways, this desperate bonding of the everyday to a larger world history worked first to incorporate its unassimilated remainder and residue into the framework of the nation-state; at another level it attempted to efface the frictions of noncontemporaneous contemporaneity by subordinating the everyday to the larger spatiotemporal chronotope provided by Japan's world-historical mission. While acknowledging that the everyday was the principal site of action, it was a lesser principle of actualizing which he reserved for the larger stage of world history. The everyday remained outside the historical, as such, but gained its meaning from world history to form a unity with it. The implication of this move resulted in thoroughly spatializing everydayness and extending it to empire.

Like so many of his contemporaries, Miki was drawn into discussions engaged in determining what constituted concrete "reality" in a world already dominated by the commodity form and abstract exchange. He was convinced that the answer to the question was to be found in "historicality" (*rekishisei*), echoing prior and parallel debates still taking place in Europe, notably Bergson and Lukács, which had expressed as Heidegger demonstrated in *Sein und Zeit* (1927) a growing impatience with and even rejection of a regime based on quantitative, measurable time (clock time, the time of science) for forms of interior experience and psychological time. In Heidegger's powerful account this misrecognition of the nature of temporality led fatefully to historicism and the establishment of a world dominated by the They (*das Man*).

The logic of Miki's intervention was driven by a conviction that the real referred to the realm of "actuality" (*jissaiteki*), implying action (*kōiteki*) (Miki 2000, 210). In this formulation, the actual would thus signify the meaning of everydayness, and specifically the situation humans find themselves living in the everyday. But Miki's construction failed to conceal an unease with the contradictory claims of historical representation and the presentation of everydayness, especially the potential conflict between history made to progressively reveal meaning and reason and an everyday dominated by endless repetition. To finesse the separation between two domains he recommended situating action, history's vocation, in the everyday, even though he recognized the distance between the routines of everyday living and the activity of people on the stage of world history, the latter constituting the precinct of eventfulness, the former a realm spare in events and fixed on the repetition of custom. There would be no contradiction, he declared confidently, between an "actual standpoint" and a historical one (Miki 2000, 211). Accordingly, the aporia surfaces when the original standpoint of anthropology, which seeks to emphasize everydayness, will be seen to be incompatible with a historical anthropology. History, Miki observed, was invariably understood as opposed to the everyday and concerned principally with events, the great and extraordinary who act on the stage of world history. The question he posed, but never really answered, was how to move from the eventless world of everydayness to the register of an event-filled world history, from experience to nonexperience, a temporality of the present, mixed and entangled to a linear trajectory heading for a specific destination.

Miki plainly grasped history as national narrative, whose content differed significantly from the mundane experience of time in the everyday present. Moreover, history pointed to the singular and unique, while everydayness was the context of averaging and the commonplace, routine and repetition. For this reason, the everyday could never be seen as identical with history, which presumably occurred elsewhere and in a different zone of temporality. How Miki sought to resolve this knotted contradiction was to link the everyday and world history to a ground called "originary historicality," which authorized the procession of a steady evolution progressing from the first to the third level (Miki 2000, 215–16). The different and mixed temporalities signaled by the everyday and world history were restructured and smoothed into a narrative succession supposedly illustrating the inevitable maturation of time, its "ripening" (*zeitigen, kairos*) (Miki 2000, 229–30). In other words, Miki sacrificed the temporality associated with the sentient claims of everyday life—experience and memory—to the higher necessity and abstraction of narrative movement and the final (Hegelian) revelation of history's meaning. Regardless of his decision to employ the unity of the three categories in a linear progression representing the achieved "ripening" (*jijuku, jukusuru jikkan*) of history's reason— the world historical—he, nevertheless, opened the path to recognizing the aporia of differing and distinct temporalities belonging to the separate spheres of everydayness and world history and the necessity of pursuing historicality from within the precinct of the everyday.

"Matsuzakaya Joins Culture and Life Together"

In the postwar, and especially after 1960, the everyday has largely been succeeded by space-bound categories like public realm, publicity—the triumph of liberalism and its transmutation of civil society into a public sphere, marked by public opinion and the quest for greater communication, reflecting still the primacy of individual interests. But even before the installation of postwar society, we can recognize the attempt to relocate the everyday outside the historical and detemporalize it by subordinating it to the space of nation form and its world-historical mission. This spatialization effected in a number of discourses effectively emptied the everydayness of its crucial temporal dimension and robbed it of its capacity to foster a politics of actualization. Moreover, the drive to spatialize the everyday ultimately prefigured the later move to restructure it in such a way as to remove its capacity for producing dangerous and unanticipated excess. The postwar state finally secured the promise of dominating it, as Max Weber had once observed.

We can see the beginnings of this arrangement with the attenuation of everydayness announced in the films of Ozu Yasujirō described by Gilles Deleuze as the "banalization" or trivialization of everyday life and the determined effort to physically and materially resituate everyday life from the streets (where it was lived in the 1920s and 1930s) to the suburbs through the public implementation of housing policies and the construction of *danchi* targeting the middle class. But where the prewar perceived the everyday as the site of the subaltern masses who had made the modern everyday in the first place and thus remained ever ready and positioned to rewrite it, if necessary, the postwar saw it as the habitus of the middle class and a category now more spatial than timeful, more rooted in consumption than production, and unavoidably more committed to culture's incorporation of the political. What postwar planners learned from the prewar experience was to identify everyday life with space—often diminishing its temporal force—thereby restructuring the crucial chronotopic relationship between time and space and the possibility of actualization in the now. In this way, postwar state and society were thus able to recognize the organizational necessity of routinizing and standardizing it in order to assimilate the dangerous residues of the everyday to a new conception of civil order variously called the public sphere or civil society.

In the end, Tosaka's struggle to redefine the relationship between culture and politics and avoid the incorporation of the latter into the former, which was at the heart of fascism and the Japan ideology, was transmuted into an advertisement found on delivery trucks of the large department store Matsuzakaya, which promised to fuse culture and life through the mediation of commodity consumption. But this promise already rejects the establishment of the "endless everyday" (*owaranai nichijō*) of "our future," observed by the pop sociologist Miyadai Shinji, and now marks the dominant rhythm of Japanese life. What Miyadai is referring to is an endless everyday occupied by a body navigating its way through it with ceaseless consumption that provides "the means to live daily life" and its meaning (Miyadai, Fujii, and Nakamori 1997, 147–57).

References

Deleuze, Gilles. 1994. *Difference and Repetition.* Trans. Paul Patton. New York: Columbia University Press.

Fujii, James. 1993. *Complicit Fictions.* Los Angeles: University of California Press.

Harootunian, Harry. 2000. *Overcome by Modernity: History, Culture, and Community in Interwar Japan.* Princeton, N.J.: Princeton University Press.

Horkheimer, Max. 2005. "On Bergson's Metaphysics of Time." Trans. Peter Thomas, rev. Stewart Martin. *Radical Philosophy* 131 (May/June): 9–19.

Kawakami Tetsutarō and Takeuchi Yoshimi, eds. 1979. *Kindai no chōkoku.* Tokyo: Fuzambō.

Lukács, Georg. 1997. *Lenin.* Trans. Norman Jacobs. London: Verso.

Miki Kiyoshi. 2000. *Miki Kiyoshi essensu.* Ed. Uchida Hiroshi. Tokyo: Kobushi shobō.

Miyadai Shinji, Fujii Yoshiaki, and Nakamori Akio. 1997. *Shinseki no riaru.* Tokyo: Asuka shinsha.

Tanabe Hajime. 1976. *Kaisō no Tosaka Jun.* Tokyo: Keisō shobō.

Tosaka Jun. 1977–1989. *Tosaka Jun zenshū.* 5 vols. Tokyo: Keisō shobō.

——. 2001. *Tosaka Jun no tetsugaku.* Ed. Yoshida Masatoshi. Tokyo: Kobushi shobō.

CHAPTER 8

ALLEGORIZING HISTORY

Marxism, Hani Gorō, and the Demands of the Present

I. Allegory, Actuality, and the Present

When, in the 1930s, the historian Hani Gorō was prompted to turn to the writing of intellectual history, forcefully invited by political conditions constraining him from further pursuing an examination of the Meiji Restoration as a refeudalizing process leading to absolutism, it was not simply to criticize the prevailing practice of cultural and spiritualistic historiography. Even though he had early leveled a scorching assault against cultural and spiritualistic historical practice, Hani paradoxically shared its own struggle with the hegemonic claims of a positivistic historiography prepossessed with preventing the insinuation or hint of subjective desire from slipping in unnoticed in any "reconstruction" of Japan's past. Under the command of historians like Kuroita Katsumi this brand of historical practice resulted only in confirming the state's official version of the country's history. Now, in the conjuncture of the 1930s, Hani was in a position to draw upon the resources of his powerful critique (made in the late 1920s) as a condition of envisaging a proper intellectual history, which would address the question of his present without actually doing so directly. While his critique generously credited cultural and spiritualistic historians for having successfully broken the grip of a positivist historiography and its narrow protocols, recognizing in it an openness to other disciplinary practices and their diverse knowledges, he also saw the political dangers of a perspective driven by an idealistic conceit that prioritized and essentialized cultural value and spirit above all else as transcendent principles of synthesis. In his view, a history that relied on unhistorical principles of synthesizing was no history at all but rather an "antihistoricism."[1] For Hani, the defect of spiritualistic historiography lay in its overwhelming desire to find the timeless "marrow of history" (*rekishi no kotsuzui*), its relentlessly obsessive preoccupation with essences, unchanging and eternal, frozen emanations, as Adorno would have put it, "spiritual things" (*seishintekina mono*) replacing materiality, such as "personality" (*jinkaku*), "ancestors" (*sosen*), the "native land" (*kyokoku*), configuring tropes in such a way as to convey a religious aura to produce a form of religio-spiritual history for the modern, secular state (*HGRC*, 1:38, 39). Yet he also knew that such a modern historiography had already been prefigured by nativism (*kokugaku*) once it had abandoned its critical vocation and turned its hermeneutic assessment of classic narratives (*kiki*) into a veneration and worship of them as sacred texts. In this regard, spiritualistic history appeared as an immense caricature of earlier religious narratives, replacing only the terms: "personality" for "deity" or "god," "native land" for the kingdom of god or *shinkoku*—the land of the deities—and a particularistic individuality in exchange for divine revelation (*HGRC*, 1:38, 39). By the same measure, Hani similarly complained against the claims of folklorism and its own atemporal narrative of folk and custom, accusing it of promoting a fantasy that studied the "native place" (*kyōdo*) when no "native place" any longer existed (*kyōdo naki*) (*HGRC*, 1:298–308). It should also be said that Hani's turn to intellectual history represented somewhat of a departure from a version of Marxism that had already discounted the role played by ideas for the primacy of their conditions of production—that is, base for superstructure and the materiality of social life for mere ideology. Hani needed to find a way to both circumvent the direct causal connection that linked the immediate past to his present and the dictates of second international Marxism, as practiced by the Japanese Kōzaha (Lecture Faction), and its insistence on reducing superstructural formations to a material (economic) base. In short, he confronted the difficult prospect of avoiding both causal rectilinearity and reductionism. Hani found in allegory and the process of allegorization the means with which to resolve this double problem and, perhaps, exemplified a practical prefiguration of what Walter Benjamin would elsewhere call historical construction.

What apparently bothered Hani most was the presumed grounding of spiritualistic history (or cultural value) in a timeless and atemporal presence, expressed throughout historical time in indelible forms manifesting the irreducible spirit of the folk, and escaping, therefore, the status of historicity which would subject them to analysis rather than uncritical praise. In his view, such a history was already completed, finished in an indeterminate but distant past. This proposition conflicted with his own conviction that history's primary synthesizing principle must conform to "our own historical existence" (*HGRC*, 1:45), which, in this instance, meant the lived present. Even more worrisome was the aptitude of cultural and spiritualistic historiography to easily fall prey into cooperating with political forces of reaction, as was the case in the 1930s, a habitual aptitude the philosopher Tosaka Jun attributed to the collusion of liberalism and archaism.

But despite the power of critique and its hold on Hani, the turn to a form of intellectual or ideological history in the 1930s must also be read as a move toward allegorization, necessitated by the current situation through which he was living that would enable finding a method capable of addressing the actuality of his present without taking on the risk of doing so directly and attracting the attention of further policing. The fears articulated in the earlier critique of cultural and spiritualistic history were already ratified by complicit historians willing to put up their scholarship to serving the fascist state. The best known were historians like Nishida Naojirō, a cultural historian at Kyoto Imperial University, already recognized for having produced an idealistic cultural history of Japan (paradoxically, the basis or model for George Sansom's *Japan: A Short Cultural History*), who joined the government-sponsored Kokumin Seishin Bunka Kenkyūjo in 1932 and was thereafter involved in the formulation of ideological policies for the state, and Hiraizumi Kiyoshi, whose *Kokushi no kotsuzui* of 1927 had already fixed the coordinates for a new spiritual and ultranationalist narrative, which he and his students busily filled in during the decade of the 1930s. In this ideologically charged environment, Hani made the crucial decision to probe the formation of nativist discourse in the late eighteenth century, especially its inaugural critical engagement with its own present, and its subsequent erosion into a proto–national history preoccupied with antiforeignism and the workings of the gods and ancestors in a mythic time of origins. But before turning to Hani's seminal text on nativism, and the reasons governing this choice, it is necessary to say something about the structure and operation of allegory as a displacement of the actual present and how it worked.

The technique of historical allegorizing required a movement from an immediate present to a present past, a doubling which would permit a prior present to stand in for the contemporary now and the prior present on top of the contemporary present to constitute the figure of a transparent palimpsest that allowed the lower layer—the image of the contemporary present—to show itself through the imposed stratum that illustrated the earlier present of the late eighteenth century. An allegorical history thus entailed seeing the past for another present which would stand in for the absent contemporary present of Hani's time. Its operational strategy substituted a past, which had once been a present in the late eighteenth century, for the now-time of the present lived by the historian. This movement implied the possibility of repetition, but Hani would probably not have approved of this effect, owing to his commitment to the linearity of onetime occurrences (*HGRC*, 1:146). Rather, the allegorized past must be seen as an unscheduled spectral episode whose presence flashes up to momentarily occupy the present, as a ruin, perhaps, but also as a reminder (and remainder) of a past present, which was capable of offering both a lost exemplar for contemporary action (or critique) and the record of its own limitations and failure. As a ghost, it needed to be requieted, which meant working through its experience in the register of a different present, the kind of rememoration Hani would undertake in his examination of *kokugaku*. But working through this past present disclosed the pathway to connecting it with the actuality of his moment, which he was prevented from addressing directly. In this way, the eventfulness of the now is removed and replaced by the ruined landscape of a prior present—eighteenth-century Japan—now passed, to be sure, whereby a "kind of mystical movement becomes the now (*jetzt*) of contemporary actuality—separated from the events of the nation's history or story, leaving only a living image open to diverse revisions by the historian, a concern for transience of things and to rescue them for eternity."[2] Hani clearly saw this concern for mounting a rescue mission in Motoori Norinaga's project and the shared immanence, if not urgency, of the great nativist theorist's effort to retrieve an archaic moment, not as a form of knowledge, as such, or a nostalgia driven by a yearning to recapture a fictional golden age, but as a timeless presence that would make the present present again. Hani would subsequently pursue, in the hope promised by Motoori's example, the recovery of the silhouetted figure of the "mystical movement" that would become the now of his "contemporary actuality," an image distant from their originating events.

We know that the impulse empowering allegorization undoubtedly grew out of Hani's personal and professional circumstances in the 1930s, the failure of an unstable political liberalism in the world depression, the breakdown of Japan's international relations with the West and the subsequent fallout, notably with the United States and Great Britain over the status of the Western Pacific and Asia, imperial frenzy in China and the drift to fascism, which was, in fact, related to these setbacks and offered to resolve them. But it is important to add that his turn to intellectual history was also impelled by a desire to locate the "premises" of modern Japanese thought precisely at the moment when, as a Marxist, he was deeply implicated in the epic historiographical debates over the origins and development of Japanese capitalism and the country's modernization transformation, which focused on assessing the meaning of the Meiji Restoration in this epochal narrative. While it's hard to know exactly why he turned to an examination of ideas at this time, especially within the framework of a Marxian discourse that had already dismissed their role as either superstructural emanations or, worse, trivialized them as misleading idealist secretions, part of the answer stems from his relationship to the philosopher Miki Kiyoshi and his own conceptual reflections on Marxism, philosophy, and history.[3] Particularly important for Hani was Miki's formulation of a concept of contemporaneity authorizing the primacy of the present and role played by experience, precisely the form of consciousness workerist Marxism had already discounted as a lingering idealist residue.[4] (It is not surprising or even accidental that Kyoto philosophers like Koyama Iwao and Kōsaka Masaaki would later privilege the category of the present in their own meditations on Japan's "world-historical position.") In this regard, Motoori's intervention in the late eighteenth century exemplified for Hani an eventful encounter with the present and its relationship to the formation of a critique indexing the historicity he (Motoori) and nativism constantly acknowledged in their texts. What drove this critique was not simply the longing to restore an archaic prelapsarian precedent in his present but rather to revive the freshness of an inaugural ancient present and resituate its presence—manifest in "freshness"—in eighteenth-century Japan. But in insisting on the necessity to restore the freshness of an archaic exemplar in late eighteenth-century Japan, Motoori and nativists were registering a critical complaint against the course of contemporary history and the failure of Tokugawa authorities to adequately address it. They were also offering a solution in their assessment that their moment had drifted away from the ancient precedent. In a certain sense, the nativist program had already defined the design of an allegorizing operation by returning to a distant past and employing the optic provided by the Japanese classics to show the present (late eighteenth century) how it needed to resuscitate the novelty, originality, and inventiveness of antiquity in the present time to become an actual present. Hani's strategy was thus a doubling of this gesture, which allowed him to confront his present with the past of Motoori's present and appropriate his example to remind his moment of a paradigmatic promise and the dangerous consequences of failure. With this doubling move, Hani also hinted at a logic of comparability between different presents rather than merely past and present. But his most enduring contribution was to provide Marxism with a way of approaching the task of intellectual and cultural history that was at the same time capable of avoiding both the excesses of an idealistic preoccupation with spiritualism on the one hand and the narrow materialism of contemporary Marxian practice which had already assigned ideas to the secondary register of reflecting the effluences of the superstructure. Yet it is important to recognize that in this logic it is the present that necessitates allegorical reflection and its capacity to erase the distance between two temporalities by making one moment a spectral presence of another yet preserving the shadowy silhouette of a prior experience. In history allegory and actuality are brought together.

Hani's immersion in the present was thus empowered by Miki Kiyoshi's conception of basic experience produced by the proletariat as the only mode available for grasping the contemporary moment. While for Miki Marx's theory of the commodity form privileged the present and its commitment to novelty (and with it the temporality of everydayness) and opened up the route to rethinking the category of modernity and the status of history, he was also fully aware of how this present invariably encouraged the illusion of eternality and anti-history reminiscent of bourgeois aspirations for a timeless order. It should be pointed out in this connection that Hani early perceived in bourgeois history the claim of untimeliness. There was, he believed, a contradiction between the bourgeoisie and their historiography, one which inflected the growing inconsistency between productive forces and the given form of the relations of production (*HGRC*, 1:133–36). Whereas the modern bourgeoisie continually insist that their age will last forever, like capital, without periodicity, as Simmel once observed, the viewpoint of its historicity must see the historical process as having a distinct beginning and end, which meant that the bourgeoisie, like other classes, will rise, fall, and disappear. In Hani's reckoning, bourgeois historians were thus compelled to promote a "turnabout, which referred to studying the past for and in of itself" (*HGRC*, 1:138). The change cut bourgeois historiography off from the present (*genzai*) and obliged it to abandon its fundamental vocation to "grasp the present as well as the transformation leading to the present" (*HGRC*, 1:138). And it resulted in delegating bourgeois historiography to a "static past" (*HGRC*, 1:139) and the activity of trivialization that has nothing to do with the "moving potential of the present" (*HGRC*, 1:137), which, in fact, severs history from "our present existence" (*HGRC*, 1:140; see also 236–47, "Chiriteki yuibutsuron no shikan," for a prescient defense of the present, the site that "desires to understand the world and humanity and its history"). Grounding in geographical materiality escapes the errors of transcendent naturalism and its mythical origins. Furthermore, this turnabout removed the perspective of the whole or totality (*zentai*) from the study of history (*HGRC*, 1:140, 159). What is so significant about this early critique is that Hani's later assessment of nativism mirrors it precisely, as if it was a prior form of emplotment of what the bourgeoisie would later repeat, in order to serve as a prefiguration of the failure his present will live through. Hani seized upon this displacement of present for the past to demonstrate the importance of the former for grasping the latter. In an essay on late-Tokugawa ethics, he declared his conviction in both the primacy of the everyday present (*konnichi*), the now or today, as against yesterday, and in the importance of contesting the claims of eternality by bringing to surface its repressed historicity.[5] Hence, the present for both Hani and Miki constituted the appointed and only moment to begin the difficult task of constructing a critique of it capable of leading not simply to emancipation from "material desire" but rather from the "totality of material life."[6] What Miki named in his *Rekishi tetsugaku* as "history as actuality," the substantive purpose of history, Hani reworked into a historical practice made possible by his allegorical program. Here, Hani was able to show that a concentration on the present, as such, did not mean forgetting the past but rather demanded its retrieval—its rememoration, through spectral figuration offered by allegory.

Hani, it should be remembered, had been deeply implicated in the historio-graphical debates on the origins and development of Japan's capitalism and thus committed to a narrative plotting that sought to reveal the formation and unfolding of the absolutist state in the transition from Tokugawa feudalism to Meiji modernity. This counterrevolutionary refeudalization process worked to repress and even abort the development of the appropriate liberal political forms that were said to accompany industrial capitalism elsewhere. As a result, this distorted narrative, temporally linear and short-circuited but not necessarily progressive, locked Japan's history into a causal trajectory dedicated to show-ing how the past had inevitably led to an incomplete present. Yet the narrative placed great emphasis on the singularity of historical movement, which Marx, especially in mature texts like *Grundrisse* and *Capital*, explicitly dismissed for a more complex relationship between history and the logic of capital's catego-ries (already sighted by Uno Kōzō in the late 1930s). What differentiated Miki, Tosaka, and others from the historicist linearity dominating the study of Japan's "transition" to capitalism—never far from its bourgeois adversary whose model of narrative it had appropriated—was plainly the status Marx accorded to the commodity form as the principal structuring agent of capitalist social forma-tion, not the nation-state. This perception informed Miki's understanding of the importance of the present as the temporal site of history as actuality, as it also appeared in the reflections of Tosaka Jun, who rarely spoke of historical narrative, as such, only to dramatize its identification with national history. On his part, Hani endeavored to put into practice the idea of "history as actuality" by incorporating both its privileging of the contemporaneity of history and the historicity of the contemporary. In this act of rethinking, he produced his sem-inal essays on Tokugawa nativism and affirmed his commitment to locating the "premises of modern thought" in Japan, whose origins resided in the act of criticizing the present.

In these essays, Hani was able to circumvent the fixed and completed nar-rative which explained how absolutism grew out of unresolved and unsublated social contradictions originating in the Tokugawa period that subsequently diverted the transition. (But it should be stated that he never abandoned the absolutist interpretation and actually reaffirmed it when he demonstrated how nativism forfeited its relationship to the people by aligning with the feudal regime, an act that undermined the possibility of a later middle-class revolu-tion.) By addressing the actuality of his present through the prism of late-Tokugawa thought, he was able to override both the causal logic driving the narrative of absolutism and its commitment to a different conception of tem-porality for Japan's modern history. Moreover, Hani was positioned to finding a detour around the organizing unit of the dominant narrative that centered on the Japanese race-nation form. At the same time, he was sensitive to the narrative's failure to successfully conceal its most damaging contradiction, which could lead only to exceptionalizing Japan in the international division of modern states. Here, Hani's critique of thinkers like Watsuji Tetsurō and the idea of national particularity came close to actually calling attention to how Marxian historiography itself remained constrained by the unity of the nation form. While he drew from both Lenin's and Bukharin's texts on imperialism and the global spread of capital to propose a differentiation between a "worldly generality" from "national particularity," he argued that the move to the latter was a response to the homogenization of capital on a global scale (*HGRC*, 1:58). Even though the nation had once been a progressive force in the formation of the modern state, in time it had became "mystical," "overbearing," and "fatalistic," directing historians like Ranke to misrecognize the plural histories of nations for a genuine world history (*HGRC*, 1:68, 82). But by the time Watsuji inverted Heidegger's understanding of being and temporality into the spatial dominant and its claims to universality, the nation or national being was bonded to the particularity of climate and culture, which he— Hani— described as a "particular individual cultural history as imperialistic history" (*HGRC*, 1:78–82). For Hani, a true world history, free from the entanglements of the mystical nation form, lay not in a miscellany of diverse national histories gathered together as a kind of collective singularity, devoid of a binding dialectic connection, but rather in a history of the universal which is "cosmopolitan" and in communication with others. Such a history, he was convinced, recalled Marx's "Preface" to the *Contribution to the Critique of Political Economy* and Engels's *The Origin of the Family, Private Property and the State*, which provided the crucial precedent for envisioning a genuine "world history" capable of resolving the antinomy between "international universality" and "national particularity" (*HGRC*, 1:89–90). Marx and Engels, it is important to recall, had already worked out this relation in *The German Ideology*, where they showed how the world market brought together the local and the universal in a continuous interaction. But it is important to suggest that the Marxian narratives on the development of Japan's capitalism were not only rooted in the nation form, rather than indexing a broader universal or international division of labor, but often risked as a result falling into exceptionalizing the Japanese experience.

In any case, this commitment to the temporality of the present conformed to his earlier and later concerns to finding the terms for envisaging a proper world history and Hani's continuing interest in the role played by the city as the spatial container of capitalism. But it was, I believe, the figure of the commodity form itself that authorized establishing the present as the site of historicity and necessitated the labor of unveiling its concealed and effaced history. By the same measure the present, like the commodity, demanded to be read for its own, hidden history, what Tosaka named as the "kernel of the secret."

Such an approach would invariably clash with a concept of historiography whose story line of the nation form in Japan was already known, completed in its own way, as its destination followed a causal chain inaugurated in an earlier time, and whose originating social contradictions triggered a historical process that would inevitably arrive at the figure of absolutism. In this perspective, the present was a foretold outcome and thus the effect of an inexorable causal process. But in Hani's allegorical reading, the present worked to determine and identify a past for itself and promised to supply it with resources of possibility for actualization—similar, perhaps, to what Benjamin once called "a tiger's leap."

If Miki believed that the starting point of history is not the past but in the present, what Paul Ricoeur would later name as the "historical present," Hani reinforced this observation by insisting that "reality can't do without the today" (*NKSZ*, 111). He was thus persuaded that the "yesterday," though departed, still pulsated in the today. In this regard, Hani's desire to collapse the distance between his present and a past reflected his earlier passion for the historical thinking of Benedetto Croce, whose *Filosofia dello spirito*, volume 4, *Teoria e storia della storiografia* (1917), he had translated into Japanese in 1926, which aimed to show that all history was fundamentally contemporary. In Hani's rearticulation of this principle, historical consciousness derived from the "structure of contemporaneity" (*gendaiteki kōzō*) determined by "historicity" (*HGRC*, 1:58)

II. "A Historiography of Struggle"

In many ways it is probably difficult to differentiate Hani's life in the interwar period from his historiographical practice and ambition of its political direction. He was born in 1901 and died in 1983—the fifth son of a wealthy banker. Hani attended the elite First Higher School (Dai Ichikō), enrolled in the Law Department of Tokyo Imperial University in 1921, only to soon leave it in disappointment with the bureaucratic educational system it served. Like many gifted contemporaries, he migrated to Germany to study philosophy of history, represented by the Baden School of Windelband and Rickert, the principal agency of neo-Kantianism at the time, and with his friend Miki Kiyoshi and others like Ōuchi Hyōe he eventually turned to a study of Marxism. Upon his return to Japan in 1924 he entered the History Department of Tokyo Imperial University and received a rigorous education in positivist historiography as taught and represented by Kuroita Katsumi. Two years later he married into the family of Hani Motoko, wedding a daughter named Setsuko, who became Japan's first woman journalist. In the same year, he changed his family name from Mori to Hani.

Hani's first, major published work was a translation of Croce's *Theory and History of Historiography*, as mentioned earlier, which immediately attracted a large audience of historians and even a favorable review from Hiraizumi Kiyo-shi, who, though already known in academic history circles, was to become a prominent proponent of nationalistic and patriotic historiography in the 1930s. Hani graduated from Tokyo Imperial University in 1927, after success-fully submitting a thesis on the late-Tokugawa agrarianist and follower of the nativist thinker Hirata Atsutane, Satō Nobuhiro, and secured temporary employment in the university's prestigious Shiryō Hensanjo. He resigned from the historiographical institute in less than a year after speaking publicly to endorse the candidacy of the old Meiji Christian Socialist Abe Isoo, who in 1928 was campaigning for election in the first popular vote in Japan (after the enactment of the Universal Manhood Suffrage Law of 1925), on the platform of the Social People's Party. As a result of having become the object of criticism at the institute for his political commitments, Hani was persuaded by the absence of intellectual and political freedom in government-sponsored institutions and began looking elsewhere for an outlet for his talents and skills. In the fol-lowing year, he established a publishing house, with Miki and Kobayashi Isamu, and began bringing out a journal titled *Shinkō kagaku no hata moto ni*. The purpose of the new journal was to offer a broad forum for Marxism and the more established academic disciplines, recruiting articles from young intellectuals like Tosaka Jun, Sakisaka Itsurō and Kurahara Korehito. In 1929, Hani's New Science Corporation merged with the Industrial Labor Research Bureau (Sangyō Rōdō Chōsajo) and the International Culture Research Bureau (Kokusai Bunka Kenkyūjo) to form an umbrella research organization called the Proletarian Science Institute, in which he served as the chief of the history section. In these closing years of the decade, Hani wrote a number of seminal articles criticizing the prevailing conventions of bourgeois historiography, which established the foundation for what he would later consider as a proper Marxian historical practice in Japan.

In 1932 and 1933, Hani was actively participating in the epochal Marxian his-toriographical project devoted to examining the development of capitalism in Japan (*Nihon shihonshugi hattatsushi kōza*). Under the leadership of Noro Eitarō, this symposium literally changed the nature of historical scholarship in Japan by aiming to provide both a powerful narrative template for under-standing the process of capitalist development in Japan but also a connecting link to the broader world of capitalist accumulation. At the heart of the sym-posium was the concern with assessing the status of the crucial temporality of transition between Tokugawa feudalism and modern capitalism in Japan, a question that would also be posed by Marxian historians in China at about the same time in the social history controversy and in England and France after the war. Hani's several contributions were important essays on various aspects of the Meiji Restoration, the struggles leading to it, whose pivotal eventfulness determined the direction of Japan's subsequent modern history. The symposium produced two contending but overlapping interpretations: the Kōzaha and its theorization of a transition to capitalism derailed by refeudalization in the form of emperor-centered absolutism and the Rōnoha, with its accounting of the Restoration as an achieved bourgeois revolution. Hani favored the former over the latter, but his acknowledged originality seemed to exceed both positions, as his own historiographical practice, constantly informed by a profound grasp of theory, began to attract the attention of younger scholars, especially those at Tokyo Imperial University who were able to break ranks with Hirai-zumi's brand of patriotic ultranationalistic and spiritualistic narrative. These defectors established a study group in 1932 called Kōgōkai, which regrouped further in the following year and renamed itself Rekishigaku Kenkyūkai. Even though many of its founding members were not involved in Marxism, they were all, nonetheless, interested in Marxian historical analysis and the examples supplied by Hani's practice. Moreover, some students from Tokyo Imperial University, who were active in the Marxist movement and went on to organize yet another study group that was annexed to the Japan Communist Party, studied privately under Hani's tutelage and were often joined, as well, by members of the newly founded Rekishigaku Kenkyūkai like Nezu Masashi, Matsuda Hisao, Suzuki Shun, Endō Motoki, Suzuki Ryūichi, Imai Rintarō, etc.

Immediately after the publication of the proceedings of the symposium on Japanese capitalism, Hani was arrested on the charge of violating the Peace Preservation Law. At the same time, he was also fired from his position at Nihon University. But he was soon released after several months of imprisonment by agreeing to write a "prison memoir" wherein he declared his "intention" to establish a scientific view of history capable of overcoming both the Hegelian idealistic view of history and the Marxian materialistic perspective. It is interesting to note, in this connection, that this promise had already been voluntarily offered by the sociologist Takada Yasuma in his well-known "third view of history" as a solution sympathetic to fascism. Despite the hint of recantation (tenkō) such a confessional implied, Hani had no intention of converting and in the years after he ceaselessly continued to think through the presupposition of a methodological agenda for Marxism by seeking to envision an intellectual history consistent with the premises of historical materialism yet resistant to being reduced to an authorizing base that it supposedly reflected. He was also bent on pursuing an intellectual program that would also seek to broaden the arena of historical analysis into a genuinely world or universal history based on the proletarian experience instead of the particularisms of the nation-state and the repetitious narrative of the unchanging folk (minzoku). In a sense, Hani's long career after the war, which I cannot consider here, followed the aspiration of achieving a cosmopolitan history he envisaged first in the late 1920s, and it is clearly the interwar decade, especially the conjuncture of the 1930s, that formed and shaped his subsequent intellectual program.

In the remaining years of the decade after leaving prison, Hani resumed writing after a brief hiatus of self-imposed silence and published an essay in 1935 titled "The Meiji Restoration," which meant returning to a familiar terrain he had earlier charted. While his output continued, under the watchful eye of Special Higher Police surveillance, he was finally forced to stop in 1942—approximately the same year his friend Miki Kiyoshi was sent to a prison from which he never returned. By the late 1930s it was plainly impossible for him—Hani—to criticize the historical ideologies employed by a fascist regime, which so many of his contemporaries had already embraced in the environment of panic that induced denunciations of their earlier radicalism to serve the very state that Marxism had targeted for revolutionary overthrow. In this time of what Ernst Bloch described as "the moment of darkness," all the principal Marxian outlets were closed down, its theorists silenced or jailed, its hopeful critical agenda on its way to becoming a dim memory of incompletion. It was in this setting that Hani turned to Tokugawa intellectual history and Japan's precapitalist epoch immediately prior to the Meiji period and its momentous transformation into a modern nation-state. In this distant premodern past, Hani was convinced he had found a possible historical configuration removed from the events that had formed it that was capable of being employed for allegorizing the historical actuality of the present through the figure of a parallel past, one whereby its leading thinkers took up the question of their own present and the particular conjuncture that had produced it in order to assess the status of its historicity and its failing political mechanism manifest in the growing instance of peasant disturbances. The object of this quest was to construct a critique adequate to the present's failures. But Hani also turned toward the possibility of realizing a general history in these years, focusing on the Italian Renaissance, not only because of the censorship constraints he faced but, as well, out of a Marxian conviction that demanded a broader universal and cosmopolitan history able to overcome the claims of what he had earlier called the "illusions" (*gensō*) of individual particularity (*HGRC*, 1:58–74). Even after he was prohibited from writing any longer, younger scholars would often visit him regularly to form an informal "Hani group," which became a prominent historiographical force in the postwar period. One of these scholars, Inoue Kiyoshi, described Hani's historiography in these years as a "history of struggle," which offered "hope and encouragement to the peoples' fight for freedom and democracy against the war and fascism."

III. Past for Present/Allegory for Actuality

While Hani's theoretical preoccupations with the theory of history imbricated empirical research covering a wide diversity of subjects, constituting a complex, arabesque tapestry of history, it is important, at least for our purposes, to pause briefly to account for the reasons governing his choice to examine late eighteenth-century nativist discourse (*kokugakuron*) and use it to address the current situation he was living through in the 1930s. For Hani, the choice of *kokugaku* was, paradoxically, the condition underlying his decision to engage the present and was thus seen as undoubtedly indistinguishable from the present from which it drew its own authority for constructing a critique. Two interlacing factors informed this bonding of a contemporary political crisis with the subject of nativism in its eighteenth-century formation, a theoretical shift to valorizing the present and a tradition of scholarship on nativism which had matured in the 1930s. Hani, it is well to remember, easily fused a Marxian commitment to interrogating the "current situation" to Miki Kiyoshi's conceptualization of a basic experience, rooted in the concrete everydayness of contemporary existence as the ontological structure of history as actuality, merging the role accorded to the commodity form with the imperative required by phenomenological reflection. This constituted a combining of an earlier Crocean impulse that recognized the contemporaneous character of all history, which Hani constantly reiterated in his meditations on the historical present as the temporal site of "making" (*tsukuru*), glossing Miki's philosophic concept of *techne*, and a phenomenological Marxism rooted in the wish to capture the immediacy of experience (especially the "basic" experience of the proletariat), mediated by the force of the commodity form. Hani, like Miki, was convinced that the circumstances of capitalism and the domination of the commodity form provided the occasion to repress actual history but also close off the opportunity to configure a critique of the present that might represent the "starting point" of any effort to rescue history from its concealment. The present implied the place of novelty and ever-repeating newness—sameness and homogeneity—which meant designating it as the appointed moment to begin the difficult labor of envisaging a critique capable of eliciting its true history that might lead to an emancipation from "material desire" and, more importantly, the "totality of material life." What Miki subsequently called the "history of actuality" Hani renamed the "history of the present." But for both, acknowledging the centrality of the present and its meaning for history reflected the commanding role played by the commodity form in structuring a capitalistic social formation. Yet it must be recognized that any analysis of the contemporary social formation from the perspective of the commodity form ran the risk of undermining the claims of a narrative of the past development of capitalism within the framework of the Japanese nation-state, which, like bourgeois historiography, never seemed to arrive at the present. Moreover, an identity of the present represented in the figure of a social hieroglyphic demanding to be deciphered and read for its repressed history could be considered as inconsistent with a conception of historiography whose story line was already known and completed. Where Hani departed from prevailing Marxian historiographic practice was in his decision to start from an incomplete present rather than a completed past. Here, he solved the apparent disjuncture between the location of the present and the problematic status of a categorical past by turning to *kokugaku* and its own anxious encounter with a contemporary now-time in the late eighteenth century that no longer resembled the present of an archaic past whose presence had been obscured and ultimately hidden by its reliance on Chinese thought and language. But, as will become clear, Hani read in the history of nativism's confrontation with its feudal present a figure for his own moment that made it possible to pair the ultimate failure of eighteenth-century nativism with its later bourgeois counterpart in the 1930s. At the heart of this bonding was a parallelism between Hani's conception of a contemporary ontological structure founded on a fundamental experience of the proletariat and nativism's valorization of the ordinariness and the constantly renewing freshness of everyday life as lived by the ordinary people. Both nativism, and its later avatar, bourgeois ideology, forfeited a fixation on concreteness, based on a connection with the working and farming classes—actuality—for the abstraction of supporting the claims of a timeless and unchanging political order. It was at this point that *kokugaku* shifted its attention from interrogating the classic texts as a hermeneutic exercise to venerating them as containers of unassailable sacred truths. In this regard, bourgeois historiography similarly abandoned the study of history concerned with explaining the "dynamic present" for the later preoccupation with a practice concerned only for and in itself that resulted in portraying the past as static and a historiographical procedure consumed by the trivialization of facticity, a preoccupation with "big data" before the letter. Yet it interesting to notice closely how this appeal to eternality recalled capitalism's version of its own history as natural, not subject to history, and eternal. In both cases, the concreteness of the historical present was abandoned for the claim of the illusion of eternality. It was this forced parallelism that sanctioned Hani's appeal to allegory.

It is equally important to also observe that the subject of nativism was foregrounded in the 1930s by a number of historians and writers. What I mean is that the 1930s witnessed a maturing of scholarship on nativism and a growing popularity that reflected its attraction to diverse interests. The really important question is why nativism appeared to be so compelling a subject for so many writers and historians at this time. What, in fact, occurred in the 1930s conjuncture to prompt so many different writers and thinkers to embrace the subject of nativism? It is well known that this interest was either inaugurated by historians encouraged to rescue the residues of premodern culture in the 1920s or quickened by a historical scholarship searching for signs of an enduring spirit, as represented by the work of Muraoka Tsunetsugu and others, who felt bound to resituate what was genuinely Japanese—in this case religious sentiment—before it disappeared altogether in the march to modernization. In this regard, Muraoka's examination of Motoori's philological method and his subsequent reassessments of nativist belief (*shintō*) paralleled the work implemented by Yanagita Kunio and his followers and even Kuki Shūzō's hermeneutic of Edo "style." In Muraoka's text, Motoori is made to appear as a prescient example of hermeneutic rigor, coincidentally recalling the work of eighteenth-century German hermeneuticists he could not have known, presciently bordering on the scientific method, which would prefigure the later adoption of scientific method in modern Japan. Others like the historian Itō Tasaburō identified the evolution of nativism by Motoori's successors like Hirata Atsutane and its successive transplantation from the cities to the villages and its appropriation by local elites to become a "grassroots nativism" (*sōmō no kokugaku*). This populist form of nativism became the basis of a gradual yoking of religious belief and the moral imperative of work as a form of worship which, it was believed, would not only confirm rural local elites in their position of leadership in the Tokugawa arrangement of power but also act as an ideological brake on peasant discontent. In other words, "grassroots nativism" furthered *kokugaku*'s alignment with the Tokugawa system of authority, even though it contained the potentiality to defect and secede from the central Tokugawa authority, like other discursive practices as the new religions, when it became evident it was no longer capable of meeting its political obligation to maintain order. Still others, like the public prewar public intellectual Hasegawa Nyozekan, located a Rousseauian naturalism in *kokugaku*. Yet nativism also absorbed the attention of a diverse group of progressive writers like Nagata Hiroshi, Hani Gorō, and even Maruyama Masao, to name the best known, at the same moment it was being appropriated by conservatives like Tsuda Sōkichi and reactionary groups like the Nihon Rōmanha, who, perhaps ironically, fastened attention on its call for a return to an archaic imaginary, a program that was rearticulated by Kobayashi Hideo after the war. Although there were undoubtedly a variety of intentions motivating choice, there clearly must also have been a common conjunctural inducement they all shared. I would suggest that the moment already called into question Japan's hurried modernization experience and its consequences for those residues still surviving from a prior, premodern era, which now were in danger of disappearing entirely from the scene of modernity. With the fear of this passage came the recognition that late eighteenth-century nativism represented a lasting self-conscious identification of what it meant to be Japanese in a society long dominated by cultural exemplars adopted from an alien civilization—namely, Confucian codes of conduct and Buddhism—appearing on the eve before the country was opened to an even greater tidal wave of cultural transformation under the impact of yet another foreign culture. After all, it was *kokugaku* that supplied the trope of "Restoration" (*ōsei fukko*) which ultimately empowered the subsequent political transformation leading to the establishment of the modern race nation. But at the same time Tokugawa nativism also provided the modern present with the authoritative claims of an incipient nationalism in its distancing from China (before there was a nation form), a protoscientific method, the subjectivity of folkism, a native and natural aesthetic sensibility, not to forget a system of beliefs linked to it, and an involuntary submission of the population to emperor-centered absolutism. In the various accounts, there was already a close identity between nativism and the strategy of displacement, substitution, and allegorization. With Hani Gorō, what it offered was evidently the displacement of a critique of a contemporary crisis, which seems to have been lost to history.

In Hani's reckoning, nativism derived from the perception of contemporary crisis, which it steadfastly sought to appraise, rather than an overwhelming desire for a literal return to a misty, indeterminate archaic past. It appeared before him as a form of immanent critique, inextricably braided with the contemporary scene in late eighteenth-century Japan, which sought to mobilize a past present from which to draw its measure of expectation rather than a future which it was scarcely able to conceive. Temporally, there was only the present in nativist meditations, and when thinkers like Motoori detected difference they were marking the distance between their now from what it had originally been thought to be. Above all else, Hani was convinced that Motoori 's texts revealed a troubled but profound sensitivity to the spectacle of an evolving contemporary crisis he and his contemporaries were living through and whose conditions he managed to instantiate in a number of writings. Here, it seems, Motoori's conjunctural awareness provided Hani with the perspective of comparison with his own time and the prospect of employing its imagery of political address to speak for his present. Long before he turned his attention to *kokugaku*, Hani had proposed that a new historiography must always be based on a "contemporary ontological structure of [our] life and learning" that fulfills the demands of our "historicity"—namely, it is nothing but historical materialism (*HGRC*, 1:45). In an essay on "real facts," he returned to this identification of the "contemporary ontological structure" determined by "historicity" that accords to the "basic experience" of social classes. With this gesture toward a "basic experience" identified with social classes, Hani was clearly summoning Miki's powerful formulation of the "foundational experience" (*kisoteki keiken*) of the proletariat. "New facts," he wrote, are revealed in the field of history because the "contemporary structure of being manifests itself as a selection of new facts and requires a new interpretation of them" (*HGRC*, 1:56). Only those who stand before the "contemporary ontological structure" are able to solve the "dialectical contradiction between a selection and interpretation of fact," and, he further added, only those who occupy the place of "self-alienation" are in a position to recognize "self-negation" and the "unreality" of an inhuman being

(*HGRC*, 1:56–57). Hence, the problem of contradiction between making a selection and interpreting facts can be resolved only by means of a historiography for and of the proletariat. In short, the ontology of the present—constituted of self-negating experience, what Miki had described as the fundamental experience of the proletariat—Hani envisaged as a comparable present to the one lived and recorded by Motoori in the late Tokugawa period. The primary purpose of historiography, he observed in "Rekishigaku no hōkō tenkan," is to "grasp the true historicity of the present," as well as its "transforming process" (*HGRC*, 1:138). Bourgeois historiography, he argued, presents the image of a "static or quiescent past" and has nothing to do with the present it rarely manages to reach. Because it removes the perspective of the "totality" (*zentai*) from the historical account, it leaves open the way to playing down the past and reducing it to "particularity," as expressed in categories like the "folk" (*minzoku*), "state" (*kokka*), and "race" (*shuzoku*), all of which divert the direction of history from the "positive universality of class struggle" to the "individual exceptionality of national war" (*HGRC*, 1:143–47).

In the "Birth of Nativism," Hani seized upon Motoori's *Hihon tamakushige* as the text that best embodied both an accounting of the social and economic conditions recording the contemporary crisis and the social attitudes that attended the formation of *kokugaku* in the late Tokugawa period. This meant that Motoori first saw the heaviness of land tax—feudal rent—and the crushing burden imposed on small cultivators as a symptom of the contemporary crisis and the source of agitation, dissatisfaction, and discord. In his view, the peasantry was subjected to growing immiseration and impoverishment (*NKSZ*, 5–7), since those who were in positions of leadership had forgotten the standpoint of people below (*NKSZ*, 9). What Hani underscored by citing this crucial text was the extent to which nativism was not formed in a vacuum and developed in empty space (*NKSZ*, 10) but rather originated within the crucible of these social and economic conditions. Accordingly, Motoori discerned in the circumstances of his present its crucially defining historical watermark—the overburdening of taxation, rent, the surfacing of commercial capital radiating outward from urban centers, and the emergence and spread of money, together with the "pitching of the feudal managerial" order, and the increasing incidence of protests manifest in unscheduled *uchikowashi* (peasant trashings) driven by peasants and urban classes. In Hani's assessment, Motoori was so acutely sensitive to the circumstances of his time that he obsessively recorded in his diary the price of rice at the end of every month. For the fifth month of Temmei 7, for example, he concluded that prices had risen so high that widespread (*shōkoku*) poverty had become visible and had begun to spread to major cities like Osaka and Hyogo, where large-scale disturbances had exploded that increasingly lasted for longer periods. He had heard reports that not even Edo was immune from such out outbreaks (*NKSZ*, 11).

Hani recognized that despite its sensitivity to the current situation, nativism aligned with the leadership rather than the overtaxed poor (*NKSZ*, 11, 14). This alignment with the feudal leadership led nativists to quite naturally fail to see that the agricultural and laboring classes worked only for the lords rather than the broader region. Because they were committed to supporting the system of vassalage nativists could never see beyond the horizon of the immediate domain. In this regard, their view matched opinions held by the samurai, who were never able to see beyond their own domainal interests and lived only according to their capacity to expropriate the product of peasants (*NKSZ*, 14). But *kokugaku*, in Hani's evaluation, was able to perceive that the feudal leadership was hobbled by an attitude that excluded all "self-respect" among the ruled that naturally generated a "feeling for emancipation and opposition toward the feudal slave system" (*NKSZ*, 15). Convinced that despite the deepening of oppression inflicted by the managerial class, the "spirit of the people" had not been totally repressed and remained available (like Lukács's "soul of the proletariat" that resisted full ideologization) for the gradual growth of a desire for opposition to the conditions of their present and relief and ultimate emancipation from it. Oppression could no longer avoid provoking expressions of discontent and even prevent the willingness to act on them directed toward alleviating the harsh circumstances of contemporary life. In this connection, Motoori had no trouble in imagining the incompetence of the feudal leadership and worried about its consequences. Nativism responded to the contemporary scene by reflecting on and thus conveying the reasons and necessity by explaining why the popular classes were driven into the frenzy of riot and rebellion. But it saw these events as a signal for alerting the leadership to embark upon reform in order to rescue and maintain the received political system. Here was Hani's principal complaint against nativism and its ruinous reformist impulse (resembling the bourgeoisie of his day), even though he could acknowledge the importance of its critique of the present and the "momentary connotation" of the emancipating movement and expression of futuristic and progressive discontent demonstrated by the lower classes (*NKSZ*, 18).

If nativism worked to resolve the crisis of its present in order to reaffirm the received feudal order, it was forced to rely on a strategy that promoted a naturalist perspective epitomized in Motoori's theory of *mono no aware* that would encourage the ruled to act naturally, to accept "things as they are," so to speak, and accept the status quo. Hani read this impulse, as he did of the religious inclination in nativism, as a conservative impulse that worked to defuse the budding emancipatory movement of the popular classes and deactivate its revolutionary force to become "powerless." What nativism risked producing was thus a contradiction between a disposition to align with the regime and an ambition to advance a critique of its policies as a means of salvaging its authority. Aware of the self-interest blinding the feudal warrior class and its isolation from society's masses, nativism was particularly critical of its lack of affection for their home and country and their total inability to see beyond their declarations of loyalty to the lord. Owing to the absence of a broader concern in the samurai class, Hani reasoned that a "sense of nationalism" was nurtured only among the people, who was already beginning to show symptoms of struggle against feudal oppression. The people's struggle reflected an embryonic nationalism, which had not yet acquired the proper social foundation to achieve unity, lacking the necessary political and intellectual resources with which to express this new "progressive" attitude. Since this energy had no adequate outlet, Hani explained, its "revolutionary ethos" was absorbed into the "middle opposition group" within the feudal social order—namely, *kokugakusha*—who were intent on maintaining the feudal regime by reforming it. Yet the progressive demands for broader national identification and liberation released from feudal fetters emanating from the masses were mediated through nativist aesthetic concepts that worked to discount the "Way" and "antiquity" for a commitment to "freshness" and a concreteness that aggregated into a genuine critique of the present circumstances, with audible echoes from Hani's own time. But this critique was still more concerned with straightening out the status of archaic and classical texts and judging the aesthetic quality of an affective sensation and sensibility than with projecting a program for action. Where nativism faltered and thus failed, in Hani's estimate, was in its reluctance to sustain the people's struggle. To the end, it remained curiously removed from any activity that attempted to realize the demands it had willingly reflected and incorporated into the content of its critique, thereby risking the forcing of an further distancing that ultimately resulted in a slide into abstraction from the "actualities" of power propelled and represented by the explosion of popular energy dedicated to shaking the foundations of the feudal order (*NKSZ*, 39). Because of this commitment to retaining feudal authority at all cost, nativism easily fell into complicity with official ideologies pledged to reorganizing and reinforcing feudal domination. With this move, the fate of modern Japan was doomed to absolutism.

Nevertheless, Hani was convinced that instead of emphasizing nativism's defects it was equally important to reevaluate its role in the construction of a critique of the present. If nativism often seemed overly preoccupied with the significance of Japan's archaic heritage, an obsessive bondage to cultural origins, it was not to blindly praise it. Nor was it a simple gesture calling for a return to an Arcadian archetype. Rather, the nativist appeal to a remote mythic past functioned to break down the feudal ideologies of the Tokugawa present, which had originated in the medieval period. The purpose of this tactic was to demonstrate the existence of a "natural" state of things that had once prevailed before the introduction of constraining ideologies replaced them with artifice (*NKSZ*, 46). The original simplicity and freshness of outlook informing the

antique present contrasted starkly with Motoori's present, dominated by a sur-
feit of abstract moral constraints derived from an alien philosophy. The idea of
the "Chinese mind" (*karagokoro*) required adherence to an "antiforeign exclu-
sionism" and even "chauvinism" that had suppressed the more natural sentiments of the "life of the people's nation" (*NKSZ*, 45). In fact, antiquity—
ko/inishie—was concerned with observing things (*mono*) in their sensuous
presentness (*ima*), their immediate nowness. A present restricted in the way it
is today becomes inferior to antiquity (*NKSZ*, 47). But a progressive present is
superior to the past (*NKSZ*, 47). In Motoori's reckoning, the state of pastness
constituted what had despoiled the present and now needed to be removed. The
principal limitation of *kokugaku*, in Hani's reading, was its inability to define
the content of the "people's nation," failing to account for the true feelings of
the working people who constituted the axis of the state (*NKSZ*, 56). This failure was particularly evident in the blurring of lines between the various social
estates in Tokugawa Japan, whereby all were subsumed under the category of
the nation's people, without acknowledging that its generality did not refer to
workers and peasants and divisions were grouped according to status rather
than class. Even though nativism never tired of emphasizing the primacy of
"true feelings" (*makotogokoro*), it remained locked in the register of abstraction, remote from "real circumstances" (*NKSZ*, 59). The invocation of true sentiment, Hani asserted, never permitted nativists to grasp the real "feelings" of
workers and peasants, striving and struggling to achieve a measure of freedom
from feudal oppression. (A similar sentiment was being expressed directly at
the same time by Tosaka Jun as a description of contemporary reality, in an
effort to rescue the everyday from the domination of metaphysics.)[7] Once nativism reached its limits, it lost its progressive momentum and became a reactionary instrument of feudal control. Hani explained that when *kokugaku*
retreated from its relationship with urban workers and rural peasants, it also
forfeited its vocation to "reflect" their real "feelings." This failure drove nativism into the arms of an "ultranationalism" it once opposed, what Tosaka Jun
called the "Japan Ideology" in the 1930s, which resulted in handing over their
intellectual skills to the feudal regime and joining more established ideological partners already committed to devoting their energies to maintaining the
received arrangement of authority. Here, Hani could have been describing the
collapse of contemporary liberalism in his present and its own complicity with
the forces of fascism and militarism. After all, *kokugaku*, in Hani's apprehension, shared with liberalism its middle class "orientation" and reformist propensities to maintain the established political order. It also shared a comparable penchant for abstracting reality and separating its concerns from the
working poor. Liberalism's own limitations led to supporting any political
offer to maintain the status quo yet save capitalism from itself, which in the
context of the 1930s meant embracing the fascist solution. But this parallelism

was never made explicit by Hani since his allegorizing made such a move unnecessary.

Hani pointed to further limitations undermining nativism that resonated with contemporary relevance: (1) While it endeavored to criticize Tokugawa feudalism and its Confucian, ideological underpinnings, it overlooked the economic basis of the polity from which the politico-ideological system derived its authority. This blindness derived from a conscious avoidance of addressing the exploitative propensities of feudal rent and peasant resistance to it. In this regard, Hani referred to the example of Andō Shōeki, a contemporary of *kokugaku*, who had managed to acutely dissect the anatomy of Tokugawa feudalism and denounce the structure of exploitative social relations. (2) Nativism not only assumed a critical stance toward the Japanese classics of antiquity but also came to regard them as repositories of "facts and realities" and even paradigmatic sacred narratives demanding veneration, reenactment, and worship since they were dictations from the gods. Here, *kokugaku* departed from its initial scholarly and intellectual trajectory, which had managed to disclose a protohermeneutic approach based on philological inquiry promising to supply a method of reading texts for their meaning, "scientifically" and "objectively," for a perspective which looked upon them as objects of reverence, conveying "eternal" truths about Japan and the Japanese. In this sense, they ceased to be subjected to rigorous analysis to become revelations demanding belief in their truths (*HGRC*, 1:72). (3) As *kokugaku* turned away from philology to pseudoreligious ideology, it lost its original critical edge completely to become an instrument for taming the very popular masses whose aspirations for freedom it once embodied. (Here, Hani came close to a critique of the archaism and Japanism Tosaka identified with fascism.) Hence, the nativist denunciation of Confucianism emphasized its "foreignness" rather than its falsity, signaling the formation of an identity between what now was clearly Japanese and the Tokugawa order. That is to say, the assault on a foreign ideology now meant replacing its support with an authentically native worldview, one which, in Hani's thinking, sought to divert the people's energies against the feudal regime toward foreign countries like China (*HGRC*, 1:76–77). Significantly, this incomplete and aborted critique dissolved into producing sophistries that denied knowledge itself and rejected the value of a rational approach to the study of ancient Japan.

Once Motoori mandated this move, all that remained was the singular obligation of believing in the archaic temporality as the "age of the gods." This form of "self-negation," Hani declared, and especially its aggressive anti-intellectualism, ordained *kokugaku* to willingly submit to feudal ideologemes, recently rearticulated by Mito scholars in the early nineteenth century, which announced the necessity of people to obey order rather than to secure knowledge (*HGRC*, 1:79). Here, nativism slipped easily into the ranks of complicity with feudal ideology to keep people in a state of permanent ignorance, requiring of them only the expression of voluntary submission to the ruling class.

For Hani, nativism qualified as a "premise" of modern thought only in its momentary capacity to articulate a critique of the present against feudalism. Its limitations were derived less from history than intention, since its own class basis led to an alignment with the feudal authority. It was neither a Renaissance as it appeared in Italian cities nor a "democracy" or even a protoscience or a naturalism with inalienable rights but only a prescient critique of the present. It is interesting to note that this failure to nourish the capacity of the people to know and carry through their political project rather than simply accept things as they are was at the heart of Tosaka's call for an enlightenment encyclopedia that might supply the masses with scientific knowledge and rational, critical faculties in the dark moment of the 1930s. When Hani concluded with the observation that nativism had abdicated its original vocation once it severed its reformist ambitions from the task of reporting the lived conditions of eighteenth-century Japan—the true feelings of workers and peasants—to validate "ultranationalism," what better description was there of the actualities of his present and the political failures that led liberalism to open the door to fascism? With his powerful allegory of the present he was able to satisfy a Marxian conviction to engage the actualities of the current situation with the immanence of critique to recall for us what Antonio Gramsci, at about the same time, was advising when he proposed that "all history is contemporary, that is, political."

Notes

1. Hani Gorō, "Hanrekishisghugi hihan," in *Hani Gorō rekishiron chosakushū* (Tokyo: Aoki shoten, 1969), 1:38–40. Hereafter cited as *HGRC*.
2. Walter Benjamin, *The Origin of German Tragic Drama*, trans. John Osborne (London: NLB, 1977), 223.
3. Hani produced some stray essays on Arai Hakuseki and Ogyū Sorai before his work on nativism. See *HGRC*, 3:126–66.
4. For Hani's reflections on Miki's importance, see "Nihon bunka ni okeru Miki Kiyoshi no chii," in *HGRC*, 2:109–12.
5. Hani Gorō, *Nihon ni okeru kindai shisō no zentei* (Tokyo: Iwanami shoten, 1984), 111–12. Hereafter cited as *NKSZ*.
6. Miki Kiyoshi, *Miki Kiyoshi zenshū* (Tokyo: Iwanami shoten, 1966–1967), 3:76; see also Harry Harootunian, *Overcome by Modernity: History, Culture, and Community in Interwar Japan* (Princeton, N.J.: Princeton University Press, 2000), 358–99, for an account of Miki's conception of "history as actuality."
7. Tosaka Jun, *Tosaka Jun zenshū*, 5 vols. (Tokyo: Keisō shobō, 1978), 4:138.

CHAPTER 9

PHILOSOPHY AND ANSWERABILITY

The Kyoto School and the Epiphanic Moment of World History

Philosophy has come to be a discipline such that, within history's movement, it clarifies one's own standpoint and has thus become a learning [gakumon] that provides suggestions on which direction we might proceed. It is because of this [reason] that we must analyze the contemporary [moment]. Yet analysis of this present is in fact nothing more than the analysis of a particular moment of the present within the context of world history.[1]

I think philosophy must also be mediated by historical fact.
Historical reality and . . .[2]

—Kōsaka Masaaki

Solutions which once were impossible within the study of history until now will become the necessary philosophical motifs for the study of world history. . . . For overcoming the unsatisfactory side of historicism . . .[3]

—Suzuki Shigetaka

This is what contemporary philosophy must be.[4]

—Nishitani Keiji

I

Ever since Georg Lukács exposed the affirming method of philosophers like Heinrich Rickert as simply a "prolongation of the state of pure immediacy" that reflected the failure to take into account the process of mediations, there could only be the inescapable conclusion that any analysis of reality "ends by returning to the same immediacy that faces the ordinary man of bourgeois society in his everyday life."[5] What apparently troubled Lukács was the perception that the "facticity of bourgeois existence . . . now acquires the patina of an eternal law of nature or a cultural value enduring for all time."[6] Under such circumstances, "history must abolish itself," owing to the "unhistorical character of bourgeois thought [which] appears instantly when the present is seen as an historical problem." Lukács insisted that the problem of the present has become the problem of history, one that refuses to go away despite bourgeois denial, whose elucidation must constitute the task of a proper historiographical vocation. The reasons for this "blindness" stemmed from the preoccupation of philosophy to ground its theoretical approach in unmediated "contemplation," which itself has produced an "irrational chasm" dividing the subject and object of knowledge. Since World War I bourgeois thinkers and historians have been prevented from seeing the "world-historical events" of the present as an expression of an incipient universal history. As a result, their work has never risen above the "pitiable" level of the worst kind of "provincial journalism." In other words, philosophy's dedication to sustaining the separation has originated in the decision to bracket the historical present of its world and thus exonerate some of the century's outstanding thinkers from accounting for their thought and its moment of temporality. Years later and in a different part of the world this was the same estimate made by the philosopher Tosaka Jun, who pointed to how philosophy had abdicated its principal vocation to interrogate actuality for a flight to transcendence.

Paradoxically, the present is the philosopher's primary precinct of occupancy, not the historical past. It is the place where thought and reflection are carried out. Yet as Paul Ricoeur reminded us, despite the differences between thought, literature, and history, they ultimately share a common referent, which is the human experience of time or the "structure of temporality." In the decade of the 1960s of the post–World War II era, the philosopher Louis Althusser revisited the question of philosophy and history and their putative relationship and the space they might mutually share. With his lapidary declaration that "philosophy has no history," echoing another familiar announcement asserting that "ideology has no history," Althusser called into question the necessity of rethinking the relationship. But the proposal should not be understood as recommending a thoroughgoing formalism immunizing philosophy from its world, even though some have seized upon this interpretation as a divergence from conventional Marxism. But as Marxists, Althusser and his followers granted to philosophy neither an independence from "an objective, historical existence," its claim to timelessness and universality, nor its unknowing complicity in dimly reflecting social reality.[7] Rather, philosophy, as a practice, was linked to other practices and produced effects (from absent causes) that needed to be accounted for and revised according to a changing historical situation it could never fully grasp.[8] This departure from an immanent critique manifest in Lukács, which the Althusserian inflection partially shared, required philosophy to thus confront its present and reflect upon its historicity, that is the "theoretical conjuncture," in order to "stake out a position" on and in the temporality of the present. For Althusser, since philosophy has already occupied every space, what thus appears necessary is the act of taking a position against the prior occupants. According to Pierre Macherey, Althusser was apparently objecting to any attempt to reduce philosophy to a historicity external to itself that would "denature the fundamental operation."[9] Because the philosopher thinks in the present, meaning that the present provides no priority as a given circumstantial "actuality," what is being expressed is the "pure presence of thinking to oneself." Thought thus affirms itself to the present in the act of thinking, which is proper to a "pure practice" since it is not related to anything but itself. Unlike other forms of knowledge shaped by relations to exterior objects defining their domains, philosophy has no history because its "object" is itself, dedicated to speculative reflection in a temporal moment proper to it that cannot be measured by any other time. But lingering in the shadows of the present is the conjuncture, a historical moment demanding an accounting in any explanation of philosophy's presentness and the present of philosophy.

If philosophy has no proper history as such, history has a philosophy that works on it and transforms it. In this regard, history marks philosophy by exposing it to the risks and promises of temporality, rather than thinking solely in and for its own time in a necessarily singular manner.

Hence, philosophy is induced to think with and for time, ideally for all times, by moving beyond the circumstances that have made it contemporary to itself;[10] it thus confronts other forms and figures of thought and is conserved or altered. In this way, history is not external to it but rather internal to its operation since it can in no way be bonded to a fixed object and its appearance. Philosophy is in fact history, a history of its relationship to itself—that is, its present. But the present is not so much merely a moment but rather a vast conjuncture marked by traces of coexisting pasts, uneven temporalities between different domains of activity, heterogeneity, irreducible divergences that foreclose the possibility of linking social reality to the appearance of an unmediated immediacy. In fact, the philosophic text is no longer separated from an external history, nor is history external to it, no longer reflecting a world outside it or merely representing it since it is both "fully historical and real."[11] The sign of this kinship is recorded in the temporal discordance and disorder that traverse and crisscross the philosophic (and indeed any) text fashioned out of a social reality, which itself is indicated by conflicts and uncertainties unevenly developed that can only be described as a "historical present" rather than "the simplicity of the present."

Whatever distance some philosophers sought to impose between their philosophy and moment in the 1930s, it was not nearly as great as the effort of the postwar reflex in Japan to rehabilitate Kyoto philosophy under the steady drumbeat of periodically and repetitively reminding us that its philosophic reflections never refracted the force of the historical present in which it was produced. The reproach calls attention to yet another context, more implicit than explicit, which is rarely articulated but clearly refers to the text(s) under consideration, as if it (or they) possesses an invertebrate knowledge of itself. Such attempts to spare philosophy from the world that produced it, or in which it was produced, can only lead to denunciations that discount the scholarship informing accounts that seek to explain the historicity of texts. What appears to be at stake in this defense of an indefensible formalism is the presumption of a transhistorical truth claimed for philosophy (as if history has no truths of its own) and the impossibility of securing assent or agreement on what constitutes the proper "context" for the elucidation of philosophic reflections. Those critics who have made careers in defending the claim of exemption of Nishida philosophy from its world ultimately remind us of Marx's penetrating critique of Stirner and the effort of Young Hegelians to separate thought from history: "Philosophy and the study of the actual world have the same relation to one another as onanism and sexual love."[12] The resulting consequence is a rejection of both the singularity of situations and the importance of its specificity.

While it is not my purpose to assign political guilt and rehash the insistence of philosophic formalism and contemporary appropriators seeking to "correct" misinterpretations that serve the present rather than either past presents or its thinkers, I will be concerned with what we might identify as the practice of separating philosophy from history and reflection from its world, the reasons informing this impulse, and the corollary question of philosophy's answerability to history. I should say, in this connection, I am not referring to the history of philosophy, as such, a mere history of illusory ideas, spirits and ghosts, as Marx observed,[13] since it sustains the very formalism that is at the heart of the question. Rather I want to focus on how both philosophy and history must be answerable to each other in the present they commonly occupy, how each must be used against the other in the effort to seek a way to offset the impression that they are not mutually implicated with each other, even though such a relationship is often disavowed on both sides. Instead, I want to suggest that many of the very people who have been exonerated from their historical present by the appeal to a timeless formalism were deeply involved in and responsive to the imperatives demanded by their present. Specifically, I will be concerned with the relationship of a historical present and the formation of what Kyoto philosophers called a "world-historical standpoint" at the outset of World War II.

The Russian philologue, comparativist, and literary critic M. M. Bakhtin is our best guide to the problem of answerability, as exemplified in one of his early texts dedicated to explaining art's answerability to life. Bakhtin perceived in discursive thought a split between the "content or sense of a given act" and the "historical actuality of its being." For this reason, he feared the loss incurred in every instance of knowing the value and "unity" of a given art's actual "becoming and self-determination." Hence, he declared, "two worlds confront each other," two worlds that fail to have any communication with each other and are thus "mutually impervious." "The world of culture and the world of life, the only world in which to create and the world in which these acts and cognition proceed and are accomplished once and only once." What Bakhtin was apparently calling to attention was the recognition of acts that moved in two different directions and the necessity to reflect on both simultaneously, to achieve the "unity of two-sided answerability." Moreover, the accomplishment of this reciprocal answerability must become a constituent moment of the act or what is given, since it is the only way the "pernicious non-fusion" and "non-interpretation of culture and life could be surmounted."[14] A human, he wrote, has no right to an alibi, to an evasion of that unique instantiation of answerability, which is constituted by his/her actualization of a unique, never-repeatable "place." In fact, a human has no right to avoid that once-occurring "answerable act or deed" which his whole life must constitute.

It seems to me that it is this reluctance to satisfy the imperative of answerability that has resulted in the narrowing of our understanding of philosophy's moment of historical production. Driven by a fear that philosophy, like all other forms of expression, will be merely reduced to a material historical determination, the act of denial risks undermining the necessity of mutual communication between philosophy and history. Yet from philosophy we must expect an accounting of the historical location of its reflective act, while history will be asked to acknowledge its reliance on forms of philosophic enablement in its pursuit of meaning. It is instructive to note that Tanabe Hajime, in his lectures on historical reality of 1940 (*Rekishiteki genjitsu*) expressed this sentiment, whereby he saw philosophy's task to be sorting out what we know or do not know about historical reality and especially the contemporary history Japanese were living in the late 1930s.[15] Tanabe was merely reiterating a shared response among Kyoto philosophers, who had increasingly turned to history and the present to grasp the nature of their relationship to it as a condition of understanding the meaning of their moment. Like many of his contemporaries, Tanabe saw the challenge of the contemporary present as the singular vocation of philosophy to grasp the reality of history and its meaning for the future.

We must thus recognize the importance of the irony of a philosophic discourse that sought to surmount the conventionally received separation of philosophy and history for the more difficult task of inducing a mutual answerability to each other by focusing on the present in order to ascertain the demand of contemporary history. In this encounter, both philosophy and history would be transformed into a proper form of address leading to action. Yet this response represented a far cry from later custodians (the epigoni) of Kyoto philosophy, who have consistently persisted in their resolve to reinstate the cleft between history and philosophy. However much this engagement of the present might today summon critical denunciation, it cannot be discounted for having shirked the gesture of responsibility for attending to the more difficult decision to find an "answerable unity" of thinking and "performed action," in the interest of trying to align life (history) and politics.[16] We can detect in this sensitivity the leitmotif of the now infamous symposium on world history of 1942 (*Sekaishi tachiba to Nippon*), which, in Kōsaka Masaaki's admonitory proclamation, proposed that the central question at hand is the present and constituted a preoccupation found in the writings of virtually all the people who, in one way or another, were associated with Kyoto philosophy, like Tanabe, Tosaka Jun, Nishitani Keiji, Kōyama Iwao, Miki Kiyoshi, and indeed even Nishida Kitarō himself. But none was more engaged in this question than Miki Kiyoshi, who answered the compelling question of the conjunctural present in a philosophic idiom that fused into pragmatic and political analyses for the formulation of policy in the current situation. When he departed from his philosophic vocation to work in policy-oriented research units associated with the state, his intent was to supply an example of how philosophic analysis could be used to grasp and address the current situation to make policy. Yet we can see in all these thinkers the effect of Marx's early identification of a world history yet to be written but that would fuse the "local being" to the "universal being," region to world, as he already had perceived occurring in the formation of the world market demanded by capitalism and its aptitude for expansion. However, this is not to say that Kyoto philosophers were Marxist, excepting Tosaka; far from it in fact but only captive to this singular insight that saw capital as making possible world history.

What Miki shared with his philosophic cohort was the conviction that the resolution of the present's status required finding ways to overcome it and thus exceeded its entailing historical associations to reach the goal of a temporalization no longer burdened by the claims of the modern. It should be remembered that this rejection of the reviled category of a degraded modernity had become the subject of both philosophic discourse and common sense in the late

1930s and echoed Martin Heidegger's earlier dismissal of the modern and the "them" (*das Man*) who inhabited this specious temporal and historical register. With Miki, and Kyoto philosophy in the late 1930s, the present offered an urgent occasion for continuing the "reckoning of time," as Heidegger had named it earlier, and the opportunity for rethinking the figure of a true temporality. In Miki's reflections this trajectory led to envisaging a new conceptualization of time and its relationship to space capable of accommodating Japan's world-historical position and an emergent Asia yet preserving capitalism in a new configuration. Part of this preoccupation with the present in the form of a persisting presentism derived from a modernist impulse already established in interwar Japan that had pronounced a verdict on the past as a necessary condition for securing a separation from the burden of the present's antecedents. Kyoto philosophers also shared a modernist distrust of received forms of historical representation. But an equally important source prompting it was the interwar conjuncture that literally sought to fuse the future with the present or condense the one into the other for its promise of immediacy, presence— progressively made more demanding by the deteriorating world situation.[17] In this environment, philosophy moved to emphasizing the importance of what might be called the phenomenological "now" and proceeded to provide it with a diagnosis that would open the way for it to become the temporal tense of the future perfect. Here, it seems, was the meaning of an "overcoming" that would surpass the contemporary present. Yet inscribed in the heart of the conjunctural imperative privileging the immediacy of the present and urgency to meet its demand for resolution was a set of historical presuppositions pointing to the nature of Japan's modernizing experience that eventually would prefigure the philosophic intervention and configure its discourse. I am referring to the appearance of the great Marxian historiographical controversy of the late 1920s and early 1930s over the historical nature of capitalist development in Japan and its subsequent effect on sensitizing the conjunctural generation to the consequences of capitalist modernization in Japan. More than anything else, it was this debate that called attention to the various aporia of capitalist modernization, and which would ultimately prompt the recommendation to "overcome modernity." Even though its own agenda was narrowed to emphasize the economic nature of capitalist development in Japan since the late eighteenth century and the political fallout of the transformative events leading to the Meiji Restoration of 1868 and its aftermath, the debate, owing to its Marxian orientation, would also identify the social contradictions put into play by the new state and its commitment to establishing a capitalist political and economic order, which, it was believed, would have to be overcome if Japan was to enter the new world history Marx had envisioned but was yet to be conceived and written. Hence, the effort to supply the view of a new world history, no longer yoked to either Hegel's systematic presentation of a universal history and the unfolding of reason or Marx's incomplete reflections, with a philosophic analysis that assigned the task of overcoming all antinomies to a state rooted in folk and community as the response to the contemporary Marxian debate on the origins and development of Japan's capitalism. Both Marxian historical discourse and Kyoto philosophy sought to resituate Japan in a new global and temporal register: the Marxists in capitalism and the formation of a new international division of labor that would announce the triumph of the proletariat as a fulfillment of Marx's own unfinished conception of world history, and Kyoto philosophy in discerning in the present the temporal moment as the occasion for Japan to embark upon a world-historical mission to construct a "true" and universal world order that would surpass the particularistic manifestations of the past.

Hence, philosophic discourse turned toward the assignment of addressing the status of contemporaneity—genzai—by paradoxically taking up the task of rethinking the status of history and historical consciousness. The purpose of this seeming detour was, according to Kōsaka Masaaki, to reconfigure the matrix of the present in such a way as to make history anew in a temporal register no longer weighted with associations burdened by the category of "modernity." To be sure, this new history was the world history valorized by the famous symposium named after it, a new temporal and spatial formation, which, Kōsaka proposed, was the problem posed by the present itself that would lead to its (the present) surpassing. In Kōsaka's thinking the present and its overcoming were "above all" reducible to "the problem of Japan."[18] In his opening statement of the symposium on world history, Kōsaka highlighted the importance of history and especially the philosophy of history. In his reckoning, he divided Japan's interest in the philosophy of history into three stages, which reflected stages in the country's modern history, the last being the present now dominated by a consciousness and philosophy of world history, which has succeeded the previous moments of Rickertian epistemology and Diltheyian hermeneutics (STTN, 3–4). In other words, the identity of an achieved world-historical status in the present underscored its contemporary significance and its importance for the future. Moreover, it is precisely this identification between a consciousness of world history and the actual demands of the present (genzai Nippon) that accentuated philosophy's responsibility toward history: "Philosophy has come to be a discipline such that, within history's movement, it clarifies one's own standpoint and has thus become a learning [gakumon] that provides suggestions on which direction we might proceed. It is because of this [reason] that we must analyze the contemporary [moment]" (STTN, 3–4). As a result, the "philosophy of world history possesses the obligation to direct the course in world history," as it now serves as a foundational discipline for "orienting" and "advancing" "anew, step-by-step" (SNR, 61).

At about the same time, Tanabe Hajime was advising that "historical reality" must be seen as the mediation of possibility, which determines the self freely for "our future" (*RG*, 20). What is important is the overdetermined activity of philosophical discourse in the 1930s conjuncture to privilege the present moment at the virtual expense of diminishing the role of the past (Kyoto philosophy's response to the Marxian historiographical date on the development of capitalism in Japan and its contradictions). While this intellectual impulse brings to mind one of the principal planks of the modernist platform, it also draws attention to the philosophic desire to refigure the present and world historicality into an epiphanic moment positioned to shatter the narrative reminders of the past for the attainment of a new level of consciousness, which would induce a defining interruption leading to intense change. In this regard, I think it is possible to suggest that Kōsaka's decision to discount both epistemology and hermeneutics for world history represents a shared rejection of the claims of narrative itself—especially all those narratives that had, like the Marxian historical debate, highlighted the development of a specific capitalist modernity made in the West. Since the events announcing the arrival of world history were beginning to disclose the vague silhouette of a world still in process of "coming" into being and in its "making" in the present, as Tanabe anticipated, it would be necessary to continue the effort to actualize a course of action committed to overcoming and moving beyond the older narrative of modernity. (Here, it should be noted, Tosaka Jun also shared a distrust for narratives, especially those dominated by the unity of nation-state but substituted the hegemony of the world market and the international division of labor for world history [*RG*, 25–26].) The determined purpose of the philosophy of world history was the achievement of a new present, a time different from the "modern," once associated with an anticipated future and directed at realizing the what will have been of the future anterior. Moreover, this project of the present leaned increasingly toward defining Japan's destiny as the subject and substance of the category of world history, which aimed to replace the older stage dominated by the reign of the world market as the arena of the nation-state and its political alignments, marking Japan's entry into capitalist modernity.

II

The central problem that aroused the interest of Kyoto philosophers in the present was the question of historicism and the urgency of resolving the crisis of value resulting from an excess of history. Beyond the immediate task of resolving a surplus of historical knowledge and the uncertainty of values in the face of relativism, the attempt to address the crisis of historicism ultimately paved the way to "overcome the modern," which meant surpassing the present itself for a new contemporaneity. Japanese thinkers in the 1930s, especially those associated with the Kyoto school, responding to what Ernst Troeltsch had named earlier as both "the problem" and the "crisis" of historicism, reinforced the conviction that in their present they were living though a crisis in historical thought manifest in the production of an excess of historical knowledge and the runaway relativism of values it unleashed.[19] Moreover, it was observed that this excessive production of history was principally derived from accelerated specialization and fragmentation among the disciplines resulting in a collapse not only in the stability of values making the permanence of evaluative judgments impossible but also in the crumbling of whatever coherence history may have once commanded. Ever since World War I it had been progressively noted that historical specialization was undermining both the claims to standardized, enduring values by seeking to understand the past in and on its own terms (as if such a utopian mastery was ever attainable) and the acknowledgment that the discipline had consistently failed to explain convincingly how the present has been produced by its pasts, prompting Paul Valéry to declare that "history will justify anything" and "it teaches precisely nothing." Valéry, along with numerous contemporaries, saw the ultimate inutility of historical knowledge in its failure to foresee and anticipate the coming of World War I.[20] But this failure signified an exclusive preoccupation with the past to the detriment of ignoring an analysis of the current situation as history's true vocation, as Marx and successors like Lukács had advised. This discounting of history was especially true of the immediate present of the late 1930s and the defiance of a world conjuncture to submit to the protocols of historical understanding, as it was already forecasting the contours of yet another global conflagration.

Kyoto philosophers were quick to turn away from the faded promise of historical knowledge to teach about life to understand the historical present, which they designated as the locus of history. In this new assessment, the present thus required a rethinking of the structure of historical practice conforming to a philosophy positioned to provide a coherent image of world history, rather than merely a history of the national past. The purpose of this rethinking was to make history once more meaningful—universal—and its value free from the oblivion of relativism. The task was assigned to the construction of a philosophy of world history, one that would exceed Hegel's idealist trajectory of the unfolding of "freedom" and overcome the crisis-ridden historicism of a European consciousness dominated by a regime of abstraction for a return to the concreteness of "real life." Kyoto philosophers thus seized their moment as the occasion for redefining Japan's special world-historical mission to rid Asia of an implacably exploitative white man's imperialism and release its various societies from colonial bondage for the realization of independent nationhood under a new putatively cooperative regional arrangement of authority called the Greater East Asia Co-Prosperity Sphere.

Under Japanese supervision, the new regional authority would create a spatial site for capitalism (making some suppliers, others producers) and a different temporality for its operations, which, it was believed, would transport a hitherto absent Asia, languishing invisibly in the shadowed eclipse of Western colonialism, into the light of a new age of world historicality and put on an equal footing with the West. In the meditations of Kyoto philosophy, it became evident that the past, which was rejected for the present, was the temporality that had been assigned to Japan, whereas Asia would now occupy the new time of the present. As Kōyama proposed, time and again, Europe and its world-historical moment now belonged to a different temporality and the past. While this proposal implied an inversion of the Hegelian historico-temporal paradigm, I think Kōyama was trying to move beyond Hegel by pointing to both the installation of a new temporal present, one that would accommodate the new with the received past and which was consistent with the thinking on "overcoming," and a new kind of social and political configuration that was ultimately concretized in the Greater East Asia Co-Prosperity Sphere that aimed to "federate" new Asian nation-states. It is important to recognize that Kyoto philosophy pursued the promise of a new, universalized world history, first systematized by Hegel as the march of reason and later revised by Marx as a moment yet to come once the "world market" appeared. But Marx envisioned (as did non-Marxian thinkers of the Kyoto school) not the "universal history" propelled by Hegel's reason, which posited the trajectory of a one-way street endowed with meaning all societies would eventually realize but a world history that would show the uneven interplay of contingent forces that made of history moments marked by the appearance of world historicality and its "closing down," as Kōsaka put it, its disappearance, and the overcomings that would lead to its reappearance only in a new present. Or as Marx might have envisaged, "It breaks up into branches, large and small, that always begin afresh. Each critical point of bifurcation poses its own questions and demands its own answers."[21] Hegel's "universalism" pointed to the achievement of homogeneous sameness, precisely the modernity Japanese were committed to overcoming, whereas Marx's worldly history conserved the past in the new present—that is, the mutually interactive relationship between the "local being" and "universal being" Marx and Engels first envisaged in *The Germany Ideology*.

Kōsaka Masaaki announced that the present was "spatially" an "unprecedented turning point," inasmuch as new worlds were emerging that the West heretofore had ignored, especially the historical world of Asia. "Temporally," he added, the modern will be immediately changed to a "new present" (*SNR*, 60). His colleague Kōyama Iwao constantly returned to the centrality of a "turning point" as the occasion for "constructing" and establishing a new world-historical presence in the present. Above all, the prevailing intellectual impulse informing this quest for a new world-historical imaginary at the outset of World War II was the resolution of the historicist crisis, which had gripped the attention of leading thinkers throughout the 1930s conjuncture in Japan and western Europe, not, as some today suppose, Japan's putative cultural identity. But it was also clear that the question confronting all participants in the 1930s was the meaning of the present, as a growing complex conjunctural configuration began to show signs everywhere of overdetermination and question the status of historical consciousness and knowledge to actually determine what was happening.

In Kōsaka's reckoning, there were three world-historical views that represented a typology of subjectivity. Convinced that world history symbolized particular human destinies, the trinity represented a history of symbolic humans. World history was not merely spirit wending its way through time, manifesting itself along a certain trajectory, since it inevitably realized its potential in the land (*tsuchi*), the soil, ground. Its appearance was modulated by the oscillation of diversity and historical repetition (*SNR*, 77). Land, in fact, was connected to the absolute and embodied in forms that changed appearance with expansion (*SNR*, 92). Even though the absolute was dispersed in diversity, its symbolic remained firmly rooted in the soil, a distinctive principle that meant that naturalistic phenomena like earthquakes could never be disregarded in the making of a world-historical formation. (Here, Kōsaka was evidently echoing the earlier mediations of Watsuji Tetsurō's *Fūdo*). The history of the Orient, he remarked, whether in Japan, China, or India, has always been achieved through the mediation of a profound naturalism. Hence, world history, illuminating the dispersed manifestation of the absolute through the principle of land, constitutes the movement of the "great earth" seeking its symbolic center. Despite the practical positioning of world history down to the present, Kōsaka was confident that it constituted an organic unity that grew out of the soil. Why this organic principle of growth loomed so importantly in the present is that the current situation now appears crowded with several past worlds being reshuffled to become contending candidates as grounding for a tendency to build a new civilization. World history is thus not like a "necessary tidal current" that flows incessantly and on schedule from the past but rather is a reorganization that derives from the symbolic center of the world history in the present. It is a "symbolic event that occurs anew" and marks the ceaseless repetition of the present. "The present" is therefore the period that announces the arrival of an awareness that recognizes its message of unique meaning (*SNR*, 92). Kōsaka warned that when the present grows out of the past, as imagined by German idealism and rejected by Marx, the peculiar meaning of the present is extinguished; there can be no true creation or history under this circumstance (*SNR*, 86). When past, present, and future are universally divided, the finite nature of human existence becomes insurmountable, and, as with Hegel, there is a correspondence between history and a self that eliminates the "true thou."

Here, it seems, Kōsaka's referral to the universal, the transcendental, pointed to the folk (*minzoku*), timeless yet ever changing, and the imperishable world it has made. As for the accomplishment of world history, whether it expresses its particularity in the individual or the folk, it is complicated since such a subject must be said to have a "world-historical existence." What Kōsaka pointed to was the perception that regardless of the forms of either spatially or temporally driven world histories, the question of a "true subjectivity," one embracing both the particular and universal, had hitherto always been disregarded "burying" the true subject, which meant forfeiting the transcendental and absolute in history. Where the current move toward a new world history constituted a superior improvement over earlier types was precisely in recognizing the present's awakening and bringing to surface the importance of a true subject.

Historically, past world histories failed because of their denial of the universal. They instead relied more on worlds of particularity, which can never change into the world historical. In this regard, the universal should never be exclusively identified with Christianity, which, in his opinion, had already "exited" from the scene, played out its particularistic role in the mask of the universal, and was no longer in a position to foster a continuing process or development of the universal in the historical world. The way out of this troubling prospect lay in an analysis of time. Kōsaka, in this connection, recapitulated Tanabe Hajime's argument that historical time could take diverse forms and directions. Specifically, temporality's course is not narrowed to a linear, horizontal register (*suiheimen*) but is capable of simultaneously moving vertically or perpendicularly, not to forget circularly in repetition. If time is limited to the horizontal, the world historical will no doubt be considered only from the perspective of progressive development. But when time simultaneously moves vertically, it will possess dimensions of both continuity and discontinuity in world history. By the same measure, if time ordinarily begins from the present (its sole state of existence in its presence), so too the world historical. What makes the past a mediation of the self, rather than having the mediation take place in the past, is the true present (*SNR*, 93). This view implied a concurrence of the temporal tenses of past and present, an identity that Kōsaka called the "eternal now," and proposed that the circumstances of world history must be the same. While world history has begun in the past, presumably the present of a past, its identity derives from the present, not the past. Its possibility resides in the present, "a labor of resolution," and all the proper instances of the world historical, whether in China or Greece or even modern Europe, are products of the present and its confrontation with things that are made new and fresh again. For him, the world historical was identified with the mission of relieving people and thus aligned with the world's religions in antiquity. In this sense, the kinship with world history was in its discovery of the absolute no-thing, inasmuch as it—world history—was the symbolic (and material) embodiment of something that had no objective existence. In fact, Kōsaka's argument implied that world history was an effect of an absent and unseen cause. Beyond this relationship to the absolute, world history represented humanity's symbolic history that marked the selected paths of destiny in different pasts and places, which referred to those moments when subjectivity was formed.

But Kōsaka was convinced that world histories did not always establish conceptions of "true subjectivity." True subjectivity hinged on a notion of universal rationality. "It is not," he explained, "a rationality produced according to having been connoted under the universal whereby the particular case mediates the unique; to the contrary, the universal connoted within the particular mediates the unique." This distinction called attention to a relationship to the domain of the symbolic or representation and signified what he described as the "characteristic of historical rationality" (SNR, 94–95). At the same time, such historical rationality is not inscribed in the individual but rather in the world-historical individual, which maintains the "ethical substance" of a self linked to the folkic subject that accompanied the formation of the modern state. In other words, world-historical subjectivity is the world-historical folk sustained by the state. To this extent, world history is the history of the symbolic folk and clearly constituted a substitute for Marx's world proletariat proposed in a conception of world history that had yet to be written. Not only did an ethnic folk take over the role assigned to an international laboring class but one now equipped with the capacity to overcome the interiority of the solitary and individual self, which had once been the classic emblem of class consciousness. Moreover, it is the state that supplies the "nucleus" of this possibility for realizing folkic subjectivity, that gives it form, through which it must create a world-historical culture. The expression of the world-historical mission Japan had begun to undertake was marked by the folk, state, and culture as its principal constituents. Japan, Kōsaka remarked, had not hitherto followed "the failed path of established world-historical models that have disregarded the opportunity offered by the objective spirit." A true overcoming, which implied seizing the opportunity at hand, is impossible without the mediation of the historical formation that will lead to the absolute. In this sense, an overcoming is always an overcoming of history (SNR, 96). The true future utopia remains within the act of overcoming in the present, the now of eternity, as he put it (in contrast to Tosaka Jun, who looked to the present as the now of the present—that is, the everyday as the source of history's temporality). The difference was the following: Kōsaka's now eternity was a utopian imaginary linked to the accomplishment of overcoming the contemporary present, whereas Tosaka saw in the present the nowness of making history rooted in the daily performance of labor, with no hint of a utopian moment. World history symbolized this eternal now.

A subjectivity that fails to "blast open" and construct the world anew, Kōsaka asserted, is no subjectivity at all, and a "world-historical world" without a constructive overcoming will simply close up again. Under this circumstance the subject will remain buried in the world and disappear into world history (*SNR*, 97). Hence, world history symbolizes the overcoming of immanence and the mission of humanity that makes the eternal its destiny; it is thus a symbolic stage of humanity's eternal mission. If history is the world symbolizing the absolute no-thing, inasmuch as it flows eternally, it will be carried out in the "eternal now." "We must see," he concluded, "the eternal history of Japan there."

Kōsaka, like a member of a relay team handing over the thematic baton to a successor, turned these themes over to Kōyama Iwao, who would bring them to completion. In fact, Kōyama's lengthy *Sekaishi no tetsugaku* (Philosophy of world history), a compilation of a number of essays written beginning in the late 1930s, reflected, perhaps as no other contemporary work, the fullest assessment of the nature of historical production as the vocation of the present and force of answerability demanded of philosophy by the global conjuncture of the contemporary moment. It was necessary that the response be equally worldly to satisfy the immense task of overcoming the liabilities of the past and ridding the present of its unwanted and inhibiting problems of untimeliness. Much of this project was enshrined in the various symposia conducted by the Kyoto school in 1942 devoted to its enunciative presentation, whose discussions disclosed the prescient range of their philosophical analysis "before the letter" that would reappear in altered form to meet the circumstances of a different world after the war in texts like the Mombushō's *Kitai sareru ningenzō* and in European poststructural philosophy, which could not have known the earlier Japanese articulation.[22] While this analysis prefigured later discourses that put into question the status of the subject, especially the instability of representation and conceptions of history no longer bound to the limited unit of the nation form, chronology identifying past with present and the authority of empirico-positivism as the ground of historical knowledge, it often subordinated this philosophic analysis to the demands of the Japanese state and its agenda calling for "total war" and leadership in Asia.

Even more than Kōsaka, Kōyama's analytic perspective was driven by the "crisis of historicism." The present constituted a temporal "turning point" or even a transition that required "deep reflection on the question of historical consciousness."[23] Such moments inevitably arouse the impulse to resolve vitally important problems that have been transmitted from a prior time, which the past has denied or declined to address, that necessitates its rejection by the present. Kōyama argued that historical practice had proceeded to simultaneously convey what effectively was relative to its moment while presuming it also constituted an instantiation of the absolute. The awareness of a critical turning point in the present demands an immediate recognition of the relativity of the moment as a condition for subsequently assessing how it might be linked to the absolute. "We often forget about the death of many in everyday life," he wrote, echoing Heidegger's earlier condemnation of an everyday life that seeks to forget about death, "and live and act as though there were immortality" (*ST*, 401). While this sentiment clearly resonates with Heidegger's meditations on the death of *Dasein*, it is evident that Kōsaka was actually seeking to absorb the death of many in everyday life to the figure of *Dasein*—"Being There"—even though commentators on Heidegger have presumed that *Dasein*'s did not refer to others but only *Dasein*'s singular death. Yet it did not necessarily exclude the possibility of referring to the death of people in everyday life. But a singular death has the capacity to call attention to the possibility of the death of many. People ordinarily have little consciousness of the periods in which they are living but acknowledge this fact once they confront a turning point in the present, as they do when they face the conditions of dying and death. Moreover, this attitude is conducive to believing that because life is lived in modern culture its idea of itself is eternal and passes unchanged for all times to come. Echoing Marx's critique of political economy in *Grundrisse*, which he could not have known, the same attitude, marking the absence of a critical reflection, prevails toward politics and economics. Under such circumstances, Kōyama suggested that it was difficult to be shaken from a condition of noncritical lethargy, which has completely lost any sense of awareness, into a state of consciousness that is fully capable of recognizing the powerful temporal unevenness constituting the historical world. What is so important about this observation is the role Kōyama accorded to the "turning point in the present," which throws the present into dramatic contrast to what has come before and manifests both a temporal unevenness that undermines the supposed identity between past and present, the claims of succession in a continuous causal relation, and, most importantly, an attitude that has assumed the givenness of life as unchanging and eternal. It is here, he reasoned, that the relativity of the moment is made apparent, the limits of its temporal boundedness established. By the same measure, he insisted, there is also now the possibility of discerning the absolute in such moments, since the fleeting nature of human life intimates the absolute because the encounter with death is with an absolute and thus a confrontation with the immortal and eternal. The quest for the absolute comes to be embodied in the action of constructing (*kensetsu*) a new historical structure in the present (*genzai*) (*ST*, 401). In other words, the necessity of compelling a resolution of a problem inherited from the past transposes the period (*jidai*) and accomplishes resolving the task (*kadai*). Such a resolution is a "new creation." "When the act of construction is directed to penetrating the historical consciousness of relativity, it realizes the eternal in the present, makes the present the beginning of the universe [*tenchi*] and carries out a creation of the universe in the creation of the present" (*ST*, 402). For Kōyama, this singular act pointed to pursuing the historical simultaneously with the transhistorical, the instant with the eternal, the relative with the absolute.

In this oscillating movement, historicism is the name of the spiritual attitude that pierces the center of historical consciousness. While historicism venerates history it is also a spiritual attitude that comes to the heart of historical reality, and because of this it shows its typical structure on those occasions when periods are transposed. But Kōyama warned that this spiritual attitude is not solely all there is to historicism. The spiritual in historicism exists everywhere there is "deep reflection" on all history and organizes the immanence of one philosophic world view with historical studies (*ST*, 402). On the one hand, historicism is bonded to a consciousness of historical relativism and on the other to the search for the absolute of construction. It is this recurring impulse for construction in the present that converts the relativity of the time-bound moment into the sign of the absolute and eternal that thus drives the ceaseless repetition of a dialectic between *kadai* and *kensetsu*, whereby the same always produces something different, that is to say different presents. Nothing, he proclaimed, is outside the pursuit of creation in history, which is always the creation of the present itself (*ST*, 346). What Kōyama was implying is that historicism, in its inordinate valorization of the past heritage and cultural value, invariably forgets the present as the site of construction. The sense of construction that informs creation denies the utility of the past, and the resulting discontinuity that severs present from past makes sure that history is no longer founded on continual chronological or genealogical development (*ST*, 351). In the temporal succession of historical worlds there is always a discontinuous rupturing since history is an intricate web of unlimited necessity and contingency interacting with each other to produce change from possibility. When the creative will of humans is braided with history's internal demands, there appears the creative moment, a history men make but not always according to their wishes, so to speak. But Kōyama was convinced that what is produced is the new without the weight of the past (*ST*, 354).

Kōyama was particularly sensitive to the European (Hegelian) conceit that history and a critical tradition of philosophical history had failed to develop outside Europe. Even though it had been Ernst Troeltsch's important *Historismus und seine Probleme* (1922) that later had sparked Japanese responsiveness to the relationship of the problem of historicism and the crisis of the world conjuncture in the 1930s, it was also this work that foreclosed the possibility of societies like Japan and China from envisioning a world history. In this work, Troeltsch was dedicated to demonstrating how the attainment of a future was consciously derived from a past preserved by Europeans. Kōyama's task was to show the cultural bankruptcy of Europe's claim to singularity (*ST*, 357–60). The real reason for claiming this monopoly, he reasoned, stemmed from an impulse to expand to other regions of the world that was not always propelled by economic considerations but frequently accompanied by the political reason of the sovereign state to implant Anglo-Saxon supremacy (*ST*, 380). While Troeltsch failed see the world beyond Europe's borders, he was still able to propose a

promising solution to the question of historicism—its relativization of values—
that Kōyama was able to employ in accounting for the relationship of the particular and universal. Troeltsch had argued that the solution lay in a cultural
synthesis of the absolute and relative that might bring particular and universal
together. Yet, as Kōyama observed, this solution relied on a conception of the
absolute rooted in Christianity, with its transhistorical fixation on the eternal,
universal, whereas he advised that it was better to start from the particular like
the ideal of folk spirit or ethics of nationality. The problem was to envisage a
conception of world history that was able to include a nation's history yet remain
distinct from it. In this endeavor, Kōyama recommended abandoning Troeltsch's reliance on Christianity (but not necessarily the idiom of spirituality)
and the particularity of Europe masquerading as a universal endowment for
all to follow and advised the construction of a true and secular world history
in the present that was genuinely worldly. In fact, he designated the vocation
of the present to imagine a new world history, commensurately reflecting the
facts of the day, which would mark its capacity to fulfill the task of producing
the contemporary.

The issue at hand was how to determine the relationship of history and value.
Kōyama agreed with Troeltsch and other writers of the epoch like Oswald Spen-
gler and Christopher Dawson, the Irish Catholic medievalist, that historical
philosophy embodied two significant themes: the realization of cultural synthesis in the present as subjective premise of world history and the selection of
ideals that would constitute the content of world history (*ST*, 436). In this
arrangement, whereby world history performed as the concrete materiality of
cultural synthesis, the principles assigned to determining value that grasp the
meaning of historical structure derive not from theory, as such, but from conditions of subjective life that correspond to the living association of people
themselves. But cultural synthesis, the capacious power to integrate diverse
practices, risked an internal strain—contradictions—that inevitably inhibited
the achievement of realizing a genuine "theoretical unity." Kōyama explained
that connection to the absolute made for an "idiosyncratic unity," symbols representing the trace of an unknown principle, which undoubtedly constituted a
true unity that could only be imperfectly reflected in effects as partial revelations. Here, it seems to me, Kōyama was reaching back and rescuing an earlier
form of cosmopolitanism that momentarily reigned in the post–World War I
decade of the 1920s, following Nishida Kitarō's earlier pathway charted in *Zen
no kenkyū*, which called for the gathering of national cultures into a world
cultural unity greater than its parts, whereby the distinct or singular parts contributed to a blending or even a unity that remained unseen and unknown.
However, the difference between the earlier cosmopolitanism, implying a met-
onymic strategy by which the part stood in for the whole and thus privileged
the unique contribution of each national culture, lay in Kōyama's appeal to a

new world-historical configuration that clearly prioritized the whole at the expense of incorporating elements of diverse cultures under Japan's guidance. This difference disclosed the immense seismic shift in world conjunctures and a virtual inversion from what had taken place in the postwar of the early 1920s down to the beginning of World War II. The cultural synthesis Kōyama thus recommended required abandoning first, as much as possible, received cultural dispositions, in order to plunge into the world's several cultures. It is, he believed, necessary to change received circumstances as a whole, and this demanded objectively recognizing cultural ideals from different societies and pasts that might be enlisted in the project of constructing a new present (*ST*, 438). It is important to point out that in Kōyama's reading of Troeltsch it was evident that the German thinker's analysis had managed to exceed the practice of mere positivist historical research and a hermeneutic approach to the past. What he— Kōyama—thus perceived in Troeltsch was rather the promise of an intellectual range of options that opened up a historiographical perspective empowered to induce "creative action."

Here, we must turn to Kōyama's representation of the current situation that authorized his promotion of a new conception of world history. Kōyama was particularly concerned with considering the "necessary conditions" that "will imperil" Japan's program to overcome the European-based worldly history that had excluded non-Europeans (*ST*, 360). "Our Japan," he exclaimed, "is now [positioned] to enact the leading role in changing world history today. Japan's world-historical activity had begun by entering the contemporary century and separating the movement of emancipation from the European world by those who had been outside it" (*ST*, 445). In other words, the significance of Japan's arrival on the world scene was foremost *the* act that put the world outside Europe on an equal footing. But what had appeared immanent now became a different temporal order. At the heart of this observation was a view that classified the European conception of world history as belonging to the past (the epoch of modernity)—the history of overseas expansion, imperialism, and the establishment of the world market in the late nineteenth century. In a sense, Kōyama seemed to shift from what earlier had looked like relativism to a universal temporality embodied in Japan's realization of a present (and thus conception of the modern) it had now surpassed. What apparently had occurred is simply a transformation of the historical configuration, whereby Japan now represented a new temporality when before it remained locked in the indeterminate atemporal zone of "catch-up." Now societies like Great Britain were consigned to a timeless past that had passed. Specifically, Kōyama was referring to Great Britain's compulsion to install its hegemony in the "Orient" and legitimate its status militarily, which, in the interwar years, was progressively enhanced through a series of international conferences seeking to regulate the relations among states in the postwar years by controlling relative military size that clearly were directed at curbing Japan's role in Asia, what he described as "energetic opposition." It is interesting to note that Kōyama's account of the reasons raising the necessity for a new world history guided by Japan clearly saw Japan replacing Great Britain's hold on the world, which had been centered on European hegemony (*ST*, 381). In this recent history, he compared Japan's seizure of Manchuria in 1931 to "the great wave" that inaugurated a new world history (following up on Japan's earlier and momentous victory over Russia in 1905, an event that turned all of Asia toward Japan), succeeded next by further involvements in China envisioned to keep in check British and American ambitions in the region, and finally Japan's decision to join the Tripartite Pact with Nazi Germany and fascist Italy. The purpose of this recounting of events was to show how one conception of world history was already in process of being replaced by another, whereby a "particularistic" form was being overtaken by a universalistic one. But the leading structuring agency was intimately linked to the experience of Japan's national history. Kōyama's discourse aimed at explaining how the newly emergent formation was pointing to the installation of a new universal world history—nourished by the nation's history that would qualify as a "worldly world history" (*ST*, 390), one capable of containing the subjectivities of both Europe and Asia rather than Europe alone. This immense transformation was principally historical, since the "turning point" that animated the present to such an act resulted from a "thematic" (*kadai*), which had been formulated by the failures of the past the present had inherited to now resolve. Hence, recognition of the contemporary meant the end of an older history and the beginning of the new—actualized in an "instant" (*ST*, 400, 429, especially 452). "The instant of contemporaneity [*genzai*] is time [that] overcomes time. During such a turning point instant there is a consciousness of relativity in one direction and a connection to the pursuit of the absolute character of construction in another" (*ST*, 402). Even though the different historical worlds signify the relative and embody a diversity of histories, possessing their own temporalities, a universalistic world history of the present would be able to transcend these discordant times by incorporating the particularistic histories they represent and unify them. Unification for Kōyama meant sharing a singular temporality. The transformation already announced a new temporal immanence that marked the change from a declining world order to an emergent successor led by Japan. It should be noted in this connection that Kōyama's recommendation to transcend the temporal diversity of historical worlds and integrate them into a new immanence was consistent with colonial policy everywhere, which demanded the recalibration of a standard social time and the subordination of all local times to it. In his program the different temporalities would be incorporated into a single worldly time that would unify the historical world.

In the new global configuration, Europe would be consigned to a particularized past, to play the role of a vanishing remnant but discredited claim to world-historical status, while Japan would command the present through its actualization of a true world history. Kōyama named this universalist history as the "absolute no-thing" (*mu*), because of its ability to transcend the local character of historical worlds, unify times with the world and the relative with the absolute (*ST*, 448). Ultimately, this absolute "no-thing" exceeded time itself for the "unlimited" and "eternal." This appeal to (and reminder of) Nishida Kitarō's conception of an all-incorporating and eternal absolute—recalling the "absolute contradictory self-identity" (*zettai mujunteki jiko dōitsu*) and its powerful but complex "logic of integration"—a virtual absent cause—unified all antinomies and was the place (*basho*) that manifested the world historical, indeed the eternal (*ST*, 450). What Kōyama wished to emphasize was that concurrence of the relative in world conditions with the simultaneous perception of the absolute, the historical (time) with the eternal, that is a correspondence between temporality and sociality into what, in effect, became an absolute present no longer causally bound to a past and indistinguishable from a future it already embodied (*ST*, 455). In other words, history, deriving from relative conditions determined by the moment, produced values that at the same time could claim the status of the absolute and eternal. It was this "absolute present" that reconciled all oppositions to "overcome the modern." Yet it is difficult to separate this absolute present from the eternality claimed by capitalism's conception of contemporaneity.

In Kōyama's reckoning, it seems that the process of realizing the absolute present signaled the final becoming of the folk, which meant permanently reconciling all oppositions since the present was no longer shackled by its past. Once identified with an enduring and unchanging past the present was positioned to represent an achieved future. This philosophical formulation was not far from more familiar political programs in Germany declaring the establishment of a Thousand Year Reich and Italian fascism's commitment to continue imperial Rome's eternal glory and actually opened the way for the return of a fictional archaism Tosaka Jun saw as the core of the "Japan Ideology." In other words, this "natural" history was realized by homologizing the categorical structure of capitalism with a logic preoccupied with forms that would result in bracketing empirical history presenting a natural, timeless, and synchronic history, much in the manner Marx had observed of political economy. As a result, the absolute present claimed by capital provided the ground to eternalize the archaic and to subsume the present to the past into a timeless and unchanging unity. It is important to recognize that Kyoto philosophy, like others, was never far from the conjunctural crisis of capitalism, even though it was a topic rarely and directly addressed. In the end, it was Miki Kiyoshi who tried to envisage a temporally and spatially different kind of capitalism embodied in the regional Greater East Asia Co-Prosperity Sphere as the solution to both a crisis that required saving capitalism from itself (and liberal failure) and satisfying the need to emphasize distance and difference from the "modern"— that is, overcoming the West.

It is important to suggest here that all the attributes Kōyama invested in explaining the creation of a new world-historical order he inscribed first in the act of creating culture and the role of the folk (*minzoku*). Yet this new world-historical order assumed the form of the imperium, which Japan had already begun to construct and expand but which merely expressed the centrality of the state itself. In this regard, we must propose that whatever link Kōyama had to Hegel, his conceptualization of the state as the source of absolute and eternal morality and value derived from Nishida's philosophy, which offered both to supplement what he believed was missing in Hegel and to exceed him by appealing to a philosophical configuration grounded not in being, as such, but in no-thing that presumably grew out of the Japanese folkic experience of the world. In fact, it is the state that mediates all social oppositions like "class struggle and national conflict" and constitutes the "truest expression of the 'world-historical mission' of the Volk as creator of the 'new world order.' "[24] But if the state produces and reproduces value, it is because the folk have come into being through the act of "self-formation" or self-consciousness by creating culture from the experience of its daily working existence and thus distinguishes itself from the "human species" first by representing itself in the form of a social imaginary characterized by communitarian relations (*kyōdō*). This prior construction, undoubtedly the model for the later figure of world history in the present, signifies the presence of subjectivity—that is, the state. Kōyama identified history (temporality) and culture because they shared the same dynamic of production: "The foundation of culture exists in the self-formation of a folkic life" (*ST*, 67). Moreover, "Culture possesses historical temporality together with a territorialized folk character" (*ST*, 398). As a result, the presence of the folk, especially the history of the folk, becomes the basis of world history. By the same token, the folk is formed and re-formed by culture.

Despite the later evolution of the nation-state from earlier forms of social imaginaries, Kōyama was convinced that it continues to express a folkic component. The trace of this folk endowment in the modern state appears in the desire to maintain continuity and survival through reproduction and through the will to sustain unity based upon the communal character of culture. But the state also continues the work of the earlier folk community by becoming the subject, which constructs culture in the widest sense and preserves the ethical and moral systems that set limits and regulate. The most enduring folkic residue is the sense of collective solidarity and thus the differentiation between inside and outside other and the subordination of the self to the group whereby the individual is integrated into a totality that is the state. Yet there is something circular about this achievement of integration since it was secured by appealing to a prior identity achieved as a member of the folk and its culture, which might be described as an "always already" identification with the primal folkic cultural community even before its ultimate manifestation in the state. We can only point to the dire and obvious political consequences of this idea once yoked to the imperium and its world-historical countenance upholding the principle of exceptionalism and exclusion that designated the Japanese state to act "instant[ly]" (*setsuna*) to begin its historic "mission" of constructing an absolute present for East Asia.

III

If thinkers like Kōsaka and Kōyama sought to address the question of answerability between philosophy and history, expressed in the relationship between the present and the past, Miki Kiyoshi took the next logical step that had remained unattended in these discussions, which was to consider the relationship between historical time and action. In a certain sense, Miki's discourse followed the path charted by Kōsaka, Kōyama, and Tanabe. But where he significantly departed from them was in a willingness to think through the consequences of contemporary eventfulness for the proper formulation of policy and action. Throughout his writings in the crucial decade of the 1930s, the common theme of crisis appeared regularly, accompanied by articulations of the condition of angst and the circulation of expressions of permanent anxiety over the contemporary state of the human condition, driving it ceaselessly into ever more desperate attempts to find a practical solution. This concern was verbalized in his essays on Marxism, where he first sought to construct a humanist philosophical anthropology positing an I-Thou relationship grounded in a putative materiality. In subsequent texts on angst, the philosophy of crisis, Pascal, Lev Shestov, Nietzsche he deepened this sense of the existential dislocation of humans as he backed off from his earlier encounter with Marxism. Yet he retained his interest in the role played by history in both its Marxian theorization of alienation and its existential conceptualization of a hermeneutic necessity that demanded addressing the question of self-understanding the current human condition, which, he believed, might offer or reveal a way to overcome the anxiety-ridden present. Specifically, it seems that Miki's effort to overcome the present was driven by a desire to realize the creation of a new human being, indeed a new philosophical anthropology, whose profile was already disclosed in literary figures like Don Quixote, Hamlet, and Othello. Yet it is important to recognize that the urgency fueling Miki's quest to find an adequate anthropology was reinforced by the conjunctural force of his present and thus the concourse of local, regional events and global occurrences leading to full-scale economic failure and the unwanted promise of an evolving political totalism committed to resolution by war. Under these dire circumstances, Miki proposed a conception of double overcoming that clearly pointed to Japan's inadequate adoption of borrowed elements from foreign cultures since the Meiji period—its superficial adapting and imitation—and the misrecognition that the country's pace of development lagged behind the advanced, modern states of the West. (I should point out that this misperception of developmental lag persisted well into the postwar years and was dramatized by the party of modernization led by Maruyama Masao.) Here, Miki was particularly animated by the defects of the narrow understanding associated with action and conduct (kōi).[25] Actions, he believed, were linked to a chain of causes, but there was something more to their structure. While the course of acting and performing a deed reflect the movement of an internal disposition, this interiorized impulse is still not merely reducible to consciousness. Interiority must always overcome what is internal—externalized—since action can never be considered solely from the standpoint of the interiority prompting it. In this sense, the performance of an act must always involve the gesture of a "double overcoming" that entails a surpassing of both the external along with the internal (MKE, 225). Action's meaning, resembling the figure of an angle, seeks to accomplish the unity of inside and outside. Moreover, Miki envisioned the expression of enactment as the manifestation of an "occurrence" (dekigoto), whose meaning unveiled a destiny yet to be realized, deriving its authorization from a theory of historical action grounded in the vocation of poiesis and "making" (techne) rather than simply practice.

The very historical present that supplied empirical authority to Miki's categorization of a pivotal contemporaneity, which now required surpassing, convinced him, like Tosaka Jun, that philosophy should pursue a more practical calling. To this end, Miki turned increasingly to assessing the significance of events implicated in the crucial relationship between local and global historical happenings that occasioned the production of a number of policy-oriented papers seeking to design the shape of a world-historical Japan and its mission to reconfigure the East Asian region into a new kind of "cooperative" union. At one level, he was treading the path Marx had earlier (in The German Ideology) recommended when he proposed that true world historicality could be achieved only when the "local being" was connected to a "universal being" in the world market; at another his commitment to a solution personified in the Greater East Asia Co-Prosperity Sphere ran counter to Marx's conception of the world historical because it privileged the domination of the local (Japan) over the universal (Asia). It is important, in this regard, to be aware of how he sought to reconnect his understanding of contemporary historical reality—a "practical present," as Michael Oakeshott has proposed in another venue—to a philosophic ground far removed from the "lecture pulpit" (Uchida, in MKE, 320). By referring to what he classified as world-historical events like the Sino-Japanese War, the Soviet purges, and the Nazi burning the books, not to forget the assault on academic freedom in Japan symbolized by the Takigawa incident, Miki was able to gradually resituate his own position within the larger precinct of world history, which, as a category, acquired empirical and existential substance by the end of the decade to become a major preoccupation of Kyoto philosophy. For, as Kōsaka proclaimed, the figure of world historicality "touched upon" the subjectivity of Japan (*SNR*, 61). According to Kōyama Iwao during the symposium of 1942, world history is felt differently by Japanese and more intensely and "bodily" than by Europeans (*STTN*, 7). What seemed at stake in these considerations of the current situation was the conviction that humanity was in a process of fusing with a worldly historical experience already foretold by both Hegel and Heidegger. In Miki's thinking, Japan had no other hope for existing but to open itself to the world. We must thus see in Miki's engagement of the present and its demand both the formulation of philosophy's responsibility to contemporary history's insistent challenge by specifically responding to the task of overcoming the double aporia of a philosophic discipline turned in on itself and its willingness to now confront an external world crowded with facticity claiming the status of an eternal law of nature in its immediacy. It was the reality of contemporary human existence embedded in history and the necessity to change this relationship that constituted the fund of experience informing anthropology, which Miki would rename as historical anthropology. And it was action itself that provided the key to overcoming, the act of making, recalling the still audible echo of Marx's designation of the first, inaugural historical act of social cooperation that revealed the contours of an anthropology steeped in the authority of the paradigmatic experience of collaboration. For Miki, it was especially the experience of lived everydayness that marked this sphere of practice humans initiate in encountering their immediate environment (*MKE*, 209). But it must also be added that Miki shifted his tactic to not only merge the everyday with the contemporary present but also reconstitute it as a the sedimented reservoir of historical deposits.

For Miki, custom played an ambivalent role in his equation on how the everyday related to history. It was custom that made history part of nature and supplied the everyday with its link to it (*MKE*, 225). While this identity of custom, standing astride nature and history through the mediation of the everyday, secured for everydayness a relationship to nature and the natural world, Miki would try to demonstrate how daily life was still subject to the broader movements of historical change. It might be noted that this formulation departed from Tosaka Jun's reflections on custom (*fūzoku*) which, despite the appearance of eternality that effaced its conditions of production, was still produced by specific historical circumstances. Miki departed from many of his Kyoto philosophic contemporaries (excepting Tosaka), who ultimately saw in the present of world historicality a category that was already skilled in subsuming the everyday and its materiality. While he avoided clarifying what this material subsumption of the everyday actually involved, it conceivably referred to how world history, the ongoing arena of the production of events, acted similarly to the human intervention and conquest that subsumed and subordinated nature. With Miki, it should be recalled, the everyday was spare of events and belonged as much to the order of nature as to the human sphere, whereas world history, like Hegel's unfolding of Spirit, was the product of human action. In this regard, his position was sandwiched between the conference on overcoming modernity, with its inordinate emphasis on the materiality of modern everyday life in Japan, and the symposium on Japan's world-historical position, which remained somewhat distant from everydayness for the more abstract configuration of a world history that had not yet been achieved and the role of the moral energy. During the first conference on world history, Kōsaka recognized, like Tosaka before him, that philosophy appears to have been "separated" from the everyday, insofar as the ordinary person has forgotten that they embody a philosophy conforming to a "new world image" and live according to its requirements (*STTN*, 94).

But it was Miki's interest in the current situation as it was daily unfolding in events that captured his interest and disclosed both the historicality inscribed in everyday life and its imprint in the changing status of custom. Convinced that the task of anthropology should focus on the "actuality" of human action in the present, the meaning of "actuality" must invariably refer to the everyday and thus relate to the situation of the lived everydayness of humans (*MKE*, 210). "What we call real life," he exclaimed, "is the active, everyday life." Here, Miki wished to differentiate his conceptualization of anthropology rooted in the humus of everyday activity from Kant's earlier meditation on cosmopolitanism and its association with a complete (and completed) philosophy, whose basic meaning appeared to be "unhistorical." In this view, there was no real incompatibility (*mujun*) between actuality and history since his logic presupposed an anthropology claiming equivalence with the standpoint of historicality—that is, actualization. Similarly, he discerned in this formulation the hint of a possible aporia. If, for example, the original viewpoint of an actual anthropology emphasizes everyday things, then it might be seen as contrary to the advocacy of historical anthropology. When speaking of history ordinarily understood as a narrative of "great men," the "extraordinary," as such, then it usually appears to be concerned with "noneveryday things" (*MKE*, 211). By the same measure, the actions of everyday life are rarely visible in historical practice, no more so than the fact that everyday humanity mirrors the actions of historical personalities. Even though these two spheres of activity must remain distinct and differentiated from each other, Miki proposed that everydayness should be the "basic presupposition" of the historical. At this juncture he tried to yoke the everyday, through the mediation of its historicality, to the wider categorical unit of the "world historical." "Even though everyday personalities are not world-historical personalities," he wrote, "they are still [part of] a historical humanity."

In this equation, Miki distinguished between what he named as an "original historicality," the "character of everydayness," and "world historicality" as basic categories in a "chain" or "series" securing the figure of a coherent, sequential relationship, if not necessarily a shared temporal kinship. Returning to the question of philosophy's "answerability to history," he proposed that the problem of history, if envisioned from a philosophic perspective, must not be grasped at the level of a preference that privileges "historical consciousness" and thus a specific narrative dedicated to an unfolding (Japan's modern history) but rather from an inquiry embedded in its sources as a question of a wider human historicality. With this move, world historicality and everydayness become mutually bound to a generative originary historicality, which makes available a perspective that permits viewing the coupling as an interactive unity (*MKE*, 216). At bottom, he added, everydayness provides the grounding of history since the actions that gain entry into history are bolstered by it, insuring its constant development and the shifting of its grounding. Quick to acknowledge that the everyday is a subject on which there is rarely any serious reflection, Miki saw in it an eternal countenance—its "pure, constant conditions," which recalled its affinity with nature (*MKE*, 218). Even so, history and the everyday were still separated by their respective contents and their distinct temporalities. Whereas the everyday is spare in its capacity to produce eventfulness, more preoccupied with circumstances encountered daily, the repetitions of custom and habit rather than the more exciting world teeming with dramatic events, the amateurs who pursue the study of history favor events and constantly express a desire for them that invariably captures their attention. Needless to say, the two domains do not stand in a direct causal relationship to each other since history and everydayness remain unconnected in substantive ways. Accordingly, Miki reasoned that because the two realms are circularly bound to each other, they are sure to clash with the implicit temporal linearity attributed to the unfolding of history's reason.

Yet it is important to see in this decision to elevate the figure of circularity one of the possible forms of time Tanabe Hajime enumerated later in his *Rekishiteki genjitsu*. Just as the scarcely perceptible movement of a continent constituted of custom and habit, with its rhythms seemingly obeying a circular motion, could clearly collide with the temporal claims of a forward moving narrativity, so the conception of the everyday Miki envisaged shared with the world historical an eternality—in fact an "eternality of the now"—that would manage to occupy a different register of time that was timeless. In trying to resolve this knotted problem, he thereby sought to demonstrate how custom corresponded to everyday things and vice versa, and how inevitably the customary of life changes with history, however glacial the movement, because it possesses the aptitude (*nōryoku*) to produce a trajectory that continually moves (*MKE*, 226). Indeed, "it premises change" as an internal endowment. What Miki apparently meant was the "indwelling" of possible change in the customary of everyday life. Additionally, the division between possibility and reality, inner and external conformed to the basic structure of things and created custom. And that which makes or creates custom must possess an inner spontaneity, but not to excess since custom always represents the "mean ratio between [human] will and nature."

In these reflections, the presence of custom pointed to a structure comprising interiority and exteriority and sanctioned a relationship marked by the binary of possibility and reality. We might recall in this connection Tosaka Jun's dim estimate of custom as a figure of pure, calcified exteriority, whose informing will and history remained concealed and obscured in imitation of the conduct of the commodity form. He saw custom as the "skin" on the surface that brackets its historical production by misrecognizing it as a natural phenomenon—that is, as the phenomenon itself that induces unquestioning consensual assent. Because it was modeled on the figure of the commodity, it signified the presence of reification and necessity of imitation since its objective appearance claimed there was nothing behind it, concealed or hidden. The importance of Tosaka's account of custom's capacity for reified existence derived from the observation that its demand of consensual assent encouraged only conformist imitation, not action. In this respect, Miki, by contrast, saw in the changeable tendency of the customary the creation of new customs that ultimately would have the force to destroy the old and thus realize the renewing promise of the relationship between inner and outer, possibility and reality.

Still, by situating custom on the side of nature and delegating it as the mediator between human will and natural existence, Miki was obliged to differentiate it from history. History's basic principle is time, he wrote, whereas space determines the shape of nature.[26] If nature is considered to be an interior moment (keiki) of history, then it is possible to detect in history the shadow of spatiality and its force on the making of events and custom. In this sense, history is not only temporality but also participates in both time and space. Similarly, if the everyday participates in the historical, it too shares its temporal dimension, and the combination will produce a special characteristic of real historical temporality toward physical nature, which he called "spatialized time."[27] Although Miki had already distinguished between the two directions of linear and circular limitations of time (MKE, 228), he nevertheless acknowledged that historical time is circularly limited at the same time that its pulsation is also marked by a linear limit to constitute the Zeitraum—the time/space that resembled a chronotopic relationship determined by differing directions assigned to history's time and space. This binary was further reduced to what he named as generation (sedai) and Zeitalter (jidai), which enabled seeing the relationship as a coextension of two different temporalizations represented by the idea of generational change based on circular time and the category of period (*Zeit*), with its emphasis on linearity (*MKE*, 229).[28] For Miki, this conception of time/space structurally encompassed the reality of the historical present, inasmuch as "real historical time . . . finds [its] completion in the [movement] of the two directions" of circularity and linearity. A constant oscillation of one to the other, the movement of the specific direction authorizes either the installation of a period or an epoch, the former expressing linearity, the latter circularity, employing the category of period to denote the linearity of "transition" and epoch to signify the passage to maturation. I would clarify this distinction further by suggesting that the concept of a rectilinear transition implied production, while epochal circularity and its world of settled maturation represented the operation of reproduction. The point to configuring time/space into a historical unity and breaking it down further into differing temporal directions and durational subdivisions was to reinforce the relationship between history and everydayness (clinging to the domain of the natural). Beyond this purpose, Miki's apparent objective was to locate the placement of the larger and more advanced category of world historicality. Both everydayness and world historicality matched up to the structure of opposites constituting his conception of history's structure: with the everyday constrained by space and its destination veering circularly, world history driven by a linear trajectory aimed at reaching a permanent present. In this sense the establishment of world history signified the end of chronology, an abstract, quantitative marker, and its replacement by real, lived time.

Clearly, a world historicality identified with history as endless historical movement was the principal problem that remained unresolved. How Miki sought to solve it must be seen in his decision to appeal to the "maturation of time" and in the meaning of a completed time which supposedly brought the two temporalities of history and the everyday together. Events and occurrences would reveal the meaning of "completed time," what he named as *kairos*, which itself possesses the signification of the instantaneous (distantly echoing Walter Benjamin's "flash of lightning"). Action finds its conclusion in the fullness of time, its ripeness, as time's completion in the event and occurrence. In this way *kairos* contains the meaning of destiny yet to be fulfilled, which only the completed event and thus the ripeness of historical time will finally disclose.[29] "The differentiation of world historicality from everydayness is considered from the [standpoint] of *kairetic* time. . . . In order to concretely grasp our problem it is necessary to clarify the meaning of the world. From beginning to end both the idea of world historicality, as well as the idea of the everyday, are connected to the world," and "both are indivisible from the idea of the world (*Welt*)" (*MKE*, 230). In other words, Miki managed to substitute the identity of world historicality for everydayness (incorporating the latter into the former) by replacing the structure of time shared by history and narrative with the structure of the world as it was encountered in its immediacy. As a result, he risked forfeiting the force of temporal form for the static countenance supplied by space, ultimately embodied in the epochal figure of the imperium. The closest he came to making a persuasive linking of the domain of world history and everydayness was to propose that the everyday was the circumference surrounding the world historical since it is everywhere the "center of history" (*MKE*, 222). More to the point, the form of world historicality was mediated by the nation-state, which seizes the occasion offered by the present to give it a new direction and leadership, which eventually took the political form of the Greater East Asia Co-Prosperity Sphere. In this respect, everydayness, the "lived," was subordinated to and assimilated by the broader narrative of nation—that is, the conceived. Where Tosaka Jun departed from the fixed historical form was to see the everyday as the source of historical time and prior to the construction of any national narrative, which ultimately must be derived from its experience instead of personifying "history's reason."

In Miki's accounting of the current situation, the so-called China Incident announced the advent of the world historical (*MKE*, 281). Even though the "incident" had occurred recently, the event had ripened in time, by bringing to a close a process that had been long in the making. The meaning of the moment had already been foretold by history's reason, which had proclaimed its designated arrival in the present. "We must endeavor to pursue history's reason," he wrote of the occasion, "within the occurrences that have taken place in the present," because such events provide the promise of realizing self-independence from the subjective intentions of certain classes, groups, individuals, and concerned persons (*MKE*, 269). Plainly pointing to the corrosive divisiveness caused by capitalism in the more settled industrial regions of Euro-America, Miki viewed the Japanese invasion of China (an "incident") as a moment in the creation of a new regional cooperative union in East Asia that would lead to the successful realization of a world-historical mission directed at recognizing the distinctiveness of each of its constituent members and implementing a new kind of capitalism without capitalist class conflict. The model for this world-historical epiphany was ancient Greece. Recalling for his contemporaries the lessons of the ancient conquests of Alexander the Great and the resulting worlding of the Greek culture he revered, Miki was convinced that this transformation to Hellenism exemplified the momentous turn from a local Greek culture to a worldly one. It also represented the unfolding from classical Greece to contemporary culture that fulfilled the meaning of world history because it decisively demarcated the maturation of time. More importantly, this moment disclosed the necessity for Japanese to reapprehend the meaning of historical reason within the events taking place in the present, as they will inescapably lead to other events, corresponding to and enlarging them. This vision sharply contrasts with Kōyama's program, which would not have appealed to the example of Greece and all prior instances of world-historical epiphanies as a model for Japan's entry into world history but rather as necessary failures that provided little or no instruction for the conduct of the "absolute present."

But, for Miki, it was the search for "new meaning" from the position of "history's reason" that drove his pursuit, even though he acknowledged the possibility that he might see no meaning at all in the crowded eventfulness of his present and thus fail in the effort to extract history's elusive message. Anticipating the opening remarks of Kawakami Tetsutarō at the time of the meeting of the conference on overcoming the modern in 1942, Miki insisted upon the expression of duty (*gimu*) toward the expenditure of "flowing blood" to give world-historical meaning to the "China Incident," as it is "the way of living our own bodies today." Discounting reliance on abstract theory to explain world historicality, Miki advocated a view founded on the "concrete historical situation of reality," which required an expressed reverence for the special and distinct characteristics of Chinese and Japanese cultures. As such, it made no sense to merely base Japanese action in China only on the valorization of Japan's distinct culture. What appeared necessary was the identification of a genuine mediation competent to connect the two. This mediation was supplied by the category of the "Orient" (Tōyō). Henceforth, the Orient, in his thinking, would not become simply a world that possessed a single internalized unity in the manner of the West since the time of Greek culture and the spread of Christianity but would be committed to observing the different cultures that formed it. For Miki, the problem of the "Japanese Spirit" could not be separated from the Orient, which meant that it was also possible to discern a broader meaning of world history that included the "China Incident" in the formation of the Orient. Anxious to avoid misunderstanding, Miki warned that it was important not to confuse imperialist ideals with Japanese despotism in the Orient. Yet it was equally necessary to recognize in Japan's emergence on the stage of world history an immense transformational event that was still related to the modern culture of the West. Unity in the Orient in the present has become possible through the powerful mediation of a scientific culture born in the West but which now has entered the East and recalls the prior unification of the West mediated by a Christianity born in the East, which had subsequently migrated to the West. "The day on which the 'Orient' is formed is the day on which the 'World' is formed in its true meaning" (*MKE*, 272). By the same measure, Miki could not but acknowledge that Japan's contemporary mission to unify the Orient would have consequential effects for the contradictions of capitalism and how they might be overcome. Just as he was certain that the realization of "true world-historical meaning" and Oriental unity was not possible without a "plan" (*kōsō*) directed toward resolving this problem, so he granted that this project could no longer remain a speculative one.

Ultimately, Miki's conceptualization of a world-historical present trumped his considerations of everydayness by subordinating its politics of time to the demands of a present dedicated to actualizing Japan's world-historical position. This was, it seems, a final reworking of his earlier Marxian formulation that envisioned the historical present as actuality. Where Miki differed from Tosaka Jun's powerful intervention that opened the way to rehistoricizing the everyday, as suggested earlier, was in his decision to yoke it to the mission of world history and required emplotting the everyday within the framework of world history that already signified the status of an achieved nation-state. But he could only accomplish this act of conjuration by taking on the additional risk of making the everyday complicit in Japan's vocation of fascism at home and imperialism abroad in Asia. If his formulations emptied the everyday of precisely the fund of never-completed experience, memoration, and coexisting temporalizations which had made it the scene of constant rehistoricization, the aporetic nature of the problem of aligning everydayness with world history (the calling and domain of the nation-state and the purpose of actualization in the present) was manifest in the desire to nudge differing temporalities inscribed in the now of everyday experience into agreement with the more abstract principle of Japan's world-historical destiny. In many ways, this desperate bonding of the everyday to the larger space of the world historical (actually mixing a temporal unit with a spatial one) worked first to incorporate its unassimilated remainder and residue into the framework of the nation-state; at another level it resulted in the attempt to efface the frictions of the noncontemporaneous contemporaneity by subordinating the everyday to a larger spatiotemporal chronotope provided by Japan's world-historical aspiration. While Miki fully recognized that the everyday was the principal site of action, it was downgraded to the level of a lesser principle since he had reserved the space of actualizing for the larger stage of world history. Hence, the everyday remained outside the historical as such and gained its meaning from world history to form a unity with it rather than from the act of producing history. The implication of this move resulted in thoroughly spatializing everydayness—making it appear as a given ready-made instead of seeing in it a temporal unit of formation—ultimately extending to and equating its atemporal husk with empire. In this regard, world history subsumed the everyday, despite Miki's attempt to show they constituted equivalent space/times. Tosaka widely diverged from Miki's formulations by initially rejecting the unity of world historicality as it was being discussed by Kyoto philosophers. His reason for this stemmed from his rejection of national narratives or national history, which the category of world history simply enlarged and expanded into the broader space of an imperium. By the same measure, the privileging of world history and subsequent eclipsing of the everyday meant a diminishing of the importance of historical time for historical space, despite Miki's effort to salvage the significance of time's maturation. The problem Miki confronted with his appeal to kairetic time was to position the centrality of eventfulness and thus chronology, not the measure and action of historical time. In Tosaka's reckoning, everydayness was always a combination of space, specific place and time, nowness, that might be mediated by a nation-state but was still apart from it since it constituted the source of historical production. Under this circumstance, the category of world history was little more than an enlarged reified version of the nation form.

In the end, Miki grasped history as national narrative, whose content differed significantly from the mundane experience of time in the everyday present. Moreover, historical narratives centered on the nation-state pointed to the singular and unique, while everydayness was the context of averaging and the commonplace, routine and repetition found everywhere and always leavened by the force of unanticipated contingency. For this reason, the everyday could never have been considered as identical with history, which presumably occurs elsewhere and in a different zone of temporality. How Miki sought to resolve this tangled contradiction was to link the everyday and world history to a commonly shared ground called "originary historicality," which authorized the procession of a steady evolution progressing from one level or stage to another. The different and mixed temporalities signaled by the everyday and world history were restructured, smoothed and flattened into a narrative succession supposedly illustrating the inevitable maturation of time, its "ripening" (*jijuku, zeitigen, kairos*). In other words, Miki's "answerability" to history sacrificed the temporality associated with the sentient claims of everyday life—experience, memory, and its vast tableau of uneven temporalizations—to what appeared to him as the higher necessity of totalization and the very abstraction of narrative movement he eschewed and the final (Hegelian) revelation of history's meaning in reason. Yet we must also perceive in the project how closely Miki's program inadvertently managed to recuperate Lukács's verdict on bourgeois thought's penchant for "prolonging the state of pure immediacy" that masquerades as an enduring natural law. With Miki, it is thus possible to see the steady slide into the unhistorical miasma of provincial journalism once he recognized that the present constituted a compelling historical problem. But it is also possible to imagine in this reconsideration of the overheated attempt of Miki and the Kyoto school in the late 1930s and early 1940s to rethink the philosophy of world historicality in order to resolve the problems of their present by beginning the difficult labor of determining meaning for our global present. Such a revisiting must avoid the baneful effects of missionizing the world historicality the prewar philosophers enthusiastically embraced. At the same time postwar Japan must reject its entry into the American imperium and the domestic politics that supports it, as if it promised a return to a world free from its prewar adventure in imperial missionizing when, in fact, it was the reverse that substituted what it had lost.

Notes

1. Kōsaka Masaaki et al., *Sekaishiteki tachiba to Nippon* (Tokyo: Chūō kōronsha, 1943), 5. Hereafter cited as *STTN*.
2. *STTN*, 94.
3. *STTN*, 94.
4. *STTN*, 94.
5. Georg Lukács, *History and Class Consciousness*, trans. Rodney Livingstone (London: Merlin Press, 1971), 155.
6. Lukács, *History and Class Consciousness*, 157.
7. Pierre Macherey, *In a Materialist Way: Selected Essays*, ed. Warren Montag, trans. Ted Stolze (London: Verso, 1998), 5.
8. Macherey, *In a Materialist Way*, 6.
9. Pierre Macherey, *Histoires de dinosaure* (Paris: Presses Universitaires de France, 1999), 283.
10. Macherey, *Histoires de dinosaure*, 283, 284.
11. Macherey, *Histoires de dinosaure*, 10.
12. Karl Marx and Frederick Engels, *The German Ideology*, in *Marx and Engels Collected Works*, vol. 5 (London: Lawrence and Wishart, 1978), 236.
13. Marx and Engels, *The German Ideology*, 130.
14. M. M. Bakhtin, *Art and Answerability*, ed. Michael Holquist and Vadim Liapunov, trans. Vadim Liapunov (Austin: University of Texas Press, 1990), 3.
15. Tanabe Hajime, *Rekishiteki genjitsu* (Tokyo: Iwanami shoten, 1945). Hereafter cited as *RG*.
16. Bakhtin, *Art and Answerability*, xxiii.
17. For an articulation of this condensation of the present's eternality and the future, see *RG*, 31–42.
18. Kōsaka Masaaki, "Sekaishikan no ruikei," in *Sekaishi no riron*, ed. Mori Tetsurō, vol. 11 of *Kyōto tetsugaku sensho* (Kyoto: Tōeisha, 2000), 59. Hereafter cited as *SNR*.
19. Christian Uhl, "What Was the Japanese 'Philosophy of History'? An Inquiry into the Dynamics of the 'World-Historical Standpoint' of the Kyoto School," in *Re-politicising the Kyoto School as Philosophy*, ed. Christopher Goto-Jones (London: Routledge, 2008), 125–26.
20. Hayden White, *Tropics of Discourse* (Baltimore, Md.: Johns Hopkins University Press, 1978), 36.
21. Daniel Bensaïd, *Marx for Our Times*, trans. Gregory Elliott (London: Verso, 2009), 34.
22. My thanks to Steven Platzer for making this connection between Kyoto philosophy and the postwar Ministry of Education.
23. Kōyama Iwao, *Sekaishi no tetsugaku* (Tokyo: Kobushi shobō, 2001), 400. Hereafter cited as *ST*. I have also consulted Kōyama's wartime book *Nippon no kadai to sekaishi* (Tokyo: Kōbundō shoten, 1944), which he saw as a companion volume to *Sekaishi no tetsugaku* and dedicated to the spirits of the war dead who "fell in defense of the fatherland in the Great East Asia War."

24. William Haver, *The Body of This Death: Historicity and Sociality in the Time of AIDS* (Stanford, Calif.: Stanford University Press, 1994), 34.

25. Miki Kiyoshi, *Miki Kiyoshi essensu*, ed. Uchida Hiroshi (Tokyo: Kobushi shobō, 2000), 224–25. Hereafter cited as *MKE*.

26. Miki Kiyoshi, *Rekishi tetsugaku*, in *Miki Kiyoshi zenshū* (Tokyo: Iwanami shoten, 1967), 6:151–200.

27. Miki, *Rekishi tetsugaku*, 180.

28. Miki, *Rekishi tetsugaku*, 153–54.

29. In Miki, *Rekishi tetsugaku*, 165, Miki assigns a more modest role to the ripening of time.

CHAPTER 10

REFLECTIONS FROM FUKUSHIMA

History, Memory, and the Crisis of Contemporaneity

The philosopher Paul Ricoeur once asked whether history was actually the remedy to the subjective and experiential excesses of memory or its poison. He seemed to be concerned with the separation of the two forms of retention and the order of their relationship. If history was a remedy, it could act as a necessary supplement, taming by mediating memory's experiential self-indulgence; if it was its poison, it would bring an end to its claims to rescue the past.[1] He failed to recognize that a little poison might be just the right remedy. Ricoeur recognized that history, as a domain of knowledge, had, since Hegel, freed itself from memory, not by rejecting it out of hand but by putting itself at a distance from it. He knew that any attempt to short-circuit the relationship and forcibly bring history and memory together and close the distance separating them could produce serious consequences for history by contaminating its own vocation committed to securing a verifiable knowledge. But the threat of such contamination of history and historiography by memory lay not so much in its capacity to singularize history as it was in its propensity to privilege the profoundly subjective. This was especially the case when making the selections that often designated the determination of chronologies that disclosed an indifference to the reconstruction of a group and to identifying the global rationalizations that might ultimately explain an event.[2] The real problem implied by Ricoeur is precisely the appearance of those unscheduled moments when an occurrence exceeds historical expectation and spills over, when temporality accelerates and events overlap, to involuntarily throw history and memory together, blurring and diminishing their differences.

The earthquake in northeastern Japan—Fukushima—and the subsequent tsunami that swept away so many thousands of lives and left only the rubble and residues of a once-lived and stable everyday was such an event; its aftermath has consistently shown this involuntary encounter of history and memory in the lives of the surviving victims and their search for new ways to assert the veracity of one over the other to supply meaning in an environment marked by continuing crisis.

I would like to propose that the forced convergence of history and memory in Fukushima resulted in singularizing expressions of experience and memory, thus inducing survivors to focus on the immediate context of the everyday itself rather than the nation and national history, which increasingly were seen as distant and abstract manifestations. In other words, the response to the historical event was to individualize experience and recall it at the level of the everyday the survivors had actually once known and lived through; the disruptions they were forced to endure would result in the writing of their own history. This move was enabled because history, especially national history, was already formed into a fixed representation of a now-completed past. History, in this respect, was usually centered on large-scale events that occurred on the national or global stage, whereas the everyday, in a more diminished scale, occupied the temporal register of the now. This unity of space/time resembled the philosopher Tosaka Jun's conception of the now (*ima*), marked by a scarcity of events and the prominence of affairs of the immediate locale.[3] Owing to this relationship of scale between history and the everyday, the latter was positioned to inflect catastrophic events only as distant rumors, unless the events directly struck one's immediate regional habitat. With the Fukushima earthquake and tsunami, the inhabitants of the immediate everyday of the locality reacted by resorting to singularizing and individualizing expressions, which became the basis of remembered experiences that will never be completed. The difference comes down to one between the formed and forming that remains unformed, a past present now passed and a present that refuses to become a past.

Few observers have registered the significance of how this combination of nature and history overdetermined the catastrophic environment of the event. It is important to recognize that this collision of history and memory was provoked by a combined assault of the energy of nature and history, which refers to the history of the region in modern times and the continuing activity of the state in the aftermath of the event. For survivors in the region, it often came down to the same thing, since both nature and history were implicated in the destruction of their lives. In the immediate aftermath of the occurrence, one elderly woman who lives in central Tokyo ratified a traditional political wisdom when she was quoted as saying that "when a country's leaders are bad, natural disasters occur."[4] In Japan's remote pasts, occurrences brought on by nature, such as drought, pestilence, volcanic eruptions, shooting stars, earthquakes, and the appearance of foreigners were invariably read as signs of a leader's moral failure. Because the social order was aligned with nature, and thus obliged to mimic it, any divergence such as a calamitous natural event would be interpreted as a reminder of moral failure, surely followed by even worse catastrophes portending the imminent collapse of a political regime. This renewed perception links up with the rejection of history, especially in the form of mounting national distrust of the state and the political classes directing it, which has prompted the inhabitants of the stricken area to increasingly turn to their immediate experience and appeal to a memory of then and now. Yet a difference persists, and 3/11 has begun to look more like its predecessor 9/11 as a world-historical event that exceeds its local and regional contours, inasmuch as it has become a historical marker—what one writer called the "hinge of history"—indicating that something "irrevocable and transforming has occurred [and] will not fade soon."[5]

In the wake of the event, then prime minister Kan Naoto recalled the end of World War II and the fires of the Tokyo earthquake of 1923 that destroyed much of the city. There were even nervous evocations of the more recent earthquake in Kobe in 1995 and revelations of shoddy highway construction and the state's tardy response. The event inspired the governor of Tokyo to blurt out that this combined earthquake and tsunami represented "heaven's vengeance" (*tembatsu*), which called attention to divine judgment against the habits of "selfishness," rampant materialism, and the "worship of money" that should point to the necessity of eliminating this wayward life and putting Japanese on a correct path.[6] (Not surprisingly, this was an echo of both an older plaint to explain the 1923 earthquake and former emperor Hirohito's 1946 proposal, in an act designed to escape the gallows, that war was brought about by the moral laxness of the people who had been seduced by materialism and consumerism.) The influential intellectual Azuma Hiroaki saw in the event the opportunity for constructing a theme park, while the writer Murakami Ryū wondered if it might provide an occasion for regaining hope. What unfortunately was swept away was an everyday life now displaced for countless homeless survivors and the thousands who perished in the waters of the tsunami; what was left behind is the historical record of the state's failure to prepare for such an inevitable disaster, in view of the past history of the region, and its incapacity to provide accurate information to the general populace, as evidenced by the former prime minister's avowal that he didn't know what was going on, and the consistent underestimation of damage reports by TEPCO, the company in charge of the facilities in Fukushima for over forty years. For some time, TEPCO operated on the presumption that the reactors could be saved, but now the company has admitted that the facility will have to be scrapped. This acknowledgment is accompanied by more recent recognition that leakage into the soil and into the

Pacific from holding tanks has continued. In fact, it has taken TEPCO, the hybrid company created by the bureaucracy that straddles the barely visible boundary between public and private sectors, more than two years to finally acknowledge that its preparations on the site were inadequate to withstand nature's impact. But no accounting has been made for the accompanying history, which has been as damaging as nature's ill-tempered ferocity. This history has shown that TEPCO built the nuclear plants along the disaster-prone Pacific coast. The facility was erected and operated without adequate protection against tsunamis of more than seven meters, even when there was ample historical and geological evidence that tsunamis of that magnitude had struck Japan repeatedly during its recorded history and would undoubtedly continue to do so. By the same measure that TEPCO functions as a stand-in for the state, TEPCO's nominal overseers in the Japanese government have still not called it to account for its errors. One of the lasting ironies has been the implementation of a reconstruction program driven by a campaign to actually persuade the populace that the risks of radiation and contamination have dissipated and today pose no real danger. The logic informing this campaign derives from the experience of Hiroshima and Nagasaki and the belief that pollution and radiation were "washed away."

But even before the event occurred, the region was marked by continuing forms of economic unevenness dating back to the late nineteenth century and was noted for the depths of poverty its inhabitants endured during the great depression of the 1930s. Historically, northeastern Japan lagged behind much of the country in development well into the postwar period. The state's decision to construct American-designed nuclear reactors in Fukushima in the 1960s must therefore be seen as a gesture to offset the deficit of historical repetition and to stimulate regional economic development and employment. But the new nuclear reactors would generate electric power south, to Tokyo and the Kanto sector. In this connection, the state and TEPCO deliberately earmarked the building of such plants in areas like Niigata and Fukushima Prefectures, at a distance from its chief beneficiaries in the Tokyo region. The bureaucratic optimism that shaped this calculation was off the mark, since the status of distance or nearness in the planning of nuclear facilities had nothing to do with the long-term effects of radioactive contamination and the conduct of dispersal, which is governed by wind direction, velocity, temperatures, and topography. Worrisome levels of radioactivity have reached beyond Fukushima to the entire Kanto region and beyond. This haphazard and uneven patterning of the trajectory of contamination began the moment the reactors imploded and released their deadly substances. What seems important about the state's historic failure to account for its own role in exacerbating the current circumstances is that it became the basis of an official bureaucratic assertion that sought to uphold the principle that the pain should be shared. Paradoxically, interpreters of this scene claim that the "sharing of pain" is the product of an egalitarian society and a desire to distribute equality to all by putting all lives equally at risk. In other words, the state used the occasion of what it perceived as a regional crisis to emphasize national solidarity, requiring all Japanese to share the pain. This resulted in proposals that the nation should trust the government and its leaders and learn how to live with radiation. One of the more spectacular schemes designed to renew national solidarity in the face of the unyielding crisis was to suggest that radioactive waste materials be distributed evenly through Japan's prefectures. The attempt to reintegrate the everyday into the nation before it completely severed itself thus prepared the ground for subsequent campaigns to minimize the risk of hazard. It was presumed that once radioactive substances were airborne in a wider space, their density would soon dissipate and their power to contaminate would weaken. A conceit apparently long held by electric power companies supporting the installation of nuclear facilities, its target was to diminish the fear of leakage by assuring clients and customers of the possibility of swift dissipation. As late as 2012, the Ministry of the Environment, charged with incinerating polluted remainders, announced that there was no reason for fear among the populace since there appeared to be little concentration of radioactive debris in the atmosphere. While in the case of short-lived substances this might be true, it is still far from reassuring; in other instances involving substances like cesium and strontium, whose afterlives are much longer, eventual disappearance is more extended. Evidence has been found that even in the event of incineration, substances have been released and allowed to enter an atmospheric register where their density is diluted and temperature lowered. The substances are dispersed again, to accumulate and aggregate in new habitats. Even houses distant from the afflicted zone have been found to be infected with toxic residues, and while they can be mapped and measured and detected, the water that may run below them is not accessible for such testing. The fear of contaminated foods is well known, but the simple truth that has emerged is that one can't really tell how toxic the food and water are. One tactic consumers have adopted is a form of avoidance of producers from the affected areas, of food from remote areas, despite Prime Minister Abe Shinzō's recently and well-publicized demonstration of his willingness to eat raw fish from the region. To offset this reaction, the government has resorted to a campaign organized against this practice aimed at dispelling "harmful rumors" (*fūhyō higai*). Unfortunately, the population's growing distrust has not generated any real political change, as attested by the Liberal Democratic Party's recent electoral victory. But distrust opens the way to indifference and withdrawal. Emergent groups in the area have dedicated themselves to self-reliance and a greater distancing from the state. Much of this, I believe, has been spurred

by the turn to everyday life, especially the village or household, and the subjective and singular precincts of experience and memory.

The crisis has demanded attempts to restore some semblance of the rhythms
that once anchored a routine and familiar life that vanished and to put into
practice in a new present those impulses that seek to conjure the memories, revenants, and remnants from the reservoir of its pasts. The evidence of the traumatic collision of history and memory that produced permanent uncertainty
is sadly overwhelming. It should be recognized that the event of 3/11 has, with
time, evolved into a montage in which it is virtually impossible to untangle the
devastation of nature's wrath from the threads of history's failures, by which I
mean the received, uneven past of the region and the contemporary state's continuing production of it. The resulting crisis has been heightened by the temporal entanglements people must negotiate daily, in the new and uncharted
present, as the sense of centered order has departed with their villages, households, and the countless lives that once inhabited them. Under the unanticipated and unexpected emergency, survivors find they are forced to fend for
themselves in the grim idiom of simple repetition and reproduction. They must
adapt to living in what might be described as a permanent parenthesis. Ethnographers have reported the examples of women who feel they are now living
in an endless present, even as they are told otherwise by the state and want to
be believe that it is still temporary, that they have some sort of purchase on an
unforeseen future. In such cases, there is little to induce the survivor to hang
on to the past, which, according to one woman, was already beginning to pass
with the eventual demise of her village, even before the earthquake had struck.
With another, there is the articulation of hope, but this reflects only an optimistic conviction in rebirth (but, nevertheless, another form of repetition).
Some express nostalgia and a longing for an imaginary everyday past linked to
their now-vanished village. Others have appealed to the necessity of returning
to the lives they once led. Most are repelled by the promise of brighter futures
that easily has become the common rhetorical mantra of politicians and have
concluded that such visions are pointless. While outsiders sought to give spiritual, ethical, and even political meaning to the first anniversary of the event,
most survivors in the area made no observances and spent the day quietly. This
was seen as a rejection of any thinking about or imagining the future and represented a refusal to separate the now—that is, the today—of their lives from a
special anniversary day commemorating the anniversary of the disaster.[7] A
consideration of the now revealed the crowding of different moments in an
uncertain space embodied in the multiple reasons that surfaced in discussions after the event. The disaster revealed a catalog of complaints relating to
the possible root and nature of Japanese society that have hitherto remained
repressed or concealed: the malfunction of the presiding Liberal Democratic

Party government; the impugned collusion of government, power companies, and universities; the "nuclear villages" established under postwar Japan's unbalanced and uneven regional development. Others blamed the elite culture, the loss of national solidarity, capitalism, and the like. In other words, it was difficult to determine when the now began.[8] The difficulty of thinking about the future was directly linked to a present that no longer provided the platform for anticipation and expectation. If the future could no longer be anticipated, and the past had become a phantom, people were limited to relying on the resources offered by the individual experiences and memories they were able to summon in the present.

One moving story from Iwate Prefecture involved the experience of cars stopping at a railroad crossing. After the event, cars were still stopping at the crossing, and the drivers were looking both ways even though the line's track had sustained major damage from the tsunami and the train was no longer operating.[9] On one level, this gesture reflected a habitual reflex. Yet on another, the drivers knew that the trains were no longer running on the tracks. The ethnographer proposed that the hesitation signified that the drivers, even for a few seconds, needed time to accept the present in which they were now embedded. Stopping at the crossing momentarily recalled for them their past, perhaps representing a mournful gesture commemorating what they had lost, before moving on, not necessarily toward the future but rather the present. There are numerous accounts of people trying to return to their abandoned homes and vacant villages near the damaged nuclear site. One woman regularly made the dangerous trip to her former home to pull out weeds from the yard. The act signaled a desire to not yet give up on the past, and she attempted, by all the memorable associations invoked by her home and garden, to continue a routine that had ended two years ago. The continuation of this routine resembled the act of drivers who stopped at the railway crossing no longer in use. The woman who revisits her home knows that she and her family will never return to this place to continue a life that belongs to her past, which now exists only as an experience in memory, providing purpose in the form of a repetitive personal commemoration and meaning because it is still her home.

For the thousands forced to move, most know they will never return home and that the permanent parenthesis, which has become the principal precinct of their existence, has replaced the habitat with which they once identified. Villages in the region have become ghost towns, the young have increasingly migrated to other areas and new lives, while the old seem stranded in "cramped temporary" quarters living off measly monthly handouts from the state. If the figure of the ghost town now stands as a spectral testimony and even unwanted monument to where villages and a vibrant everyday prevailed, the human cost of thousands of people who have lost jobs and the means of providing their own subsistence is a problem the state has scarcely begun to approach in a period still preoccupied with cleaning up an environment dominated by mud and sludge and the random debris of household things that have been captured. For the most part, it is important to recognize that it is mainly the old who seek a momentary return to relive, reenact, and thus recall a familiar activity from their lost everyday, whether it is pulling out weeds from a useless garden, sweeping the tatami in empty houses, or, for so many, performing traditional religious observances, like washing the grave of a spouse who perished in the earthquake. There are also stories of people who have taken the responsibility of caring for individuals, and even the Japanese Kanji Proficiency Society announced that the character selected through national ballot to best reflect the year 2011 was *kizuna*, or "bond," in an effort to encourage greater ties among people both in and out of northeastern Japan.[10]

The anthropologist Anne Allison, who spent a good deal of time volunteering in the afflicted region, reports in a new study how one woman, whose husband is missing, refuses to claim him dead, which would bring her compensation.[11] But she is not ready to do so and instead visits the municipal office daily to check the list of reported dead. She talks to her missing husband for long periods, visits his truck, where she last saw him alive, sits in the driver's seat, strokes the dashboard, and recalls what happened to their town and house; she also reports who survived and who did not. This is how we manage, she says, and confesses how hard it is to keep on without him, steering the wheel of the lifeless car. "When are you coming back?" she asks (*PJ*, 188). Allison recounts another story of a retired man in Tokyo who, since the crisis, has been traveling regularly to Iwate Prefecture on the weekends to offer help. On the first visit, he met an elderly woman walking up and down the littered beach who was thinking of throwing herself into the sea to join her husband, who had been swept away in the waves. His purpose is to keep her alive, and he succeeds by telling her that if she dies, there will be no one to give her husband *kuyō* (service for the dead), no one to pray for his spirit as it makes its journey to the other side (*PJ*, 188). In short, another reason for living is to provide service to the dead and departed. Allison speaks of another survivor, tormented by the fact that his grandmother's body has never been found, so the family cannot perform the proper memorial rites. Her spirit is trapped in an indeterminate zone, and the man apparently dreams incessantly about this conundrum (*PJ*, 188–89). Here, the effect of 3/11 plagues the mental health of survivors, and large numbers have already committed suicide.

Finally, we have stories of outsiders who come to prefectures like Iwate to clean up mud and sludge. In the process, they retrieve objects that have been arbitrarily cast into these mud and sludge pools and begin to wash them. One reported instance describes how a team of volunteers was assigned to remove mud-infested things (*mono dasu*) from a home. Photos and images are washed and hung out to dry. The work of preserving images is increasingly seen as saving "memory images" (*omoide no mono*) and has become a nationwide effort. At the heart of this project is the belief that cleaning photos and personal objects, of "washing memory things," extracts from death and destruction a forced opening capable of disclosing the fragments and traces of a life once lived, its singularly historic index (*PJ*, 193–95).

These stories reveal an intimate relationship between memory formation based on recalling momentary experiences and its immediate context in the everyday. In fact, the crisis implies a separation of contemporaneity and the lived present at the level of the everyday and the nation's own repeated attempt to reorder the present according to the narrative templates of the nation's past history. In this regard, the separation shows how the everyday meets the task of constructing a different form of political temporalization that combines the past, through the memory and experience of what is near at hand, with the new demands of the present, which enables the writing of its own (the everyday), different history.[12] In its most recent manifestation in Fukushima, this alignment of the then and now is centered on the household and unpaid women's labor power and the appropriation of what is near at hand in the struggle to protect the immediate members of the family from the ubiquitous and daily threat of radioactive contamination in the stricken environment. The occasion for turning to the immediacy of the everyday in the face of the state's reconstruction policy entails a form of rejection of a program that clearly was seeking to diminish the fear of hazard by inducing people to live with radioactivity as a condition of their everydayness instead of having its cause removed.

Observers like Yabu Shirō claim that the agents of this emerging movement committed to self-reliance include homemakers in the affected region charged with overseeing households. It should be recognized that this assertion of self-reliance in the everyday that now writes its own history echoes a prior historical impulse. The gesture recalls the historical examples of withdrawal of localities from the political center represented by Tokugawa authority in the mid-nineteenth century that prefigured the Meiji Restoration of 1868. But in a larger sense, the more recent instance of groups in Fukushima relying on their own resources near at hand in the everyday implies a form of secession from the distant political abstraction of the state. Many of these earlier communitarian groups had been founded by women as a means of preserving their version of the commonness of everyday life from the dangers posed by both nature and history. Yabu claims that the agents of the Fukushima groups are ordinary homemakers, principally housewives dedicated to managing the everyday political economy of the household, occupied with what he reports as "reproductive work," which had once played a central role in a precapitalist division of labor. Under a capitalist reorganization of the division of labor, reproductive work reappeared as invisible, unpaid labor.[13]

I can only briefly summarize the basic dimensions of this initiative centered on the household as the fulcrum of everydayness. Those opposed to the state's reconstruction policy see in it the eventual disappearance of both the household and the everyday. Practices toward devising protective measures on-site derived from the received experience of the household and the long tradition of care informing it. These included cooking, cleaning, washing, childcare, and so on, and their implementation meant producing a mode of knowledge that preceded capitalism. It thus involved putting into daily use practices that had been integral to the idea of a natural economy but were now marginalized with the advent of capitalism in Japan and the privilege accorded to productive labor. Such activities have become the responsibility of homemakers—women—since it is the family, the smallest social unit of the everyday, that has become the object of the attempt to protect, which, in turn, has led to asserting the self-reliance of the everyday. By the same measure, unpaid homemakers have, as a result, incurred continuing discrimination from advertising agencies bent on representing the state's point of view in campaigns aimed to alter the image of women by emphasizing feminine beauty, the "beautiful woman," "fashionable moms," urging a "disciplinization" of their bodies by making available information on health and beautification, antiaging, and the like. In addition, agencies have begun to circulate advice concerning the necessity of "accepting radiation bravely" at the same time that people are being asked to accept government risk estimates that report the lowering levels, if not the complete dissipation, of toxic substances. Implicit in this move is the presumption that radiation is an integral party of the lived everyday, an important campaign in view of the forthcoming Olympics in Tokyo. Finally, the activity of "reproductive" labor aimed at protecting everydayness from disappearing is being described as temporally different from wage and contract work, which is defined by a much shorter working day and serves capitalism's penchant for surplus value. For these workers, the temporal horizon of their working day, like their life, is considerably expanded since it derives and is in part still embedded in economic practices that haven't been separated from other household activities regulated by incomparably long patterns of cyclic time.

Whether this example of withdrawal from the everyday present will become a model of broader political application is hard to know. But the return to the everyday through memory and recall dramatizes the "problematic nature of the past's manner of preserving in the present." Memory always appears as an actual, living link with the everyday present. "If memory is a capacity, the power of remembering is more fundamentally a figure of care," that basic (philosophic) anthropological structure of our historical condition by which we hold ourselves open to the past.[14] If, moreover, the everyday is the smallest cellular unit of the social, it is also where the "small nothings" prevail to reveal what is truly important—how people live their lives: "a reality that can only come from practice and more precisely the most trivial acts, as well as the most necessary, for everyday lives, those by which we clothe and nourish ourselves."[15]

Notes

1. Paul Ricoeur, *Memory, History, Forgetting*, trans. Kathleen Blamey and David Pellauer (Chicago: University of Chicago Press, 2004), 141–45.
2. Enzo Traverso, *Le passé, modes d'emploi: Histoire, mémoire, politique* (Paris: La fabrique, 2005), 21.
3. See Ken C. Kawashima, Fabian Schäfer, and Robert Stolz, eds., *Tosaka Jun: A Critical Reader* (Ithaca, N.Y.: Cornell University East Asia Program, 2013), for the first set of translations from Tosaka's key writings, accompanied by a number of essays on various aspects of his thought.
4. Norimitsu Onishi, "Reeling from Crises, Japan Approaches Familiar Crossroads," *New York Times*, March 19, 2011, www.nytimes.com/2011/03/20/world/asia/20future.html?page wanted=all.
5. R. Taggart Murphy, "3/11 and Japan: A Hinge of History?," April 21, 2011, japanfocus.org/events/view/77.
6. Onishi, "Reeling from Crises"; see also, in Japanese, "Daijishin wa tembatsu," *Asahi shimbun*, March 14, 2011, https://www.asahi.com/; Lee Jay Walker, "Tokyo Governor Ishihara Says Earthquake and Tsunami Was 'Divine Punishment,'" *Newsvine*, August 1, 2015, http://www.newsvine.com (originally appeared in *Modern Tokyo Times*, March 15, 2011, http://moderntokyotimes.com).
7. Reported in Shuhei Kimura, "Between Hope and Nostalgia" (unpublished manuscript, 2013), 3.
8. Kimura, "Between Hope and Nostalgia," 4.
9. Kimura, "Between Hope and Nostalgia," 6–7.
10. Kimura, "Between Hope and Nostalgia," 16.
11. Anne Allison, *Precarious Japan* (Durham, N.C.: Duke University Press, 2013), 188. Hereafter cited as *PJ*.
12. Peter Osborne, "Temporalization as Transcendent Aesthetics," *Nordic Journal of Aesthetics* 44 (2013): 10.
13. My thanks to Sabu Kohso for having brought the texts of Yabu Shirō to my attention. See, in particular, Shiro Yabu, "Radiation Exposure Is Unequal," https://jfissures.wordpress.com/2013/04/24/radiation-exposure-is-unequal/.
14. Ricoeur, *Memory, History, Forgetting*, 508.
15. Pierre Macherey, *Petits riens* (Paris: Le Bord de l'eau, 2009); Warren Montag, "Avec Pierre Macherey, à la recherche d'un quotidien insaisissable et obsédant," *La Revue des Livres*, no. 011 (May–June 2013): 27.

PART IV

IDEOLOGICAL FORMATION

Colluding with the Past

CHAPTER 11

VISIBLE DISCOURSES/INVISIBLE IDEOLOGIES

There are several discourses on the social in twentieth-century Japan devoted to making sense of the effects of industrialization and of new forms of instrumental knowledge, including its vast propensity to differentiate spheres of learning into specialized disciplines reflecting more basic social divisions. Yet among these discourses I hope to show that none more clearly and enduringly sought to resolve the aporia of social indeterminacy (in which declining remnants of a precapitalist order coexisted in an antagonistic relationship with a capitalist society, working to presumably prevent the fulfillment of an uncompleted past) than the 1942 symposium on "overcoming the modern" (*kindai no chōkoku*). This uneasy cohabitation of earlier modes of cultural production alongside newer epistemological strategies in the same social space (what Ernst Bloch, rereading Marx's conception of "unequal development," would call nonsynchronicity) was further exacerbated by a war against the West; it demanded a resolution of the question of social determinacy, concerning the principles bonding Japanese society, if the survivors of the past were not to be altogether eliminated by a capitalist present and its theory of social relationships. But what began as an effort to reimagine the social as distinct from the prevailing social imaginary (how societies seek to represent the "real" by calling it reality and endowing its signification, even though the "real" remains outside representation) in prewar Japan became, forty years later, a social discourse. In other words, a discourse which tried to account for history as a principle of social constitution was transformed into an arrangement in which the distinction between representation and the real was effaced in order to make society appear without history. Whereas the instituting discourse, calling for the overcoming of modernity, still conceded the importance of history for explaining the development of a traditional order into a modern society as a condition for moving to another level, the later "conquest of the modern," promoted by the government of Ōhira Masayoshi in 1980, sought to displace history, or simply to get outside it, in an effort to proclaim a narrative in which premodern and modern elements comingle as if they now constituted a natural and timeless coupling.

Yet before this narrative pastiche was constructed to take the place of the older discourse on the social, the Japanese intellectual Takeuchi Yoshimi, in a desperate and lonely intervention to forestall the elimination of the social by the state, reread the critique of modernity in the early postwar period as a prerequisite for the resolution of the aporia between discourse and the social, in order to find a model of modernity that belonged neither to the West nor to a dead and discarded past. Takeuchi's text on *kindai no chōkoku* represented a superimposition on the symposium's text; it functioned as a palimpsest that allowed the critique of modernity to glimmer through while it blotted out the more strident justifications of war. Although he sympathized with the symposium and the task it set for itself, he was neither insensitive to its ineffectualness nor indifferent to its moral hypocrisy with respect to the war in Asia. But the palimpsest, bringing together different times and texts, risked duplicity, insofar as Takeuchi sought to combine views discordant and ceaselessly contradictory. *Palimpsest* gave way to the construction of a pastiche, which had no need for articulating a reasoned defense or synthesizing seeming opposites, since the operation was founded on the composition of random shards of life and history, which obeyed no other logic than the frame that contained it.

This last moment was inaugurated by the Ōhira brain trust in a remarkable text announcing the advent of a new age of culture. Whether or not it can be considered a postmodern moment depends entirely upon how the category is understood. If, by postmodern, we are willing to recognize that it aims to condemn the modernist separation of politics and culture, thereby attributing the cause of disorder to this momentous division, then it is possible to read as postmodern all those efforts that seek to reinstitute the regime of a political totality at the expense of dissolving the social, without resorting to the more coercive methods usually associated with established forms of totalitarianism. According to Claude Lefort, postmodern polity manages to eliminate the opposition between the state and civil society by dissolving the social into the "pure generality" of the political.[1] Its discourse will radiate the signs of its unity and, hence, of the homogeneity of the objective domain. By manifesting the presence of the state throughout the social space, it conveys, through a series of representatives, the principle of power informing the diversity of activities and incorporates them into a model of common allegiance. It carries out this operation by "diffusing itself throughout the circuits of socialization, by elaborating signs whose representative function is no longer identifiable," by taking actors, turning them into subjects, and inserting them into systems so that the discourse almost speaks through them and almost abolishes the space, implicit in modernist ideology, between enunciation and that which is enunciated.[2]

While the postmodern would, in its denunciation of an adversarial culture, says Hal Foster, "confound cause and effect" in order to reaffirm prevailing political and economic arrangements, its conception of order would conform to all those efforts to re-present a totalized polity in the simulacrum of the social, even as the social is effectively eliminated. This will become evident from a reading of the *Bunka no jidai* (Age of culture) text. This text proclaims, in comparison with earlier attempts to imagine an "overcoming" of modernity, that the time has come for "conquering the modern" (it is important to note the tone of militancy of this forced march) in order to implement the new age of culture. This new age of culture will constitute the final contraction and reversal of the categories of the "real" into a dense, seductive, and entirely cynical communal or consensual order which appeals to cultural uniqueness for its certainty even as it is held together by commodities and signs signifying signs. Jean Baudrillard has proposed, quoting Ecclesiastes in one of his more hallucinatory texts, that the simulacrum is "'never that which conceals the truth, but is, instead, the truth which conceals that there is none.'" "It is the generation by models of the real without origins or reality: a hyperreal," "the map that precedes the territory." By this measure, the so-called real can easily be produced from "miniaturized units, from matrices, memory banks and command models," to form a pastiche which can be reproduced indefinitely and which need not appear rational, since it is not measured against any idea or "negative instance."[3] Under these circumstances, culture remains an operational an instrument largely or principally at the disposal of state control and is projected to conceal bureaucratic "rationality." As a result, the earlier modernist critique of 1942, and even Takeuchi's later courageous intervention, became a postmodern "therapeutic," not to mention a "cosmetic," employed to justify a return to the solidarity of the traditional family and the truths of morality and a Japanized culture. In this scheme, modernism is reduced to a style and consigned to a moment in history, a moment which has now been "conquered" and condemned as a "cultural mistake." Elements enlisted from premodern and modern experiences are easily combined and conflated to erect a false unity, whereas culture and history are smoothed over to appear natural, difference is subsumed by identity, and the Other is finally banished from the social order.

In contemporary Japan there has been a relentlessly obsessive "return" to "origins": an orchestrated attempt by the state to compensate for the dissolution of the social by resurrecting "lost" traditions against modernism itself and

by imposing a master code declaring "homogeneity" in a "heterogeneous present." It is precisely an effort to install a master code, an effort systematically
announced in the official statement of the Ōhira government but surely prefigured in the discourse of countless intellectuals, including Yoshimoto Takaaki,
Nakane Chie, Murakami Yasusuke, Hamaguchi Eshun, Kimura Bin, and others too numerous to mention. This master code would eradicate the scandal of
difference, for all times to come, in the name of an "affirmative culture" rooted
firmly in reified values. Such a culture has characterized the program of Japanese governments since Ōhira's prime ministership proclaimed an end of the
modern—that is, since the postwar era and the "advent of an age of culture."

In the case of the *bunka no jidai* program, all hope of a referent is discarded.
Moreover, this loss of reference is accompanied by a rejection of the point of
certainty outside society, in favor of an affirmation of discourse solely as discourse, now extricated from the social, to mask the "bureaucratic fantasies" of
abolishing the historical in History, restoring the logic of a "society without history" and identifying "the instituting moment with the instituted," denying
the unpredictable and the unknowable, and firmly establishing an order that
will not "tolerate the image of an internal social division." This order claims to
be homogeneous, whether racially or socially, inasmuch as everybody belongs
to the "middle stratum" despite all the differences which exist in fact.

* * *

In July of 1942, a group of distinguished intellectuals, academics, and critics
were summoned to Kyoto by the Literary Society (Bungakkai) to discuss the
theme of "overcoming the modern." All the participants believed that the
debate, convened six months after the outbreak of the Pacific War, would mark
the end of "modern civilization" in Japan and would reveal the outline of a "glorious new age." Composition of the debate was divided along a line that distinguished two major intellectual groups: the Literary Society and the Romantics.
Among the better-known participants were figures like Kobayashi Hideo,
Nishitani Keiji, Kamei Katsuichirō, Hayashi Fusao, Miyoshi Tatsuji, Kawakami
Tetsutarō, and Nakamura Mitsuo. Under the shadow of war, the debate's principal purpose was to discuss the larger "world-historical meaning" of the event
itself, and how this understanding might relate to the vision of a future that no
one could immediately perceive but which all anxiously sought to envisage. One
of the organizers of the conference, Kawakami Tetsutarō, stated this overall
concern most clearly in his concluding remarks. He proposed that, apart from
the question of the success or failure of the discussions, it was an indisputable
fact of immense importance that such an intellectual encounter had taken place
within the first year of the outbreak of the war. He felt that the discussions
reflected a struggle between "the blood of the Japanese, which truly motivates

our intellectual life," and "Western knowledge, which has been superimposed upon Japan in modern times." He was convinced that the ensuing conflict would be a desperate and bloody one.[4]

If the intellectuals who discussed the question of modernity in Kyoto believed that the task before them was to envisage a social order beyond the contingencies which plagued contemporary Japanese society, they also saw the war as the agent capable of finally conquering the modern. This is not to say that there was complete unanimity or consensus among the participants, but all could agree that the war, however they felt about it, now made it possible to construct a new social imaginary that would "overcome" the innumerable contradictions of Japanese society. For the most part, "modern" meant the West, its science, and the devastating effects it had inflicted on the face of traditional social life. A number of writers, like Kamei and Hayashi, recommended that the inappropriateness of science and even technology had, in fact, alienated the Japanese from their founding myths and their gods, to such an extent that the real meaning of "overcoming" required the reintegration of the Japanese with the spirit of the kami (gods) and the elimination of the effects of reason, with its ceaseless propensity to divide and separate. Here was revealed the ideology of the debate, insofar as the discourse was made to suppress all those signs which, many believed, threatened to imperil and even destroy the sense of certainty concerning the nature of the social: that is to say, signs of genuine historicity, of contemporary daily life, of precisely all those things fractioned and fractured through the "dispersing effects of socialization, autonomization, differentiation" and signs—which, in other words, now promised to make society in the 1930s "alien to itself." In this respect, the "secondary discourse"—the "folding over of the primary, manifest discourse"—could easily become an ideology in search of a representation which, by invoking a juxtaposition of tradition, modern, and a transcended modern, could establish a society "without history" at the heart of a historical society. This goal was never fulfilled for a number of reasons but was, as we shall see, at the heart of the later projection of a holonic society in the new age of culture.

While the debate's most perceptive participant, the critic Kobayashi Hideo, early expressed an ambivalence toward any effort to overcome the modern, as he felt that Japan was already modern, this sense of timeless essences unmediated by history constituted a principal part of his own intervention. Kobayashi proposed that conceptions of progressive history inevitably misled modern men and created false expectations by deluding them with a "poetry of the future." But forms of beauty remind societies of a timeless quotient, perhaps, though he never said it, a "poetry of the past," which has successfully overcome history, especially those conditions attending the production of the particular object. Beauty, he insisted, never "evolved" in a progressive, purposeful manner and can never be understood from the historically motivated perspective of the modern.[5] Thus, Kobayashi called for a knowledge of essences; these essences could be easily identified with enduring artifacts from "tradition," inasmuch as they had survived the limitations of their own history and outlived the moment that had given them expression. Yet his understanding rarely strayed from a more familiar Platonic conception of beauty as a form of eternal truth. Overcoming the modern did not mean an "advancement" to a new period but a reunion outside history with the eternal forms of truth and beauty, possibly an encounter with the unrepresentable, the sublime. Such a view supported a program calling for the traditional cultural ideals, allowing them their own space and time, not because they were necessarily and uniquely Japanese but because they had survived time, as tradition, in such a manner that they might serve as sources of renewal, creative inspiration, and identity in a world insisting on the sameness of the modern. For Kobayashi was most troubled by the fear that Japan would become a replica of Western society. He dramatized this concern by enlisting Marx's own irony, which itself constituted an ironic gesture; Kobayashi described the modernization of the West as a "tragedy" and the second manifestation of it in Japan as a "comedy." The quintessential comedians of Japan had not yet captured the stage, he remarked, but they would soon.[6] Only art, he observed, would save Japan from the contingency that he associated with history, despite the effort to represent the historical as the succession of reason and progress, and to make it appear orderly.

The debaters concentrated on one further issue. In interrogating the meaning of civilization, identified with the Meiji achievement, participants like Kamei Katsuichirō and Hayashi Fusao drew attention to its epistemological consequences—the specialization and compartmentalization of knowledge. Kamei observed that this effect generated a profound loss in the sense of "wholeness" in life among the Japanese and constituted a serious disruption of traditional spirituality. Specialization had proceeded at a relentless pace in the twentieth century, driven by a relentless utilitarianism that accompanied the idea of progress willfully promoted by the Meiji enlightenment. In this fateful process, Kamei remarked, the real "philosophers of life" were destroyed—by which he meant those courageous figures like the Christian leader Uchimura Kanzō who had resisted the assimilation of modes of specialization and instrumentality for a unified vision of knowledge in which all things were informed by an intrinsic and divine spirit. Kamei spoke for most of the participants of the debate when he called for the restoration of a philosophy of "wholeness" and the "unity of knowledge" as it related all things, creatures, and beings, a unity he believed had been the mark of Japanese civilization from the time of its origins. In his harsh condemnation, Meiji civilization and enlightenment had introduced "deformed specialists" into contemporary Japanese culture and had produced incalculable consequences for the quality of life, which only the war would be able to arrest and unmake. This rejection of rational knowledge resulted in the conviction, articulated by the former Marxist and writer Hayashi Fusao, that the "civilization and enlightenment of the Meiji period meant the adoption of European culture, and resulted in the submission of Japan to the West."[7] Although the Meiji achievement represented the last opposition of the East against the West (for only Japan managed to withstand the Western wave that had already swept over India and China), the price paid for this resistance was the incorporation of the rational instruments of the enemy. The time had come for a final confrontation between the East and the West if the plague was to be exterminated, if, in fact, this epistemological domination was to end.

The debate singled out something called "Americanism" as the principal force empowering the global expansion of utilitarian instrumentality and extinguishing the spirit everywhere it was applied. The participants specifically referred to the immense importation of what they described as "hedonistic" and "crass" materialism among Japan's urban youth after World War I, exemplified by faddish groups calling themselves "modern boys" and "modern girls." This critique showed how the visible marketing of mass culture reflected the absence of a deeply rooted sense of cultural purpose in the United States, rather than an obsessive concern with the circulation of commodities and the reproduction of consumption. The danger of this "Americanism" lay in its capacity to spread a new "universalistic" culture of simple materialism and to destroy the foundations of older, ancient societies, whose values had withstood the test of time and had survived until this latest onslaught. Because of the duplicity of Meiji civilization, Japan confronted the spectacle of a consumer society driven by a desire for commodities which could never be satisfied, even in the last instance; moreover, it faced the concomitant loss of quality and the beauty of scarcity and restraint. In the final analysis, the problem appeared to be how Japan might retain its own technological accomplishments yet preserve those irreducible elements from culture which, it was believed, made Japanese Japanese. When faced with the choice between traditional and modern modes of production, none of the participants ever conceived of turning back the clock, so to speak, and returning to a simpler and undifferentiated agrarian order. But they were clearly concerned with trying to constrain the "machine" into the role of the servant rather than the master and to restrain what all perceived as the ceaseless commodification of their lives.

* * *

When Takeuchi Yoshimi wrote his long meditation on this wartime symposium concerned with the critique of modernity, like so many of his contemporaries in the postwar period he did not mean simply to recall the half-forgotten discourse of an earlier time in order to remind Japanese of an intellectual

episode lost to history. Nor was he primarily interested in salvaging the repu-
tation of many of the symposium's participants, especially those associated
with the Japan Romantic faction, recently discredited because of their supposed
complicity with fascists and ultranationalists. Takeuchi acknowledged that it
was customary after the war to refer to the debate and its title—"Overcoming
the Modern"—as "infamous" (akumyōdakai), and he wondered if the great
"havoc" it allegedly had caused was not simply a case of overdetermined criticism, since the intellectual content of the proceedings was nonexistent.[8] As a
result, he thought it best to offer a new reading of its text, as a condition for
resituating his own critique of modernity in the postwar discussions of the
questions of modernism, subjectivity, the promise of political democracy, and
the problems of war responsibility. While he sought to provide a genealogy for
his own developing critique of the forms of modernism, it would be wrong to
accuse him of antimodernism or some variation of an invertebrate tradition-
alism. He was nonetheless convinced that, once the earlier text had been
stripped of its unjustified ideological associations and the charges of complicity in Japan's war goals, it would reveal a prescient awareness of the problems
Japan encountered when it fatefully decided to transform society into the
Western image. By the same measure, he was equally certain that the war and
the postwar reconstruction of a new order dramatically necessitated his decision to retrace the steps of this earlier discourse, in order to imagine the terms
in which writers and intellectuals understood the modern and why they felt an
urgency to overcome it. Writing in the 1950s, Takeuchi recognized that the
war did not bring an end to the modern in Japan, as many in the kindai no
chōkoku debate had fully anticipated; it merely laid the groundwork for an
even more powerful modern order that was already on its way to completion.

     Takeuchi connected with the symposium at the moment when its partici-
pants recognized that the shock of the opening of hostilities was manifest in
an "intellectual shudder"; for they knew they were now committed to a struggle between "Western knowledge" and the "blood of the Japanese." He heeded
most closely the symposium's ardent pledge to dissolve the "autonomization"
of cultural spheres. This autonomization had come to dominate the landscape
and to separate genuine cultural production by intellectuals from political practice. With this move, Takeuchi believed that it was possible to differentiate the
symposium's consequent ideological associations from its substantive and critical discourse, which had effectively problematized the question of Japan's
modernity. Supplementing what he believed to be missing in the text of the symposium, Takeuchi carefully separated ideology from thought, or, as he stated
it, extracted thought from ideology. He confessed that this operation might well
be impossible to accomplish; yet if he did not attempt the effort to understand
thought as reality and if he did not take the risk to acknowledge its independence from event, he could not possibly tease out the thought "buried" in those

discussions. More importantly, Takeuchi's decision to uncouple thought from event called attention to a recurrent proposition of the critique of modernity, which was to escape (outside) history altogether. By burying the symposium as an event in a past history, Takeuchi advised, and pacing the difficult ground of its thought, it might still be possible to give life and presence to its legacy in the present.

Takeuchi hoped to install as a living presence in postwar Japan the critical possibilities inherent in the self-perception of the "blood of the Japanese, which has acted as the true motive power of our intellectual activity and its rivalry with Western knowledge, which has unhappily been superimposed on it"[9] If recognition of this seeming bonding prompted a record of a bloody struggle, the motivation for releasing Japanese intelligence from its Western dependence was no less compelling in the first year of the war than it was nearly two decades later. The disjunction between native wisdom and Western rational knowledge opened up, for Takeuchi at least, a space within which to reassess a modernization process that slavishly aped the West while subverting Japanese intelligence. Such a reassessment also offered to sunder the virtual identification of the two as a condition for a reunion with suppressed alternatives, for rediscovering the path the Japanese had not taken. This was a well-known, major driving force in Takeuchi's own writings, and it prompted his valorization of the modern Chinese writer Lu Xun, who represented best the choice all Asians encountered in selecting routes to modernity. Lu Xun's example projected an image of defending a modernization process which relied neither on Western models nor on reified traditional forms but on the energy of the masses. Furthermore, his example constituted for Takeuchi an eloquent reminder of the promise inherent in the play of cultural differences rather than of sameness.

It was for this reason that Takeuchi, whose sympathies were often with the left, devoted so much energy to resuscitating the tarnished careers of prewar right-wing activists, such as Kita Ikki and Ōkawa Shūmei. Takeuchi saw in these prewar intellectuals analogies to Lu Xun, especially in their thinking about Japan's modernity. The kinship of these various writers and thinkers, as well as of other Asians such as Tagore and Gandhi, lay in a common refusal to accept either a Western model of modernity or its reified double in traditional and archaic forms—this was, he believed, the meaning of *kindai no chōkoku* the symposium hoped to convey. Here, Takeuchi agreed with Kawakami Tetsutarō, the symposium's principal organizer, who announced that the times necessitated giving substance to the idea of a new spiritual order. Since the late nineteenth century, the specialization of knowledge had prevailed and the cultural sphere was fragmented into autonomous disciplines. However one attempted to avoid such autonomization of the fields of knowledge, one inevitably ran counter to the "rule of special terminology," theories concerned with epistemology and methods, and the historical stages of manufacturing. Within this framework, Takeuchi recognized that the effect had been to erect barriers between different areas of culture, causing mutual isolation and preventing genuine self-understanding; "communication requires striking a wall in order to talk to inmates inhabiting the next room of the same ward."[10] The reference to the ward, and its special association with disease, was not lost on Takeuchi and functioned as a constant metaphor throughout the 1930s to call attention to the baneful effects of Westernization.

Hence the symposium was represented as a "lone beacon of light piercing the wall of each person's isolation and illuminating what had already been before them, but they had not been able to see." Takeuchi acknowledged with the participants of the symposium that they were all modern intellectuals and writers, driven by necessity to assess the actual cost of Japan's assimilation to the West, even as they knew the impossibility of separating themselves from what had apparently become common sense. The problem was to find a way to conceptualize a modernity that was made in Japan, not in the West. Rather than launch an antimodern attack, the symposium ought to have imagined a modern order in Japan that would be accountable to native intelligence and indigenous experience. To overcome the modern, then, meant liberation from the West and from the constraints of a model of modernization that insisted upon a sameness which had successfully suppressed the other and the play of cultural difference. According to Takeuchi, it was this critique which compelled so many of the participants to examine their own modern endowment in Japan, and which represented a "beam of light" illuminating the path to follow in the postwar era.

If the modern had a consistent meaning, it referred to historicism (according to Suzuki Shigetaka); therefore, overcoming it demanded a program of getting out of the straitjacket of developmental historical emplotment and rejecting the legacy of *bummei kaika*, the Meiji commitment to an enlightened civilization of rational utility and instrumentality. Yet on closer examination, these two targets represented different sides of the same coin: if one started from an assessment of the theory of historical development, whether Marxist or non-Marxist, it would lead directly to a critique of the Meiji commitment to an evolutionary and progressive conception of historical development. Or, if one began with a rejection of Meiji instrumentalism, it would invariably lead back to its authorizing historical mission. In other words, both historicism and rational utility, as embodied in the state, inevitably led to modernism and its double—Japanism (Nihonshugi). Within the framework of this critique against historicism and utility, Takeuchi situated his own text as a condition for connecting the charge to overcome the modern with his present. If *kindai no chōkoku* was to make sense for his own moment, it was necessary to problematize how the symposium grasped the structure of modern Japanese thought at the time that it convened. While Takeuchi rejected the temptation of differentiating the two moments, he acknowledged that something was lacking in the original text which he proposed to supplement. This missing element was the incapacity of the symposium to distinguish between an intellectual struggle with the West, leading to war, and Japanese colonial expansion in Asia.

By problematizing the structure of modern Japanese thought, the symposium disclosed a profound aporia, a doubt and a "necessary hesitation" before the claims of Westernization and modernization. This doubt produced theories leading to conflict as a form of resolution. It was the task of the present to discover where such theories went wrong. Takeuchi proposed reversing the normal course of history in order to uncover the particular blindness that had prevented both the past and the present from finding an adequate resolution of Japan's relations with China and Asia, without making this resolution a condition of an intellectual revolt against the West. In this respect, the debate on modernity represented a kind of "condensation of the aporia of Japan's modern history."[11] At the heart of this discourse of doubt, Takeuchi noted, were a number of binary oppositions demanding resolution, such as restoration and renovation (*fukko* vs. *ishin*), loyalism and expulsionism (*sonnō* vs. *jōi*), opening the country and keeping it closed (*kaikoku* vs. *sakoku*), national essence versus civilization and enlightenment (*kokusui* vs. *bummei kaika*).[12] According to Takeuchi, the symposium failed in its inability to make the aporia itself—the doubt—the object of consciousness. The reason for this failure was its refusal to separate an intellectual struggle from the idea of total war. Hence the doubt dissipated "like scattered clouds," and the symposium's promise to overcome the modern degenerated into an explanatory "label" for a public ideology of war. "The dissolution of the aporia," Takeuchi wrote, "prepared the intellectual ground for the postwar devastation and the colonization of Japan."[13] Takeuchi argued that, while the symposium could hardly serve as a source for creative thought, it is, nevertheless, necessary to set right the aporia as a central theme if Japanese are to restore creativity to thought. Advising contemporaries to return to the ground traveled by people like Ōkawa Shūmei in order to understand why the Sino-Japanese conflict really differed from a struggle with Western intelligence, Takeuchi was convinced that the energy invested in Asia was an extravagance that inhibited the formation of thought according to tradition. The problem for contemporary Japan was not in sustaining "myths," referring to Etō Jun's defense of them, but in avoiding an "easy knowledge" emptied of self-reliance and incapable of conquering or overcoming myths.

Among his contemporaries, it was the modernists Takeuchi wished to contest, especially those adherents of political democracy who dominated postwar discourse down to the early 1960s. His critique against modernism revealed an impulse to decenter the agency of a subject who made history, as well as to release a suppressed other—the energy of the masses—in the hope of realizing a new kind of history. In the process of reinstating the human subject as the agent of a new history, he believed that postwar modernists evaded any confrontation with the idea of the folk, owing to the wartime valorization of *minzoku* (a racially specific folk). Despite this unhappy episode, the folk or the masses, whom he increasingly identified with Asia, remained a historically viable constituency, in contrast to the reified conception of subject authorized by a theory of ideal types. In his words, the folk had always been the "real antithesis" to civilization and enlightenment and modernism, since the time the country had been opened to the world. The refusal of contemporary modernists to come to terms with the folk, regardless of their unfortunate ideological appropriation during the war, was not substantially different from the policies of the prewar state to mobilize the masses for capitalism and a ruinous war. Yet they alone, as the China of Mao Zedong already showed, offered the hope of a genuine revolution in contemporary Japan.

To overcome the modern in this postwar context, therefore, meant liberation from the very mediations used to articulate a program for contemporary Japan. Takeuchi's text sought to show in this environment that the war did not forestall or even foreclose the real critique offered by the *kindai no chōkoku* symposium, and that, in their identification of an aporia, the participants had hoped to avoid closure itself. In a remarkable presage of what was to come, he feared most that the alliance between modernism and Japanism would decenter the subject, armed precisely with those practices which hitherto had been identified with instrumentality and utility. In this transformation of a class model, the bourgeoisie—the object of earlier critiques—was redefined now as Japanese and human; it established its regime of truth under discursive practices that functioned to maintain its rational advantage and to provide a culturally exceptional justification for its economic privileges against the West. Even when Takeuchi wrote his essay, postwar Japan was, in fact, in the process of realizing the very form of historical narrative that earlier writers had identified as the problem: the ideological form of modern Western society, the inevitable slippage into sameness. The struggle in postwar Japan, as it had been earlier, encompassed differing "systems of narrative" and the necessity of establishing one that was particularly resistant to assimilation.

For Takeuchi, overcoming modernity meant finding a way to reunite thought with the practice of the people, tapping the energy of the masses which had been suppressed throughout the long night of Japan's modernizing history. Here, he believed, might be found the promise of a genuine Japanese revolution. Convinced that the model for this reunion with the practice of the people was already exemplified by the Chinese revolution, he was emboldened to propose that Asia itself should become a method for transformation, which would successfully avoid either the course of Japan's slavish dependence upon the West or its reverse in the reification of traditional forms. Postwar Japan had failed to resolve the claims of modernization for those, like himself, who looked increasingly to Asia for a release from the West: his government and people still looked down upon China and other Asian nations. But, he warned, quoting the critic Odagiri Hideo (who had written earlier about *kindai no chōkoku*), since "we have not worked to settle the past with our own hands," calling attention to the American Occupation's control, "so the past is beginning to take reprisals against us."[14] To avoid this dark future, indeed, sameness itself, Takeuchi plunged into political action in 1960 in order to complete what he believed to be unfinished business: to bring about the Japanese revolution he feared might already have been lost.

＊＊＊

In 1980, thirty-five years after the end of a disastrous war the Japanese fought to "overcome modernity," the government of Ōhira Masayoshi announced a plan for the eighties and beyond, to the twenty-first century, in the establishment of a new age of culture. The new age of culture marked a "conquest of the modern," which referred to the postwar epoch between 1945 and the late 1970s. The text established a comprehensive chronology of the genealogy of Japan's modernization since the Meiji Restoration. Before the war, periods seemed to follow fifteen-year cycles: 1885–1900 constituting a time of politics and the installation of the political framework for modernization; 1900–1915, when capitalism was formed; 1915–1930, a time of culture—Taishō culture—which saw the efflorescence of the "democracy movement"; and 1930–1945, a "time of conflict" which led to war. After the war, the same pattern of periodization resumed. The fifteen years from 1945 to 1960, principally guided by Prime Minister Yoshida Shigeru, represented the "age of politics," which reestablished the political infrastructure for Japan's subsequent progress. The span of time between 1960 and the late 1970s, inaugurated by the Ikeda cabinet and continued by Satō, initiated the "age of economy" with the expansion of "high economic growth" (*kōdō keizai seichō*). Once the Japanese people entered this stage and experienced the benefits of economic abundance, they were ready to pursue the "fruits of spirit and culture." What the text excludes is a discussion of why the cycle ends here, why the last stage of "conflict" would not inevitably be repeated.

According to the text *Bunka no jidai no keizai un'ei*, in each age there is an appropriate requirement (*yōsei*) that must be satisfied; for Japan, standing at the beginning of the 1980s, the time has come to meet the demands of culture and spirit. This means "implanting" in the folk the superiority of specific cultural values. Yet on closer inspection, it becomes apparent that the values this program seeks to instill are derived from a "managerial" experience which now promises to displace, if not eliminate outright, the possibility of social surplus, manifest in mass democracy and its necessary valorization of human rights. The managerial dimension is, in fact, masked by appealing to a revitalization of values associated with the older quest to salvage a traditional way of life.

At the first meeting of the group selected to envisage the new "age of culture" (April 1979), Prime Minister Ōhira proposed that "thirty years after the war, Japan has pursued the goal of economic abundance and pushed on ceaselessly without looking aside. We have reaped remarkable results. As for these results, especially in the century since the Meiji, they represent the great essence of modernization and industrialization advanced by the model of several European countries."[15]

Moreover, the resulting "unprecedented freedom and abundance have stimulated reflection on the important side of human character, which had been lost sight of under the regime of industrialization and modern rationalism." When people turned to the pursuit of a "restoration [kaifuku] of warm human relationships in the family, workplace, and local regions," they would see that "material civilization based on modern rationalism had reached its saturation point [hōwaten], and the time had arrived to transcend the modern [industrialization] to an age that stresses culture."[16] Writing from this perspective, Ōhira's brain trust stated that, in an age that demanded "modernization" and "economic growth," the objective and model were provided by the West, which "disregarded our traditional culture and fixed for us progress and standards and goals pursued by others." In the new age devoted to culture, the text intoned, the requirement would be the installation of a genuinely "comprehensive Japanese culture." But in order to confront the end of modernization and overcome the modern, it was necessary to systematically assess anew the "special quality of Japan's culture."

What counted as the special quality of Japan's culture was reflected in the determined opposition to a structure which "contrasted sharp distinctions between two things," such as those between God and Satan, a winner and loser, white and black in European and American cultures. Resembling the child's game of scissors, rock, and paper, Japanese culture has always been characterized by the avoidance of binary oppositions, thereby emphasizing the model of a three-legged contest or the structure of a circle "where none are superior and there are no absolute winners or losers."[17] As a result of this tradition, Japanese have rejected both a totalistic holism (zentaishugi) which disregards the individual and an extreme individualism that promotes the "self differentiated from the other" (tasha), found throughout European and American societies. This contrast demonstrates Japan's "cultural particularity," which has been described as a relationalism (aidagarashugi) that privileges the relationship between human and human, between part and whole, as expressed in words like ningen, "between people," nakama, "within relationships," and seken, "within society." Japanese, therefore, emphasize the importance of essence (ki) embedded in human relationships and subsequently stress the centrality of one's participation in a larger complex—*bun*, as found in terms like *kibun, jibun, hombun, mibun, shokubun*, etc. Discerning the quality of *bun* requires exhausting oneself in it and is thus linked to *en*, "binding ties," as represented in the following relationships: *ketsuen, chien, gakuen,* and *shaen*.[18] All signify the characteristic of the "*nakama* society" or the "*ie* society," a social constellation held together by fundamental and culturally irreducible relationships that determine how one is to behave with reference to others within the confines of Japanese society.

When Japan is compared with either the holism or the individualism of the Western world, the special features of this relational social order are even more apparent. This form of social imaginary, the text implies, has remained unchanged since the Stone Age, despite historical upheavals, and constitutes Japan's claim to exceptionalism. Since it was now believed that the Japanese had already reached a high level of technological and industrial achievement, the "citizenry should no longer make the modern its goal." Instead, they must define their objectives through the mediation of a more precise opposition between the "Western thing" and the "Japanese thing."[19] It should be stressed that where the earlier prewar discussion had forcefully tried to reify tradition in an effort to counter the onslaught of the modern, the new postmodern inflection changed the terms of discourse entirely and thereby undermined the whole critical program which had informed it. While the invocation to overcome the modern summoned powerful associations of an earlier antimodernism, its presumed connection with the later *bunka no jidai* vision was, at best, spurious, since the earlier discourse aimed principally at contesting the imperial claims of Western epistemology, while its "successor" has been unfailingly associated with it. At their most intense moments, the earlier discussions produced a critique which called into question a rational, instrumental knowledge and its differentiation into spheres of specialization as a condition for social and historical progress. If prewar thinkers agreed on nothing else, they nonetheless shared a profound distrust of politically rational forms, represented by and in the bureaucratic state and its corresponding conception of a civil society. To be sure, the associations evoked by the new age of culture immediately suggest their genealogical descent from this prewar discourse. Yet it is the purpose of the postmodern ideology to secure this effect of an uninterrupted and seamless process. The ideology inscribed in the call for a new age of culture seeks its authority in a science of society, which derives its authority from the earlier reconstruction of social theory before the war. Any effort to unpack the genealogy of the postmodern would reveal the origins of the present more clearly in the period and experience, rather than in the 1930s, and the resemblance of its own narrative to little more than a pastiche, rather than an uninterrupted "history."

The "scientific" authority of the postmodern ideology derived from social sciences developed in the postwar period, which matured in the texts of Nakane

Chie, Doi Takeo, Kumon Shumpei, and Murakami Yasusuke, notably in *Bummei to shite no ie shakai* and other texts that successfully eliminated historicity as a condition for eliding and conflating disparate elements into essence. According to Murakami et al., for example, a continuity of essences linked the prewar concerns for traditional social relationships to their postwar retention as a primary principle of social organization. But they also recognized that the prewar effort to retain the principles of a "household society" was compromised by a "trial-and-error process aimed at synthesizing differing principles of European and Japanese society in order to industrialize."[20] The accomplishments of this "synthesis" escaped dismantling by war and defeat; instead, they were reinforced by this experience. In fact, the "revolution" sparked by the American Occupation and the transformations it introduced affected only the "outer layers of thought" and failed to alter the "basic patterns of people's behavior." The household (*ie*) and the view of the family state that prevailed before the war disclosed their "brittleness" precisely because they constituted an "adulteration" of the fundamental model of social relationships. Although the household—*ie*—was "dismantled," the *ie* society remained intact, and it even replaced the destructive features of the older social imaginary with a "functional, household-type corporate body." Even after the war and the vast changes implemented by the military occupation, Japanese society was able to resist the blandishments of "individualism" because it was constituted by a variety of "*ie*-type groups," such as enterprises, firms, household businesses, and religious organizations. However, this model of the social was less an enlargement of the household than a homology of the "peasant collective organized to press demands" (*ikki*) or the "village" (*mura*).[21] A typology of social patterns founded on the model of traditional peasant organization would operate functionally to contain the "new middle classes" (*chūkan, nakama*) once the economy and polity were reconstructed after the war. In this way, the values of an agrarian order have been made to serve the requirements of a postindustrial society.

While this "scientific" argument tried to instate a continuity in social relationships since the remote past (the period of "clan society"), according to its authors it was possible to concentrate on the status of the group *only* at the expense of effacing historical differences between prewar experiences and the principle of the new middle class, proposing that what survived was a "functional form" and not its adulterated content. This move required rereading the history of the prewar discussions so as to establish a shared identity between an antimodernism which, before the war, was fueled by "enlightened and progressive intellectuals" and epistemological colonialism and, after the war, was stimulated by "progressive intellectuals" bent on establishing a democratic society on the model advocated by the American Occupation. This is not to say that Murakami et al. did not see differences between earlier concerns for community and the postwar reestablishment of a household-type society. They readily acknowledged that the model of society before the war had suffered from "brittleness" and "adulteration" and was ultimately surpassed by a new pattern free from history and competent to organize the new middle class. Moreover, this new social arrangement guaranteed exemption from the very changes, the so-called age of conflict, which had led to the dissolution of the "family state" (*kazoku kokka*), although not to the dissolution of its "form." Once a *mura*-type state is put into place, according to Murakami, a pattern will be established that will not change, even after the attainment of "high economic growth." In the context of this surge for economic abundance, a new middle class will be formed according to (1) an equalization of the distribution of income, (2) homogenization of "life-forms," and (3) an advance of "mainstreamism" (*chūryūka*) at the level of life consciousness.[22] Writing in the late 1970s (the *Ie shakai . . .* book was published in 1979, at precisely the moment its authors were beginning to prepare the statement on the age of culture), Murakami et al. saw the attainment of moderately high levels of personal income and a corresponding increase in the standard of living—consumption—as conditions for imagining a new "middle' class," one in which opportunities, and capacities for fulfilling them, would level all the distinctions marking older forms of class division. The effect of homogenizing social and economic differences within the population, to create a broad or mass middle stratum managed by principles governing the household-type system, resembled Nakane Chie's earlier social-scientific analysis which showed how groups in Japan "formed on the basis of commonality of attribute" invariably possess a strong sense of exclusiveness founded on this commonality. It is important to note that this sense of leveling, made possible by organizing people according to the village collectivity, functioned only at the intermediate levels beneath the government, which, according to Murakami, is free from the "influence of the family state." It would not only produce a high rate of growth preceding the age of culture but also sustain this style of life against the corrosions of historical change. In short, the household-type society would secure the promise of similitude, now read as homogenization (a move made earlier by Nakane), against the spectacle of difference—history. Along the way, writers like Nakane and Murakami have also noted how other groups in Japanese society have conformed to this typology of interaction and concluded that when, say, the family is compared with its counterpart in Western industrial societies, it reveals a far greater degree of social solidarity than that found in "individualistic Western societies."

This vision of the social order was presented as a natural necessity mirrored in Japan's history. Even though history was extensively emphasized to enhance the argument for the endurance of the *ie* society, nothing seems to have changed very much since the *uji* period of Japan's prehistory. Yet this discounting of historical change, denying history as the site of genuine difference, prefigured the assertion that, once the modern has been surpassed, the age of culture and the new middle class will finally realize their exemption from the uncertainties of change and the caprice of history. This reworking of what Hegel elsewhere had called a "historyless history," firmly at the heart of Japanese social science, promised to relieve the present from the determinations of the past and the unpredictability of the future. By the same measure, it authorized the state ideologues to separate themselves from the discourses of the prewar period, even as they claimed genealogical kinship with them. They must do so as a condition for producing their own "scientific" discourse and for revealing this genealogical "past" as merely ideological, or, as they described it, "adulterated," "trial and error," and "brittle." What this science managed to project as "natural" to the Japanese was a vision of a society in which, as Hamaguchi Eshun and Kumon Shumpei stated elsewhere, the "dynamics" of the "Japanese managerial system" are applied to the totality.[23]

By contrasting the Ōhira program to the wartime debate, we can conclude the following: (1) Whereas the earlier discourse seized upon the surviving traces of tradition as the condition for calling attention to an organic totality (*zentai*) that had always been in place since the beginning of the folk, the later, postmodern version transmuted these reified elements of fixed and enduring social relationships into functional prerequisites which authorized a "holonic path" (*zentaishi*) ever capable of harmonizing differences."[24] (2) Before the war, social theorists produced their critique in an atmosphere of urgency, fearful that the modernist transformation would soon eliminate the spiritual traces of an authentic life. But the planners of the new age of culture and the twenty-first century acknowledged that the thirty-five years from 1945 to 1980 were spent reconstructing a political infrastructure competent to augment high economic growth—as if to suggest that considerations of spirit (that is, culture) appear only after the folk have achieved "abundance." This means that, while the earlier discourse wanted to alter the order of priority, so as to situate culture at the head of the signifying chain for determining subsequent political and economic content, the postmodern state sees culture as merely a product of the chain of signification, determined by a technocratic bureaucracy devoted to rational and instrumental control. (3) Both the premodern discourse against modernity and the postmodern ideology sought to repair the split or lack of fit between the social and the political as a means of avoiding social surplus; however, the earlier discourse sought the solution in rethinking traditional structures, while the latter has made the business firm the model for the wider sociopolitical order. (4) Despite the extravagant claims for a new age of culture and spirit, the new program differs dramatically from the expectations of the earlier discourse precisely in its thorough commitment to materialism and commodification, which the prewar debaters would have rejected *tout court*. It should be recalled that one of the purposes of the earlier discussion was to prevent the contamination of the spirit of creativity—culture—by the materialism of the commodity fetish, which the United States and its shallow sense of culture signified. In the new age of culture, scarcity of goods will have been eliminated and abundance will serve as the bond for reinforcing forms of "Japanese-like" social relationships between human and human, in order to secure the promise of a unified and homogeneous community.[25] (5) The new cultural age juxtaposes the "Japanese thing" (*Nihontekina mono*), rather than "tradition," against the image of modern Western society. Although the pre-war symposium was concerned with the aporia between tradition and moder-nity and was fearful of the eradication of the former by the latter, the debaters were still willing to risk the realization that these modes of social existence con-stituted moments in an ongoing history that characterized all societies, not simply Japan and the West. Still, the new representation appeals to the ethos of an exceptional culture (identical with "nature") in order to explain the irreduc-ible and unique source of Japan's status as a world "industrial power" and a global "economic giant." And no doubt it dispels older associations which had yoked modernity and progress to the West and tradition and stagnation to Japan. Yet clearly the new representation no longer conforms to the simple opposition between traditional and modern, seen as moments in an evolution-ary narrative. Rather, it reveals the operation of a newer division between what the *Bunka no jidai* text describes as the "Japanized view" and the "Western-ized view," now facing each other as absolutes standing outside history, account-able only to an unchanging "nature" (read as culture) and "race."

* * *

After the so-called conquest of the modern, the Ōhira government's proclama-tion of a new age of culture disclosed the formation of a new discourse, whose ideological implications, concealed and invisible, differ vastly from the puta-tive antimodernism of the wartime debate and from Takeuchi's recommenda-tion to make Asia itself a method for the modernist transformation. In the case of the debate and Takeuchi's subsequent gloss, the question did not relate so much to whether Japan ought to be modern or not, since it was already a mod-ern society according to Kobayashi Hideo; rather, the issue was the appropri-ateness of the modern West as a model for Japan and, indeed, for the rest of Asia. If the debaters were blinded by the necessity to make sense of a war which they quickly misrecognized as a struggle to rid Japan of the baneful effects of psychological and epistemological colonialism, so that it might lead Asia to a new order under Japanese tutelage, Takeuchi was able to separate this identifi-cation of an Asian war of liberation from the modernist critique in order to reapprehend the status of both in the postwar period. Unlike the debaters, Takeuchi made no effort to suppress his antipathy for the prewar and postwar states, and he linked this criticism to his general renunciation of the Western

model both had recklessly adopted. He believed that such an assault on the postwar political order was necessary, since it was beginning to show signs of
reproducing the discredited past with even greater intensity. Takeuchi never
lived to see the polity promoted by the Ōhira government, nor even to imagine
the rush among responsible intellectuals to "scientize" reified conceptions of
the totality, renamed by people like Nakamura Yūjiro as *sensus communis*. Yet
he was still certain that unless Japan was able to find a ground outside its recent
historical experience of modernization, then the call to overcome the modern
would signal the completion of a process which he and others before him had
sought to arrest and redirect from the imperial claims of identity to the place
of radical difference. Whereas the war defeated the aspirations of the *kindai no
chōkoku* symposium, the "second chance" envisaged by Takeuchi met a similar fate in the period of "high economic growth."

In the vacated space, the new age of culture declares a kinship with an imagined past from which it derives authority and a separation from a history of
cultural mistakes. This is no familiar dialectic, which, in its movement, ceaselessly incorporates moments of its past as it supersedes them in the itinerary
toward the end of history. It is, instead, a truncated version and cynical closure
which proclaims the end of the historical with the "conquest of modernity"—
that is, the twilight of the Hegelian idol.

To this end, the program of the holonic society aims to eliminate the distance between the discourse on the social, marking both the prewar debate and
Takeuchi's rereading, and a social discourse—the practice of socialization—by
collapsing the former into the latter. Hence the new discourse conceals the distance between the representation and the "real," which consistently imperiled
the modernist ideologies of the *kindai no chōkoku* symposium and Takeuchi's
replay. At the same time, this discourse renounces all those efforts to "realize
the representation in the form of the totalization of the real," which has always
threatened totalitarian ideologies.[26] Its strategy constantly calls forth the "ruses
of the imaginary" in order to dismiss them; even though it is a process that
is both "unconscious" and "without history," it must still account for the
effects of knowledge and history by binding them into new configurations in
the service of tasks that are always the same. In Japan, and perhaps other
societies showing the symptoms of postmodernity, the "group" is fixed as a
"positive entity" and envisaged as both the expression and objective of social
communication; it operates effectively to obscure the apparatus of domination
from the masses, who are without power. The representation of the group—
the broad "middle stratum" to which all Japanese belong—as put forth by the
Ōhira brain trust and inscribed in countless articulations by serious social
thinkers, excludes from its domain the question of the "origin" (or takes it back
to a remote and mythic time too far removed from contemporary Japan) as
well as the "legitimacy and rationality of the oppositions and hierarchies" that

have been instituted in each sector and continue to exist. Seeking to elicit a belief in the "mastery" of the very experience of socialization which means being Japanese in the present, the new representation attempts to conceal itself as a representation and divert attention away from itself as discourse.

Employing advanced techniques of communication, the new discourse pretends to propagate information, to make the contemporary order into (what has been called) an "information society" (*jōhō shakai*); in this incessant communication of unwanted information, it does not take hold of the Other at a distance but uses information and the technology of communication to include its representatives within itself. In this way, the individual is situated in the group, an imaginary group (called "relationalism"—*aidagarashugi*), inasmuch as individuals are "deprived of the power to grasp the actual movement of the institution by taking part in it." If this new faith in social communication and group centeredness still leaves open the possibility of social division, even when attempts are made to disguise it as a "flaw in the dialogue between classes," the representation of social relationships is made unconscious for the express purpose of assuring both the facilitation of communication and "the implication of the subject in the group." The effect is expressed in the ready way people call attention to the identity of their group in the obligatory utterance "we Japanese," which seems to prefigure and preface all discourse between Japanese and the outside world. But, however efficacious the expression "we Japanese," it is invariably posterior to the conditions of a network already in place, in which the agents are linked together in a national subjectivity devoid of regional, class, or even gender distinctions, "by being deprived of any mark of their opposition to one another."

We have also seen that the new representation derives from the model of the organization of the firm, which is applied to the rest of the social formation; but it no longer tolerates a division between managers and those who carry out their orders. One need not recall the countless books and articles that have recently bombarded us, which testify to something called the "Japanese style of managerialism," with their "inspiring" accounts of quality-control sessions, the cooperation of managerial-worker teams, heroic self-sacrifice, stirring examples of the boss rolling up his shirt sleeves to pitch in with his workers, etc., to accept this picture of an arrangement which has effectively eliminated the division between labor, management, and the mode of production, linking them together within a structure capable of functioning on its own, nationally and independently of human choice and desire: the model for robotics.

With this in view, we can see how, in the Ōhira vision, supplemented by numerous social-scientific and cultural texts, the organization constitutes the reference of the real, a representation that is disseminated throughout the whole of society. According to Claude Lefort, "the incantation of social communication is complemented by an incantation of information."[27] Experts abound everywhere, he says, dispensing the truth of everything, since everything can be said. But this proliferation of information, deemed necessary for carrying on daily life in contemporary Japan, marks the indeterminacy of knowledge and places a high valuation on perpetual novelty, the newness of the new, the latest and most recent bit of knowledge: this is the sign that is mobilized everywhere these days, in order to stave off the threat of the historical. Which brings us back to Baudrillard and the role of consumption: if consumption is generated not by locating a need whose origins lie in an individual or group but by representing a "system of objects" which stands in place of the social as an illusion, the resulting simulation is an effort to present the historical again by making change invisible and promoting the new. What is consumed is always new and everything is within the means of everybody, whatever one's capacity to pay for it. Every dream is marketable and directed toward everyone in society, not merely the few, thereby effacing the difference between one consuming subject and another, since they are made to appear to belong to a common world populated by objects which they must consume. Only the signs of human beings—the "system of objects"—are perceived. But to employ communication and organization in order to stimulate consumption means that ideology has completed its task, by making invisible the "great closure,"[28] since it no longer needs to make statements about the nature of man or society as the condition for a discourse on the social.

Notes

1. Claude Lefort, *The Political Forms of Modern Society*, ed. John B. Thompson (Cambridge, Mass.: MIT Press, 1986), 215; see also Ernesto Laclau and Chantal Mouffe, *Hegemony and Socialist Strategy* (London: Verso, 1985), 93–148, for a brilliant critique of the "positivity of the social."
2. Lefort, *Political Forms*, 216.
3. Jean Baudrillard, *Simulations*, trans. Paul Foss, Paul Patton, and Philip Beitchman (New York: Semiotext(e), 1983), 1–2.
4. Kawakami Tetsutarō and Takeuchi Yoshimi, eds., *Kindai no chōkoku* (Tokyo: Fuzambō, 1979), 166.
5. Kawakami and Takeuchi, *Kindai no chōkoku*, 219–20, 222, 226.
6. Kawakami and Takeuchi, *Kindai no chōkoku*, 219.
7. Kawakami and Takeuchi, *Kindai no chōkoku*, 107, 239.
8. Kawakami and Takeuchi, *Kindai no chōkoku*, 275.
9. Kawakami and Takeuchi, *Kindai no chōkoku*, 290.
10. Kawakami and Takeuchi, *Kindai no chōkoku*, 290.
11. Kawakami and Takeuchi, *Kindai no chōkoku*, 338.
12. Kawakami and Takeuchi, *Kindai no chōkoku*, 338.
13. Kawakami and Takeuchi, *Kindai no chōkoku*, 339
14. Kawakami and Takeuchi, *Kindai no chōkoku*, 284.
15. "Ōhira sōri no seisaku kenkyūkai hōkokusho," in *Bunka no jidai no keizai un'ei* (Tokyo: Ōkurashō insatsukyoku, 1980), 21.

16. "Ōhira sōri no seisaku."
17. "Ōhira sōri no seisaku," 4.
18. "Ōhira sōri no seisaku," 4–5.
19. See Kawamura Nozomu, *Nihon bunkaron no shūhen* (Tokyo: Ningen no kagakusha, 1980), 147–48, for a perceptive discussion of this juxtaposition of the "Japanese thing" and the "Western thing." See also "Ōhira sōri no seisaku," 16.
20. Murakami Yasusuke, Kumon Shumpei, and Satō Seizaburō, *Bummei to shite no ie shakai* (Tokyo: Chūō kōronsha, 1979), 466.
21. Kawamura, *Nihon bunkaron*, 259–62; Murakami et al., *Bummei to shite*, 473–78.
22. Kawamura, *Nihon bunkaron*, 259.
23. Hamaguchi Eshun and Kumon Shumpei, *Nihonteki shūdanshugi* (Tokyo: Yūhikaku, 1982). This is, in fact, the central argument of this ideological tract, masquerading as "managerial science."
24. "Ōhira sōri no seisaku," 12–15, 104.
25. Actually, this achievement of a unified and homogeneous community, expectantly announced by proponents of cultural exceptionalism (*Nihonjinron*) and secured by following the so-called holonic path, signifies the accomplished existence of a unified national subjectivity everywhere in Japanese society. While such a goal is still incomplete, there is good reason to believe that the publicly instituted tendency of the state to secure the promise of uniformity and homogeneity—by reminding both Japanese and foreigners of the uniqueness of such irreducible values as consensus and group centeredness—is very much the point of all those "scientific" declarations, which attest to the primacy of the *ie* throughout Japan's history. Needless to say, the *ie* permits the constitution of an "imaginary Japanese" in discourse and thereby eliminates any explicit connection with the usual divisions, such as class, gender, and regional affiliation, to gain forceful representation in the ideal of a "mass middle stratum." The idea of an "imaginary Japanese" is suggested in Michael Bommes and Patrick Wright, "'Charms of Residence': The Public and the Past," in *Making Histories: Studies in History-Writing and Politics*, ed. Richard Johnson et al. (Minneapolis: University of Minnesota Press, 1982), 264–69. On "group as subject" and the requirements of the *ie*-centered society, see Murakami et al., *Bummei to shite*, 257–58.
26. Lefort, *Political Forms*, 225–29.
27. Lefort, *Political Forms*, 233.
28. Lefort, *Political Forms*, 235.

CHAPTER 12

THE PRESENCE OF ARCHAISM/THE PERSISTENCE OF FASCISM

Thus, "nationhood" drives time, indeed history out of history: it is space and organic fate, nothing else; it is that 'true collective' whose underground elements are supposed to swallow the uncomfortable class struggle of the present as totally superficial and ephemeral.

Ernst Bloch, *Heritage of Our Times*

"The Reckoning with Time"

It is instructive to note that the successful return of Abe Shinzō to Japan's prime ministry has been heralded as a return of conservative leadership and values and the prospect of ultranationalist patriotism to provide the country with new direction in the form of radical "regime change." Some observers have even seen the surfacing of the shadow of fascism after a long putative democratic dormancy. Since the conservative control of the Liberal Democratic Party (LDP) has lasted for over half a century, with brief interruption, the question is raised why Abe's reappearance now is seen as different from the politics over which the party has presided since the days of the military occupation. While his return has been accompanied by bold declarations of forthcoming new policy shifts directed to the domestic economy and a more aggressive foreign policy, these rhetorical announcements constitute no dramatic swing or departure from the LDP's political line since the 1960s, even though they gesture toward more reactionary political enactments. Such moves now appear as necessarily immanent as Japan's relations with the United States become less steady, implying that the country can no longer rely on its client status in the American imperium and must make its way in the world. (But this also represents no real change from the past and works to mask American support of a more aggressive line toward the People's Republic of China [PRC].) As its relations with the PRC deteriorate, there appears the need for greater strengthening of the country's independent military capacity, which reinforces Abe's obsessive desire to eliminate the constitution's peace clause (Article 9), if not embark on full constitutional revision that conceivably will recall the content of the older, discounted Meiji Constitution. In any case, the rejoicing among the political class was occasioned less by his return signaling the reinstatement of conservative values, which never went away and the prospect of a remilitarized Japan that has been on its way for decades, than by the reappearance of a form of fascism, which promises to fortify the nation's independence through the implementation of the authority of greater moral discipline among the populace and increased military expansion. To authenticate this directional turn, Abe, in his public performance, has abandoned a traditional pacifism for militancy, especially in declarations vowing retribution for the beheading of Japanese hostages by the Islamic State.

Despite Abe's decision to tighten control of political society in ways that are beginning to recall for us the more familiar profile of prewar fascism and its collusion with liberalism and dedication to saving capitalism from itself, the prewar conjuncture that saw the rise of fascism as a global political phenomenon was not only concerned with rescuing a frayed liberalism and its role in preventing capitalism's world crisis. It was also fixed on the peril posed by international communism. This was as true of Japan in the 1930s (as manifest in the "undeclared" war with the Soviet Union in Manchuria in the late 1930s) as it was of the capitalist bastions of western Europe and the United States. Japan is a principal participant in the contemporary global conjuncture, in spite of a long postwar parenthesis that has allowed the country to play a recessive role because of its client-state status in the American imperium. Yet we must also acknowledge that it differs in decisive aspects from its prewar predecessor (the older threat of international communism has passed and nation-centered liberalism transmuted into global neoliberalism and an even more expansively savage form of capitalist capture), but the relationship between capital and fascism never disappeared and has once more begun to appear in a new historical register housing familiar political discourses, practices, and movements to form a silhouette of repetition of an earlier time yet with a difference. Whatever else is driving Abe's politics toward a reunion with forms of Japan's prewar fascism, it is also an index of the force of a contemporary conjuncture that has announced a return of organic nationalism in a number of societies, the mobilization of mass movements often described as populist (less so in Japan, given the population's traditional unpoliticality), and wide-scale assault against neoliberal policies that have been dominated by unrestrained financialization, privatization of services, nationwide austerity, and galloping social inequality. Japan, I would propose, is part of a growing "landscape that now includes France, the Netherlands, Austria, Sweden, Denmark, Finland, Germany, U.K.," and the United States, with less-developed states like Turkey, Hungary, Poland, and Romania trailing close behind.[1] The initial impulse in western Europe—within European Union members—has been the massive influx of immigrants from Africa and the Middle East and a growing resistance to the difference (especially religious and cultural) they represent, the dangers of attacks by radical Islamist groups, and the tightfisted austerity policies that undermined Greece and threaten countries like Italy, Spain, and Portugal and growing unemployment among many of its states. In the United States, the triumph of Donald Trump behind a rightist movement denouncing neoliberal policies, loss of jobs, sluggish recovery since the collapse of 2008, and the flow of immigrants from Mexico and Central America has been accompanied by promises to withdraw the United States from policing the world to tend to its own domestic needs (a new isolationism?) and the failing fortunes of its white middle-class and working-class populations it has won over by masking oligarchy for popular democracy, which has already begun to openly betray in vague outline a renewal of organic nationalism and its reliance on fascist political principles to maintain order and protect the people from outside enemies. Turkey under Recep Tayyip Erdogan has moved quickly away from a superficial democratic or republican idea down a road marked by neither the secularism of the Kemalist state, misrecognized as "freedom," nor democracy, a road that has veered quickly into nervous pronouncements of organic nationalism masquerading fascism in a new environment. Inaugurated by Mustafa Kemal before World War II as part of a capitalist modernization program, it has morphed into an outright dictatorship that has hysterically identified literally thousands as the enemy of the state, dispossessing and imprisoning them, along with closing down the press and publishing houses. In the Erdogan state's renewed effort to constrain and contain its Kurdish population, resulting in massive deaths in response to political demands for independence, we can detect the familiar face of earlier genocidal murders of other ethnic minorities like Armenians, Greeks, and Assyro-Chaldeans in Anatolia for the same reasons. Erdogan has also displayed an ambiguous history in Turkey's dealings with the Islamic State, and it is unimaginable to think what is happening to the Syrian refugees interred in concentration camps in Turkey that Europe paid to have deposited. Japan shares some similarity with Erdogan's descent into the formation of a fascist political imaginary in its attempt to curb criticism through forms of coercion and ostracism bordering on violence, constraining teachers and punishing "offenders" daily to comply and conform and by multiple ways to remove the presence of difference in Japanese society, as represented by a long-resident Korean population now under daily attack in the internet and their neighborhoods. In contemporary Japan forms of political criticism, especially of the imperial court, regularly invite the present danger of threat, intimidations, and violence. What Turkey and Japan share is a tradition of distrusting racial difference that inevitably has led to violent forms of elimination. There are some who have named this present conjunctural direction as "antisystematic movements" that purposely avoids the identification with fascism, which, they believe, has safely passed away with the past in which it originated. Yet this allergic avoidance ignores the relationship of capital to fascism, which constitutes a part of its DNA structure and may remain dormant under certain circumstances but never fully disappears, unless capitalism itself vanishes. What this avoidance overlooks is in fact the nature of political violence that invariably accompanies the implementation and realization of these efforts to remove the specter of difference and resolve economic failure by addressing what is defined as a state of emergency to maintain civil order and protect the population from its enemies. Moreover, the political impulse promoting some form of imperishable national identity obliges the act of drawing upon deeply rooted nativist cultural roots to provide specific and familiar expressivity resulting in the production of multiple fascisms rather than a singular fascism. In the case of Japan, this reliance on a deeply rooted nativist sociocultural and political endowment was occupied by emperor and imperial institution and the recurring historical imperative of restorationism. While it is not possible here to account for the diversity of these emerging movements and their specific forms of expression they all share a common ground of revolt and withdrawal, which call to mind the still audible echoes of the prewar conjuncture. We must, in any case, situate contemporary Japan in the broader conjuncture, despite the locally specific ways it has chosen to express this global force.

In the second prime ministry of Abe Shinzō, there has thus appeared a rather sudden resurgence of radical conservativism bordering on recalling the forms of prewar fascism and a concerted state effort to remove all difference with breathtaking speed by demanding from the general population sacrifice, conformity, and acquiescence. All of this has been carried out behind the insistent but veiling screen provided by the image of Japan as a democracy. Yet Japan still remains within the temporal eclipse cast by American hegemony established since the military occupation, which constituted the chronological category of the "postwar" Japanese still employ to name and often describe the parenthetic moment they believe they are inhabiting that has stretched out to become a permanent present imminent with the presents lived by others but signifying a different zone of time. As Ernst Bloch perceived of Germany in the early 1930s not all people live in the same now-time, but they do so only externally, inasmuch as they can be seen by others. But they are not yet living in the same temporality as others.[2] This peculiar relationship to other presents has resulted in an ambivalent attitude toward the world that has often periodically induced withdrawal from it, as if to underscore its untimely countenance of acting like a spectral revenant, empowered to reappear and disappear at unscheduled moments.

Hence, regardless of the great expectations announced by these contemporary shifts in Abe's Japan and how they are interpreted, the presence of fascism has always been inscribed in the country's political and social endowment since the end of the war. While continuous with what had existed in the 1930s that led the country to imperial war, utilizing similar elements, the fascism of the postwar is no simple repetition but one that more closely resembles a second coming since it occupied a dissimilar conjunctural formation. In many ways, this apparent return of fascism in a new face and different temporal register suggests both the adaptive resilience of the political form and its continuing identity with capital, its role as the ghost in the machine now reappearing to summon accession of the "principles of the imperial state" that had existed down to 1945 and the correctness of its conduct that had inaugurated an East Asian war aimed to liberate the societies of Asia from Euro-American colonialism and reconstitute them as new and independent states.[3] In this invocation of the prewar imperial state and what it stood for, Abe's Japan appears now to be on course to identifying a new set of legitimating principles to replace those provided by the United States. In Abe's thinking this points to virtual regime change and scrapping the postwar order.

Temporally, the country remained in the zone of a timeless postwar parenthesis that continued long after the Occupation ended; spatially Japan was early restituted as a client state within the expanding territoriality of the American imperium, whose presence is still manifest in the existence of some one hundred fifty military bases. The Japanese historian Shirai Satoshi has recently named this postwar temporal parenthesis as a period of "permanent war defeat" (*eizoku haisen*) and the dominant "*kokutai* [political body or structure] of the après war."[4] In this perspective, Abe's leadership is envisioned as a completion of the postwar state of permanent war defeat. But nothing is gained by renaming the postwar as the time of permanent war defeat, other than a capacity to finesse an earlier description that referred to the period as "embracing defeat."

What I am thus proposing is that Japan's persistent ambivalence toward the world is yoked to the identification of autonomy and independence with the untimely rhythms of a failed past. Here, there seems to be renewed efforts to reinstate what the Russian writer Svetlana Alexievich has named as "secondhand time" to indicate how in post-Soviet Russia there has been a significant groundswell of popular opinion calling for a return to the old days of Soviet

Russia and Stalin, a memory that is now recalled as superior to what is presently being experienced under Putin. By the same measure, the category of postwar in Japan, originally a chronological marker, has demonstrated the political capacity of time to give form to relationships of power and domination, as evidenced by Japan's effort to restore forms of political leadership and strategic components of the prewar political and social order sanctioned by its client and dependent status in the American empire. For the United States, and especially those who continue to valorize the Occupation's grandiose experiment, "postwar" was supposed to show that Japan had finally entered the time of a contemporaneity with other advanced industrial democracies. Some writers have proposed that Japan, after the war, was caught up in the gaze of the United States and incorporated into its hegemonic system to forfeit whatever claim to autonomy the country once possessed. In this way, "postwar" became a kind of no-time, a permanent present housing the dream fantasies of both archaists and modernizers to reconfigure.

If incorporation into the expanding American imperium offered both security (in the U.S.-Japan security pact that rendered Article 9 pointless) and the promise of rapid economic recovery, accelerated by America's war in Korea, subordination brought the benefit of forgetfulness and memory loss of the past immediately before the war, especially political fascism and capital's need for imperial expansion. The reason for national amnesia is undoubtedly related to more complex reasons like historically ingrained dispositions of unpoliticality among the population and other complex sources. But it also had something to do with surviving prewar participants in postwar Japan, especially politicians, bureaucrats, and intellectuals, who sought to remake their world through what might be called an act of historical repetition that would promise contemporary Japan the prospect of assimilating its historical antecedents and make a different past and its desire appear identical with the present. This reflex was powerfully reinforced by the Occupation's decision to continue the socioeconomic endowment that had been fixed since the Meiji era. With Japan, the steady slide into the temporality of a permanent postwar also seemed linked to a well-known process of self-victimization induced by a combination of convictions that blamed the military and prewar state for bringing about the war and the American decision to end it by devastating Hiroshima and Nagasaki with nuclear bombs. This explanation required assuming no responsibility for starting the war and spreading its depredations in Asia since it was the work of the state and the military. In this scenario, the destruction and deaths caused by the unprecedented employment of atomic weapons meant that the Japanese had suffered more than their Asian victims. Such a stand was also consistent with a position that had already absolved the emperor from war responsibility before the Tokyo War Crimes Tribunal, even to the extent that no reference to the emperor was permitted in subsequent testimony. It should be further noticed that echoes of this traumatic war's end experience vanished in the wake of the Fukushima earthquake and tsunami and the damage they inflicted on the area's inhabitants and its nuclear installations that the state had established beginning in the 1960s. Fukushima invalidated a long domestic antinuclear campaign and disclosed the state's incompetent response in relocating the thousands who had lost everything in the calamity and its ineffective program of cleaning up the affected region.

But the really consequential effect of the war and the time of the postwar was the silencing of the immediate past. Silencing a specific past worked to elevate the moment of defeat ending the war and inaugurating what came to be the permanent present of the postwar. Its "eventfulness," scaled to the status of the Holocaust itself, required only sustaining an act of mourning, according to some determined critics, and a continuation of the portrayal of self-victimization into an endless present without an apparent future, which will occur only when the grieving ends and the present is finally overcome to become past. But even in this formulation, the prewar past resonates in the noisy demands to overcome the present. In Abe's Japan, above all else, the drive is to make the present look like the past.

If Abe's return to power has sparked a yearning for fascism that immediately awakens memories of an earlier episode before the war and the prospect of a déjà vu, it would be wrong either to assimilate the contemporary impulse to its prewar predecessor or weight the present with a mimetic demand. Too often the content of a specific historic manifestation of fascism is mistaken for its form. Much of this false recognition stems from Hannah Arendt's Cold War book *The Origins of Totalitarianism* (1951), which sought to provide the emerging struggle with a genealogy of totalitarianism in which fascism simply represented the first stage in a continuing history of totalitarianism succeeded by communism, American social science, which pitted value-neutral science against ideological distortion and judged fascism as a category with no descriptive and analytic utility, and historical narratives like that produced by Germans like Ernst Nolte, who tried to freeze the content of fascism in its historical epoch to conclude that it had now passed into the past and would never return. To focus on fascism's form and its relationship to the continuing objective conditions of capitalism, as both Karl Polanyi and Theodor Adorno advised, releases it from the content of a fixed specific historical time and spatial register. Maintaining a separation of form from a specific content guaranteed the former's independence from and supremacy over the latter and thus the capability of producing history but whose future was not constrained by a singular and originating historical content. There is, as I have proposed, always the possibility of a more contemporary manifestation of a phenomenon constituting a repetition of an earlier experience. But while differing occurrences may utilize similar components, as the Japanese example shows, the appeal to a repetitive déjà vu reflects more about the present than the past it supposedly is imitating since the "false recognition" appears to supply the very circumstances that are being perceived in the current moment. "What can be more unavailing," Bergson once asked, "than the memory of the present?"[5] Such a rescued past is an illusion and its desire for mimesis a sign of the present's excessive memory of itself and the resignation that apparently set in to capture affect in the wake of the 3/11 catastrophe and the state's failure. The kind of repetition I have in mind sees it as a "condition of historical action" that drives actors to identify themselves with figures of the past. It is production, of the effort to produce something new "only on the condition that we repeat—once in the mode which constitutes the past, and once more in the present of metamorphosis." When it falls short and thereby fails to lead to metamorphosis and the production of something new "it forms a kind of involution, the opposite of creation." It becomes comic.[6]

Still, Abe's return to power inadvertently recalls for us an earlier episode of the political form before the war, and the present's mimetic desire for a similar eventfulness necessitates a renewed interest in its career in Japan. In fact, the principal question is the form of fascism, which manages to outlive and exceed specific historical contents, to reappear in new temporal registers under altered historical circumstances. Abe's comeback compels us to reflect on the example of a prior manifestation and thus identify the possible genealogy of components shared by the two moments. This specter of fascism thus demands envisaging the ways presents preserve a past that is either taken for granted and thus unacknowledged or possesses a presence that is misrecognized as absent.[7] Presence, in this regard, manifests itself in the sense of feeling or expression of symptoms "to account for the fact that the past, though irremediably gone, may feel more real than the world we inhabit."[8] This interest should not be construed as a conventional search for meaning. But because it resembles how custom works in the present by absenting or bracketing its past conditions of formation, it is able to disguise itself as eternal yet appear as the sign of the past in the present empowered to moving people to act according to prescribed behavior without their knowing and wondering why. It is for this reason that the past in the present is invariably dehistoricized in such a way as to ensure its identity with the present, even though its historicity remains unseen and unnoticed, like Poe's purloined letter, there in open visibility but unseen. That is to say, it is an "unrepresented way the past is present in the here and now."[9] In contemporary capitalist societies it is the unevenness of development, resulting from capitalism's aptitude to appropriate what is at hand for the pursuit of value, what Marx named as its fundamental rule—formal subsumption—and the capacity to make of every present formation a mixture of different and uneven historical moments that misrecognizes the contemporaneity immediately before it as temporally smooth and completed.

"The Cold Forgetting of Fascism"

Two principal events have converged to shield postwar Japan from confront-ing the political horrors committed in its recent past and paradoxically worked to actually rescue a sense of continuity with it by retrieving the form of its prin-cipal or dominant sociopolitical components. The first was the Cold War obsession to divide the globe into opposing ideological zones competing to win the unaligned to their respective ways of life by defeating the other: the United States' promotion of "democratic freedom," which meant the expansion of cap-italism and market accessibility promising to peacefully modernize societies, and the Soviet Marxist-Leninist offer pledged to represent the model of revo-lutionary transformation seeking to enlist societies for socialism. The second was the U.S. military occupation, which easily converged with the Cold War moment to ultimately pave the way for the restoration of prewar political com-ponents leading to the installation of an archaic presence in the form of neo-emperorism.

The American Cold War campaign projected an imaginary to new nations (recently liberated from colonialism) in the name of a value-free science to counter the apparent distortions of ideology, embodied in the Stalinist com-mitment to Marxism-Leninism, with the effect of reducing the struggle to diverse ideological claims representing truth and falsehood. In the United States during the 1950s social science had already discounted and ultimately pro-scribed ideology as a useful concept because of its propensity for distortion, announcing "the end of ideology." Yet the pronouncements of ideologically free scientific neutrality were hardly any more persuasive and invariably failed to conceal the economic and political interests propelling it. At the same time, there already was a tendency to reduce fascism and communism to their shared political kinship by identifying both with totalizing regimes. This proved to be an immensely favorite reflex in the postwar period, as evidenced by the lasting success and popularity of Arendt's epochal study *The Origins of Totalitarian-ism*, issued soon after the inauguration of the Cold War. Arendt's book sought to provide substantive authority to the American claim of scientific neutrality and its critique of ideology by seeking to demonstrate how fascism (German and Italian) and communism were devoted to implementing state violence on a genocidal scale. In this regard, Arendt had no trouble in coupling Hitler and Stalin and drew especially from the experience of Germany (ignoring Japan altogether) to dramatize fascism's goal to realize total reorganization and polit-ical integration. In her perspective, Soviet Russia personified the communist analogue to fascism as the postwar's representative of totalitarianism. But what Arendt dropped from her new equation of totalitarianism (apart from Japan's own genocidal impulse in Asia, brutalization of prisoners of war, and coercion of Korean and other Asian women into sex slavery) was the role played by vitalism in the 1930s and its contribution to fascism. Here again, she gave Japan a pass. (One marvels at Arendt's complete indifference outside Euro-America, excepting her discussion of South African racism and the origins of bureaucracy as quintessential Eurocentrism at a time when new nations in Asia and Africa were appearing daily to virtually change the global map.) But Japan, like Germany and other European societies, experienced its moment of vitalist thinking in the late 1920s, which, combining with the destructive force of new technologies, responded to the threat posed by the excess of mass culture and politics by attempting to prevent the descent into chaos and overcome the meaninglessness of everyday life that ultimately laid the groundwork for the articulation of fascism and its vocation for violence. In its full fury, vitalism signified the end of civilization and culture and was joined at the hip with the desire of totalism to perpetuate the loss of freedom in self-estrangement and unreality. But it is important to recognize that vitalism, as such, and totalitarianism in the 1930s were seen as opposing forces, just as fascism and communism were separated by political and economic differences. The effects of this strange collusion of vitalism and totalism in Japan was imprinted in calls for overcoming the modern, Kyoto school philosophy's formulation of Japan's world-historical mission and the "philosophy of total war." The move to link socialism, even the Stalinist inflection of a corrupted and distorted Marxism, to cultural nihilism and a frenzied Spenglerian civilizational dance of death worked more to reinforce the Cold War conjuncture than to account for the actual historical differences that divided fascism and communism before the war. Arendt's eagerness to reduce fascism and communism to a shared totalitarianism also overlooked the obvious fact that fascism was dedicated to saving capitalism from itself, ridding it of its conflict-producing divisions, whereas communism was opposed to it. Arendt's alternative was to return to the scene of the prewar conjuncture and rescue a discredited liberal democracy that had already failed to prevent capitalism from succumbing to its own propensity for generating periodic crises. Her subsequent reconfiguration made the Cold War into a struggle of the West and its civilization with a generic totalitarianism ironically centered in the East and as a continuation by other means of World War II's effort to dispose of one local version of authoritarianism before embarking upon the destruction of its avatar. There is more than a hint of congruence between this arrangement and Ernst Nolte's later explanations that Germany's principal aim in the war had been to prevent the spillover of the peril posed by the East. By the same measure, it would be wrong to underestimate the role played by anticommunist sentiment in Japan as an explanation for military aggression in Northeast Asia.

In the scholarly literature, this powerful intervention—the Arendt effect—encouraged the widespread practice of envisaging fascism as a variant of

Marxism, an offshoot sharing common properties and often similar political, economic, and social emblems, ideas, and aims. The result of this twining was to remove fascism from the contemporary scene, sweeping it under the carpet of communism and constraining it to its historical epoch, closing off its future occurrence, what the reactionary historian Nolte called "the epoch of fascism," signaling its final passage to an irretrievably irrevocable past. Safely removed from the future, social theory turned toward a form of programmatic development and the possibilities of capitalist modernizing makeovers that facilitated the effacement of fascism from the screen of contemporary consciousness. This program was carried out by substituting the category of modernity, symptomizing scientific rationality for capitalist accumulation, even though the means of reaching modernity were reducible to realizing a capitalist social structure. Former fascist countries like Japan, Italy, Germany had a decisive developmental advantage since they were already committed to capitalist modernization, and Japan, especially, was easily made to exemplify a model of imitation among new nations of the decolonizing world.

It is not surprising that in the impulse to present dramatic empirical evidence attesting to the success of peaceable modernizing makeovers Japan stood out as a classic textbook model, even though a great effort had to be made to minimize the political violence involved in the country's revolutionary transformation and to renarrativize and explain away the subsequent adventure with fascism and imperialism as a momentary aberration or departure from the proper liberal democratic course. This attempt actually began with the American occupation's experiments with reforming Japanese society and was later taken over by scholars and social scientists, many of whom had officially participated in the Occupation. Moreover, it was in the formation of modernization theory that democracy was identified with market capitalism as a natural relationship, when before the war the contradiction of equality and inequality made them incompatible.

If the collapse of the Berlin Wall paved the way for reintroducing all those memories buried in what had been designated to forgetfulness in the political and cultural unconscious, the surfacing of fascism demonstrated it never really went away. Even before the Cold War ended, there were audible voices willing to confront the specters of fascism and express its dangers as a living reminder that its occurrence could easily recur in any present. In the 1970s the Italian writer Primo Levi had no trouble in consistently declaring that every age could expect the return of fascism in newer and different forms, what he named as the "silent Nazi diaspora," which could encourage nostalgia for a world in which order supposedly prevailed once that presumption leads back to all those devices employed to maintain the illusory fear of disorder. His renaming of fascism said it all: fascism, as a silent Nazi diaspora, appeared unannounced and unacknowledged and empowered travel and dispersion beyond its original homeland. Years before (1959), Levi's contemporary the philosopher Theodor Adorno revisited the terrain of fascism to recall for his present that the "past one would like to evade is still very much alive." Adorno was persuaded that "fascism lives on, that the oft-invoked working through of the past has to this day been unsuccessful and has degenerated into its own caricature, an empty and cold forgetting . . . due to the fact that the objective conditions of society that engendered fascism continue to exist." Cautioning contemporaries that fascism cannot be derived from subjective dispositions, implying that both state and collective ethnic claims to subjective status constituted an effect, Adorno proposed that the "economic order, and to a great extent also the economic organization modeled upon it, now as then renders the majority of people dependent upon conditions beyond their control and thus maintains them in a state of political immaturity." Adorno was neither convinced that democracy had yet been "naturalized to the point where people see themselves as subjects of a political process" nor confident that they would reach that level anytime in the near future. It was simply one among a number of items on a menu offering political choice. People are not identified with democracy, nor was it a sign of their political maturity. Instead it was nothing more than an instrument of special interest to which people "submit to given conditions" that force them to "negate precisely the autonomous subjectivity to which the idea of democracy appeals."[10] Adorno's reflections on the failure of democracy and the central importance of "objective" conditions to any understanding of fascism echoed observations made a generation earlier by Karl Polanyi, who, in 1935, had pronounced on fascism's desire to erect a society founded not on the "conscious relationships of persons" but rather on the conviction to "transform and structure" them in such ways as to extinguish the development "towards" socialism.[11] What Polanyi unveiled in his overlooked analysis of fascism made on location was the continental historical experience that democracy inevitably led to socialism and how this economic outcome necessitated the elimination of the former before its transubstantiation into the latter. Fascist anti-individualism thus derived from a rationale rooted in the belief that capitalism and democracy were incompatible, parading as the liberal fantasy of an unregulated market capitalism that he dissected in *The Great Transformation* (1944), which showed how liberalism morphed into its neoliberal successor, even though it was not named as such. Fascism was committed not merely to destroying democracy (and thus the inevitable prospect of socialism) but also to establishing a new social order rid of the possibility of its return. He saw, at roughly the same time as both Tosaka Jun in Japan and Herbert Marcuse in Germany, how liberalism was linked to fascism, inasmuch as fascism envisioned its task to prevent interference in the price system and thus diminished the sum total of goods produced as promoted by both communism and democracy. Hence, "fascism is condoned as a safeguard of liberal economies through the elimination of a democratic political sphere and the subsequent reorganization of economic life"—market capitalism—on the template of different branches of industry to become the "whole of society." It is for this reason that fascism appeared everywhere under the banner of solving the crisis of capitalism by calling into question the utility of all forms of political representation and demanding, in many instances, a moratorium on them. To this end, it promised the installation of an arrangement of authority that would conform to the template of economic life—by superimposing on it the figure of a natural, organic, ethnic community.[12]

In this way, fascism channeled its energy into expunging the social from the social formation by removing economic life of all impurities that had created conflict, like class division and racial heterogeneity and even considerations of gender differences, that had impaired its full development. But the principal condition of this putative communitarian condition, which Slavoj Žižek called *Gemeinschaft* capitalism, required the extinguishing of all traces of subjective autonomy underlying the claims of individualism and its replacement by the restoration of a timeless natural order repetitiously enacting the everyday life lived by the folk that was said to have been lost to history and the now of the present. This was precisely the world signaled by the militant right-wing radicals in the 1930s who demanded a Shōwa restoration symbolized by the return of direct imperial authority. If in the postwar direct imperial political authority could no longer be summoned, the figure of the emperor and associations of an archaic presence empowering him as the embodiment of both political and social communities into a single unified identity still remained available as an archetypal template on which to structure the social formation that would inevitably trump the division of state and civil society.

It should be recognized that in Japan's postwar Marxism sought to keep alive the question of fascism and the dangers it continued to pose. The economist Uno Kōzō wrote in the late 1940s that he feared a revival of fascism because of the peculiar historical evolution of capitalism in Japan, which had retained feudal villages, instead of undergoing the dire consequences of enclosure releasing large numbers of the populace from their means of subsistence. This policy kept peasants in the villages and farms and continually connected to their means of subsistence, long enough to accommodate the development of industry and the growth of a new labor force. Uno worried that even though the feudal system had been formally eliminated, feudal custom, behavior, and ways of thinking had been internalized, like a feudal unconscious, by a peasant population because of the retention of villages still persisted to represent a clear roadblock to the development of democracy. But others—namely, adherents of prewar Kōzaha Marxism—were not so farsighted. Their problem, as I will explain later, was an inability to shake loose from an unyielding attachment to a mode of analysis locked in prewar constraints and language that in the postwar they continued to embrace by misrecognizing its relevance in the changed political environment. It is striking how tenacious prewar expressive modes of meaning, which once, by necessity, had to be disguised to look neutral or at least politically uncharged to pass the attention of censorship, continued to exercise the Marxian imaginary as if nothing had happened or changed. Yet everything had changed: the Comintern had vanished and police oppression, for the time being, was on hold.

"The Emperor's Shadow in Daily Life"

The moment fascism began to pass into forgetfulness Japan was in process of being resituated in the solar eclipse cast by the emerging postwar American imperium.[13] Despite losing a vast territorial empire at war's end, baptized as the Greater East Asia Co-Prosperity Sphere, the new dispensation permitted Japan to secure what might be described as a surrogate empire, which also satisfied the well-known equation linking fascism to imperialism. Yet, as if to make a distinction between seen and unseen worlds, phenomenal and noumenal realms, and the primacy of the latter over the former, the retention of the emperor and panoply of the imperial institution (Kunaichō) entailed recognizing his status as custodian and him—in this case Hirohito—as the principal performer of rituals and ceremonies that thus included the invisible spiritual empire inhabited by the creation deities, spirits of heaven and earth, and imperial ancestors. In other words, the emperor was not only saved but was also able to continue grounding his authority in the supremacy of the invisible world of ancestors and deities over the visible world. While the affairs of the visible world would continue to be managed by an army of bureaucratic specialists, the affairs of the invisible world were imparted by the emperor's performance of archaic rituals and ceremonies, the interruption of the untimely in timefulness, increasingly accompanied by an expanding institutionalization of supporting Shinto associations and a swelling constituency of faithful adherents. In recent decades Shinto has moved from functioning as an agent of bereavement representing the families and relatives of the war dead to political activity yoking government and business to religious observances like attending controversial shrines, promoting the restoration of "spiritual values," and publicly expressing greater patriotic sentiment. I shall return to this subject later. The postwar's retention of the emperor in symbolic form was supposed to represent the transformation of an absolute, divinely appointed monarch into a petit bourgeois paterfamilias who was no different from anybody else, as Hirohito is made to say in a conversation with one of his court chamberlains in the opening frames of Aleksandr Sokurov's great film *The Sun*.[14] Sokurov believed that Hirohito's disavowal would establish the foundation for a genuine democratic order in Japan. But, as I will show, Hirohito's dedivinization could hardly produce the desired outcome because the imperial figure was endowed and empowered with even a greater force.

We are all, by now, familiar with narratives valorizing the American Occupation attempt to "democratize" Japan and the necessary Japanese talent for "embracing defeat." It is also common knowledge how this putative narrative was early divested of its democratizing vocation as the United States entered the Cold War and needed to identify a reliable ally in the Asia-Pacific region once the Chinese Nationalist regime collapsed in 1948. The earlier reforms were either abandoned or watered down in such ways as to diminish the chance for carrying out the establishment of a genuine social democracy. It is not even clear that the military occupation was really committed to realizing this grand democratic goal, given the easy turn away from punishment and reform. In its place, the Japanese were made to settle for its palest replica, emphasizing at most procedural forms that depended upon naming what was in place as democracy, inaugurating an American bad habit that has been followed to the present day that calls any client, whatever its politics, "democratic." What the Occupation was interested in is restoring Japanese capitalism and the political conditions that would enable its realization. The restoration of capitalism in the Cold War was far more important for the American military and the policies of subsequent Washington administrations, as well as the recently returned Japanese political classes, than realizing the requirements of political and social democracy. The Occupation narrative underscored the early importance of imposing a constitutional framework envisioned by foreigners in order to fill the vacated place of the discredited Meiji Constitution of the late nineteenth century. On the face of it, the contrast could not have seemed more dramatic: the new constitution conferred rights on the people rather than duties and vested sovereignty in a popular will instead of a divine emperor. But instead of ridding political society of the emperor and imperial institution, the new constitution recoded the emperor as the "symbol of the state and the unity of the Japanese people." The emperor was obliged to acknowledge his lack of divinity, which, paradoxically, simply reinforced the conviction that only a divinity can declare he or she is no longer a god. But more importantly, the new constitution transmuted what since the Meiji period had been a deliberately configured imperial institution into a ready-made designed, like national shrines, to serve the development of capitalism and now into an abstraction whose symbolic status meant that it could refer only to itself. Yet this effort to return to an archaic imperial institution while at the same time seeking to weaken it by removing its source of divine legitimacy created an ambiguity in national consciousness. The decision to spare Hirohito from the hangman's noose (on which both MacArthur and leading Japanese bureaucrats agreed) meant installing him back to a position he effectively occupied before the war as the principal custodian of all the rituals and ceremonies binding the monarch, the national deities, and ancestors to the people that constantly called attention to the primacy of an invisible realm or empire. The Japanese *tennō* was still called emperor, even though his earthly empire had shrunk and his reign was still the measure of imperial time, different from socially normative time. He presided over an unseen realm of gods, with whom he communicated through the exercise of a calendar of rituals capable of enlisting and cementing the people into a permanent solidary group provided by his mediation. This figure of an emperor was further reinforced by the military administration's decision to put Hirohito on the road for the population to see him in his new humanity, circulating throughout towns and villages of the nation in the immediate postwar years to buttress what American authorities believed was a new imperial status quo. But what the military administrators and MacArthur may have intended with this public relations campaign produced the unexpected effect of staging an ongoing national epiphany whereby the nation celebrated an emperor "who now appeared a victor after all."[15] What these tours managed to reaffirm was the status of emperor and imperial house rather than a monarchical representative of democracy.

In revisiting the retention of the emperor in postwar Japan, we must remember that since the Meiji period, when the institution and figure were reconfigured anew, it was the combination of its temporal anachrony and contemporaneity in every present that constituted the structure that bound the population to working and dying for the emperor, condensed in the period's slogan *fukoku kyōhei*. In the 1930s, the philosopher Tosaka Jun, constrained by state censorship proscribing any criticism of the emperor (and thus the state), named this relationship between archaism and anachrony as "animistic primitivism." What appeared so extraordinary about this refiguration and reinstallation of the emperor in the Meiji is that it represented a deliberate decision to resituate the noncontemporary or nonsimultaneous in the figure of a monarch, embodying a divine genealogy and thus presence that stretched down to the archaic depths of the mytho-history of origins, at the heart of a society committed to capitalist and technological transformation. Even more startling is the decision of the U.S. military occupation to retain this archaic figure and the domination of his presence in the reconstruction of Japanese capitalism, which meant recuperating and maintaining the historic contradiction marking the foundation of Japan's modern order. What resulted was not any contradiction but an absolute one that elicited the aura of authority integral to both the development of capitalism and the formation of its corresponding social structure: a divinely derived emperor who was still, according to the philosopher Tanabe Hajime, inside and outside history, despite Hirohito's strategic disavowal and putative symbolic status. Owing to the retention of sacred religiopolitical ceremonies over which the emperor still presided, the imperial figure was nonetheless filled with the reality of its imagery, and the symbolism recaptured what it supposedly

symbolized.[16] Because of his divinity he possessed the capacity to hold the contradiction between archaic residues and capitalist demands in a more or less
constant balance and relatively free from convulsions capable of tearing Japan's
social fabric. This aptitude was later (in the postwar) harnessed to Nishida
Kitarō's capacious concept of *mu* (nothingness) that would, in Tanabe's reckoning, mediate, bring together, and unify colliding opposites. Only the emperor,
owing to his divinity, was above the fray of conflict and could transcend it at
the same time he was also actively part of it at the human level. In Tanabe's
postwar reformulation, the emperor's divinity was replaced by nothingness
(*mu*), which he symbolized.[17] In this way, the emperor was still positioned,
especially after Hirohito's disavowal of divinity, to unify contradictions and
oppositions yet retain his distance from partisan entanglements. Beneath the
formation of this recent contradiction lay the crisis of the structure of the
communal system's (*kyōdōtai*) consciousness brought by the economic collapse
of the Tokugawa premodern village sparked by the appearance of capitalism
in the countryside. The structure of the ideology of the modern emperor system was an expression of the formative living consciousness of the crisis-ridden
premodern communal order incorporated within the imperial ideology. In
other words, the imperial system itself remained latent to and internally
implanted in the unconsciousness of the village (*mura*) and household.[18] In this
way, the implementation of a restoration of the emperor could never have been
an accident but rather a necessity. The Restoration sought to resolve the crisis
by superimposing the restored emperor who embodied the contradiction
between the archaic and new on top of the crisis of the communal order that
had already been undermined by the forces of capital in the countryside.

Absent but implied in Tanabe's formulation as the source of divine empowerment was the effect elicited by the emperor's inherent capacity to continually
summon the national deities and imperial ancestors through his enactment of
rituals and ceremonies. In these moments, the emperor communicates with his
divine ancestors and the national deities, beseeching them to confer good fortune on the country and protect it. The act of making the emperor a symbol of
the unity of the Japanese people and investing sovereignty in a referent that
never existed meant that the symbol referred back to only him the emperor,
whose power now was as great as all of nature; that is to say, returning from
the symbolic to he literal, "from the illusion to the reality of the illusion."[19] The
critic Yoshimoto Takaaki gave this expansive sense of imperial power in the
postwar a direction different from the route Tanabe had charted. For Yoshimoto the "masses [*taishū*] are affectively absorbed in the emperor system." They
pursue the moment to be politically swallowed up in the emperor system in a
"disposition or mentality that brings folkic expansion." (In Yoshimoto's reckoning, it made no difference whether the object one encounters is related to
humans or nature or toward the objects of life like labor; they still possess the

same form of approach and way of distancing as they would take toward the "false authority" called the emperor system.) The emperor system remains behind as a residue, another shadow in folkic mentality, latent, dormant, a remainder that constitutes a powerful uninterrupted undercurrent in folk life, paradoxically recalling Maruyama Masao's conceptualization of the *basso ostinato* in Japanese culture.[20]

Yet even in defeat, Hirohito was able to cash in on the charismatic and sacred authority associated with the throne, especially its allegedly divine origins and traditions he ritualistically performed. Some of these rituals derived from a distant archaic agrarian and mythic time and were routinely revitalized through the emperor's enactments of them as they and their framing of the antique agrarian order were constantly summoned in the present. Here, I believe, the unevenness constituted by situating the figure of the archaic at the heart of a modern industrial society must be juxtaposed to the observation that when Japanese are asked by foreigners whether they believe in all this imperial mummery the question is dismissed by responding that nobody takes it seriously. In this respect, the Japanese historian Kan Takayuki has proposed that even though Japanese live daily with the dominant thought that they have no relationship to the emperor, they encounter the shadow of the emperor every day in numerous ways, from being made aware of the reign name that bears his name, thus partially living in the regime of imperial time, through family genealogies and remembering ancestors, shrines, religious holidays, the national anthem, flag, and the acceptance of the idea that the emperor system is embedded in the hamlet order itself, "in every blade of grass and tree leaf," making him inseparable from the environment in such a way as to serve as the containing framework of the population.[21] In other words, the reminder of the emperor's presence is suffused and saturated throughout the daily life of Japanese society in countless ways one need not be conscious of that can hardly be dismissed by a mere verbal gesture that he is not thought about. Yet this mere verbal gesture aims to displace a complex belief system—a virtual cultural unconscious—so deeply embedded in Japanese society that acknowledging the emperor's unimportance announces a disavowal that signifies submission to the institution. Such an automatic utterance behaves very much like accepting a custom that goes without saying or questioning because it comes without saying. If this attitude reflects the relevance of the emperor and everything the institution implies, it also denotes at the same time acceptance of the spurious nature of its claims, but never questioning it or the continuation of the institution in Japanese life in the twenty-first century. What this suggests, in Slavoj Žižek's view, is an inversion of Marx's famous observation that "they do not know it and do it" (*Capital*, "The Commodity") into a more Freudian mind-set that is able to say that "even though they know it, they do it." That is to say, even though the emperor is naked people act and live as if he were not but fully clothed. Here, the Japanese emperor comes close to resembling Hamlet's king, who is a thing of nothing. But the Japanese emperor is also at one with the no-thing (*mu*) of Kyoto philosophers like Nishida Kitarō and Tanabe Hajime, which overcomes oppositions. Ideological illusion, according to Slavoj Žižek in *The Sublime Object of Ideology*, no longer resides in a demonstration of knowing, as such, or even in seeing but in doing and acting as if the emperor was the embodiment of the national community, one with the mystical *kokutai*, instead of the reverse as proposed by the new constitution. This expression of denial closes off whatever space was provided for a civil society by the postwar constitution, whereby the emperor is positioned to stand in for both the political and social (ethnic) communities as symbol of the state and the unity of the Japanese people.

In this perspective, what people appear to misrecognize is not the everyday reality they actually live but the illusion that has structured it. Like behavior ruled by custom, as Tosaka Jun proposed before the war in *Shisō to fūzoku*, they act according to directives and accept such commands without either questioning it or knowing how it became customary. Tosaka equated custom to human skin—that one takes for granted and is lived in the register of second nature. But in this scenario the illusion supports reality itself by providing not an escape or exit but rather a masking of some fundamental disorder that cannot be symbolized. For Japanese, the emperor, as a persisting archaic presence in a modernizing society, offers a resolution and the promise of managing the unimaginable antagonism and inexpressible disorder produced by the unevenness and imbalance that have always shadowed their capitalist modernization, if not their entire cultural history. He remains the mark of Japan's modernity and its unfulfilled completion, but his presence also represents the archaic moment *in illo tempore* of a realized origin and state foundation; that is to say Japanese have assumed that a completed modernity that had not been reached was the goal of the modernizing process. What was not grasped was the fact that modernity's condition everywhere always remains incomplete and uneven. This truth was shielded from Japanese, and other latecomers to modernity, by the stigma associated with the status of late development itself and the temporal lockstep of backwardness they were all forced to endure in their pursuit of catching up, which would be realized only in the last instance. In other words, the Japanese, like others who came late to capitalist modernization, would live a temporality simultaneously imminent with the modern West yet belonging to a different present.

Hence, the emperor's dual role of serving as a monarch of a modernizing society who, because his position derives from a remote, archaic imaginary, continues to perform rituals belonging to this ancient agrarian order in the heart of a rational, industrial society. He is thus the sign of both continuing unevenness and the compatibility of differences it constantly produces now achieved through the performing of rituals. This sense of unevenness was so deeply inscribed in the political unconscious that Marxists before the war tried to explain it away as simply the manifest trace of feudal remnants—a hangover from the past—which had stalled the development of capitalism into a frozen state of semifeudalism but in time and other political circumstances would realize full modernity into a completed totality. This argument was also made by non-Marxists like the political theorist Maruyama Masao, who, in the postwar, called for a second start of Japan's modernity in the belief that this time Japan would get it right and complete its modern project, instead of seeing in it the actuality of unevenness characterizing all such experiences.

But the emperor was no simple feudal remnant, despite the determined logic of the Kōzaha Marxist analysis. This form of Marxian critique was formulated under the constrained conditions of the 1930s and the watchful surveillance of the state. Under these circumstances, criticism was forcibly muted and settled on showing how the state bureaucracy—named the emperor system (tennōsei)—constituted a feudal survival, a remnant that represented the immaturity and incompletion of capitalist modernization. What state censorship proscribed was any critical language targeting the emperor, as such, and the subsequent critique of the bureaucratic apparatus as a feudal remnant constituted a displacement of the emperor, a concealed substitution. In a recent work (Tennōsei no jāgon [ingo]) the critic Suga Hidemi has proposed that the mode of Kōzaha strategy resulted in a jargonized critique yoked to the idea of the primacy of the imperial bureaucracy, which after the war was redeployed to show itself increasingly irrelevant and out of touch with the historical circumstances of the postwar environment. The continuing appeal to feudal remnants gradually had no referent in postwar Japan, even though forms of unevenness persisted by the mere presence of the emperor. The paradox of this position is that even though the prewar constraints of censorship had been lifted after the war, Kōzaha Marxism remained obdurately committed to the "jargon" of an older critical argument and its now frozen language preoccupied with the primacy of feudal remnants masking the real object of the emperor, as if, in fact, they remained stuck in an older, past temporality rather than a new one offering the possibility of a new time and different possibilities for critique. Suga remains silent on the question of why Marxists, like others, failed to recognize the nature of the capitalist modernizing process as a constant work of uneven development in progress rather than an expected completion.[22] (But in this respect they were no more misguided than generations of European thinkers who inflicted the myth of a completed Enlightenment project on the rest of the world.) What is even more extraordinary is the Marxian refusal to see that in the postwar the real problem all along was revealed to be the figure of the emperor, not the bureaucratic apparatus ruling in his name. Long before Suga presented his argument, the sinologist and independent critic Takeuchi Yoshimi was able to explain why both Marxists and modernizers had failed to grasp how the retention of the imperial institution had, in fact, become the central problem for postwar Japanese society which, if left unresolved, risked recuperating prewar fascism in the future. The recognition of such imperial durability prompted him to excoriate both the communists and modernists alike for having misunderstood the nature of the institution: the communists because they envisaged the emperor system as a thing of materiality that could be opposed and destroyed by simply attacking the managerial order that ruled for it, that is to say the imperial bureaucracy, and the modernists, who simply misrecognized the nature of the institution altogether by situating it in a modernizing process that imagined it merely as one system of values among others, rather than the composite grab bag of all values, a sort of untranscendable horizon, that provided space for the incorporation of differing perspectives. Both Marxists and modernizers woefully underestimated the power of ideology to persist and retain assent even after it had been repudiated and unmasked.[23]

Rather than turning to devise a new analytic strategy to meet the postwar necessity of holding the emperor responsible for the war and calling for the removal of both Hirohito and the imperial institution as the condition for constructing a new social and political imaginary, Marxists and modernizers alike, radicals and conservatives failed to call for a national discussion in the early years of the postwar concerning the status of the imperial institution and its war responsibility. Instead they upheld agendas that fastened onto forging a proper political subject formation among the populace, implying along the way that somehow the war occurred because of their political immaturity, and resorted to endless discussions on war responsibility that consistently avoided the figure of the emperor (the elephant in the room), which eventually morphed into the whining and wailing of reactionaries like Katō Norihiro accusing America of preventing the Japanese from mourning for their war dead. Political modernization for the Japanese was nothing more than what the American military had proposed, which was a procedural form of democracy primarily defined by an electoral system—that is, voting. Under these circumstances, it is not too surprising that leading thinkers would push for a broadened franchise composed of informed voters, which weighted postwar discussions with preoccupations concerning the formation of proper political (male) subjectivity. It is true that today when such criticism is made against the imperial institution, however indirect, it risks intimidation, injury, and even loss of life from the right wing and their criminal thugs whose behavior has been fully sanctioned by the LDP and even, in some instances, institutionalized, by being overlooked. But in the early days of the postwar, the opportunity was available for a serious discussion of emperor and institution and was bypassed just as the emperor's war responsibility was absolved by the American-dominated Tokyo War Crimes Tribunal.

This silence and the resulting incapacity to begin a national discussion on the status of the emperor in the immediate years of the postwar and to seize the genuine possibility of constructing a political society no longer dependent on the structuring agency of a contradictory archaism seemed to be reduced to finding new ways to displace the real source of society's antagonism and the reasons underlying war, destruction, and defeat. This failure, as will be clear, resulted in bringing back leading political components that had shaped and controlled Japan's prewar society. What Marxists overlooked was the fact that both emperor and shrine were reconfigured in the Meiji period in such a way as to enable the new state, without either a working class or a bourgeoisie, to realize its aspiration for capital accumulation. Each, in their way, provided legitimating force to induce the population to work and die for the "ancestral land" (*sokoku*), relaying the deeper meaning of the Meiji state's principal ideological slogan of wealth and power. Ultimately, the recalling of the political past in the postwar has led to a restructuring of "gangsterism" as an accompaniment of the retention of the emperor, thus recuperating a governmental form of racketeering resembling the shift perceived in Nazi Germany in the 1940s by Friedrich Pollock, Theodor Adorno, Max Horkheimer in their accounting of how state political organization and bureaucratic cliquism of leading interests worked to replace liberalism's reliance on the market to solve the crisis of capitalism.

The Mosaic of Neo-emperorism: Gangsterism and Ultranationalistic Shinto

Instead of following the more critical path to constructing a new strategy in the postwar, founded on the basis of discounting the structuring role of archaism as embodied by the figure of the emperor, postwar Japan's putative reconstruction resorted to enlisting precedents from the past. Rejecting a working through of the past by embracing some of its more retrograde components like archaism was a formula for retrieving the form of fascism rather than deepening a dedication to a realized democracy. The postwar imaginary Japanese cobbled together consisted principally of neo-emperorism, bureaucratic control of the political, and what might be named as gangsterism. Despite soothing narratives that have celebrated the American role in rebuilding Japan and sustained by the complicity of professional scholarship that has continually praised the Japanese democratic achievement, both have veiled the fact that military occupation acted as much in the interest of resuscitating leading elements of the old order at the cost of undermining its own program of reforms. The formation of a professional area studies relating to the study of Japan and the proliferation of specialists since the early postwar years have dutifully performed

as the mouthpiece of narratives that have studiously avoided any real examination of the relationship between prewar fascist elements and their postwar
appropriations. With few exceptions there are no critical discussions of the role
played by a rescued imperial institution and those who have occupied the
throne. This studied silence must be counted as a contributing factor to aiding
and abetting what might be called the achievement of a second but lasting
Shōwa restoration centered on the form of neo emperorism. To secure the success of this imperial restoration American troops have been continuously stationed in Japan and Okinawa since the end of the war, as they still are, to become
permanent tenants of the landscape and reminders of the temporality of the
postwar. Those peace activists who have emerged in recent years have highlighted a nonissue, comparable to the defense of Article 9, since the American
military presence is a lasing guarantee of both Japan's peace and a repudiation
of the empty fear that Japan will go to war once Article 9 is abrogated. Abe's
seizure of the initiative immediately after the American election of Trump and
his mercurial two visits to Washington, D.C., putting him at the head of the
line before other national aspirants wishing to visit the White House should
be a reminder to the all those who have worried about the maintenance of
Japan's peace and relieve those who fear the threat of military expansion.

During the late 1980s and 1990s reactionary critics like Katō Norihiro, as
already suggested, amplified the complaint that the United States had effectively
denied Japanese the right to grieve and mourn for their war dead while being
held accountable for the millions in Asia who perished because of the war. Katō's
grievance obviously referred to the "proscriptions" discouraging LDP politicians from visiting Yasukuni Shrine, even though this remains unmentioned.
In recent years the shrine precinct has witnessed crowds of politicians falling
over each other in their eagerness to make regular visitations to honor Japan's
war dead. Accordingly, this kind of self-serving self-victimization, coupled with
earlier charges of censorship by critics like Etō Jun, have not only sustained the
categorial status of the postwar as a colonized temporality in the American
imperium but also, as the indictment further goes, encouraged only a distorted
and twisted image of what it means to be Japanese in such ways as to permanently alienate them from themselves and their own history. At the moment
Japanese were being told they were living a disfigured and deformed existence
there appeared an aggressive call for a total revision of history textbooks and
thus an overhauling (and inverting) of the prevailing conception of history to
show the nation that Japan had not been responsible for the war. According to
this new story line, the destruction inflicted upon Asia has been overstated and
exaggerated. Accusations of having started the war with the seizure of Manchuria and enlarging it in China prompted putting forth explanations that
Japan sought to maintain its own security and independence and a historic mission to relieve Asia from Western colonialism rather than embarking on a

path of mere imperial expropriation. There have been recent attempts in the Abe government to repudiate earlier scholarship validating Japan's role in fostering the practice of "comfort women" serving the military during the war. But these demands are merely effects of the Occupation's decision to not foresee in 1946 what now appears as a determined disposition to reemploy earlier myths and resituate the content of archaism. If it is hard to imagine that the very myths that once again have become leading elements of a reviled ideology, now daily being stoked by Shinto associations, rapidly becoming the guiding principles testifying to Japan's democratic and anticommunist credentials in the emerging Cold War struggle, one must pause to wonder what all those Japan specialists who served in the U.S. State Department and Occupation actually knew and understood. It is astonishing to believe that they were making the case for retaining the emperor on the grounds of the fictional historical continuity of emperorism authorized by the mythic claim of divine origins that constituted the basis of Japan's fascist ideology. It is even more unconvincing that they were driven by some sense of strategic realism that persuaded them to align with prewar bureaucrats in rescuing the emperor as a necessary first step to restoring important prewar components and personnel to political power. In this regard, America's reverse course in Japan paralleled similar policies in West Germany. In this scenario, anticommunism took precedence over the establishment of democracy. The emperor was apparently saved because of the belief that his removal would undermine the principle of social solidarity and open the way to a communist revolution and bloodbath, sentiments Hirohito himself "heroically" expressed in his vindication statement of 1946 (*Dokuhakuroku*) and which conformed to MacArthur's own convictions. It is important to recognize that while the idea of an emperor symbolizing the unity of state could refer to a concrete and historical reality, to a political community based on the interests of the ruling political classes, an emperor who was made to symbolize the unity of the people referred to nothing but the emperor. This relationship never existed since there was no historical precedent symbolizing a unified people embodying the principal of sovereignty. It is, I believe, precisely because of this attempt to retain the emperor as a symbol that makes it more significant and far-reaching than any of the Occupation's democratizing reforms and contributed to undermining whatever promise they might have possessed. Rescuing the emperor made the Occupation inadvertently complicit in retaining the imperial bureaucracy (what had been known as the *tennōsei*). In many ways, this formula was merely a simple inversion of the location of sovereignty from one source, the emperor, to another, the people. But he still presided over a calendar of rituals and ceremonies, calling forth the image of *illud tempus*, sacred time, the time of origins, directed to expressing thanks for the blessings of life to the national deities and imperial ancestors. These rituals functioned to elicit continuing good fortune and bounty for the nation from the deities and reflected the archaic principle that made no distinction between the performance of religious rituals and governance. What had to be avoided was "heaven's vengeance," which was often recruited to explain national catastrophes like the earthquake of 1923 that the former mayor of Tokyo reminded Japanese of in the wake of Fukushima, events showing the disapproval of the deities of the people's behavior. Hirohito employed the same technique in his early apologia (*Dokuhakuroku*), when he claimed that the war was an outgrowth of the immoral conduct of people addicted to consumption and pleasure in the preceding decade. The emperor's performance of rituals and ceremonies also signified conducting political affairs. In spite of the Occupation's attempt to separate religion and politics, the reinstating of the emperor ensured both the continuing identity of the two in the body of the emperor and the archaic power that mandated this combination of sovereign authority as the basis of legitimation.

By the same measure, rescuing and salvaging the imperial institution was accompanied by the Occupation's decision to actively return large numbers of prewar bureaucrats, which further guaranteed the continuation of the principal governmental form of the old order. This was particularly true of high-ranking bureaucrats installed in leading positions, many of whom, like Yoshida Shigeru, an early postwar prime minister, were vocally strong advocates of maintaining the imperial house. In this arrangement, the emperor's unsurprising return supplied the necessary legitimation of the emerging political order that would continue to be more bureaucratic than democratic. Despite the existence of political parties and the early and long domination of the LDP, electoral politics as such would play a progressively diminished role in decision making since the two-way traffic (*amakudari*) dispersing former bureaucrats into the party and business guaranteed an intimate relationship between the state and private sector, often making them and their class identities indistinguishable.[24] Bureaucrats, most of whom already shared a common educational background at elite schools like Tokyo and Kyoto Universities, who became future capitalists and party politicians, were able to reinforce this single class identity through the development of a common interest to see capitalism succeed. "Where the transition from state functionary to capitalist is so well known beforehand," the political theorist Bertell Ollman perceived, "the interests of the capitalist also become the interests of the bureaucrats."[25] The hegemonic role played by the bureaucracy over the parties—nonelected officials—falls far short of reflecting the popular sovereignty implied by the constitution's recognition of the unity and sovereignty of the Japanese people but rather owed its immense decision-making powers to some other source, as it did before the war when the same officials were known as imperial retainers. In other words, the emperor continued to serve capitalism, as the institution was configured to do so in the Meiji period, in a way that neither the new constitution nor free elections or indeed any other source in Japanese society are able to deliver legitimation.[26]

(We should not forget how the current Heisei emperor, when he was Crown Prince Akihito, and his wife appeared in an advertising campaign promoting "My Homism" that required hawking household labor-saving devices in the late 1950s.)[27]

In such a system that has historically depended on the role of a divinely absolute emperor to provide authority for the maintenance of governmental functions, carried out by his imperial retainers, the new dispensation offered by the postwar constitution that invested such power in the "will" of the people or the supremacy of a democratic electoral procedure was an abstraction. It should also be remembered that in the early postwar the Japanese population could still remember that Hirohito spoke on radio to bring the war to an end; and after 3/11 his successor went on television to ask the country to remain calm in the face of the Fukushima earthquake and tsunami and specifically asked them to follow their leaders. While these episodes represented instances of the emperor stepping out of his usual role, which was not to act and speak publicly, they reflected how he was the most indispensable source of legitimation in Japanese society. Empowered to perform rituals and ceremonies as forms of governance, an investiture of authority he alone embodied trumping all other exercises of legitimation, any act or utterance would constitute a representation of the unity or identity of interests of the political and social communities in which he stood "astride."[28] In other words, state and civil society were conflated and the putative will of the people was "integrated" with the will of the emperor (at least in the Japanese translation of the constitution).

This matches the arrangement of authority the writer Takeuchi Yoshimi described in the immediate postwar years when he concluded how the emperor appeared to be indistinguishable from the representation of a "hamlet communal order," upon which the institution was supposed to be based. It is interesting to note how closely this description corresponds to the later observation of Deleuze and Guattari (*A Thousand Plateaus*) that fascism derived its strength from microcosmic structures. Takeuchi was, in fact, saying that representation required projecting the "quality of being a sign or person that holds the place of another, an image—and importantly—a political body," an "empty coffin on which to stretch a cloth for a religious ceremony."[29] For this reason he was prompted to propose that contemporary Japan marked the place of "any number of miniature emperor systems," that could be found everywhere, in "every single blade of grass, in every tree's leaf."[30] In his reckoning, then, the emperor system had come to resemble the "torso that had been made to stand in for all of ancient Greece," a magical metonymy empowered to represent the national body, and was, therefore, inseparable from the whole of society. If the institution functioned metonymically to call attention to the totality, the totality—culture—invariably summoned the imperial institution. Each was meaningless without the other. Yet this substitution and Takeuchi's understanding of an emperor who had been both an absolute despot and a monarch constrained by laws disclosed a central paradox he had failed to recognize: the emperor played both the role of a referent who supplied authoritative recognition and that of a symbol which referred to a referent capable of limiting his margin of authority. Because of the existence of referentiality, especially in the performance of imperial rituals, there appeared to be yet another space of unevenness between representation and power that bureaucracy and emperor would strive to conceal in the long postwar. In the years after the U.S. military occupation officially ended, the bureaucracy has endeavored to enhance and deepen imperial authority, often in violation of the constitution, to present the emperor as the principal of authority and to induce the popular mind that he stood as the head of state.[31]

As an archaic sign, a symbol, and titular head of the Japanese nation, the emperor was positioned to secure the people's acceptance of the existing political arrangements, to enlist without question their assent to things the way they are. This was achieved by transmuting sentiment and people's loyalty toward their social (ethnic) community into the political community of the state. By embodying and enabling the conflation of the two (social and political domains), their coalescence, by resorting to the operation of inversion and interchangeability, people were persuaded to misrecognize or confuse the form of rule with that which has constituted Japanese as a social group, encouraging them to thus act politically as if they are a social group.

Ramifications of this arrangement have affected every aspect of Japanese society, and it appears now that the return of Abe Shinzō to the position of prime minister represents an awaited culmination of this process. I can only barely consider the principal props instrumentally buttressing the deepening of this fascist imaginary in contemporary Japan: the role played by a program of thuggish yakuza coercion reflecting the alliance between criminality and neo-emperorism and the growing presence of Shinto nationalism in everyday life. As Japanese society prospered, inviting closer attention from the world for the level of its economic and technological achievements, it became evident that one of the enabling factors of the economic order was the cycling of the older elements in the national myth of racial homogeneity and social solidarity founded on familial consensus, symbolized and enacted by the imperial family and its capacity to eliminate opposition and conflict and encourage claims of cultural uniqueness. This campaign dedicated to demonstrating Japan's culturally exceptional endowment from the 1960s on, rooted in the solidary connection between emperor and people derived from the country's archaic origins, was the sign of Japan's withdrawal from the world and its immense difference from it. (Here, it might be added, this bonding still signifies the divine nature of the relationship, even though the emperor has disavowed his divinity.) These ideologies of cultural exceptionalism have combined to establish a society marked by a network of tight social relationships modeled after the patriarchal household. From the academic world to industrial, financial organization to political parties and governmental bureaucratic structure, there are no relations unmarked by this patriarchal familial pattern. These relations are more political and hierarchical than social, even though they are cloaked as social and work to undermine its further development. It should be repeated that reification of this model of sociality was fundamentally legitimated by the machinery of what might be called neo-emperorism or even neo-archaism. While this network of relationships has resulted in guaranteeing minimal security and welfare for every Japanese until the bubble collapsed in the 1990s, by incorporating all into a national program, this very hegemonism has severely limited the spirit of criticism and opposition, if not effaced it, within all areas of society. The effort to make all Japanese as members of a vast "middle stratum" in the 1970s during the prime ministry of Ōhira Masayoshi has been immeasurably reinforced by an ideology of cultural exceptionalism that has striven to construct the figure of national subjectivity devoid of class and gender divisions, recalling early efforts to configure the folk.

But the really important upshot of this neo-emperorism is the way it sanctions a relationship between the imperial institution, as the custodian and guarantor of an exceptional culture, capitalism, and criminality. In this respect, Japan, as suggested earlier, has managed to recuperate a form of government by racketeering, whereby social relationships are condensed into a form of "racketeering" or "gangsterism" in which behavior is codified and ritualized. Japanese criminal groups—yakuza—were often dismissed as marginal but in reality have been constituted into a vast shadowy organization of political power and economic power that has developed close relations with major businesses and the leading political party, the LDP, not to forget numerous right-wing fringe groups, to become a virtual "army of crime." Significantly, the yakuza has been closely affiliated with elements within the leading conservative party— already a bulwark of permanent "one-party democracy"—and major businesses at many levels, once again serving to bridge forceful right-wing associations with both corporate and bureaucratic entities. Who would deny the relationship between gangsterism and construction companies in the reception of government contracts? In the early 1990s this was dramatically shown with the revelations of collusion between the LDP and yakuza. The case against the LDP kingmaker Kanemaru Shin for accepting a four-million-dollar bribe and using criminal assistance was initially allowed to end with the payment of less than a two-thousand-dollar fine, without any further penalty. Apparently no government agency was willing to investigate or prosecute the scandal further. The state's inability or refusal to enforce accountability to determine the nature of what might be regarded elsewhere as a criminal conspiracy unmistakably proves that those occupying the seat of power are invulnerable and have won grants of immunity. But this systematic sheltering from accountability mirrors a deeper logic of structural exemption and metalegality that can be explained only in relationship to neo-emperorism. The possibility of rooting out this system of pervasive gangsterism and state racketeering seems remote as long as the emperor is permitted to persist as the source of legitimacy in Japanese society. This coiled relationship between emperor and gangsterism was brilliantly condensed in Ōura Nobuyuki's photomontage in the 1980s, which portrays a photograph of the young Hirohito tipping his top hat to an observing, tattooed yakuza. (The work was exhibited in the Toyama Prefectural museum under the announced rubric of "new perspectives." Later, the prefectural assembly rejected it as "inexcusable" and destroyed the remaining catalogs in which it appeared, prompting Ōura to embark on a seven-year legal struggle which he eventually lost. His paintings are housed in New York City.)

The principal vocation of the yakuza is to provide a coercive arm to the state and ruling party's effort to stamp out and definitively discourage any criticism of the imperial institution and ultimately to deny its very existence. But it is reliance on criminal repression and threats of violence that have effectively silenced forms of criticism directed at the imperial house and its institutions. The yakuza have not only been designated custodians of this tradition but have frequently acted as attack dogs ready to strike at the slightest hint of antiemperor provocation. While their growing presence has poisoned the atmosphere of criticism with repression and deathly risk, it is clear they have succeeded in making a population fearful of speaking out against any aspect of the imperial institution. It is important to suggest that organized criminality has taken over the function carried out by the police before the war in keeping the population in line and fearful for their lives, what Tosaka Jun once described as the "police function." Despite this kinship and its capacity to establish self-censoring behavior, there are innumerable examples of threats of violence that have achieved the desired result without the necessity of beatings and inflicting bodily injury. The reason for this environment of fear is that people are now fully aware of the more spectacular episodes and the way they have been sanctioned by the state and leading party. Gangsterism thus manipulates with the invisible but ever-present threat of violence. While it is frequently implicated in episodes of murder and bloody mayhem, it often relies on its capacity to intimidate from a distance and discourage social analysis, which too often seeks ways to ignore its presence, bowing to the pervasive paradigm of taboo and self-censorship. The incidents of real violence and deaths have been numerous while episodes involving threats and intimidation are countless. But the violence that forces, as a result of group pressure, an individual to publicly disavow an act (like not singing the national anthem, *Kimigayo*) or a critical remark—that is, cave in—at risk of ostracism from membership of a group to which one belongs, and even greater consequences for her or his career, is as great a form of violence and reveals a new and worrisome depth of political pathology in contemporary Japanese society. While events of violence receive press coverage (like the stabbings of film director Itami Jūzō in 1992 and of a junior high school principal over a flag-raising incident and the singing of the national anthem incident) threats and intimidation go unnoticed and unreported and circulate in personal anecdotes. The violence of threat and intimidation is matched by the collusion of media, state, and gangsterism in creating the spectacle of shared unaccountability.

Fear is not the only instrument available to the political classes in Japan. The pomp staged to commemorate the death and funeral of the former emperor Hirohito and the subsequent ascension of his heir should not be forgotten too soon and calls attention to the spectacles of an earlier fascism. The announcement of yet another Olympics in 2020, displacing the ruined landscape nature inflicted on northeastern Japan on 3/11, and the state's failure to address the problem of relocating the vast uprooted population, not to forget its indifference or lack of concern for rising rates of radioactivity in the affected area have resulted in shifting funds that might have been used for the reconstruction of the region to underwrite an even greater spectacle in the near future.

If gangsterism supplied neo-emperorism with a watchdog custodian in the visible world, an energized Shinto represented its spiritual underpinning and connection to an unseen world of national deities and imperial ancestors. What they appeared to share was a strange transversal of perspectives: while gangsterism employed coercion and force to prevent criticism and discourage opposition to what in effect were religious values, Shinto resorted to secularism by persuading politicians to embrace such values publicly and act on them. Shinto's goal since the postwar military administration's policies' putative separation of state and religion and dissolution of what had been known as state Shinto has been to recover this lost ground; the yakuza thugs see themselves as latter-day "imperial loyalists" (*kinnōka*) involved in a restoration. This energizing of Shinto has been centered in the Association of Shinto Shrines, which represents approximately eighty thousand shrines throughout the nation and considers itself as a "religious administrative organization" and has become a powerful lobbyist.[32] The political arm of the association has been the Shintō Seiji Remmei, which has been translated as the "Shinto Association of Spiritual Values," when the term used to indicate "spiritual values" is *seiji*, which ordinarily means "politics."

What brought Shinto into public prominence was not simply successful recruitment of large numbers of Diet and LDP politicians but also the fortuitous convergence of their interests with the reelection of Abe in November 2014. It is clear that Abe's ideological preferences, dating back to his first term in

2006–2007, already corresponded to Shinto's tireless message that Japan had lost more than spiritual purpose as a result of the American military occupation. "We really have trust in him," Yuzawa Yutaka, director of Shinto Seiji Remmei, has been quoted as saying.[33] Yuzawa further elaborated that Abe's views "are all extremely close to our way of thinking." As suggested earlier Shinto's postwar determination has been at the heart of a strategy that moved from organizations designed to elicit support and sentiment from families of the war dead by providing the means to channel bereavement on a national scale to the center of the political arena with the establishment of a number of national political organizations that have both targeted politicians and Diet members for recruitment and acted as lobbying agents. A closely related group, the Shinto Political Alliance of Diet Members' Association, squarely reveals the intimate connection between the parent religious organization (Association of Shinto Shines) and current LDP politics and boasts two hundred forty members of the Diet (other estimates put this figure higher) and sixteen out of nineteen cabinet members, with Abe serving as the association's secretary-general.

The Shinto Seiji Remmei has composed an agenda founded on rescuing Japanese spiritual values, which, in large part, involves restoring the emperor and the apparatus of the imperial institution to its previous status. What this program seeks to accomplish, apart from reinstating Shinto's prior position in Japanese life before the American military reforms diminished it, is to restore the mytho-religious tradition centered on the emperor's divine descent and the unparalleled uniqueness of the imperial genealogy. For believers like Yuzawa, the emperor and emperorism constitute the basis for fostering patriotism, love of nation, and the reinstallation of moral discipline among the populace. "After the war," according to Yuzawa's reckoning, "there was an atmosphere that considered all aspects of the pre-war [as] bad. Policies were adopted weakening the relationship between the imperial household and the people . . . and the most fundamental of elements of Japanese history were not taught in the schools."[34] In other words, the problem troubling contemporary Japan is the absence of moral discipline that requires, above all else, teaching the young the nation's proper history. Shinto ideologues are unanimous in agreeing that Japan's youth has remained mired in unhappiness that stems from a purposelessness caused by the absence of moral discipline. Yet we must recognize that this preoccupation with a missing moral discipline represents another throwback to the prewar order and its educational regime devoted to an ethics of disciplining one's conduct (shūshin). Japanese life has thus been emptied of a relationship with the past and the aura of archaism in the present that will guarantee an authentic identity aimed at reuniting with one's self in order to secure independence. Specifically moral decline among youth was manifest in rampant individualism and unrelieved materialism, precisely the complaint made by Hirohito in his 1946 vindication statement, where he desperately sought to exonerate himself from bringing about the war by attributing the moral weakening of the population to unrestrained individualism and materialism. Hence, Abe and his new cabinet (not really different from its predecessor) have made it clear that they intend to set Japan on a new direction, which offers to undo the legacy of the Occupation as a condition of restoring the principal spiritual and political components of the prewar order.

If Shinto associations have tirelessly saturated everyday life with constant reminders of the centrality of the emperor in the matrix of ancient religious beliefs, Abe's "new direction" seeks to pursue a course that will normalize Japan, which entails an active military force, rescinding individual liberties, promoting the revision of history textbooks, especially renarrativizing Japan's wartime history by rectifying Japan's role in the war in Asia as the mission to liberate the region from white man's imperialism and reuniting state and religion that would ease the path of the emperor's return to political power and recognizing his divine right.[35]

The most recent Abe cabinet appears ideologically more uniform than past administrations, inasmuch as his ministers share common membership in a range of conservative, nationalist, private policy organizations or parliamentary associations (*giin remmei*)[36]—that is, ideological issue groups for legislators. Accordingly, there is tight agreement supporting constitutional revision, rejection of human rights legislation, and opposition to groups like the teachers' union, which has already been weakened. By the same measure Abe and his cabinet have been vociferous in their sponsorship of regular ministerial visitations to Yasukuni Shrine (the "emperor's shrine") to pay respect to Japan's war dead. But this path was already pioneered by his predecessors Nakasone Yasuhiro and Koizumi Jun'ichirō, who, especially, made six visits during his term to virtually routinize the practice. While there have been highly placed cabinet members who have publicly downplayed some of the more excessively retrograde provisions of the Shinto program, especially their consistent call to return to an older order, Abe himself has shown remarkable constancy in acknowledging the importance of an ideology that privileges the restoration of spiritual and cultural values indistinguishable from Shinto's campaign. His own conduct validates a strategy that clearly shows that ideology has trumped political expedience and pragmatism. He has made little effort to either tone down or disguise his relationship to and agreement with Shinto organizations. As prime minister Abe has been involved in twice transmitting statements honoring Class A war criminals, like his grandfather, and those classified as lesser offenders.[37] In his capacity as president of the LDP he has demonstrated no reluctance in his desire to venerate war criminals executed by the Allied powers, and he has even described them in death as "foundations of their nation," as heroic "martyrs." The ceremony is celebrated annually in the presence of a memorial denouncing the war crimes tribunal. Even more important, Abe, in

October 2013, was the first prime minister since the beginning of the Shōwa era and the only one since the war to attend one of the most important ceremonies at Ise Shrine, Japan's and Shinto's most sacred shrine. This was an archaic ceremony named Sengyo no Gi in which Ise's main buildings are torn down and rebuilt every twenty years. It should be recalled that the shrine is dedicated to the sun goddess and is considered the home of the emperor's imperial ancestors. It is also the place where the imperial accession and enthronement are enacted and the new emperor spends a night with the sun goddess. The principal moment of the rebuilding ritual is the transfer of the imperial regalia to its new residence, especially the sacred mirror, symbolizing imperial legitimacy.[38] Abe was accompanied by eight cabinet members, prompting one observer to see in the act and Abe's participation a harbinger signifying the return to the prewar order. Soon after, the archaic ceremony acquired the status of a state rite.

It is interesting to note that Abe's determination to reset the course of Japan's politics has often been described as a "regime change" by his critics, lacking a common process of beginning, a "shape of the nation" pointing to an "extreme right-wing political authority." The most familiar sign of this move has been Abe's obsession to change the military occupation inspired constitution and especially its Article 9 forswearing war.[39] The general election of 2012 was described as a right-wing seizure of political authority. Not exactly one that would lead to "Nazi gas chambers" but an equally ominous event whereby the power of might that advocates an illusory holocaust is positioned in political power. That this is so regarded is because it is a natural state of affairs.[40] Hence, the meaning of Abe and the LDP's announcement to "get rid of the postwar regime" comes before everything else to guide their constitution and revise the postwar state's *kokutai*, in order to establish as national policy a proper succession to and accession of the prewar Japanese empire. In other words, to recall the failed model of the Shōwa restoration of the 1930s, where the "double patriots," or Mishima Yukio's *homba* (runaway horses), are replaced by yakuza thugs and right-wing bullies who carry it out and impose on the present a "secondhand time." Accordingly, the ideology that has gripped these politicians who have seized political power expresses a transparent "demagoguery of form" that easily proposes that the Japanese military's comfort women were really prostitutes, a self-disclosure of the meaning of really "returning to Japan." That is to say changing the basic character of the Japanese state, similar to Erdogan's recent attempt to realize extraordinary constitutional changes in Turkey to strengthen the authority of the executive, literally strangling what's left of Turkey's putative democracy to make him sole leader. This has been matched by not only purging thousands of academics from universities and colleges but also changing the curriculum to place more emphasis on Islam. Behind this Turkish move is a vague vision of what Erdogan calls neo-Ottomanism in which his effort to eliminate the Kurds now recalls earlier genocides of minorities under the Ottoman Empire's "Young Turk" leadership, with similar aspirations for territorial expansion among Turkic-speaking peoples of Central Asia. One writer has recently suggested that Erdogan's attempt to revise the constitution and consolidate the offices of the head of government and head of state in the presidency, in himself, keeping him in power until 2029, which constitutes a throwback to the Islamic autocracy of the Ottomans, especially the reign of Sultan Abdulhamid II and a restoration of the glories of the empire before the establishment of a secular republic.

Abe may not easily qualify as a sultan or even a Tokugawa shogun like Ieyasu, but in his view the regime change he and his party have envisioned and begun to implement is to be total, embodying the image of the state itself that involves a process of rearranging Japanese society and equipping it with a different state view, principles of organization, and standards of value to ultimately change the postwar state to secure accession to the principles of the past. The move signifies a repetition anchored in the resuscitation of the figure of an archaic presence bent on altering the nature of the constitution and the political fabric it has authorized. This uncanny sense of a repetitive déjà vu was already perceived by Tosaka Jun in the late 1920s and early 1930s in his observation of what he named as "constitutional fascism."

In a draft modification, the LDP has chosen to avoid making the preamble of the constitution that lodged sovereignty in the people (*kokumin*) by replacing it with what they themselves have composed. Without notice the following marked the beginning of the replacement passage: "The Japanese nation wearing a long history and a characteristic culture is a state crowned with [*itadaku*] the emperor who is the symbol of national unity."[41] In this way it annulled and thus denied the universalistic principle previously asserting the sovereignty of the people and threw into ambiguous uncertainty the locus of authority between the state and emperor, which ultimately came down to the same thing. What is clear from the LDP draft is that there is no longer any reason for the state to acknowledge people's rights (*jinken*). Hence, the silhouette of archaism perceived in Japan and the proliferating desire to recall remote national pasts that have appeared elsewhere in fascist yearnings surfacing in a new historical register are not simply repetitions of "borrowed" names and costumes and determined efforts to unwind historical time. They are this, to be sure, but also the manifestation of a political longing to implant secondhand times in the place of a degraded present, concluding in radically reactionary attempts to reorder the present by harnessing a backward-looking nostalgia for the remote mythic past to the forward motion represented by "regime change" that aims at nothing less than replacing the entirety of the received political order.[42] The envisioned "regime change" is not quite a literal restoration or a return to the *in illo tempore* or origins but rather a renewal or rebirth in the present that looks beyond to a futural horizon. As secondhand time, it follows the traces of a prior route to realize the model of a specific past to complete, as in the Japanese case, an earlier restoration believed to have remained incomplete. In this sense the implanting of secondhand time constitutes a form of completing unfinished business, which may easily dissolve into pure nostalgics that now wishes to make the present look like a discredited and failed past.

What has thus marked the regeneration of fascist yearnings on a global scale, which now is clearly evidenced in Abe Shinzō's Japan, then, is the conscious expropriation of a remote or mythic past to complete the renewal of the present, an act that seeks to "colonize myths,"[43] yoked to Adorno's observation of fascism as "coming-to-itself of society as such." Hence, "the impossibility of portraying Fascism springs from the fact that in it, as in its contemplation, subjective freedom no longer exists. Total freedom can be recognized, but not represented."[44]

Notes

1. Perry Anderson, "Why the System Will Still Win," *Le monde diplomatique*, March 2017, https://mondediplo.com/2017/03/02brexit. It should be pointed out that Anderson excludes countries of eastern Europe because "the topography . . . is so different" and doesn't mention either Turkey or Japan, suggesting, once more, Europe's exceptional and more advanced status or that the world is still Europe?
2. Ernst Bloch, *The Heritage of Our Times*, trans. Neville and Stephen Plaice (Berkeley: University of California Press, 1990), 97.
3. Mutō Ichiyō, *Sengo rejīmu to kempō heiwashugi* (Tokyo: Renga shobō, 2016), 19–26, 56–68.
4. Shirai Satoshi, *Eizoku haisenron* (Tokyo: Ōta shuppan, 2014), esp. 122–85. Shirai's argument is that the Japanese capitulated instead of fighting to the last, as promised from the outset of the war.
5. Paolo Virno, *Déjà Vu and the End of History*, trans. David Broder (London: Verso, 2015), 42.
6. Gilles Deleuze, *Difference and Repetition*, trans. Paul Patton (New York: Columbia University Press, 1994), 90–91.
7. Eelco Runia, *Moved by the Past* (New York: Columbia University Press, 2014), 54.
8. Runia, *Moved by the Past*.
9. Runia, *Moved by the Past*, 147.
10. Theodor Adorno, "The Meaning of Working Through the Past," in *Critical Methods*, trans. Henry W. Pickford (New York: Columbia University Press, 1998), 89, 93, 98.
11. Karl Polanyi, "The Essence of Fascism," in *Christianity and the Social Revolution*, ed. John Lewis, Karl Polanyi, and Donald K. Kitchin (London: Gollancz, 1935), 390–91.
12. Polanyi, "The Essence of Fascism," 375, 376, 392.
13. The title in the subheading is from Kan Takayuki, *Tennōsei mondai to Nihon seishin-shi*, vol. 1 of *Tennōsei ronshū* (Tokyo: Ochanomizu shobō, 2014), 278. I have relied on a number of Kan's informative articles on the contemporary emperor in this volume.
14. The court chamberlain immediately responds by advising him that he must never say that his body is no different from others.

15. Herbert Bix, *Hirohito and the Making of Modern Japan* (New York: Harper, 2001), 626.
16. Herbert Marcuse, *Negations: Essays in Critical Theory* (Boston: Beacon Press, 1968), 235.
17. Tanabe Hajime, *Tanabe Hajime zenshū* (Tokyo: Chikuma shobō, 1964), 8:368–69. It should be noted that Mishima Yukio elaborated on this conception of the emperor as nothing.
18. Kan, *Tennōsei mondai*, 134–35.
19. Marcuse, *Negations*, 235.
20. Kan, *Tennōsei mondai*, 150–51.
21. Kan, *Tennōsei mondai*, 276–78.
22. Suga Hidemi, *Tennōsei no jāgon [ingo]* (Tokyo: Kōshisha, 2014), 8–38.
23. Takeuchi Yoshimi, "Kenryoku to geijitsu," in *Shimpen Nihon ideorogī* (Tokyo: Chikuma shobō, 1966), 2:382.
24. Bertell Ollman, "Why Does the Emperor Need the Yakuza?," https://www.nyu.edu /projects/ollman/docs/yakuza.php. This article originally appeared in *New Left Review*.
25. Ollman, "Why?"
26. Ollman, "Why?," 18.
27. Kan, *Tennōsei mondai*, 329–30.
28. Kan, *Tennōsei mondai*, 329–30.
29. Louis Marin, *Portrait of the King*, trans. Martha M. Houle (Minneapolis: University of Minnesota Press, 1988), 8.
30. Takeuchi, "Kenryoku to geijitsu," 393.
31. Ollman, "Why?," 30.
32. David McNeill, "Back to the Future: Shinto, Ise and Japan's New Moral Education," *Asia-Pacific Journal*, December 15, 2013, http://www.Japanfocus.org/-David-McNeill /4047.
33. Linda Sieg, "Japan's PM Abe's Base Aims to Restore Past Religious, Patriotic Value," Reuters, December 11, 2014, http://www.reuters.com/assets/print?aid=USKBN0JP2 E920141211.
34. Sieg, "Japan's PM."
35. Mindy Kotler and George Lazopoulos, "Shinzo Abe's Cabinet Reshuffle," *The Diplomat*, September 2, 2014, http//thediplomat.com/2014/09'shinzo-abes-cabinet-reshuffle/.
36. Kotler and Lazopoulos, "Shinzo Abe's Cabinet Reshuffle."
37. Kotler and Lazopoulos, "Shinzo Abe's Cabinet Reshuffle," 3.
38. McNeill, "Back to the Future," 2.
39. Mutō, *Sengo rejīmu*, 123.
40. Mutō, *Sengo rejīmu*, 123.
41. Quoted in Mutō, *Sengo rejīmu*, 130.
42. Mark Neocleous, *Fascism* (Minneapolis: University of Minnesota Press, 1997), 72–73.
43. Neocleous, *Fascism*, 72–73.
44. Theodor Adorno, *Minima Moralia*, trans. E. F. N. Jephcott (London: Verso, 2005), 144.

PREVIOUSLY PUBLISHED MATERIALS

"Tracking the Dinosaur: Area Studies in a Time of 'Globalism.'" In *History's Disquiet: Modernity, Cultural Practice, and the Question of Everyday Life*, 25–58. Copyright, 2000, Columbia University Press.

"'Memories of Underdevelopment' after Area Studies." *positions* 20, no. 1 (2012): 7–35. Copyright Duke University Press. All rights reserved. Republished by permission of Duke University Press. www.dukeupress.edu.

"Cultural Politics in Tokugawa Japan." In *Undercurrents in the Floating World: Censorship and Japanese Prints*, by Sarah E. Thompson and H. D. Harootunian. New York: Asia Society Galleries, 1991. Reprinted with permission.

"Late Tokugawa Culture and Thought." In *The Emergence of Meiji Japan*, ed. Marius B. Jansen. Cambridge: Cambridge University Press, 1995.

"Shadowing History: National Narratives and the Persistence of the Everyday." *Cultural Studies* 18, no. 2-3 (2010): 181–200. Copyright Taylor and Francis. Republished by permission.

"Overcome by Modernity: Fantasizing Everyday Life and the Discourse on the Social in Interwar Japan." *Parallax* 2, no. 1 (1996): 77–88. Copyright Taylor and Francis. All rights reserved. Republished by permission.

"Time, Everydayness and the Specter of Fascism: Tosaka Jun and Philosophy's New Vocation." In *Re-politicising the Kyoto School as Philosophy*, ed. Christopher Goto-Jones, 96–112. London: Routledge, 2008. Copyright Routledge/Taylor and Francis. All rights reserved. Republished by permission.

"Rekishi no aregori-ka: Marukusushugi, Hani Gorō, soshite genzai kara no yōsei." In *Marukusushugi to iu keiken: 1930–1940 nendai Nihon no rekishigaku*, ed. Jun'ichi Isomae and Harry Harootunian. Tokyo: Aoki shoten, 2008.

"Philosophy and Answerability: The Kyoto School and the Epiphanic Moment of World History." In *Confronting Capital: Rethinking Kyoto School Philosophy in History*, ed. Viren

INDEX

Abe Isoo, 242

Abe Shinzō, 294, 326, 352; "comfort women," 349; constitution peace clause (Article 9), 327, 348, 358; reunion with prewar fascism, 327–28, 329–30, 332, 333, 357, 360; Shinto, association with, 355–58

Adorno,Theodor, 33, 234, 332; on fascism, 337, 360

Ahmad, Aijaz, 41

Aizawa Seishisai, 74, 93n2, 107; on gamblers and idlers, 108; on *kokutai*, 114–15; on loyalty and filiality, 112; on problem of the ruled, 110–11, 113; restoration prospect of, 113

Alexievich, Svetlana, 330

Allison, Anne, 297

Althusser, Louis, 36, 49, 256–57; "ruptural unity," 65

American Council of Learned Societies (ACLS), 25–26

Amin, Samir, 18

Amino Yoshihiko, 87

Andō Masayoshi, 207

Andō Shōeki, 253

Aono Suekichi, 206

area studies, 8, 14, 23–24, 27, 36–37, 49, 51, 58, 347–48; Asia, 21–22; China studies, 26, 30, 31; field work, 31–32, 34, 54; and modernization theory, 12–13, 26, 27–29, 30, 38, 50, 60, 69n6, 185; and identity, 53, 55–56; Japanese studies, 9–10, 31, 35; and native knowledge and experience, 32–33, 51; nation-state as marker, 48, 54; Vietnam War, 11, 26

Arendt, Hannah, 332, 334–36

Association of Asian Studies, 22–23

Azuma Hiroaki, 292

Bakumatsu, 95, 105; as historical trope, 96–97, 105–6

Badiou, Alan, 55

Bakhtin, M. M., 49, 67, 184–85; on culture and world life, 259

Baudrillard, Jean, 305, 324

Benedict, Ruth, 24, 27

Bensaïd, Daniel, 68

Bergson, Henri, 215, 229, 333

Bhabha, Homi, 40–41, 43

Benjamin, Walter, 3, 5, 185, 196, 234, 241; historicism distrust of, 184, 190; now as historical present, 190; on "one way street," 4; photography model of history, 181–82, 189